Poetry Train Canada

By

John E. O'Hara aka John E. WordSlinger

By Joseph Hutchinson Colton 1855
Northern America. British, Russian, and Danish Possessions in North America.
This is the uncommon 1857 issue of J. H. Colton's map of Northern America (British, Russian and Danish.) Covers the entire area of what is modern day Canada, as well as what is now Alaska and Greenland. Divided and color coded according to province and country. Shows major roadways and railroads as well as geological features such as lakes and rivers. Like most Colton maps this map is dated 1855, but most likely was issued in the 1857 issue of Colton's Atlas . This was the only issue of Colton's Atlas that appeared without his trademark grill work border. Dated and copyrighted: "Entered according to the Act of Congress in the Year of 1855 by J. H. Colton & Co. in the Clerk's Office of the District Court of the United States for the Southern District of New York." Published from Colton's 172 William Street Office in New York City, NY.
www.geographicus.com

This is a work of historical fiction and 21st Century Poet Documentation.
Except the Poet Igloo Bill, it is a legal document for all to send to their local Senator in the United States & Member of Parliament in Canada.

All characters and events portrayed in this novel are either fictitiously
or are used fictitiously off of history in all and any form.

Disclaimer
All efforts have been made to make the information presented in this book accurate and acknowledgeable.

Poetry Train Canada
Copyright © 2015 by John E O'Hara aka John E. WordSlinger

ISBN 1517306167 / 9781517306168

Poetry Train/Poetry E Train
Poetry Train America
Poetry Train Canada
are Trade Marks of PoetryTrain.com
BMI.com Repertoire# PoetryTrain Music CA/IPI# : 682938498

All rights reserved. No part of this publication may be reproduced, distributed, or transmitted in any form or by any means, including photocopying, recording, or other electronic or mechanical methods, without the prior written permission of the publisher, except in the case of brief quotations embodied in critical reviews and certain other noncommercial uses permitted by copyright law. For permission requests, write to the publisher, addressed "Attention: Permissions Coordinator," at the address below.

Published by: John E. WordSlinger, PoetryTrain.com
444 S. Church St #220
Princeton, IL 61356

Blank pages artwork by Selena Howard: http://stronghearted1.deviantart.com

Editing and formatting assistance provided by Charles Hampton Gragg
charliegragg.wix.com/charlie-gragg

Photo Credits of John:
Mindee Beth Gonzalez & Two Angels Photography
facebook.com/twoangelsdesignprinceton
Photo of Kristin Morrison by her.
Photo of Geo Thompson by him.

Selected Poems by Various Poets
Deborah L. Kelly, Richard Doiron, Julie Catherine Vigna, Genni Gunn, Geo Thompson, Nardine Sanderson, Yotanka E. B. Aknatoy, Dominic Albanese, Glenn Shaw, Deborah Thompson, Toyota M. Safari, Candice James, Natalia Govsha, Robert Niswander, Beverly Cialone, Carlos Gomez, K.R. Graff, Yi Pang, and Glenn Meisenheimer.

John E. O'Hara aka John E. WordSlinger

Table of Contents

Preface / Dedication 7
Introduction 9
Chapter 1-British Columbia, Canada 11
   British Columbia: 24
   British Columbia Railways: 24
   British Columbia Poets: 28
Chapter 2-Yukon, Canada 45
   Yukon: 58
   The Yukon Railways: 58
   Yukon Poets: 58
Chapter 3-Northwest Territory, Canada 59
   Northwest Territories: 68
   Northwest Territories Railways: 69
   Northwest Territories Poets: 69
Chapter 4-Alberta, Canada 71
   Alberta: 79
   Alberta Canada Railways: 79
   Alberta Poets: 80
Chapter 5-Saskatchewan, Canada 85
   Saskatchewan: 93
   Saskatchewan Railways: 93
   Saskatchewan Poets: 93
Chapter 6-Nunavut, Canada 95
   Nunavut: 98
   Nunavut Railways: 99
   Nunavut Poets: 99
Chapter 7-Manitoba, Canada 101
   Manitoba: 115
   Manitoba Railways: 116
   Manitoba Poets: 116
Chapter 8-Ontario, Canada 119
   Ontario: 132
   Ontario Railways: 133
   Ontario Poets: 133
Chapter 9-Quebec, Canada 139
   Quebec: 158
   Quebec Railways: 158
   Quebec Poets: 159
Chapter 10-Newfoundland and Labrador, St. John Canada 161

- Newfoundland and Labrador, St. John: 171
- Newfoundland and Labrador, St. John Railways: 172
- Newfoundland and Labrador, St. John Poets: 172

Chapter 11-New Brunswick, Canada 175
- New Brunswick: 188
- New Brunswick Railways: 188
- New Brunswick Poets: 191

Chapter 12-Nova Scotia, Canada 193
- Nova Scotia: 215
- Nova Scotia Railways: 215
- Nova Scotia Poets: 216

Chapter 13-Th'Rising (th'Poet Igloo Bill) 219
Chapter 14-Publishers like Rawness, Poets of Tomorrow love Lawness 259
Chapter 15-Prince Edward Island Canada October 5th 2014 279

Poems by Various Poets 287
- Poetry Train, All Aboard 287
- The Railroad 288
- The Chattanooga Flyer 288
- Shaughnessy Ride 289
- On the Rails 291
- The softest train derailed 293
- midnight train 294
- TRAIN in TRANSFORMATION 295
- THE SINGING TRAIN 297
- TRACK LOOK 298
- The E-Train 299
- Ethel and Gertrude 300
- Get On the Train 301
- VAGABOND DAYS 302
- AWAY 304
- The Sorrow of Dreams 305
- The Poetry Train A 306
- The Poetry Train B 307
- The Poetry Train C 308

REST IN PEACE-POETS MEMORIAL 309
A Bill for an Act, POET IGLOO 311
POET IGLOO BILL 313
HOUSE OF COMMONS OF CANADA POET IGLOO BILL 321
Acknowledgments 329
Poet Igloo Acknowledgments 337
- American Version 337
- Canadian Version 338

Mr. Welchberrys' RxR Watch 339

Preface / Dedication

In honor of Alphonso Gerald Newcomer.
He said Canadian Poets were a force to deal with, he was very correct!

Dedicated to the Poets of Canada all through time.
Super Gorgeous Renata Augiar Rodrigues
the Youth, and *the Wicked Papoose Caboose.*

Thanks to Barb Colyott, Cherie Martin, Leo, Kevin Freeman, Paul S. Theobald for Chapter 7 ideas, Martin Pugh, Matt Anderson (Operation Jester), Olafur Gardarsson Chapter 12 lead. Emy Louie, and all that purchased Poetry Train America. Geo Thompson, Dominic Albanese, Yi Pang, Carlos Gomez, Anna Jessica Tonarely aka Lit Chick, Lilija Valis, Steven C. Schreiner and Dana-zoe Gest who have donated to the website poetrytrain.com.
PoetryTrain.com Poets & Sara Polidoro for the information and thoughts in Chapter 14. Thanks to Dominic Albanese & Alicia Young for kids mailed off fun. & Zach Wells for accurately placing Poets to chapters that are inaccurate data placed by tagging and Google errors that are found from Poet searches online as well as poets who have submitted poems.

Poetry Train Canada Book Cover Illustration by Kristin Morrison
kethenddragon.deviantart.com
facebook.com/WickedDragonArtistry

Introduction

By George Thompson aka Geo

Out of the dark and into the light at the end of the tunnel, John E Wordslinger, as in Poetry Train America, continues his creative process, with a poetic and historical journey across Canada. From sea to sea to sea, his main characters Red and Andy, whilst traversing this great nation, once again meet poets, board trains and recant their stories and adventures. Historical figures (politicians, engineers, workers) and the impact are once again brought to life.

John creates a sense of poetic wonder by touching each Province and Territory and their resident poets. Finding poets and their works creates a sense of wonder at the wealth of words and themes inherent within each piece. Red and Andy continue to weave their stories and provide humorous interludes and the many sacrifices made, as we learn of the railways and their part in building this great nation. Dreams and realties of what once was and will be are the order of the day. Moving into the present the author focuses on the Poet Igloo Bill, for both Canada and the U.S.A., and the need to link all Poets and their Poetry in unity.

With this book, John sends a message of inspiration that helped build a nation, by weaving it with poetry and using trains as the medium. Be patient and open minded. Express your imagination. The magic of words has moved mountains. Poets record the visionary impact of life. The hard work and dedication of railroaders has moved mountains and helped build this nation. It is the lifeblood that continues to play a daily role.

The engineer with hand poised on the throttle, east, west, north, south, the rails feel the pulse of the engine's thrum.

The poet, with pen poised and readied bleeds and shares, until the final rendezvous.

The Poetry of Geo Thompson youtube.com/channel/UC5usYH6iV2nEpYT7muwGnaQ
Geo also is a Literary Safe Guard like a Poets/Author body of work bodyguard.

Chapter 1-British Columbia, Canada

July 6th, 2013

Red and Andy rolled their log into the town of Arrowhead, Canada, a steamboat port, and came upon a logging and rafting camp with long bunk houses made of lumber. It was dark out, and they assumed everyone was asleep, so they slept themselves until dawn, and when they awoke, the beauty they were about to see was nearly going to take their breaths away. The Selkirk Mountains and the Lower Arrow Lake were beyond gorgeous. The scents from a near cook house awoke them, and they knew what time it was; the time for a new poetic journey. As soon as they arose from sleep, a woodsman named Alexander "Sandy" McDougal laughed at them, and asked them what crew they worked for.

"Sir, we came from Washington state," replied Andy, 'Looking for work.'

"Americans," Sandy replied, "Well, if you two think you can work well, and keep up with Finlanders and Indians; and Swedes and Norwegians, and Frenchmen, and not be a drag-along then you may have some work."

They then heard loud splashes in the lake.

Sandy wiped his beard with his hand and said, "Prehistoric fish."

Red, and Andy looked at each other and smiled.

A lumberjack from somewhere in the camp blew the breakfast dinner horn.

Sandy looked at them, and made his way towards the cook shack. He then looked back, and said, "The fish hatchery's hiring."

What's that? Asked Red.

"You put fish in milk cans, and load the cans by train," Sandy replied, "But I don't think they hire cargo." Sandy smiled and said, "I am just shaking your train, maybe."

Red, and Andy looked at each other, and Red replied, Thanks. Red then looked at Andy.

If needed, replied Red, and said, Well, we have a knack for log rolling.

"Well come on then," said Sandy. He then asked Red if he came from the Jordon, "Oh, Oh, that's right you said Washington state, and not the Detroit River."

Before entering the cook house, a group of Chinese men walked by, and right away this caught Andy's attention, and one of them, a young boy, looked like Jung Hem Sing, but it wasn't him. Andy looked deep inside, and time flashes of Jung Hem Sing came as they entered. Red noticed they looked exhausted and in discomfort.

Once inside and to a surprise Red wasn't alone, there were other black men sitting at the tables. There was a lot of talk going on. The gold rush and the brutalization towards them in California. There was talk about land, farming land, coal mines, and even the gallows. Talk about caribou cattlemen, brutal cattle drives, stockyards, and cattle shipping. The dialects were an orchestration of many colors, that displayed a verbal rainbow in Red and Andy's mind. They noticed some were being secretive. Tension? Imaginary boundary lines? Andy picked up on a conversation about the organization of construction on prairie sections, and Fort William. The Canadian Pacific Railway who were determined to retain control of southwestern Canada for mineral deposits, and there was talk about the Crow's Nest Pass Agreement.

Again Andy and Red stretched their minds to what was true and fair, furthermore their imagination for hope. A giant potato rolled out of the kitchen, and rolled near a Scottish man, the man smiled, and picked up two spoons from the table, and began to sing a song.

I like to tell you a story and I know I'll make you laugh
We couldn't take any chance, so we had to steal the calf
The old coyote got into there, and woke the farmers sleep
We couldn't take any chances, so we went and stole the sheep

A young china man with potato sacks wrapped around his knees came out of the kitchen, and retrieved the potato, and the other men were talking smack to him, because he was Chinese. Red remembered a parody, the "Immigrant Song by Led Zeppelin" from doing searches, and in his mind he remembered the lyrics.

Ah, ah,
We come from the land of the rice and roe,
from the eastern sun where the oxen roam.
The hammer of the rail.
Will set our course to new lands,
and &c &c

Red then sang a bit,

Ah, ah-

Andy looked at him and said, "Red".

Lowin Fats man, Lowin Fats man, David, and Connor. I know Andy it's just hilarious, all in fun, Red proclaimed.

"I know", replied Andy.

The scent of cooked Fung Chen sausage was strong through the cook house.

Andrew Onderdonk, an engineer, furthermore a master builder was outside the cook house, and he was looking for men to do excavation, grading, tunneling, bridging, track laying and ballasting work. Hell's gate was on his mind, and so was Fraser River, Emory's Bar and Boston Bar; Thompson to Junction Flat, The Thompson River, Savona's Ferry on Kamloops Lake and Port Moody, but mainly Caribou and Naramata. He was looking for his lambs, strong and smart men.

The fire kept going in the hearth pretty much 24-7, with various cast iron pots of numerous sizes and widths positioned above and beside the flames. Dogs were laying all around. Breakfast was served, and a man shouted, "Oh God, not pork again."

The head cook came into the dining room and said, "Whoever you are, your diet is also affected by the seasons."

Buckwheat pancakes was served, and 'Oh God' pork with boiled potato, cabbage and corned beef. Baked beans and Indian pudding was also available.

The poet E. Pauline Johnson-Tekahionwake was there, and she sat down by Andy and Red, and talked about poetry, and she recited her writing "Twin Sisters" and she told them about the Chief of Capilano Canyon but did not mention his name. She looked at Andy's pale face and Red's dark face and could see in their eyes, the knowledge of the secret of "The Two Sisters." She seen in their spirits they were warriors, brave, and shall receive much consideration in most nations.

Alexander "Sandy" McDougal, looked at Red and Andy as they ate, and didn't say anything, and they didn't say anything to him or anyone else. Red and Andy felt it again, the realm.

One man finished up, and walked out the door, and came back happy, and said, "A.O. is here, A.O. is here, and he has many horses. Railroad work is upon us."

No one got up. For many reasons they sat in their seats. The work was to hard and dangerous, and A.O. hired the Chinese, and they all didn't want to work with the Chinese, and besides that. They had seen the ecstasy of gold, and they wanted a taste of it.

Red and Andy looked at each other and said, Let's ride.

They looked into Andrew Onderdonk's eyes and said, Railroads are Poetry and in fact we are your Train.

A young Chinese boy named Kwang Ming gave Red and Andy a horse, and all four rode away to Naramata to meet Andrew McCulloch and his crew. But they didn't realize a young male wolf following them all the way, and they didn't see E. Pauline Johnson-Tekahionwake watch them as they disappeared.

Along the way A.O. told them about a poet in Princeton, Canada named Susan Louisa Moir Allison, who as he felt would be a great significance to Canada, because she wrote about poems and legends of the Chinook's, and other tribes. Andy and Red looked at each other and smiled. A.O. told them about a great railroad worker they needed to pick up along the way and his name was W. A. "Podunk" Davis. When they all got to Naramata after picking up W. A. "Podunk" Davis, who kept saying, the "Dorchester" is better than ocean to ocean "#347" speaking of locomotives, it was raining rattlesnakes. Yes, it was raining rattle snakes. McCulloch's crew blasted into a large den, and this is when Andy and Red's day began, as they finally awoke from the thuds and hisses of rattlesnakes.

Red got out of bed thinking about the Royal Canadian Mounted Police, and Andy got out of bed thinking about the Canadian Forests, and they both thought about the mysterious Ladner Trestle Bridge. The loud whistle of the train was heard, and then there was the sound of the bell. Andy and Red didn't waste any time. They hurried to get ready, and get off the train at the Pacific Central train station. Poet Laureate pj johnson and Author Robert Moore were waiting for their arrival, and to Andy and Red's surprise so was Candice James, Poet Laureate of New Westminster, BC Canada and Poet Deborah L. Kelly. Standing in line to un-board, they saw a vision; or did they? There was a steam train parked and one coming, and black smoke blew to the north. As it came they knew it was an older train, because it was smaller, but it was a moving fast. It was Locomotive #374 but was it the Dorchester?" They thought of the word "Perhaps," when a man behind them said the word and, "You two can move now, there is no one ahead of you." They turned around and were surprised again, and said, Yes, Our bad, and smiled to the man, and moved along.

It was the 6th of July, and their arrival was greeted with immense enthusiasm by those who had assembled to witness. There was quite a crowd. The scene at the station was a very lively and enthusiastic one. "Here they come, here they come." A voice said, and another voice said, "See, the Conquering Hero's Come." That voice was the voice of a man named Jonathan Rogers and he asked Andy and Red if they brought them American tea, and silk, and he laughed, and shook their hands. He then told them Jonathan Rogers, who was the first person to ever step off a train here could not make it. Andy and Red smiled, thanked him, and moved along, then curiosity got to them both about the man, so they turned around to look at him again, and he was gone.

The Poet Deborah L. Kelly came up to them excited and with a smile so big. She said, "I am happy to finally meet you both, Red and Andy" and said, "I have a poem for you, called "Poetry Train, All Aboard." Deborah put her hands to her side, and raised her head and recited the poem.

Poetry Train, All Aboard

The train wheels are clicking
travelling down this track
bringing the Spirit of the Word to all,
there'll be no turning back.

Clickety-clack on the Poetry Train,
all aboard, poetry and song.
From one great ocean of this land
to the other we keep rolling on.

Share your words, shine your light,
the engineer is riding free.
Come aboard, come aboard, the Poetry Train
shore to shore for you and for me.

Let's light up the country with every colour,
let our words reach all corners of the earth.
Let's share the gift of Peace with all -
Poetry Train is growing in girth.

The bigger the crowd, the larger she grows,
rolling on down the track.
Poetry Train gathering poets worldwide,
giving society something they lack.

The power of the Word in our heart;
travelling on wings, we are shining.
Down the tracks to cities across this land –
Poetry is the silver lining.

Shine on great poets, shine on to the world,
musicians tap your toes to the rhythm.
Celebrate the joy of the beautiful Word –
praise this treasure that we've been given.

Deborah L. Kelly 2013

The Pacific Central Train Station was huge, and it was loud. Cheers and applause to Deborah, and the arrival of the Poetry Train in Canada. Red pointed to a Greyhound bus sign and laughed. Andy pointed to a currency exchange and laughed. Poet Laureate Candice James introduced Red and Andy to many poets, and so they engaged their memory skills learned from Harry Lorayne and Jerry Lucas. They looked at each other and smiled. Once outside there were tall buildings, mainly built with aluminum and glass façade, with some cool observation decks. There was a park across the street and it was gorgeous. Andy looked at Candice and asked about the Two Sisters, the twin peaks tower above North Vancouver, and she said, "Well, you'll have to ask poet and musician David Cambell." David smiled, and sung to them his song "Looking from the Train." Red and Andy looked at Candice and said, We can't thank you enough, and they looked and pj johnson and said, You, beautiful woman, and that goes for you too, and Robert Moore, you are a soldier. Thank you all very much. Andy then thought about all of the flood damage to Canada prior to their arrival. And they both thought, were was Julie Catherine Edwards? She is a close Poet friend that kept in contact with them via Facebook on their American journey.

A taxi's brakes squalled, and visions of the owls came to Andy and Red, and so did Sir Sandford Fleming. Julie Catherine Edwards came running out of taxi, worried, excited, and finally relieved, but something was wrong, she said, "We have a long way to Dingle Tower in Hailfax, Nova Scotia." (The stones to build the tower were donated from all over the world.) "There are hidden dangers, but the mission is heroic. Oh, and the weather. Hero's among Poets, and the agenda is to inspire. You both are still on the outside, on ground level, and as I have said, a long way. You both have to climb ten stories to the observation level at the top."

Red and Andy telepathically and singularly thought of the 'Two Sisters' of the legend; Vancouver's 'Lions' and the thirteen provinces and territories of Canada, and the mysteries of the realm, they just awoke from. Andy looked at Julie and said, The taxi is leaving.

She laughed and said, "Good, let'em, because look," and she pointed and said, "We are taking the sky train, or the air train, whatever they want to call it." She looked at Andy, and sung the song "What Makes A Man?" by City and Colour.

I can hear my train comin'
It's a lonesome and distant cry
I can hear my train comin'
Now I'm runnin' for my life
What makes a man walk away from his mind?
I think I know
I think I might know

Julie then said to them, "I was hoping you'd be 12 hours early" and laughed. "Come on."

Red and Andy turned around to say something to all the others Poets, and they said, Go, and build the foundations of hope. We are going to the Heritage Grill, and you know how to reach us.

Everyone smiled. The Poet Richard Doiron spoke before they left, "In 1929, history intervened in my Father's life and his name is J.J. Doiron's, defining it. A famous train engineer named Richard Jefferson, driving the Ocean Limited, spotted him on the bank, near the Noinville brook and realized that he was looking at a hungry boy. He started throwing him food items: sandwiches, apples, oranges etc. Then one day, my father found a magazine with a story in it on Richard Jefferson, and the boy who had three months' of schooling wrote Mr. Jefferson a letter, in "broken English," telling the man how special he was. Well, sir, Mr. Jefferson wrote back saying that little boy was special too.

One day, in 1930, Richard Jefferson stopped the Ocean Limited in Noinville, and little Jerry and our grandfather, George Doiron-Gould got on, in the steam engine, at that, and J.J. was allowed to sit at the throttle and more or less assume the controls. And so was born a lifelong passion for trains. In 1931, Richard Jefferson came to Noinville with a U-Haul, as a result of that and he had clothing for all the children of Noinville.

In 1947, I was born and I got the name Richard, in honor of Richard Jefferson. Some say they don't like their names but I have always liked mine. I never got to know Richard Jefferson, who died when I was but two. My father had a passion for writing, and he wrote well. Considering his three months of schooling, way back in the Twenties, it's phenomenal. One piece of his that really stands out, a song lyric has been sung on stage. We've heard two different versions so far, and it would be hard to not see this as a hit anywhere... Six years ago, my father died. I did the eulogy at his funeral, attended by hundreds. I had just finished reading this work when the same train my father had been blessed by, bearing the same number as back then, drove by, running a bit late and let out three long and haunting blasts of its horn, something that moved us all. and Richard recited his father's poem,

"Train to Heaven"

I drove a train to heaven
One night inside my dream
It didn't run on diesel
It didn't run on steam

The power came from heaven
That made that engine strong
My helper was an angel
So nothing could go wrong

(Chorus, repeat)

The dreamer has the power
To drive that train above
But God sits in the tower
If it's to run on love

2
They came from many nations
To take the train that day
They all had reservations
Their tickets marked one way

They had their destination
At heaven's Pearly Gate
They came into the station
And not one soul was late

(Chorus, repeat)

3
I hope the Great Train master
Will keep me on this run
To take more souls to heaven
When earthly chores are done

My friends you can believe me
This is a busy line
And it will keep on running
Until the ends of time

(Chorus, repeat)"

~ Jerry (J.J.) Doiron Sr. ~

Red and Andy looked at Richard and Red calmly said, I am heart touched completely.

Andy closed his eyes, and felt something more powerful then he has ever.

Richard then said, "That poem, song is by my Grandfather Jerry (J.J.) Doiron Sr. And when J.J. was in the hospital, I wrote a poem for him. And I will recite that poem, and also in the mid 1950's, I had the same experience in that an engineer driving that old train threw me food items for some time. Unfortunately, I never did get to know his name." Richard recited his poem is entitled,

"Richard Jefferson And J.J.

The whistle blows I hear it still
As memory takes me back.
The engine strains to make the hill
Upon that mile of track.
The engineer I well recall

Was Jefferson by name,
And Twenty-Nine was quite the fall
Depression was the game.
Men road the rails and headed West
Their will was not denied.
No matter what they did their best
To hang on to their pride.
Dick Jefferson he spied a lad
Who stood upon the bank.
He knew full well that things were bad
That face was glum and blank.
Soon food and things were on the scene
Transforming life and limb,
An angel come to intervene
And Jefferson was him.
When Thirty came and rolled around
The train came to a halt.
A ten-year old was off the ground
That engine was his vault.
Near eighty years have come and gone
And memory's working still,
An act of love that's living on
To think it always will.
I was that lad in Twenty-Nine
When Jefferson came by.
I thank my stars that luck was mine
You'd know the answer why.
Those were the days of rail and steam
Of decent men that prayed
Of such as I who lived a dream -
The difference that it made!
My very son now bears his name
The legacy that's strong.
Dick Jefferson yet drives his train
I'm driving right along."
-Richard Doiron- June 28, 2008 For J.J. and for Richard Jefferson

Andy and Red felt the realm again, and this is what they knew. They knew there was something powerful in the world. This is what this journey is all about the unseen beauty. The beauty that all humanity needs to feel, read, share and express... This was and is nutrition for the soul. Hope was kicking like a train. Richard looked into their eyes and knew. Knew that Andy and Red knows the realm. Hope and Faith were flowing in their blood, and Richard said, "In the end, "Big Jerry" didn't just teach us how to live, he taught us how to die, believing in God, as he did, brokering peace between people to the end. In effect, he did more, flat on his back than the best of us would hardly ever be up to on our best of days. To us, he was always larger than life, and in the end, he surely was…No doubt at all that J. J. is up there with Jefferson and others, sitting at the controls, that big nameless kid right there beside him, taking souls to heaven, and God willing someday we'll be aboard that train too."

Everyone was speechless, even strangers to all there at the train station. Then a few minutes later, applause and cheers came from everyone. Andy and Red hugged Richard, and said, There are no words for the gratitude and grace we feel, and we shall return.

pj johnson said as they walked away, "Keep er on track," winked and said, "Remember, If just one person speaks up and speaks the truth, it could never be unheard. If many speak, it cannot be ignored."

Red and Andy said, Thank you and thought about the Wicked Papoose Caboose.

Once aboard the skytrain they discussed Joy Kogawa, her work and the historic Joy Kogawa House.

Joy Kowgawa's River of Tears as the River of Healing is powerful, Andy said, The maker made the world for fellowship. That's what the world is for, but the food of friendship is the light and good light is made up of love and the truth, and if you separate them then the light grows dim, so in order for friendship to exist, you have to have the truth, but the love has to be very strong or the truth will destroy.

Yes, replied Red, And in hatred we can be stuck forever. And in reconciling we can walk together.

"She dreams and hopes for this," Julie added.

"If there is enough grief, then reconciliation can happen," said Andy and thought about the conscious of baby elephant OP, and the damage done to the Poets of OP.

She wants the children not to be stuck in anger and hatred, Red added, and they all thought about their pots, where they all were planted, their nationalities, and their growth through friendships and poetry. Red then looked at Andy and asked, You are thinking about something, what?

"Well," Andy replied, "About what Author Martha Boone Leavell said, About sharing life's graces with children. What life means most, for us to stop and explain. Let us share with them the spiritual joys and assurances and discoveries which we are constantly finding out." He then looked out the window for the Yip Sang building before they left to go to New Westminster and King George. Yip Sang was employed by the Canadian Pacific Railroad Supply Company, where he worked as a bookkeeper, timekeeper, paymaster and then as the Chinese superintendent.

Red suggested to Julie with a smile and a laugh, Well with all the hope, we need to go to the Hope Restaurant for their famous chicken fingers, and for sure the Hope Othello Tunnels that we saw on the Roam Travel Show.

Andy laughed and said, "Well that is what we do when we are going through hope."

Red thought about some things, things learned from Mad Bear and the Great Spirit, and said, Public opinion is the most important influence in appraising, so one has to be constantly editing oneself from wear and tear. We are a poiema, the Great Spirit considers how your unique life and gifts can best make a positive impact on the world. We have the freedom to use these opportunities or ignore them. So in this onward and upward march toward life's larger meaning the ones ought to gain most from experiences are the children, they need to know in all senses from reading who has come out of the darknessi', and gave them something to hold onto, so they can get a handle on things.

Julie looked at them and said, "You two have a lot to learn before winter." She then asked them if they loved wolves. Andy smiled and said, "Yes, I had a husky in 95 and I was lucky to meet the wrestler from Nashville, named Mad Dog, and he had a male wolf. So we mated the two, but I was unlucky because a friend of mine stole the puppies."
"Awe, that is sad," said Julie.

Red just looked out the window and thought about Poet pj johnson. Red then pulled out the book "Time Lord, Sir Sandford Fleming and the Creation of Standard Time," by Clark Blaise. In fact he had three books and gave Julie and Andy one for the ride. They felt the increasing speed of time, and the journey. Time was diminishing, but not the future, and the suns light beamed through the windows gently. The pace of the new is was increasing. They did not care what people thought, because inside themselves, they were beyond man-made creation, they breathed in the realm. Condemned vanity was a facade. Their soul mirror was shattered but at the same time neo, new. Justice and Mercy pulsated as the sound of the train went ka-dewng, ka-dewng, ka-dewng. Nature's time and Standard time to Red and Andy were finally the puppets mastering the master, but don't be too naive. They knew not to get to rockety. Steady and easy, smooth was the art of just listening. They were the Dynamos and no longer the Virgins, and they wished everyone knew the wisdom of Henry David Thoreau. Mechanical the train maybe, but the Poetry Train was the raft, and faith was the lake.

Andy spoke, "I like the poet Earle Birney,' and recited his poem "Bushed."

Red smiled and said, We will be staring at amazement and excitement on this whole journey.

Earle Birney wrote numerous travel pieces for magazines and in the early 1960's took "Canadian poetry to audiences all over the world, not only his own, but that of the writers of his time," said Julie, "Just like you two."

Andy got a feeling that now they must protect poets and themselves even more, and Red picked up on the same notions. They both also thought about Charlie and was humbled by so many things, very deeply. They have come a long way since the dark days, but now things changed because they made the change, and truthfully they didn't think they would have gotten this far, in the realm of bliss, but all they could know was, they were humbled, and humbled all along the way. Charlie picked them up when they needed it, and Charlie knew when to, when they didn't. His spirit is always; his Jayhawk Spirit was in their hearts.
Julie looked at them and sensed something and said, "Maybe you two are twelve hours early," and she laughed.

Time zones sure are something, Red replied and laughed.

"And so are twilight zones," Andy added and laughed.

They laughed because of the life straw time they knew.

What they didn't know was, they were near the University of British Columbia. The Anthropology and Sociology Building. Headquarters of Canadian Literature, and Julie said, "One of my favorite poets is and fellow Canadians is Emily Pauline Johnson, Tekahionwake." Julie then recited Tekahionwake's poem, "The Song My Paddle Sings." No sooner then, the wind outside began to pick up.

Red and Andy agreed with Julie, Tekahionwake was a serious great poet, and thought about two sets of sisters and then another set. First they thought about Catherine Parr Traill and Susanna Moodie. Second they thought about the Two Sisters' of the legend; The Lions of Vancouver, twin mountains. Then they thought about the twin sisters Connie and Sophie, the waitress and the cook on the American journey. They then told Julie we never forgot the compromise, patience, and freedom in poetry. As in looking at the stars in the nights sky, stars are stars, and we are unaffected by laws, even when we apply the art of listening. Versification had always been strong and always will. Curiosity makes the ear finer.

"Then if that is the case, my dear friends Red and Andy," Julie spoke passionately, "I have a poem for you, so let's see if you can hear this."

Julie, closed her eyes for a moment, opened them and stood up to recite the poem,

"Searching For You"

Vancouver to Yukon, the train rushes on

Past cities and ports it keeps humming its song
My thoughts keeping time with the clack of the train
Oh, when in the world will I see you again

It speeds through the valleys and slows for the turns
'Round mountains and waters for which my soul yearns
My thoughts keeping time with the clack of the train
Oh, where in the world will I see you again

I'm looking for something my heart cannot find
Through mountainous Rockies and lakes where we wind
My thoughts keeping time with the clack of the train
Oh, when in the world will I see you again

There's peace in the rugged terrain we traverse
And joy in the riding when bad goes to worse
My thoughts keeping time with the clack of the train
Oh, where in the world will I see you again?

From Squamish to Dawson and Fort Nelson, too
I'm searching the province for some sign of you
My thoughts keeping time with the clack of the train
Oh, when in the world will I see you again

I pray for your safety and mourn our lost love
Each night as I gaze at the stars up above
My thoughts keeping time with the clack of the train
Oh, where in the world will I see you again

Though weeks I may wander and months may I roam
This land of BC is forever my home
My thoughts keeping time with the clack of the train
Oh, when in the world will I see you again

© Julie Catherine / J C Edwards, 2013

The whole poem was paddles, and Julie herself became the defibrillator. Not that Andy and Red were dead to the world, but when July musically used *'Oh, when in the world will I see you again'* emotional loads of memories flooded their breathing existence. And their body language spoke. Their hands covered their mouths indicating a person can only take so much. As Andy wrote a poem before called 'The Missing Jar' well that jar was full and about to break. Julie had no idea in how much light matter of the universe poured in and out of that poem, but it did, and in fact their spirits again were humbled in a new way beyond limitations, faults, blessings, appreciations, and comparisons. This new form of wonder for sure told them both the field of dreams was more powerful then they knew. This made them want to shed all bad things of themselves and the world more. Red and Andy stood up and hugged Julie, with tears no one said anything else, because she was right, when would they return to any of the poets, railroads, loves, friends, and family?

Andy turned around so they couldn't see his hurt, and the voice of the one he loved spoke to him from memory about his poem 'The Missing Jar' "Any- how about you set up a missing jar, and I'll set up a missing jar, and just like a cursing jar- every time we miss the other one- or shed a tear, we have to drop in a quarter!- then when our jars are all filled up, we can do something special together with our 'misses'!!--or put it toward our train trip fund!!!- You know when I first read this, I almost cried. You were in the bathroom, and I knew I couldn't deal with this poem, that's how great this piece is. You are able to bring the very essence of missing another front and center!

British Columbia:

British Columbia the place of North America's Crown Jewel, Glacier National Park. A land of bountiful vineyards, cherry trees, deep forests, surging waters, looming peaks, pounding waterfalls, and patches of pretty meadows. Alpine glaciers, warm sparkling crystal and glacial lakes, Williams Lake, Pinantan Lake, furthermore Islands, Moondance, and Qualicum Bays, and Crystal Cove. Fraser Canyon & River has been known as the Mighty Fraser and the place where the last spike was driven home at a place called Craigellachie in the Eagle Pass. There are numerous mountains and peaks in B.C. One of the most beautiful places on earth. I wonder if Candice James, Evelyn Lau, and Janet Marie Rogers have been to all of these places.

British Columbia Railways:

The Victoria and Esquimalt Railway Company began in 1873, the Esquimalt and Nanaimo Railway Company began in 1875, the Canadian Pacific Railway Company began in 1880, the Vancouver Coal Mining and Land Company began in 1881, the New Westminster and Port Moody Railway Company began in 1882, the Vancouver Land and Railway Company began in 1882, the Columbia and Kootenay Railway and Transportation Company began 1883, the Fraser River Railway Company began in 1883, the New Westminster Southern Railway Company began in 1883, the Pacific and Peace River Railway Company began in 1883, the Victoria Transfer Company began in 1883, the Vancouver Island Railway began in 1883, the Shuswap and Okanagan Railway Company began in 1886, the Vancouver Electric Railway and Light Company began in 1886, the Victoria and Saanich Railway Company began in 1886, the Vancouver, Klickitat and Yakima began in 1887, renamed the Portland, Vancouver and Yakima Railroad in 1897, the Delta Railway Company began in 1887, the Upper Columbia Railway Company began in 1887, the British Columbia Southern Railway Company began in 1888, the Harrison Hot Springs Tramway Company began in 1888, the Kootenay Railway and Navigation Company began in 1888, the Columbia and Kootenay

Railway and Navigation Company began in 1889, the New Westminster and Vancouver Short Line Railway Company began in 1889, the Victoria, Saanich and New Westminster Railway Company began in 1889, the Cariboo Railway Company began in 1890, the Columbia and Carbonate Mountain Railway Company began in 1890, the Okanagan and Kootenay Railway Company began in 1890, the Westminster and Vancouver Tramway Company began in 1890, the Burrard Inlet and Fraser Valley Railway Company began in 1891, the Burrard Inlet and Westminster Valley Railway Company began in 1891, the Burrard Inlet Railway and Ferry Company began in 1891, the Chilliwhack Railway Company (Chilliwack) began in 1891, the Liverpool and Canoe Pass Railway Company began 1891, the Nanaimo Electric Tramway Company began in 1891, the Nelson and Fort Sheppard Railway Company began in 1891, the Nicola, Kamloops and Similkameen Coal and Railway Company began in 1891, the Nicola Valley Railway Company began in 1891, the Upper Columbia Navigation and Tramway Company began in 1891, the Vancouver and Lulu Island Electrical Railway and Improvement Company began in 1891, the Vancouver and Lulu Island Railway Company began in 1891, the Vancouver, Northern, Peace River and Alaska Railway and Navigation Company began in 1891, the Vernon and Okanagan Railway Company began in 1891, the Victoria and North American Railway Company began in 1891, the Burrard Inlet Tunnel and Bridge Company began in 1892, the Kaslo and Slocan Railway Company began in 1892, the Kootenay Power Company began 1892, the Victoria and Sidney Railway Company began in 1892, the Kaslo and Slocan Tramway Company began in 1893, the Kootenay Lake Shore and Lardo Railway Company began in 1893, the Nakusp and Slocan Railway Company began in 1893, the Nelson and Arrow Lake Railway Company began in 1893, the Red Mountain Railway Company began in 1893, the Consolidated Railway Company began in 1894, the Delta, New Westminster and Eastern Railway Company began in 1894, the Victoria, Vancouver and Westminster Railway Company began in 1894, the Trail Creek and Columbia Railway Company began in 1895, the Ashcroft and Cariboo Railway Company began in 1896, the Columbia and Western Railway Company began in 1896, the Kootenay and Athabasca Railway Company began in 1896, the Barkerville, Ashcroft and Kamloops Railway Company began in 1897, the British Columbia Electric Power and Gas Company British Columbia Electric Railway Company began in 1897, the British Columbia Yukon Railway Company began in 1897, the British Yukon Railway Company began in 1897, the Cassiar Central Railway Company began in 1897, the Columbia River Bridge Company began in 1897, the Kaslo and Lardo-Duncan Railway Company began in 1897, the Lardeau Railway Company began in 1897, the Nanaimo - Alberni Railway Company began in 1897, the Stickeen and Teslin Railway, Navigation and Colonization Company began in 1897, the Vancouver-Nanaimo Railway Transfer Company began in 1897, the Vancouver, Victoria and Eastern Railway and Navigation Company began in 1897, the Canadian-Yukon Railway began in 1898, the Cowichan Valley Railway Company began 1898, the East Kootenay Railway Company began in 1898, the Kootenay and North West Railway Company began in 1898, the Mountain Tramway and Electric Company began in 1898, the North Star and Arrow Lake Railway Company began in 1898, the Pacific and Peace River Railway Company began in 1898, the Portland and Stickine Railway Company began in 1898, the Revelstoke and Cassiar Railway Company began in 1898, the Skeena River and Eastern Railway Company began 1898, the Skeena River Railway, Colonization and Exploration Company began in 1898, the South East Kootenay Railway Company began in 1898, the White Pass and Yukon Railway Company began in 1898, the Big Bend Transportation Company began in 1899, the Atlin Short Line Railway and Navigation Company began in 1899, the Atlin Southern Railway Company began in 1899, the Kamloops and Atlin Railway Company began in 1899, the Pine Creek Flume Company began in 1899, the South Kootenay Railway Company began in 1899, the Vancouver, Westminster, Northern and Yukon Railway Company began in 1899, the Comox and Cape Scott Railway Company began in 1900, the Crow's Nest Pass Electric Light and Power Company began in 1900, the Pacific Northern and Omineca Railway Company began in 1900, the Vancouver and Westminster Railway Company began in 1900, the Coast-Kootenay Railway Company began in 1901, the Crawford Bay Railway Company began in 1901, the Crow's Nest Southern Railway Company began in 1901, the Imperial Pacific Railway Company began in 1901, the Kettle Valley Railway Company began in 1901, the Kootenay and Arrowhead Railway Company began in 1901, the Kootenay Central Railway Company began in 1901, the Lake Bennett Railway Company began in 1901, the Queen Charlotte Islands Railway Company began in 1901, the Similkameen and Keremeos Railway Company began in 1901, the Vancouver and Grand Forks Railway Company began in 1901, the Vancouver, Westminster and Yukon Railway Company began in 1901, the Victoria Terminal Railway and Ferry Company began in 1901, the Yale-Northern Railway Company began in 1901, the Vancouver and Coast-Kootenay Railway Company began in 1902, the Velvet (Rossland) Mine Railway Company began 1902, the Victoria and Seymour Narrows Railway Company began in 1902, the Washington & Great Northern Railway began in 1902, the Great Northern Vancouver Victoria & Eastern Railway began in 1902, the British Columbia Northern and Mackenzie Valley Railway Company began in 1903, the Coast Yukon Railway Company began in 1903, the Cowichan, Alberni and Fort Rupert Railway Company began 1903-4 the Grand Trunk Pacific Railway Company began in 1903, the Kootenay, Cariboo and Pacific Railway Company began in 1903, the Kootenay Development and Tramways Company began in 1903, the Lardeau and Kootenay Railway Company began in 1903, the Morrissey, Fernie and Michel Railway Company began in 1903, the Pacific Northern and Eastern Railway Company began in 1903, the Quatsino Railway Company began in 1903, the Southern Central Pacific Railway Company began in 1903, the Boundary, Kamloops and Cariboo Central Railway Company began in 1904, the British Columbia and Manitoba Railway Company began in 1904, the Stave Valley Railway Company began in 1904, the Fording Valley Railway Company began in 1905-6, the Ashcroft Barkerville and Fort George Railway Company began in 1906, the Bella Coola and Fraser Lake Railway Company began in 1906, the British Columbia Central Railway Company began in 1906, the British Columbia Northern and Alaska Railway Company began in 1906, the Kamloops and Yellowhead Pass Railway Company began in 1906, the St. Mary's and Cherry Creek Railway Company began in 1906, the St. Mary's Valley Railway Company began in 1906, the Southern Okanagan Railway Company began in 1906, the Vancouver, Fraser Valley and Southern Railway Company began in 1906, the Bentinck Arm and Quesnel Railway Company began in 1907, the Burrard, Westminster Boundary Railway and Navigation Company began in 1907, the East Kootenay Logging Railway Company began in 1907, the Howe Sound and Northern Railway Company / Howe Sound, Pemberton Valley and Northern Railway Company began in 1907, the Portland Canal Railway Company began in 1907, the Tsimpsean Light and Power Company began in 1907, the Alberta and British Columbia Railway Company began in 1908, the Crow's Nest and Northern Railway Company began in 1908, the Eastern British Columbia Railway Company began in 1908, the Hudson Bay Pacific Railway Company began in 1908, the Vancouver and Nicola Valley Railway Company began in 1908, the Vancouver Island and Eastern Railway Company began in 1908, the Goat River Water Power and Light Company began in 1909, the Graham Island Railway Company began in 1909, the Hardy Bay and Quatsino Sound Railway Company began in 1909, the Pacific Coast Coal Mines Ltd began in 1909, the Prince Rupert and Port Simpson Railway Company began in 1909, the Vancouver and Northern Railway Company began in 1909, the Victoria and Barkley Sound Railway Company began in 1909, the British Columbia and Alaska Railway Company began in 1910, the Canadian Northern Pacific Railway Company began in 1910, the Cariboo, Barkerville and Willow River Railway Company began in 1910, the Island Valley Railway Company began in 1910, the Menzies Bay Railway Company began in 1910, the Nelson Street Railway Company began in 1910, the Northern Vancouver Island Railway Company began in 1910, the Pacific Railway Company began in 1910, the Penticton Railway Company began in 1910, the Pine Pass Railway Company began in 1910, the Port Moody, Indian River and Northern Railway Company began 1910, the British Columbia and Central Canada Railway Company began in 1911, the British Columbia and White River Railway Company began in 1911, the British Columbia and Dawson Railway Company began in 1911, the Greenwood-Phoenix Tramway Company began in 1911, the Grouse Mountain Scenic Incline Railway Company began in 1911, the Hudson Bay Pacific Railway Company began in 1911, the Naas and Skeena Rivers Railway Company began in 1911, the Pacific and Hudson Bay Railway Company began in 1911, the Peace and Naas River Railway Company began in 1911, the Pacific Great Eastern Railway Company began in 1912, the Atlin Railway Company began in 1914, the Pacific, Peace River and Athabasca Railway Company began in 1914, the Fraser Valley Terminal Railway Company began in 1915, the Northern Pacific and British Columbia Railway Company began in 1915, the Dolly Varden Mines Railway began in 1917, the Fernie and Elk River Railway Company began 1921, the First Narrows Bridge Company began in 1926-7, the Fraser River Bridge Company began in 1926, the Ladner Bridge Company began in 1926-7, the Lions Gate Bridge Company began in 1926, and the Greater Vancouver Tunnel Company Ltd began in 1931.

There was 128 Defunct Railway Companies, proposed by hopeful investors in the province's early years. Hereby declared to have wholly ceased. The Defunct Railway Companies Dissolution Act wiped out 128 railway companies incorporated in B.C. in the 45 years since 1882, compiled by Derek Hayes- bchistoryonline.com & Ian Smith, Winter 2013 issue of the Sandhouse.

British Columbia Poets:

The first Poet I found was Lindi Nolte and she studied at the University of Pretoria, and her poetry is beautiful poetry indeed, and she brings out the deepness in life for all of us. Her poetry is layered in Family, Life and Politics. She can be brutal to Despair in this world and I love that. She also has wisdom that teaches, and her poetry indeed reaches. She can be poetically lethal, so this means she is a Poet to look out for. Her poems "Elephant," "The Butterflies That We Keep," "Castro," "Nelson Mandela," and "Words Painted On Me" reveal her talent.

The second Poet I found was Julie Catherine Vigna, and there's a call for beauty, a demand! There's pursuit- okay, heartfelt, you shall get heart felt reading her poetry. So if poems had arms to hold you close, her poems are it, so relax- Her forms of poems will form and inform you. Nature unfolds, and love unfolds in her work. Warmth, warmth, warmth is all through her poetry. Her poetry, reveals her love for life, all life. Riveting, and fastening poetry. She installs poetic beauty, and brilliance into the readers heart, and Julie is very innovative, and she uses traditional forms into her own way. Her poems, "Sensual Waters," "Summer Love (A Villanelle)," "The Power of Friendship," "Sonnet Sequence: Maiden, Mother, Crone," and "The Angel and the Fairy," furthermore the poem list can go on and on.

The third Poet I found was Candice James, who is Poet Laureate of New Westminster, BC Canada. Heart in all stages of life is in her poetry. Poetry in narrative. History.! Nature, and she can go on and on. Wisdom, Woman's Wisdom. Her love for poetry is in her poetry, and here love for poets is very to the very evident & e-evident in all that she does. Candice can flip the poetic language for sure, and I took some time and read & listened in & applied to my life. She for sure also knows the definition of keep and keeping. She for sure can put the reader on any and all levels of poetry. Her poems "Ghosts of BC Penitentiary," "Our Journey," "The Parrot," "Cracking," "Sleeping Awake" and "Never Ending" are only a fraction of her heart and poetry. I also want to add that Candice introduced me and the Poetry Train to numerous talented poets, and that speaks volumes.

The fourth Poet I found was Deborah L. Kelly, and she studied at UHN, the University of Hard Knocks. Her poetry is themed in Wisdom, Nature, Spirituality, Family, Friendship, and Future Concern, furthermore Politics. She's a fighter, and a believer, and you can feel it in her poetry when you read & listen. She has beat too, most of all, her wisdom flourishes, and it's the kind of wisdom that reaches out, reaching to us now, and generations to come. Deborah's' faith poetry is superb, and you understand it, making her poetry humbling to you. Her poems "Judge Me Not," "Chorus of Peace," "The Winged Messenger," "Societal Pretense," and "Peacock Wings and Crystal Feathers" are only a small amount of her talent in poetry. Deborah also wrote a poem entitled Poetry Train Canada, and when she did when this journey began and we met online, the warmth welcome from her, and Poets from British Columbia was & still is pure soul touching.

The fifth Poet I found was Dalannah Gail Bowen, and her poetry is powerfully blues drivin to the beats of love, lost love, positivity in life, politics & spirituality. "The Spirit Within" is a masterpiece. She also sings and plays the blues, and in a percussion performance group called The Snowy Owls Drummers.

The sixth Poet I found was Shane Koyczan and his poetry is powerful in the themes of life, youth, love, family, and much more. He is mesmerizing, and his poems, "To This Day Project," "The Crickets Have Arthritis," "More Often Than Sometimes," and "Why Does This Man's Grandfather Fight Monsters?." are smooth poems that take the reader and listener to similarity's and familiarity's. I love his triplets in his poetry.

The seventh Poet I found was Chris Nelles, and his poetry has deep tones (tones themed in many things in a poem of his (a gift indeed) /deep thought, a burden perhaps? Meaningful messages layered deep in his work. I personally believe, he is well in the realm of poetry, and calling out to all; (is that the burden?) not just poets, but to readers also, because there are certain lines that convey this. He is deep in poetry, meaning mastered, but mastering in ways of realms of language that can be solid, mental solid but solid. (you know poets tools and &c &c) His poems "i am become as death, as art," "great is the yoke that yaws," "I am not strong as men count strength," "how the mooning lovers pile up," and "is it too late to put the plucked fig back" are beyond amazing. Once you read his work there is no way out. There's wordplay, great personification, and much much more to enjoy reading his work, furthermore a word of caution; it is best to read his work with a fireman's suit on so you don't get burned. His poetry is fire, and every letter is a pillar to the poems flames of imagery.

Addition by Mr. Chris Nelles, at first she will lead him by tortuous ways, at first she will lead him by tortuous ways, at first she will lead him by tortuous ways, filling him with craven fears. her discipline will be a torment to him, and her decrees a hard test, until he trusts her with all his heart; then she will come straight back to him, bringing gladness and revealing to him her secrets. but if he strays, she will abandon him and leave him to his fate.

put your feet in her fetters and your neck into her collar. stoop to carry her on your shoulders and do not chafe at her bonds. come to her wholeheartedly, and with all your might keep to her ways. follow her track, and she will make herself known; once you have grasped her do not let her go.

In the end you will find the refreshment she offers; she will transform herself for you into joy: her fetters will become your strong defense and her collar a splendid robe. Her yoke is a golden ornament and her bonds a violet cord; you will put her on like a splendid robe and wear her like a garland of joy.

Solomon

I remember only that I've forgotten, and I've forgotten all that's worth remembering. I remember odd moments that make no sense and have no time-line. I remember events that probably happened, may have happened, and likely didn't happen, as if they were facts set in stone, or flights of fevered fancy as nebulous as ether.

In my teens g-d created my heavens and earth. And I was without form and void; and darkness was upon the face of the deep. And g-d said let there be light: and there was light.

And this light shone into my mummified soul in two ways; through the love I felt for a girl and through the sublime poetic truth of the bible. I discovered both together, and my life has since involved the two entwined as I make my way up this latticed vine toward a blinding voice I cannot comprehend. A voice I have tried to apprehend in verse.

The poetry of love and justice fixed its gaze upon my razed soul using a girl and the books for its bait and drew me toward its inexorable eternal maze where beauty and truth cohabit in a contradiction that slew me to life.

Raised in blind ignorance, I did not hesitate but to immediately set my hand to imitate the prophets. I knew no better and knew not what I conceived. But I thought to employ their eloquence for more pressing matters. I wrote to win a woman's love. I plumbed my imagination and mind to find metaphors and ideas that might give justification to my enamored state in the hope of winning her affections.

Ironically, as i combed the recesses of my mind in search of metaphor to praise the object of my affection, poetry auto-plumbed the depths of my past and the black numbness of my unconscious. It illuminated every dark corner that lay paralyzed or sleeping and quickened the memories or sensations i needed to make conscious.

Indeed, it was the original intent of the prophets, flowing through the same source of inspiration, that set itself to work in my denied spirit while I believed I set it to work for more juvenile designs.

This began a contradictory cycle. As decades of deliberately forgotten feelings and experiences rushed to introduce themselves to my awareness, it created a state of ongoing crisis, which shipwrecked my love life and threw me into a lifestyle of confusion and poverty that reflected my childhood.

Poetry won me love and lost me love. It gave me my past and scuttled my future. It rushed me headlong into ecstatic arms only to entrench me in issues that left me alone in a stagnant swamp of bogged down memories which demanded attention.

Poetry taught me that truth does not need consciousness to reveal itself, that there exists something more supreme that cannot be erased, that keeps its own account of events, and measures the magnitude of injustices by a standard above and beyond man's common law which relies upon a kind of proof that is easy enough to bury.

Love poetry set me on the path of rational reality, moral outrage, and imaginative beauty. Poetry saved me from ignorance of the past and future by penetrating both with an irrefutable presence that revealed.

The meaning of justice and irony. I gathered the crumbs of clues from the four corners of my compromised mind, and stitched them into a work of art.

Once conscious of the nightmare of my beginnings I burned everything I had written related to it. A great body of work exhumed to be properly cremated. The conscious intent of the act removed much of the power of the unconscious crimes passed down from generation to generation and perpetrated personally against me.

This time forgetting wasn't about mindlessly obeying subliminal orders buried in me through arbitrary terror. Nor was it about managing pain by escaping what my life so urgently pressed me to recover. It was about realization and decision. The realization that I could remain within my family without myself or have myself with the pain of losing my family.

I chose myself with unending loneliness and pain. I chose the freedom of exile over life that felt like a thousand deaths. I disposed of the stinking corpses rotting in my mind, which my family insisted didn't exist, yet equally insisted i live with, like they were sacred relics to pass on.

And when I confronted, named, and burned them for the sake of my liberation, my original family, along with every relative I knew, fled from me, casting all manner of spurious suggestions at me and among themselves to coax the devils back into their hiding places so that they could continue to deny and cherish them and cling to their horrors still. What remained for me was doubt and the desire for a woman's touch. Poetry also remained and reassured, just as it had revealed and ruined. I trusted its conclusions, which used imagination as a medium and irony as proof. I apprehended that it embraced the intent of rational thought, and arrived at truth from an entirely unexpected angle. Poetry was my refuge, as it once was the refuge of those who are tortured into mental institutes. As it was the safe haven of those who have been driven out of their souls and into realms no one knows, by those who feed on the blood of the broken, while they seek those whom they can break next.

And because it cobbled a soul out of infinitely small shards of fragmentation and alienation it is the eternal enemy of evil. What evil perpetrates, love poetry, in the hands of one who yearns for goodness and tender justice, penetrates and dis-empowers.

For this reason the guilty fear it. Their crimes stand naked before its searching eyes. Enigmatic, arcane, allusive though lyric poetry may have necessarily become, due to mutilating circumstances, the criminal, like the injured poet, reads the true reckoning of his wrong doing , and receives his sentence within the words.

Throughout time, whether one ventures to the left or the right, among philosophers or politicians, acme artists are anathema to the functions of necessity and organization, which rely upon the law of crime, though it be perpetrated in pettiness or collusive permissiveness, for survival and aggrandizement.

Thus the true poet is born an enemy of the world and can expect only that which i inherited from the moment i drew my first breath and entered into a family which neither knew me, nor needed me.

Destined to be an enemy of the world I was delivered to lunatic alcoholics who had a proclivity for carnal cruelties. It was ensured that ignorance, every orphan's birth right, was my only teacher. I would learn only by blind impulse and the inevitable ensuing disaster. Abandoned to the state and the bare minimum, my future was left to chance without mercy or assistance.

Unconsciously perpetuating their bloodline's traditions, my parents marked me in the same manner they must have been marked. Driven by a nefarious and urgent drive to legitimize and justify themselves they reproduced their own likeness in their children, and sealed my fate with a genetic gravestone they themselves could not open.

They destroyed my youth with the coarse abuse so common among drunken Catholics. And my teen years were butchered with the religious hypocrisy known to accompany fundamentalist Protestants.

They took my mid-teen discovery messiah Jesus and turned my moment of triumph into another form of abject slavery. They chained my soul to the protestant church by co-opting the bible and used it to excuse their need to further bind me to their own petty designs. They perverted and enslaved my personality. My soul was decapitated and in its place was born an undead devotee, which lived in my place, and which still seeks to overthrow the urgent emergence of my person.

This man who I was and wasn't, lived where I couldn't. While the man who I wasn't yet, hibernated and waited for freedom's spring thaw.

Meanwhile I grew under a fierce shadow of malice, a vacuum of knowledge and wisdom, a strange and utterly terrifying superstition that gripped my parents and magnified itself through the drunkenness and hypocrisy they sought refuge in.

They ravaged my body and mind, taking reason, imagination, memory, emotion, even love as hostages to ransom to their bizarre anti-Christian Christian god who appeared, like Moloch, to require child sacrifice in exchange for favor.

I was too terrified to resist their dominance. I embraced it with abandon. I lived without thought. I was perfect in my faith. I was not troubled by questions for there simply was no mind within to ask any.

Lifeless, I became life moving as if it were dead. I moved as a perfect contradiction, an irony incarnate. I became both a mirror and a black hole. I reflected every expectation and reflected nothing at all.

The untenable contradictions created untenable contradictions. In this way my parents set their design into perpetual motion so that with or without them I would find a way to continue to abort myself through negation. From negation to negation I was inert inertia. Inert but for my need of a woman. Nothing or no one could staunch this unquenchable yearning for beauty. I blindly followed whomever I loved. She went to university so I went to university to write her poetry. Soon we were married and divorced. Soon I had left school to flounder aimlessly among the broken.

But not quite aimlessly, and not quite broken. Always the whispers of the prophets played in my mind. And when I found myself falling away from the one I had lost, they were there with their threnody.

It was as if I was being marched toward poetry's supremacy with an alternating current whose right hand did not know what its left hand did. I poured out my human love in my verse while the prophets filled me with words written with such a perfect hand that I was comforted and continued to chase love.

Poetry gave me women and women gave me poetry. Through them I was led to examine the history and future of myself, the world and nature. It was through my desire for beauty and love that strength and courage found me. Courage to confront myself in ignorance and deprivation. Strength to overcome the ensuing despair, awareness and knowledge brought with it.

Though I had applied the prophet's craft to more sexual ends, those same ends inevitably led me back to the original issues of justice the prophets spoke of. It was as if the pursuit of love led to justice and vice versa.

I began to suspect the two must be linked. Love and justice. The seers' grand demands might be implied in the rise and fall of love between the sexes. I began to believe that to perceive and record the movement of romantic relationship would lead to a universal understanding of every social, political, or personal movement of importance.

But the modern poets contradicted my thoughts. They wrote of love and failed to inspire anything other than cold contempt. They waxed poetic but not prophetic. Their poetry lacked even the eloquence the most casual prose assumed.

Here was proof that romance led to nowhere elevated. Even when they addressed social issues directly they did so with the dull drone of drudgery which fed my apathy and my yearning to return to the numb cocoon of my ignorance. Poetry appeared to plunge poets into a nonsensical world of self-inflated whim, where strings of pretty sentences led to classrooms where children were forced to swallow their frothing spit.

Or worse, it led to an avant-garde opinion of yourself which devoured even the pretty sentences of the state and school sanctioned baying and neighing, in a self-imploding whirlpool of auto-cannibalism that the poet recorded for g-d knows who
.

I noticed that everyone wrote poetry yet no one read it. I wondered at this until I understood the difference between the prophets and today's poets. I concluded that while all prophets are poets not all poets are prophets. There existed at least two unique sources of song and the song I preferred hadn't been uttered by anyone for a very long time.

Having substituted the pursuit of the aesthetic for the meaningful, the holiness of poetry lost its potency, leaving its practitioners (not knowing that holiness is beauty but beauty is not always holy, that truth is beauty but beauty is not always truth) to foster the belief that poetry, like the other arts is about appearances , which it is not.

Poetry, I realized, was not meant to be art. It was meant to be the connection with the invisibles, the conduit with which they gave men their direction. When man severed that function and took language

Into his own hands, thinking to manipulate it into his own image, true poetry escaped into the ether where it ever seeks someone through whom to speak its siren song.

John's gospel opens, „in the beginning was poetry, and poetry was with g-d, and poetry was g-d. He was with g-d in the beginning. All things came to be through him, and without him nothing made has being. In him was life and that life was the light of man. The light shines in the darkness and the darkness has not suppressed it."

Perhaps, I reasoned, it wasn't poetry that plunged poets but poets that had plunged poetry into infantile whining and arrogant apathies. Perhaps, originally, poetry had a messianic name, poetry reflected g-d, and man received poetry and conceived poetry's half-brothers, the arts and the sciences.

And perhaps some men took poetry and raped her and gave her identical bastard children of the arts and sciences: the consumptive arts and crafts created with the belief that man was the source and god a work of his hand, with the design of dominance at its heart, and cunning technique, artistic deceit, mechanized awe, and infinite financial backing upon its sleeve.
Perhaps this was why true poetry needed to be silenced or discredited or marginalized. Co-opted as an art form, men could manipulate the demands poetry makes upon one's

conscience, until it could be used by occult artists, priests, politicians, technicians, for ends other than what was intended. It could be effectively castrated in order to neutralize its original ability to uncover that which is invisible and thus expose all the slavery and torture and soul murder conceived in conspiracy to inflict upon man.

At last I understood...prophets, once heaven's rebels, whose purpose was to defy tyranny, and prepare the world for Christ, traditionally found the writing craft lent itself to their purpose. From this application poetry was born. From the dawn of culture, first the prophets, and then the true poets claimed the craft for the liberation of the people.

But another rebellion, a rebellion against rebellion, tyranny's rebellion against liberty's rebellion, along the way usurped language and has ever since pressed it into the service of the dominators who work feverishly for the disappearance of the invisibles. They use inspiration to subdue inspiration, use god to overthrow g-d, and thus they've silenced the voice men needed to remember their origins and understand their outcome.

After thousands of years of misappropriation, poetry appears as it is today: irrelevant, emasculated, effeminate masturbation's or obfuscations. A forgery, and a bad one at that. The ignominious art on death row awaiting execution. The expression of the mad perpetuating apathy.

Meanwhile poetry's bastard children rush unhindered in their age old attempt to fashion for themselves their golden man, shaped from the artistry of their hand. At last, they think, they will throw down g-d's supremacy and his prophet's rebellion. By co-opting poetry's ascendancy with beguiling crafts, they now push to visibly recreate that ancient dystopia where the few will rule the all.

Near the end of this long war between the invisible's legitimate children and the bastard usurpers you find the place where I fit in. The inheritor of eons of abdicating poets who sold their birthright to sing pretty ditties for citizen pimps who turn them out to whore their worthless masochism's.

But unlike my forbears, who rejected their origins, for effete affectations, I surprised the visible and invisibles alike by seeking the prophet's poems, which filled me with the desire to attempt to fail at a great undertaking, rather than succeed at a mediocre task: to return poetry to the invisibles and the invisibles" poems to the people.

I conceived my commission to become the present day incarnation of the ancient world's search for holy beauty.

As if this wasn't arrogant enough, having found the song of songs in the bible, that great celebration of sexual love, I returned to my belief that all the urgent wounding's that need mending are foreseen in the struggle for true love between a man and a woman. If I could understand earthly love I believed everything else would follow.

I decided, therefore, to re-experience and rewrite Solomon's, "song of songs". I imagined that this would intimately intertwine the two currents of inspiration that tied me up and set me free. I thought that I had found a way to submit myself to the same inspired flow that had arrested the prophets without needing to shift my focus away from the overwhelming beauty of women. I could thus make available to all men a reiterated way in which each person could celebrate love.

Fool that I was, I thought this self-imposed mission would provide a metaphor, the love relationship, from which people could derive an understanding of every relationship. I would give them a cryptic manual they could resort to, to discover and correct their own defects, help others better themselves, while fulfilling the search for the beloved. Wouldn't this modest ambition, then, console the outcast, succor the grieving, comfort the jilted, guide the lost, enlighten the confused, liberate the oppressed? In short I would reintroduce the passion of the prophets through my love poetry.

Yet I, the author and finisher of the text, was not consoled, comforted or enlightened. It did, however, reveal my unending shortcomings, the shortcomings of others, our inability or unwillingness to address them, and their ever growing concentric implications, as these evils move out into our world to become the harbingers of the doom that looms over us. The doomed culture, which is both mother and child of the corruptions we incubate in the closets of each other's injuries. Beyond this I have utterly failed in my task, as I have failed at knowing relationships, and myself.

Ironically, in my failure, I proved my own apprehensions. And the more I reflected on the distance separating myself from my beloved reward, the more I came to understand the age in which I lived and was called to address. The bridge between personal and social issues had emerged through my romantic inquiry. My delusion, or rather the shattering of my dream, led me to desire justice and love for all.

It led to a refusal to accept the status quo discovered in my journey away from ignorance toward awareness, which denies love and justice for anyone except the chosen, who sit upon their mounds of glittering trinkets without either love or justice, withholding the goods and services heaven wishes to pour upon our heads, for the mere pleasure of cruelty, which is the only form of love they have and the only concept of justice they deserve.

My failure to win any object of my affection forced me to master language which revealed all that psychology and psychiatry focus on as subject matter, namely the self. Everything related to romance and women came hard on its heels. Last came an understanding of the social matrix both men and women are born into. And with this knowledge I understood how ourselves, our lovers, and ultimately forces that control both self and others subordinate love's passion so that it can enslave all to the black appetites of those few individuals who own the earth.

I came to see that my work reflects no more than the profound alienation that exists between us all. It represents the complete breakdown of communication, the usurping desire of self-love over the need for the other, the abandonment of abiding affections, the betrayal of confidences and trust, the consumptive drive to devour anyone and everyone for pleasure, sport, power, distraction, or whatever else motivates someone to incarnate the limitless faces of suicidal murder that I cannot grasp.

At the same time my verse also reflects an unregenerate world's inability to drive from my inner life, the dream that love and justice for all is a reality more real than what my senses and experience gleefully force upon me. That it is only the bastard sons of god who withhold the universal blessings from us due to the attachment they bear nihilist cynicism.

With Albert Camus I have concluded that "the artist's rebellion against reality, which is automatically suspect by any totalitarian revolution or state, contains the same affirmation as the spontaneous affirmation of the oppressed. Art thus leads us back to the origins of rebellion, to the extent that it tries to give its form to an elusive value which the future perpetually promises, of which the artist has but a presentiment and wishes to snatch from the grasp of history... The two questions that are posed by our times to a society caught in a dilemma—is creation possible? Is revolution possible?—are in reality only one question, which concerns the renaissance of civilization." To this I can add nothing. Let my work be its footnote.

No longer a fool, I remain fool enough to believe in what almost everyone casts aside for immediate foolishness, that is, the belief that love and justice will prevail. Even though, with Alexander Herzen I can also say that "I no longer expect anything. After what I have seen and experienced nothing will move me to any particular wonder or deep joy. Joy and wonder are curbed by memories of the past and fears of the future. Almost everything has become a matter of indifference to me, and along with this I experience the loss of all my beliefs, all that was precious to me meeting with betrayal, treacherous blows from behind, and in general a moral corruption of which you have no conception."

Even so I cannot be turned aside from my original course. Broken I've become unbreakable. Denied I'm now undeniable. Forsaken, I have not forsaken myself, and cannot have my love of true love and justice overcome by all the worlds" cynicism heaped upon my head and forced to grow like cancer in my body.

I still believe, as John Ralston Saul believes, that "it is through language we will find our way out of our current dilemma, just as a rediscovery of language provided a way out for westerners during the humanist breakthrough that began in the twelfth century. For those addicted to concrete solutions, this call for a rebirth or rediscovery of meaning may well seem vague and unrelated to reality. But language, when it works, is the tool that makes it possible to invoke reality." To this end I have striven. Let my effort be no more than an attempt to compel others to succeed where I have failed.

Perhaps confronting, naming, exposing evil, whether in ourselves, our lovers, or our world, whatever the negative consequences, is the only optimistic act left to us who have abdicated any responsible involvement with loved ones, neighbors, or fellow citizens.

Perhaps it is now too late to complete anything worthwhile such as personal revolution or ascending the stairs to the beloved's bedroom. Perhaps all that is left us, because we have left doing anything else worthwhile, is the final overthrow of fascist corporatism which has subsumed every art and science. Certainly its arrest must be made now, before it subdues the furthest shore of civil society, and renders the issues of love and justice moot.

Let others take up the task. I am worn beyond repair from merely struggling to get to where i am writing this to you. If I have not constructed that elegant sentence which will act as a crystal which precipitates the crystallization of the whole, then I have at least laid out my scheme in plain speech so that you, who are stronger, more courageous, more gifted than i, might achieve what I could not.

A sentence rightly written, timed, aimed, released, is all it will take to begin our civilization's end and our culture's rebirth. "both nature and history are going nowhere, and therefore they are ready to go anywhere they are directed. Having neither programme, set theme, nor unavoidable denouement, the disheveled improvisation of history is ready to walk with anyone; anyone can insert into it his line of verse and, if it is sonorous..." Said Herzen, who knows what the outcome might be?

Those who rule us sense the danger. This is why they have subdued the arts and rule not only our bodies, but our ideas and imaginings. Perhaps this is why not only the ruling class oppresses us, but the majority of our intimates also seek our silence. They wish not to have their prescribed imagination disturbed, though it cost them their freedom.

Men now live without complaint, indignation, cursing and protest. Critical speech is lost, sorrow anathema. What remains is a fairyland of false optimism which, we are told, will be the panacea of all negative fears and outcomes. While distracted by the bread and circuses, this thoughtlessness lets the worst among us pave the planet black, hurling us toward a hell of Hitler's marching over our complicit minds toward oblivion.

"After monopolizing everything else," Herzen said, "the governments and corporations have now taken the monopoly of talk and, imposing silence on everyone else, have begun chattering unceasingly."

Artists and their ilk no longer call men to themselves but bray in the marketplace, enforcing their owner's agendas with billion dollar allowances, or a tawdry government grant, and an array of technological tools, from the ancient word to the most modern media breakthroughs, like avant-garde ass shadows of mammon whores.

All is false, full of sound and fury signifying nothing. But if you turn down the empty volume, the glamorous white noise and listen, really listen, you can hear the horrors they're hatching in the subtext of their get rich plots. Don't doubt they wish with relish to release them in your name, upon those loved ones you cannot love.

Unless a critical mass wakes up today and takes to resistance, tomorrow will see the rise of a fascist sun over a corporate Reichstag that will not set until we're led to our deaths, or a box that keeps us breathing for infernal experiments.

But today still exists, and today's sun, while waning still shines its free light over our decline. So i celebrate true love and self-revolt. I accept that these sublime pleasures are mine only if I also shoulder all men's righteous cry for justice.

So I speak for those who once spoke but speak no more. I stand up at the end of it. At the end of a long line of poets; Donne, Dante, Milton, Vallejo, Lorca, Merini, Akhmatova, Eliot, and many more who have faithfully carried forward the account of the prophets and the apostles of Jesus messiah. I echo Osip Mandelstam who understood, they've taken the seas, our running start, our flying start. They've weighed our steps with earth, with bars. But still we have our lips, our moving lips."

Mandelstam, acme poet king with prophet's crown and pole star eyes knew what was coming should all be left to roll on inexorably without intervention
Your slim shoulders are to redden under whips,
Bleed from scourges and to burn in frosts.
Your child hands are to lift hot irons,
lift hot irons and sew mail bags.
Your tender feet are to tread on glass,
barefoot on glass and bloody sand.
And i'll burn a black candle,
burn like a candle and dare not pray.

The eighth Poet I found was Fred Wah and he studied at U.B.C. and took an MA in Linguistics and Literature at SUNY Buffalo. Fred's poetry is unique, and playful, furthermore amazing. Some of his powerful themes are about nature, family, ethics, and he also ethical. His poems "How to Hunt," "Warp Body," "The Snowflake Age," and for sure "Race, to go," are very impressionable to me.

The ninth Poet I found was Janet Kvammen and she is a poet, artist, and photographer, and as she may say a Visual Verse artist, furthermore she is a promoter, and as she says in her poetry, Visual Verse, should be cherished in a poem. And I will leave it at that, because for one thing, she moves fast, and she takes away, and that is skills intertwined. She is skilled massively in all three arts. Her Visual Verse poems are themed in nature, animals, strength, wisdom, and love. Janet's poems "Blue Heron," "Night Diamonds," "Memories Blossom In My He (art)," "Dragonflies & Summer Daze," and "Exquisite Paradox" are prime poems of her talent.

The tenth Poet I found was Ejemen Iyayi and her poetry is keen on the human struggle. Her poem "Her Challenge, Our Challenge" is a perfect poem with that theme.

The eleventh Poet I found was Jeremy Loveday, and he studied at Concordia University. Jeremy's poetry is themed in serious issues (hard core in mellow tones, put kindly, (me guessing), and a bit comical in his "Dear Death Metal" poem, furthermore his poetry is heart touching and stamping. Jeremy for sure engages (real change) through his poetry. His poems "Ode to Courage," "Dear Death Metal," "Spirit of Giving," "Masks Off - A Challenge to Men," and "The Evolution of Love" is a small amount of his released talent.

The twelfth Poet I found was Mary Gibbs, and she studied at the College of New Caledonia, furthermore she is an artist. Her poetry makes me think, because it is emotional, with love and longing, happiness and sorrow. Her poems "Where you want to go," "The Silence," "I hope you know," "Running," "Solitude," and "Bruised," has serious passion with a calling to imagination, love and peace.

The thirteenth Poet I found was Caroline Nazareno, a.k.a. Ceri Naz, and she studied at the University of the Philippines Diliman. Her poems brighten, with love, family, nature & fun times, furthermore some soft-core erotica. There is also concern & triumph embedded. Ceri's poems, "Call Me Cypher," "Fusion," "My Name is Me," "Pandora Escapes Unto My Hands (where mystery lies)," "The Dreamer's Note," "if this piece is for peace," and many more are magical!

The fourteenth Poet I found was David Campbell, well, walking sticks are very good, very, walk and feel. All I can say about a David is, wisdom and sorrow go hand in hand, and in the art of living, and listening, there shall be tears, and years, furthermore fears: shall we try at all three, then things will grow and never fade out: David's poems, "Rusty Boat," "Walking Stick," "Oleander And Frangipani," "Working With What You've Got," and "You Remember The People" sit down the reader/listener, and his poetry does that.

The fifteenth Poet I found was Heather Haley, and she studied at Grant MacEwan University. Her poetry is upbeat, erotic, 'innovative,' visionary in technology, living the change, real change. Modica Powerful. Heather's poems, "Appleton," "BUSHWHACK," "Dying For Pleasure" and "Whore In The Eddy," are triggering & deliverance poems.

The sixteenth Poet I found was Ben Nuttall-Smith, and he studied at Western Washington University. Ben's poems, "Princess Louisa Inlet," "Billy's Bull Frog," "Of Daydreams and Seaweed," and "Rebuke to the Railway," are calming, comical, and wise, furthermore it is splendid to hear Ben read his poetry.

The seventeenth Poet I found was Dianne Tchir, and she studied at the University of Alberta, furthermore she is a retired High School English and Drama teacher. When she is not writing she is teaching English as a second language, and also facilitating workshops in writing memoir, reader's theater, poetry, freelancing for newspapers, editing manuscripts, autobiography, memoir and poetry. Right away when you read Dianne's poetry you notice her work is powerful outdoor poetry. Mainly what I have read on the journey has been Beautiful- Haiku. She is also a novelist. Diannes' poems,

"Christmas Not Destroyed By Fire," "Haibun The Move," and "Breath," show extreme originality and intelligence, because each line is a scene, so I guess where reader's theater comes into play. Her Haiku has superb perspective and environment. Dianne's poetry collection contains Northern Phoenix, The Rhythmic Cycle, Bears Bath Time, Baby's First Year, and Ants Invade The Classroom with Teacher's Guide, furthermore a Charity Anthology, a collaboration with the artist Klarissa Dreams.

The eighteenth Poet I found was Gary Geddes, and his poetry is heartfelt and strong in family and childhood; politics and war. Gary's poems, "Jimmy's Place," "Sandra Lee Scheuer," "Sullivan," and "The Last Canto," are graphic, enigmatic and mellow, but mellow for the reader to grasp the hardcore realities about some of the poems he writes. Gary reveals so much slowly to his readers, yes much slowly, a skill I have not yet found until reading his work.

The nineteenth Poet I found was Ashok K. Bhargava, and he studied at the University of Manitoba. When reading Ashok's poems you realize how beautiful poetry is along with how life and mankind can be. Love and nature is braided in his poetry, delicate & beautiful. While reading Ashok's poems, "With You," "Departure," "Celestial Treat," and "Fortune Cookie" you know right away he is very observant, and love and beauty is alive and well. Ashok is also the founder of Writers International Network Canada.

The twentieth Poet I found was Max Tell and he studied at University of Nebraska–Lincoln furthermore at the Banff School of Fine Arts. Max's poems, "Octopus Ink," "The Knight the Dragon and the Librarian," "Peace," and "The Kid Who Hid His Head in a Box" are wise, and they made me smile, and think many thoughts in happiness. Max also is an award winning songwriter for kids, Robert "Max Tell" Stelmach, dubbed "The International Troubadour" and "BC's answer to Dr. Seuss" has been delighting young audiences with his songs, stories, and poems since 1986. He has seven world tours and six acclaimed CDs to his credit. Eleven of his songs and stories have received Honorable Mention in national and international competitions, including The Australian Songwriters' Association Competition, The West Coast Songwriting Competition, and The International Songwriting Competition. His song "Cat in My Hoody" was a first place winner in the 2012 Great American Songwriting Contest, in the children's lyric category. "Sasquatch" received his most recent Honorable Mention in the 2014 American Amateur Songwriter Contest sponsored by American Songwriter.

The twenty first Poet I found was Genni Gunn, and she studied at the University of British Columbia, and she is also an author, musician and translator. Genni's poems, "wEstSCAPES," and "Dead Mail" are provocative in story like narrative.

The twenty second Poet I found was Joy Kogawa. There is connection, life hardcore or not reading her work, but it is beautiful poetry. Joy's poems, "Hiroshima Exit," "Day of the Bride," "Where There is a Wall," and "Offerings" are poems with light at the end of the tunnel, you have heard of that saying dynamite comes in small packages well, here you go, reading her poetry is just that.

The twenty third Poet I found was Evelyn Lau, and her poetry is action packed with family and life. Evelyn's poems, "Janny," "Gratitude," "Willow," "Living Under Plastic," and "Nothing Happened" surrounds you with wit and a story. Poetry with a grip.

The twenty fourth Poet I found was Daphne Marlatt, and she studied at the University of British Columbia and Indiana University. People and place is a main theme in her work. In Daphne's poems, "Wet Fur Wavers," "Animal Sheen," "bardo blues, street-level," "bardo note," "bardo: notation," you can hear her calling and pointing to the reader, "Come here and look what I have found." are superb.

The twenty fifth Poet I found was Susan Musgrave, and her poetry is themed in animals, life, and family. Susan's poems, "Rest Area," "Arctic Poppies," "Things That Keep And Do Not Change," and "The Moment" are deep and will awaken the readers spirit.

The twenty sixth Poet I found was Johnny Murdoch Macrae. He is a master at humor, and twists his poems with wisdom and reality. Johnny's poems, "B.C.," "It's Just a Piece of Paper," "Stinkweed," and "HIV," are playful and sparky.

The twenty seventh Poet I found was Shayne Avec I Grec. Science, friendship, and life are rooted in his poems. Shayne's poems, "Aqueous Solution," "The Captain of Paradise," "God Fishing," and "(Not a) Revolutionary Poem," are very interesting poems for anyone.

The twenty eighth Poet I found was Brad Cran, and he studied at the University of Arizona. Life, beauty, animals and mammals, furthermore humanity bleeds through his poetry. Brad's poems, "At Lacey Madden's Grave," "Thirteen Ways of Looking at a Gray Whale, After Wallace Stevens and ending with a line from Rilke," and "Today After Rain," are beautiful poems, and you can tell he looks for things not written about, he is sharp.

The twenty ninth Poet I found was Celeste Snowber, and she studied at Simon Fraser University, Gordon-Conwell Theological Seminary, and Southeastern Massachusetts University. Her poems are breathing with family, nature, and spiritual freedom. Celeste's poems, "Shimmering," "The Body Knows," "Random Beauty," "The Skin of Winter," and "Back to one," are heart and soul, intriguing, and thought provoking.

The thirtieth Poet I found was Nathanaël Larochette, and his poetry is witty and quick, with a layer of hope. Nathanaël's poems, "To All The Starving Artists," and "Happy News " are two poems that prove this fact, and I wish there was more to read and listen too.

The thirty first Poet I found was Linda Studley, aka Linda Connell Studley, and her poetry is witty, and about life, nature, and friendship, furthermore it is pleasant to listen to her read her poetry. Linda's poems, "Silent Legacy," "Shelide's Gift," "Cross the Existential Track," "How Like the Masts of Sailing Ships," "Sweet Clover Year," and

"The Scathing Nausic Lingle," have rhythm, and they are playful with beauty.

The thirty second Poet I found was Linda Rodgers, and her poetry is creative & wicked. Linda's poems, "Closely Watched Trains," "Except for One," "Crawling Down the Beautiful," "Silver Foil," and "Beyond the Lilies," are what they are, creative and wicked poetry as in a goodly wicked.

The thirty third Poet I found was Christine Neacole Kanownik, and she studied at the new school. Her poetry is to the point and creative as all get out, imaginable. Christine's poems, "hammer of god," "Neighbor," "11 Ways to Make Me Miss You," "I Want Milk," and "Sometimes there is a future fret," are poems classified and should be as Original, Originality.

The thirty fourth Poet found was Angelica Pohveherskie. Angelica found the train, and her poetry is fastened in family and place, history, humility and humanity. Angelica's poems, "Time God," "Facebook High School," "Trinity," "Why I Hate Poetry," "Time Machine," and "Dynasty Crayon," are like speed boat poems zooming on poetic waters, and she has her own way to the reader and listeners heart with her perspectives.

The thirty fifth Poet I found was CR Avery, and his poems, "Bird Cage," "Ode to Jimi," "Gospel According to the Purple Cotton Dress," and "Thief Behind the Mask" are story like and gripping. Political and musical and ruthless.

The thirty sixth Poet I found was Mike Cleven, and his poetry is in rhythm with love, lost love, history, place, beauty and mythology, furthermore philosophy. Mike's poems, "The Fever," "Oracle," "Refuge," "Bellerophon's Song," "Canticle," "Testament," "The Bards of Babylon," and the list goes on, are mysterious and thought provoking, enlightenment indeed.

The thirty seventh Poet I was Cherie Hanson, and she studied at Naropa University. Her poetry is alive in nature, life, beauty and humanity. Cherie's poems, "February," "In June," 'September," and "October" are entwined with great personifications furthermore are poems that are delicate and beautiful as life itself.

The thirty eighth Poet I was Ibrahim Honjo, and he studied at the Univerzitet za vciscenje dusa. His poetry is unique, in heritage, life, love, nature, and modernism. Ibrahim Honjo's poems, "Suicide Street," "Anxiety," "The Stone," "Twilight," and "Naro" are very interesting, with well put twists, as in creating new poetry tools out of old ones. He is a poet to read for sure, and to observe for his poetic craftsmanship. He for sure takes the reader to place very well.

The thirty ninth Poet I found was Jeannette Christine Armstrong, and her poetry is in her Native Heritage, history, nature, true truth, a way of life, and womanhood. Her poems, "Artifacts," "Indian Woman," and "History Lesson," are beautiful, brilliant, and sarcastic for a reason. Heart touching with a need for more.

The fortieth Poet I found was Zaccheus Jackson Nyce and he studied at BCIT Technical Institute. His poetry tells is like it is, hardcore themes, struggles of life and addiction. Zaccheus's poems, "Dominoes," "Invicta," "Of Wings," "Recovery," "Revolution," and "Uncle Mac," have inspired many and changed lives, even mine, with a brief Facebook conversation, a kind spirit.

The forty-first Poet I found was Nasreen Pejvack, and her poems, "My Garden, My Sanctuary," "Waiting" and "Woman," are beautiful, themed in womanhood, nature, peace and anti-war. Nasreen is also an author.

Chapter 2-Yukon, Canada

August 1st, 2013

Plains Cree Chief Poundmaker spoke, "We have to make mistakes in order to get along. Long and unforeseen tactics."

And the Plains Cree tribe war whooped, a war cry, Plains Cree style, while on horseback. Chief Poundmaker spoke again, "Someone has to take the road towards peace. We all must have respect for life. Why not reflect on this as a teachable moment for all races?"

A Cree Warrior yelled out, "If you do not want to be stereotyped then don't look the part. You're going to get stereotyped."

And another Warrior spoke, "Add insult to the pain of loss and further our racial, cultural and generational divides. It's not just about us. It's really about anyone who gets confronted by someone who thinks they have some power, tries to act bad ass, but can't hold their own, gets scared and uses a gun."

"How we get there matters," said Poundmaker, "Dark times, for our people." Going to Battleford was on his mind to speak with an Indian agent about peace.

Another Cree Warrior spoke, "Everything should be closed, and we must dream now of railroads filled with peaceful protesters because they did not go to work, and are marching with packed lunches and canteens. In this dream, there is no-one at the store, at the horse shoe place, the saloons, the tobacco shop, barber. Everything should be closed. We are going to scatter and build fires."

This is why women distance themselves, said Andy and thought, America is a scary place right now, and always has been, but Canada is not much different or is it?

The Stoney Warriors spoke, "Our little boys carry a weapon to protect themselves now. They follow wolves for leftovers. The lack of a benefit of doubt and the lack of certain privileges has forced us to be consciously aware of our surrounding and circumstances. Socially, I have to "stand my ground" every day. And I can't be mistaken for another race other than Stoney so this target is always on."

Andy looked at them. They wore blankets it seemed for clothing, and their black hair was long in the back, but short and spiked on top. Andy then spoke, "There's work to be done in our world internally and externally. Use your talents, blessings, and gifts to protect, educate, and inspire our youth. Or shut up and get out the way. Act with wisdom and prudence. Form a social justice organization whose mission statement you agree with, join it, and be the change you have been waiting for. Fight for your laws in every state, and we must not rest until racial profiling in all its forms are outlawed. You must put a system in place to combat a system. There is not one person who is responsible for this outcome, in-fact, every single one of us is responsible for this outcome. If you do not mentor at least one child that is not your own, you are the problem, and you are nothing but a fake Revolutionist. Who is waiting for someone else to save us."

A wagon was coming, and Andy ran to town to stop all of this. Poundmaker yelled out, "Hurry back we are going to have a Thirst Dance."

On his way, Andy ran past the clumsy buffalo hunter Gabriel Dumont, the Métis leader, who clashed with Chief Big Bear. Andy saw Canadian troops arrive, in attack mode. Andy then saw Big Bear, and the great Chief walked between the whites and his people with his bear's claw that rested in the hollow of his throat. He received this, his power bundle, song, and probably his name as a result of a vision of the Bear Spirit, the most powerful spirit venerated by the Crees. The power bundle was never opened unless to be worn ritually in war or in dance. The bundle contained a skinned-out bear's paw, complete with claws, sewn on a scarlet flannel. Big Bear wore the paw around his neck because he believed that when the weight of it rested against his soul, he was in a perfect power position and that nothing then could hurt him as long as he wore that claw there. It was as if he placed an invisible wall between his people and the soldiers. Andy couldn't believe his eyes, and he ran faster to bring the messages. The construction of the White Pass & Yukon Route Broadway Depot was ahead as Andy ran to the depot. He ran up the stairs, into the depot, and down the stairwell. He seen three workmen pencil their names and dates, "Skaguay, Alaska / July 31, 1898,"

"John Ryand / March 3, 99 / No. 3101," and "Heney" (name of the chief builder of the railroad, Mike Heney's Pacific Contract Company), followed by an obscene comment.

Bang! Ties were now being laid and rail spiked. Andy could also hear a bitter laborers' strike, but it was brief. A man walked up to Andy and asked, "Are you the painter and wall paperer?"

Andy was tired he thought, but noticed three dogs with the man. "Here look," the man then said, "Read," He then handed Andy a newspaper and it headlined "Free Gold Rush Land" "Are ye ready to get your boots wet?" The man asked. People then appeared everywhere outside the depot. The man then said as he came close to Andy's face, "All those who venture up the Pacific through the Alexandria archipelago and Lynn Canal as far as Skaguay and Dyea at least a quarter turn back intimidated and disheartened, for in front of them looms the coast range, with the terrible Dead Horse Trail, on the one hand, and on the other, only five miles north, the Chilkoot Trail from Dyea, with buzzards feasting on the carcasses of a thousand horses. Even more terrible, with its dreaded avalanches and its cemeteries of numerous dead at Sheep Camp. There was a turbulent river and climbing rocky walls was taunting, but I found my thrill on Porcupine Hill."

"Pardon me, my name is Mr. George A. Brackett. I climbed the trail to the summit of White Pass, and conclude that, though almost inaccessible to horses and dogs, it is practicable to build a wagon road through the dark and up the frowning acclivities. The whole journey is dangerous, all of it, but I face them."

Andy looked at his bald head and long beard.

Brackett said, "I need you to help me with the tents, tools and provisions. Oh yes, the dynamite. Oh, the freeze up of fall. Oh, I have to go from camp to camp. Oh to the end to which I struggle. Oh Andy, dishonesty and cupidity. Oh, I want the terrors to vanish. Oh no, you are with the White Pass & Yukon Railroad Company. Oh you are one of those new comers, Oh."

Andy wanted to laugh, and he thought of Alphonso. "I am a logger," Andy replied.

Brackett laughed and said, "I logged there too and in parts of the United States before coming to Seattle."

Andy then was taken back to when he changed his life, making him toss and turn in his bed.

"Searching out new stands of timber," Brackett said.

You people are out of control, Andy thought.

"Oh, there's school class in the barn, come on," said Brackett, "Oh my bull and dog. Oh those six kids. Oh, the Klondike Gold Rush. Oh, my wife Etta."

This was now making Andy feel odd, and Andy ran out of there, and thought, I have seen this all before, I have to warn them.

"You better hurry before the freeze-up," said Brackett.

Andy then ran to a train, and got on.

Looking out the left side of the train on the way up Andy and the passengers on the train were rewarded with many beautiful panoramic views of the valley below, with its rushing waterfalls and flowing rivers. The right side of the train offered views mainly of the side of a mountain. The smell of pine forest and the sound of the train's wheels turning was guiding us over the tallest, cantilever bridge in the world, near White Pass tunnel. Dead Horse Gulch. It got all quite as they rolled over the bridge. They all saw horses committing suicide by deliberately walking over the face of Porcupine Hill. No one said a word after seeing this as they went through a tunnel.

Someone yelled out in the darkness, "No one brought hay for the horses, no one brought hay and none is for sale in Skagway. Horses are cursed and beaten and forced to stand, fully loaded, for days on end. Downriver to Dawson City and the Klondike mines. What's your favorite railroad rhyme?"

Andy then heard G. A. Brackett say, "Take Notice! Beginning March 1 toll will be collected."

Was he on the train? What is going on, Andy thought?

No it was Falcon Joslin, a well-regarded lawyer from Seattle, and he was full of envisions.
He kept saying, "Dawson, Dawson, Dawson City. The value of natural resources on the frontier is like the value of fish in the sea. They have no value until men take and produce them."

Martin Harrais from Riga, Lithuania. A prospector who had traveled with Joslin kept laughing at Joslin, and said, "You can't cut lumber and you want to build a cabin?"

"A Coal Creek Coal Mine Railroad," said Falcon Joslin and smiled. Then said, "Let me tell you about, cooling their tempers and averting violence. I spend long hours alone in hotel rooms finding solace in my work."

Andy swallowed his spit.

"I need some sweets," Joslin demanded, "I have a pounding headache. I'll murder the next man that offers me a cigar or drink. I did not drink too much, but any is too much for me. I have immediately shipped a load of equipment and supplies so construction could begin this winter. We have miles of permafrost, covered up with three feet of moss. I did plan a golden spike ceremony on July 4th. The day before the ceremony, the Chena River flooded, washed away the bridge across the river as well as the site for the celebration. The damage is now repaired, the ceremony is rescheduled for today, July 17. Do you like the richest copper, gold and coal Andy?" Joslin asked and then grumbled. "$100 fee for every mile of Alaska railroad in operation. To make matters worse, the government helped build a wagon trail. Oh well, I am glad I am in Canada."

Joslin looked at Andy real good and said, "Perhaps this little railroad that has cost us so dearly may return us something for all our trouble in it. You have to watch out for them Wickershams! It's all bonehead work." Joslin pointed out the window and told Andy to look, and said, "That out there is the guarantee that Americans and Canadians have wilderness and resources for future generations, and that is the very resources I need to keep my enterprises viable.

Andy looked at him and said, "Yes, and the federal governments are putting in trust for all future Americans and Canadians. This is strangling development and your dreams of empire." Come on, Andy thought.

Joslin looked at Andy and said, "We are on Engine #1."

"Yes, and Engine #1 is in a snow storm," Andy replied, "And in a quagmire." Andy then thought, there is no One Eight Hundred Empire phone number.

A man then arose from a seat ahead of them and gave Andy a book, Robert Louis Stevenson's "The Amateur Emigrant." The man was poet Robert Service, and he recited the poem 'Dreams Are Best." Service then smiled and said, "And I've thought that I surely was dreaming, with the peace o' the world piled on top."

Then a man was playing rag-time on a piano. "Are you talking about the McDonald or the McGrew boogie?" Robert asked and started to play again, and Andy looked out the window at the earth tones. Browns, rusts, ochres, greens, sands, tans, charcoals, greys and clays. Then Andy looked at the stove.

Robert Service recited his poem, "The Shooting of Dan McGrew."

Andy then looked at the blues, the deep, clear, shimmering blues of giant lakes stretching along the valley bottoms, winding around the bases of mountains and filling basins behind ridges and distant passes. And the poem made Andy shiver inside. Andy looked to his left, and a seat back there was Michael J. Heney known as "Big Mike." Heney looked at Andy and said, "I ran away when I was a boy too."

Andy looked at him, and thought what the, how did he know me on the south-side of Chicago, Canaryville in 87?

A young boy spoke up on the train, and he said, "The snow is higher than the train's caboose. And we are being attacked by charging moose; I am good with stories and names but not runaway trains."

This boy was J.D. True and one day, soon to be an engineer and hoghead.

Now the train was stopping and everyone wanted to get off, and go back to Dead Horse Gulch. The Discovers of Gold, Skookum Jim, who was Kate Carmack's brother, who was married to George Carmack. Dawson Charlie, Skookum Jim's nephew, and Dawsons nephew Patsy Henderson was there. They didn't look happy, also they looked like they have been hunting moose, but not enough, because the moose were charging the train again and again, so the train was ruined. They were there to look for family; George and Kate Carmack.

Patsy Henderson was asked to look after the dogs and fish traps at the mouth of the Klondik.

Everyone got off the train and looked at them and the moose.

Martin Harrais, from Riga, Lithuania. A prospector who had traveled with Falcon Joslin was laughing at Joslin again, but now saying "You can't cut lumber and now you are going to have to build a boat."

"We are going to have to find a miners camp and contact the Royal Canadian Mounted Police," said Michael J. Heney known as "Big Mike. "Yes it's me again- Andy, and give me enough dynamite and snoose and I'll build a railroad to Hell."

A man named Sir Thomas Tancrede who was seated stood up and said, "I represent investors from London."

I knew it Andy thought. London.

The boy J.D. True then spoke again and said, "Beware, beware of Alaskan Jefferson Randolph "Soapy" Smith. A hustler and con man, Smith is known as the uncrowned king of Skagway."

Andy then thought of Jimmy New Orleans and the court in the courtyard, furthermore the Royal Canadian Mounted Police.

The boy then said, "You all are going to have to catch a steamship, but this railroad will be built by gold stampeders, including doctors, lawyers, teachers, even French chefs. And remember the Tr'ondek Hwech'in are out there."

"What about poets?" Andy asked.

"Sure, but now we must find and get on Engine #106," said Falcon Joslin, "But before that we are going to go see some cancan dancing."

As they walked to a Can Can place, Joslin said, and he was fooled by the times, "Them flamboyant dance hall queens. They like to learn and head into town. Then they rinse out their pans; toss the sticks they've been digging with down. A different kind of miner. There's nothing like an old timer."

The sun was setting and a steamship could be seen on the Yukon River. The clouds looked pink as they moved rapidly in the opposite direction of the rivers waters.

As they walked in champagne flowed, gold dust glittered and morals could be checked at the saloon door. Four women danced and one sang. They wore a cancan skirt, peacock blue corset and pink feather boa. The pianos beat was upbeat and swift, but Andy was thinking about what all he has seen before coming in here. The wooden sidewalks and to him, it looked like everyone was waiting on a train wreck with diamonds flying from it, something he has seen before on this whole escapade.

A man walked up to Andy and said, "The spirits call me Sweet Brier." and he recited a bit of the poem,

My thoughts are back in the city, I'm everything I've been;
I hear the bell from the tower, I run with the swift machine,

I see the red shirts crowding around the engine-house door,
The foreman's hail through the trumpet comes with a hollow roar.
The reel in the Bowery dance-house, the row in the beer-saloon,
Where I put in my licks at Big Paul, come between me and the moon.

Andy knew he was growing all up again, but this, this was good.

"My name is Charles Dawson Shanly, and that was a bit of my poem, "Memory The Brier-Wood Pipe. You'll want to know more. Follow me Andy, this is what you came to see," said Shanly, and Andy followed him. Charles Dawson Shanly recited his poem "The Walker of the Snow." and everything mentioned in the poem came to life. Camps glared out in haunting looking valleys, and it started to snow. Andy didn't know it, but a young male wolf followed him. Shanly then said, "The walking of the stranger left no footmarks on the snow."

Robert Service must have been following them because he appeared out of nowhere, and recited his poem "The Quitter."

It's the hell-served-for-breakfast that's hard.

Andy thought, holly molly what, oh I know, We back then.

Skookum Jim appeared out of nowhere, and said, "We are are going down river now, so come on."

Skookum Jim wore a black hat. Black. Everything black. A black tie, vest, coat and shoes. His persona impressed Andy. Jim was smooth, but Jim also has this eagle eye on you. Curious, truly wanting to see who you are, type of feeling.

Andy noticed Sir Thomas Tancrede was at the boat, and must of helped them make it because he looked over the work. Andy asked him if London Bridge was falling down? Sir Thomas Tancrede replied, "I'll have to ask my fair lady." Andy then smiled.

The young and vibrant Michael J. Heney walked up to them, and started to talk to Sir Thomas Tancrede about building a railroad. Imagine that Andy thought. Andy could feel this was going to be a long night, and Michael J. Heney and Sir Thomas Tancrede talked about this "Railway Built of Gold" until dawn. The song "Small Hours" came to Andy, because steep is the mountain which we climb. The barge was built and docked and a couple of locomotives were being uploaded. E.C. Hawkins, Chief engineer came out of nowhere and said, "You M.J. You are the Irish Prince." Michael J. Heney smiled, and gave Hawkins a little bit of scotch and a cigar and there we went, and Heney made a toast. "Wait patiently and you'll ride. Rivers I can abide with because they make a decent path through the mountains."

This made Andy think of the movie 'Stripes,' Huck Finn style.

And J.D. True sang some song he made up, "Copper River."

Heney looked at Andy and said, "I started as a mule skinner."

Hugh Foy, Heney's construction foreman walked up with his hands in his pockets and said, "Me too, and I am the mule."

Andy saw Falcon Joslin coming also, with much. Falcon Joslin and his tents, a wagon load that needed to be loaded also, furthermore we had to set up when we got there. Joslin spoke, "We are taking the horses, carriage and load in all, onto Bonanza Ridge."

John Hislop, who was Heney's surveyor, Hawkins assistant, also the Close Brothers, a London bank firm assessor came running, and said, "Don't forget about me. I want to see the Miles Glacier and the Childs Glacier."

"How can we forget about you?" A voice said from the train, and it sounded like George A. Brackett. Was he on the train?

No, it was Jefferson Randolph "Soapy" Smith and he said, "With all the pledges this morning, I am getting in while the get'in's good. I almost got killed on a train before, but that was before." Soapy started to laugh and looked at Andy smiled and said, "Please, call me Jeff, and I hope you enjoyed my can can girls? And I recite poetry when I sell my soap, and I have been on the circus train, you know about."

Soapy did very well at mimicking George A. Brackett's voice Andy thought. Then Andy thought of a telegraph office, and asked where one was. Everyone was like dumb founded, and was like Oh, I have a message or two to send. Everyone looked at each other again dumb founded, Skookum Jim, said, "Okay, there is telegraph office twenty three tents back to the left. For five dollars, you can send a message' "He reminds me of John Arkins," Soapy thought about Andy.

Everyone started walking to the telegraph office. When they got there Andy had odd flashbacks of building the tents, but knew he has never done that, but the flashbacks were real. Heney smiled at Andy and said, "You have to find middle ground."

Andy thought about copper, copper for power, electricity, and Tesla. No one was good with a hand saw, it seemed like, anywhere. The telegraph offices tent had holes in it. The suns light reflected down on the ground. Little circles swayed as the winds blew them across the floor. Creating a dance floor look with a light show, Andy thought, but the only music was the cash register.

Andy awoke thinking and thirsty, but most of all wanting his own bears claw, he never got to help Chief Poundmaker and realized something was taking a new effect on him, but he didn't know what it was but something was. Andy was a path finder, a bringer of new ideas returning to the people to deliver teachings and to allow us to learn and participate in knowing our heritage and spiritual path, sharing good medicine. When Andy met Red in the dining car, Red instantly began talking about the mass influence of the poet Robert Service in the Yukon Territory.

"Robert Service was a tunnel-digger, a white-collar wage-slave," said Andy and laughed, Andy poured some coffee, yawned and rubbed his eyes a bit.

Red looked at Andy and said, We may be like his notions of the silent men who do things. When Red said that, Andy could hear the rag-time kid play rag-time music again. Reminding him of popcorn and the circus. Andy just smiled, but Andy had this lonely feeling come over him though. Red picked up on it also. Was it the horror of the wilderness, the coming of the ruthless power of the subarctic winter, but there was also a sense of freshness, the freedom, and fairness?

All we can do is smile. There's nothing gained by whining, said Red.

"And there is no philosophy like bluff," said Andy, and laughed, but not Red because the notion came to him about cremation, from reading Robert Services work. You could feel the hours separating daybreak from nightfall in the Yukon.

And as Service writes in The Law of the Yukon, only the Strong shall thrive; and only the Fit survive, Red said passionately.

"Like picking up sticks, tools to do the job," said Andy and asked, "Who built the mountains here in the Yukon? Jagged but beautiful."

Red hummed the song "Great Crush Collision March" by Scott Joplin, and said, We need to learn to be a roisterer. Merry-make.

Andy thought about Robert Services relationship with Constance MacLean, who he lovingly called Connie and his love for it up here in the Yukon. It seemed to Andy that Robert knew he would have a happier relationship up here, far away from mankind, and as the gold rush had declined, and things could slow down some, to where maybe a man could compete. Andy then recited Robert Services poem "I am Scared of It All." While he recited the poem his eye brows a rose from the fact, and question, who was this Connie? And Connie, Constance MacLean married Leroy Grant, a surveyor and railroad engineer based in Prince Rupert. Merry-make Andy thought, and he heard the music again, but with a vision.

A long hall way, red cloth, bandana looking but thicker. Pick me up riff aura rag-time music, no it was someone seated across from them on the train, and he was listening to Hector Berlioz, Franz Liszt, Richard Wagner, and Carl Maria van Weber all this morning. He was holding a Jenny Lind cd. The Swedish Nightingale.

"Tichtkunst" (Poetry), he said to them, "I heard you all talking about poetry. I like the text of Richard Wagner. Cross-fertilization is quite common in the history of the Arts."

"Maybe so," said Andy, "I do have to ask you, Do you like his venom or innovation?"

"Innovation, of course," the man answered, and he then asks, "Do you think the power of poetry is in the wrong hands?"

"Maybe," Andy answered and asked, "Do you think the power of time is in the wrong hands?"

The man then started taking out musical instruments from a big cloth bag. A melodeon, a fiddle and a guitar.

He demanded, "Let us sing, and be indiscriminate, from sacred to popular, old songs and new ones, American, British and Canadian patriotic songs, minstrel melodies, classical and romantic." He then said, "My travel companion will accompany me in the chorus and she is a sable ventriloquist, who imitates all."

Red looked at Andy and looked up.

Andy didn't see a soul sitting next to him, so to whom was he speaking of?

The man then said, "My name is Seth Woods, and this song is called the Poetry Train Polka."

In North Truro, there is an odd stone tower
and a singers voice can be heard over the dunes
Just as strong as the Atlantic Ocean's power
Her voice had carried through ages of tunes

Theatergoers had to wait outside in the street in their outcry
While she was up in the hall in the Fitchburg depot singing high
She heard them, she heard them and the power was supra,
So she sung to them from the tower, the Poetry Train Polka

Boston, Boston, Walt Whitman is a fan
Did Emily Dickinson get her ticket to soothe, the man?
Back then you could run through the sticks,

Today you get them Massachusetts ticks

Massachusetts ticks?
Ya, the rich want to rob, so who can soothe the mob
with sticks?
Oh the Poetry Train is stopping to pick up Bob
There are no roads to the tower
So who has the power?

P.T Barnums pies and cigars, to bonnets and whiskeys
Was that Bayard Taylor, like a beagle hound named Frisky?
Just like the Swedish Nightingale, whom came to Canada
The Poetry Train shall prevail, shall prevail in Canada

In the Saturday Evening Post, and the New York Tribune
Like Ol Jenny Lind, Ol Jenny Lind could carry a tune
As literary notables as Goethe, Lessing, and Schiller
On the Poetry Train- Poetry is a thriller

all is reality and deed

Seth then spoke, "We need more Nightingales. As a recent Canadian. I first arrived expecting there to be a fully functioning railway system similar to that I had experienced all my life in Europe, especially as Bombardier was based in Montreal. After seven years I am still struggling with the fact that this government is about thirty years behind lesser countries and it is still faster to drive to Toronto than taking the train. From Ottawa I should really only have a 30-40 minute trip to Montreal or 1.5 hours to Toronto. The cost to the economy for lack of mobility in the golden horseshoe must cost us all dearly. We are told to be more efficient at work but when you take two days to do business in Toronto when it should be just a day trip. How can the Canadian economy ever compete with countries that have high speed rail installed? Build it and they will come. It was the same with the HST125 in UK and French TGV in the mid-seventies. The fact that these two high speed systems have transformed business and mobility, increased competitiveness and reduced traveling costs seems to have no bearing on future rail planning in this country. We need leaders that are bold and have a vision for this country and is not the current sycophants who buries their heads in the tar-sand and capitulates to the oil industry at every turn."

Nicole Stellon O'Donnell walked up to them, and she was there in Canada promoting her book "Steam Laundry" a story of Sarah Ellen Gibson, the sixth woman to arrive in Fairbanks in the gold rush of 1903. With her two children, she followed her husband to Dawson City, Yukon Territory in 1898.

Exciting, said Red, and it is nice to meet you.

Andy reached for the book to look at it while thinking about what Seth said, and thinking we have another person here that agrees about high speed rail. He took it from Nicole, and flipped through the pages as Nicole spoke, "As their relationship faltered and her business opportunities dried up, she fled to Fairbanks with hopes of opening her own hotel. The book weaves persona, with poems in the voices of many characters, lyric poems, and historical photographs and documents to trace her path."

Seth then spoke again, "The old "writing for publication vs writing for self" debate. Of course, there was a time when novels were one of the only form of story people had. They had more patience for backstory. Also I think television and movies have changed how we look at backstory, too. You can't get backstory in a film unless you have a flash back scene or a long exposition monologue. After taking it out, we realize we don't need it as much as we thought we did."

Red and Andy looked at each other.

Seth leaned his head forward and said, "If the internet was around starting in maybe 1800, a lot would be different by now. You gotta be a little bit psychic to see through all the deliberate misinformation in the world. When Tesla died, it was like killing or losing our first born. He had that kind of mind."

Andy has images of when he was a child, listening to stories on lp's, and holding the record cover, read along book, while the record player spun Andy's mind into another realm. "Yes," said Andy, and he wasn't the little pig that built his house with bricks."

Red looked at the book now, and the music came again.
Seth just smiled.

Andy then said, "Opportunity as far as the imagination can go, and visual language, ha, what can we bring this out into the open? Wisdom on the fly. I don't believe poets should make the same poetry over and over, but to keep in mind, poetry and music evolved parallel to each other all through time and were bred out of the same sound, but be different. Seth, play me a song please. Please play, "That's How the Yodel Was Born" by Slim Whitman."

"Ya," said Seth and laughed, and asked, "Who's going to sing it?"

"We can give it a try," said Andy. "People like puzzles and to be scared. People like the Rod Sterling type. T.V. Has a responsibility, to illuminate social conditions, and so does poetry."

Red looked at Andy, because something was surfacing. Sharing, and it was a different kind of sharing. Andy looked out the window, remembering the horses, their demise, and it was no surprise, there was an analogy, was humanity beat down and wore out also?

Seth played away, and they rode down the railroad thinking, One day we will have to rediscover ourselves. Even with our Henry Bemis syndrome.

"You can't mess with smooth" and Andy whistled, and sung the harmony to the whole song Scott Joplin's "The Favorite," and he said, "That's the song Seth, that is the song."

Red then recited a part from Henry Longfellow's poem "The Song of Hiawatha"

Ye who love a nation's legends,
Love the ballads of a people,
That like voices from afar off
Call to us to pause and listen,
Speak in tones so plain and childlike,
Scarcely can the ear distinguish
Whether they are sung or spoken;--
Listen to this Indian Legend,
To this Song of Hiawatha!

Yukon:

Beauty in Yukon, alright, Dawson City, sweetly breathtaking, Emerald lake, okay that is where I am not writing anymore, lol, I am home at Emerald Lake. Watson Lake. Five Finger Rapids, the Yukon River aka the Great River. Tombstone Mountains Park, Mount Logan, in Kluane National Park, The Yukon Mountains & Lake. White Horse and Villages, furthermore Northern Lights. I wonder if pj Johnson has been to Dawson city and was memorized by its history.

The Yukon Railways:

The White Pass & Yukon Route Railway began 1900, the British-Yukon Railway began in 1900, and the Edmonton, Yukon & Pacific Railway began in 1902.

Yukon Poets:

The first poet I found was pj Johnson, and actually pj was found on the American Journey aka Poetry Train America, and was our guide from Washington State to Alaska in 2012. Her poetry is alive and about family, friends, love, nature, and spirituality, furthermore an anthem. Pj's poems, "Set Not Your Face in Grief," "hey od," "she walks with a certain pride," "Reclaiming" "The Owl Called Your Name," "Colour Me Canadian," and "Howlin' Time" take the reader to place, and the place of heart. There is a lot of faith and positive energy in her work.

The second poet I found in Yukon was Miro, and his poetry is pounding in wisdom and spirituality. Miro's poems, "Answers," "Canada," "The Struggle," "A Warrior's Open Letter To Death," and "Where I Have Been" are quick and tight, furthermore fearless.

The third Poet I found in Yukon was Jamella Hagen, and her poems, "Dragging the Wagon," "Kerosene," and "Geomantic: Pieces," reveal how life is precious and fragile.

Chapter 3-Northwest Territory, Canada
August 22nd, 2013

Red was thinking Great, I'll be damn'd. Moose were running around everywhere. The ice carnival was gorgeous though. Igloos were also everywhere, but it was warm, but yes, it was a dream.

"Don't step over the blood of a fish, the fish of the near waters could disappear." A member of the Tlicho tribe, the Dogrib people said to Red. "Yellow Knife has funny weather," the man said, and laughed, and added, "Dinosaur tracks are everywhere. So be careful, also dog tracks" and laughed again. "What is important is teach the children using the words of the elders!"

Red laughed and replied, This New is thrown into a perpetual was, and the art of listening is no more because?

People were fishing everywhere, here at the Mackenzie River, and Yellow Knife Lake, furthermore all the way along the Nahanni River. And it does smell like fish blood. This is where lakes flow into other lakes. On one side of the river were tipi's and on the other side were tents. Red remembered Andy telling him about tents. Fish wasn't the only thing eatable around in the area. There was an abundance of rabbits, and Red wondered about the moose on the loose.

"Ah, the influence of a wigwam is stronger than the influence of a school," said Nicholas Flood Davin the Poet from the area, "And the secret young man is intertextuality. The people here care about their fish and their futures, and I care about them. They share knowledge here in hope and faith that will help and work together for everyone."

Experience in flux, consent of the enlightening moments or perpetual moments, Red replied. Red watched the women skin the fish, and put them out to be smoked and dried. The Tlicho man was helping others take fish out of nets, and placing them into baskets.

"All of this shit is Fair Grit," replied Davin and laughed.

Ya, you have to learn to stretch a camel through the eye of a needle, said Red.

Nicholas just gave Red a look.

Red looked back at him and said, Yes, But I think Nicholas the corrupted folks have learned a lot from you. They took your methods, and used them to their advantage in negative ways.

"What do you mean?" Davin asked.

Well, you Nicholas always have speculations of the future. Red replied. One of the things I foresee is in the future, media heads and the free press ha. They will use these techniques of yours to blind and deaf humanity from and for corruption, and what's sad about it all, the youth, where I come from think it's good, a necessary evil.

"Ha ha, well, welcome to my Prairie Dream," Davin replied with a sad question, "But yes that's not good, dreams do turn nightmare like, don't they? And we have disguises, if we humans can use these, what makes you think the spiritual world can't, with even more tools? Maybe dreams are disguised as nightmares, and nightmares disguised as dreams. I will tell you what. You are a black man, as I have said to the Irish, You can never lose your own respect and keep the respect of others. You can never be happy and dress yourself solely in the glass of other mankind's approval. You may as well seek to fly from your shadow as to escape from your nationality."

And a shadow appeared over them. Was it a Dogrib warrior? No it was the mountain. Mount Nirvana, actually the un-named mountain of The Mackenzie Mountains. Nicholas Flood Davin looked at the mountain and then at Red and said, "A man once said to me, 'not leave yourself be completely carried away by the glories of power. In the midst of your great and noble occupations take every day a few moments at least, for devotion and prayer and prepare yourself for death.' Tick, tick tick, I hear the telegraph. And to think me, a thee Pere Andre?"

Royal Canadian Mounted Police road by on their horses. They slowed down and looked at Red, but carried on.

Davin carried on also, "You Red, never forget the penumbra you are witnessing. There are only certain people that see these things. Also, that man once said, Our emotions are the penumbras of rapid transitions of circumstances and vanishing associations and like clouds we take the hue of the moment, and are shaped by the breeze that bloweth where it listeth."

Who was this man? Red asked knowing but showing his license.

"Louis Riel," Davin replied. Davin looked at Red and he said, "You remind me of him in some ways." Davin dropped to his knees and cried. "I am so confused by the insanity of so many things."

Red looked at him and his clothes looked to tight, every white man here looked like they wore their clothes to tight. Red thought about the 21st Century and this, the Kardashev scale. The method of measuring an advanced civilization's level of technological advancement. And Red was also confused by the insanity of so many things" but had to balance his own composer. People are everywhere, newspaper men are everywhere. Tighten up, Red demanded to Davin.

"I am old." Davin replied. A train came rushing by the prairie and Davin smiled and said, "Mount thy car!" And recited more lines from his poem "Eos: An Epic of the Dawn."

The poem was a prophecy in a way to Red, but Davin didn't know that or did he?

"Hope smiles, and airs from dawns we're never doomed."

"And she led on towards stately towers unique
In architecture and in ornament.
But when we neared the carven arch and door
She turned and said:— "Tomorrow you shall ride
With me," and like a dream she went, and blank
And desolate, I knew not where to turn."

"No more, no, never, never more comes back."

These words were seed setting, and echoed in Reds mind as Nicholas Flood Davin recited his poem.

"Yes, there's the seat of empire young,
A people destin'd to be great and free,"

"Tomorrow you shall ride With me, Tomorrow you shall ride With me."

"The hammers rang on shingle roofs, and grew
Each hour the "city" of a few weeks old"

Red and Davin walked the banks of Mackenzie River, and he witnessed the Tlicho pray for the blessings of salmon, trout and arctic grayling furthermore life period. Red took a deep breath, and looked all around him and the mountains. He was looking into the direction of Headless Valley, Funeral Range and the Cirque of the Unclimbables. Red smelled berries, and looked for them, and this reminded him of Mad Bear. Red seen something sparkle ahead of him on the ground, and it was a little rock of silver. He bent down to pick it up and he heard a steamship's horn, startling him a bit. Red looked at it and thought, the Métis are similar to the Creole. A black feather then floated through the air. Red saw sheep, grizzly bears and caribou.

"That was from Keno the last of the trail," Davin laughed at him and said, "Rebellion is in the air, and you are looking for the tower are ye? Look up to the west, and there stood the Lotus Flower Tower. And there is Fairy Meadows, a relatively flat bouldery meadow with bears, bears and bears." And Davin was right Red was knowing Rebellion was in the air, and so it was in Reds waking modes.

Red looked lost, but he didn't care, he just wanted to dive in what was beyond the horizon, and what was coming, to dive into the cosmic light that sparkled like fireworks on the 4th of July. Because Red was sensing emptiness and silence projecting images and voices, first imperial, then national, then individual, but nature was singing more than ever also. Red knew he was on railroad time, and it was his responsibility to know the difference, but he also knew the difference of internet real time. And he was in as Author Clark Baise would say, A twilight zone of competing time, and Red felt the times there, of agony, the agony of a minute, but that agony made him feel where he was into the new is. Meaning what did 'now' mean? For better or worse time was taking shape and so was Reds' dream. It began to rain, and the rain didn't stop the dancers from dancing or the drummers from drumming, furthermore it didn't stop the bison from being hunted by stampeding them over a precipice. And it for sure did not stop expansion and immigration, and Red was witnessing the British, French, and Aboriginal populations decline. And the bison was declining. And he felt that people here feared Americans, and the linguistic part of it all was in chaos.

Davin looked at Red and said, while Red was looking at the moose, "You are a mess, you need to be thinking of where to get a good buffalo coat, fur cap and mittens; moccasins, and long woolen stockings."

What book journals do you have? Red asked. You are holding them tight.

"Book journals?" Davin looked puzzled, smiled and answered, "These writing pads Red belong to Royal Canadian Mounted Police Const. Robert Hobbs, who gave the Métis leader Louis "David" Riel while in his jail cell shortly before his execution for treason."

Now Red looked puzzled.

Davin laughed and said, "Riel gave the poems to Hobbs as a gift."

Imagine that, Red replied. There was an irruption in the sky. There were a few snowy owls above, and Red looked at them then at Davin. Davin looked them and then at Red and spoke, "The journey, the distance, the quest. What beautiful animals. Riel loves animals, he uses them as metaphors in his poetry. He was also keen to inhuman schemes. He felt his rights were mere in the dirt to lie dead next to the honesty of some of his fellow people he once admired, furthermore Riel could smell the blood of broken promises in the air and the fur trade."

Jig music could be heard off in the distance, and laughter also filled the air.

Riel believed in Divine Justice, Red thought and looked behind him. He felt a presence and looked to the woods. Something was calling to him, was it the land? When he looked back Davin was walking towards a fur trading post. Red walked that way because he wanted to read some of Louis "David" Riel's poetry and most folks were looking at him, and Red could sense the collective struggle of the French Canadians and the Métis. Truthfully Red was cautious because he wasn't use to men walking around with tomahawks and rifles over their shoulders. Davin turned around and said, "These furs are good for you. Here, purchased by me."

Fox and mink, muskrat and beaver? Red questioned and it looked like marten, lynx, muskrat, wolverine, and other fur-bearing animals were also trapped. The notion came to Red, Voyageurs, Jimmy New Orleans and his French family tree. An Indian was whistling with some traders and there were big freighter canoes with painted logos on them. The trader looked at Red and said, "Steamships and Railroads have taken over, but I'll sell you a river cart real cheap."

Red said, No thanks and smiled. One man was staggering with a load of wood sacked on his back. Kids were walking around selling bowls of blueberries. Why thank you, replied Red. One man was heard while Red put on his new goods; and the man was talking about family farms, Montreal, and a Moose Factory. Red laughed inside, bred moose like cattle here, or something? Red also heard another language being spoken by people, and it was the Michif language originated with Métis people in Ontario and Manitoba. Red then walked towards a table, and there were fire strikers, knifes, axes, drowning rigs, beads, feathers, and floating bottles of beaver lure, gland sac castor oil. Red had to get some fire strikers and some feathers, for the sake of Mad Bear. Red laughed and looked at Davin and said, Thank you Davin, fits me good and feels good. I want to read some of Louis "David" Riel's poetry, Mountain Man Davin.

Davin laughed and said, "Why sure." and handed him the note book. Red thought there was another one though. Red first read the poem "The Political voice of Choteau!"

Your principal men, o Show-Tow,
Show and Tow in jail the Halfbreed,
As if, having lost the Negro,
Their rage had to have a new feed.

Red looked up at Davin and smiled. Red noticed the prophetic qualities in Riel's poetry. His poetry gave Red the sense of strength and no fear.

"He hated trains," Davin said and Red looked at him with no expression at all. Davin said, "He felt like the Métis were calling on him, and perhaps they were."

Red knew that feeling well, poetry was calling on Red, and something also was from the woods. He also knew what it felt like to be outnumbered by folks that reeked of that, and Davin knew also, that feeling of being confused by the insanity of so many things. Red spoke, He may have hated trains but according to his poem, "Minnesota, Which I Now Entered," he took one to Breckenridge, to Crookston; Then to St. Vincent.

Davin laughed.

Red did laugh a little also, and then the native art on the white spruce posts caught Red's attention. Beauties, Red said softly, Beauties. He looked at the word or name "Kahtapwao." This was similar to graffiti. Cool, Red thought, 'nineteenth century graffiti', and this was proof of the value of living things, living things in their heart. Philosophy and values were the powers beaming from the art. Red then finally heard the roaring of the Five Finger Rapids of the Yukon River. A sandpiper flew from out of the trading outpost, and into the woods. Red watched all of this and questioned himself, What was calling? Red felt this epiphany calling. How massively important animals and killing animals for their fur were to people, another insane polarity, strangely looked at now, but it made sense. The weather is a powerful force, warmth and Red thought poetry should be powerful as the weather and of money. Red then awoke and felt warmth.

Andy read aloud from the book *The Man Eaters Of Tsavo* by J. H. Patterson. An Anglo-Irish soldier, hunter, author and Zionist, furthermore who built a railway in Kenya, Africa. "This constant night watching was most dreary and fatigue work but I felt that it was a doozy that had to be undertaken as commander naturally the men look to me for protection."

Andy looked at Red as he sat down. "Well I had a dream I watched the Ghost and the Darkness, with well, you know who," Andy explained to Red, "And I am listening to the audio book. It would be scary, knowing something in the woods or jungle was following you."

Red was waking up, but that last statement awoke him up more. Red rose his head, and did a whisper laugh.

"What?" Andy asked.

Ya, following to kill you. I don't know, I feel something in my bones, something is following us, maybe not to kill us, Red explained, and it's not the Owls. I really liked that movie. Red then thought of the feeling he got in his dream, the feeling of being watched by something other than a human.

Andy didn't say anything. He did hear Red but was captured by the powerful imagery from the book he was just listening to, when J. H. Patterson described in detail, the eating of bones, when the lions devoured the railroad workers.

This place is beautiful, Red explained as he looked out the window. Just a little bit of nature's everything. So what's on the agenda today? Red asked.

"Looks like we have to back track," Andy answered, "Yes a tagging issue, and well, a skin issue, a Google glitch-go, to Okanagan." The Penticton Indian Reserve in British Columbia for the poet, Jeannette Christine Armstrong. Andy looked at Red and said, "Morning Dove. Dove, that is your new name," and Andy laughed, "No, I am just being silly. I can tell you are somewhere else today. Red, Jeanette is the grandniece of Hum-Ishu-Ma aka Mourning Dove. That is my mother's nickname also."

Red laughed. Oh ya, I like that.

Her writing has helped reveal truths about herself and her people. Andy filled Red in as Red searched and read about Jeannette for himself. "She says, The process of writing as a Native person has been a healing one for me because I've uncovered the fact that I'm not a savage, not dirty and ugly and not less because I have brown skin, or a Native philosophy."

She also helps aid in the empowerment of all Native people by teaching them writing skills, Red added to the morning research.

"She's an important poet," said Andy, "She believes in that bridge between people." Andy laughed a bit, because a quick thought of the past of him roofing came back. Of some of them people with whom he has worked with having no concept of this notion, and if so, they have no care for it neither. And another fact came to Andy, can folks read, and he means read, writing is one thing, but reading along with listening is a whole art form.

Andy, do you ever wonder through the fabric of dreams? Red asked. Also don't you think ordinary explanations are way more strange than extraordinary ones. Do you ever feel like we are constantly being separated?

"You mean, from the believing sheep from the unbelieving the goats of anything," Andy answered. "Lamb chops period. You know Red, it maybe because we are near beautiful no man's land. No civilization north of us. Not that we know of anyway. The connection. Are you home sick Red?"

Maybe Andy, maybe. Red answered. Angry spirits Andy, like something is rejecting us. Like we are opening old wounds and rekindling hatreds. Well, no, maybe not that, but something is trying to tie us to a tree, for bait.

"You want to go home don't you Red?" Andy asked. "Red you may be right. Something maybe outside our tent. We may need to move location sort of, or diverse in some way."

Rail Head camp? Red asked.

"Yes," Andy replied, "To learn more climbing ability and agility along with independence and surefootedness. We need to remember our importance of supporting others for poetry and the railroads as we move along and be more flexible in exploring new possibilities. Yes, foundations in which to stand and will guide us in building a stronger foundation if need be."

I want to make sure what is before us is strong before the next lessons begin, said Red, I am not going home. I am on the hunt for peace with you. We have bridges to build. We have our whole life Andy to do this. Maybe Andy we can complete the whole world before we die.

"We need to maintain balance and have confidence in situations and our abilities," said Andy with confidence, With agility, camouflage and blending with surroundings. Search and teach sense of togetherness and community along with how to make life easy and promote serenity. We need to remain centered in peace within the scheme of things, and maybe Red we shall. Imagine that."

Red did imagine and said, I just need to strengthen my spirit and resolve things unknown.

"Maybe we need rest," said Andy with concern, "A quiet demeanor is being balanced with a fierceness especially when family is concerned. Rest maybe needed before continuing. Another medicine besides poetry is about timing or personal power. Time for recognizing and understanding our own noble and regal attitudes."

Where are we with the animal train Andy? Red questioned.

"Chamois Hautes, Alpes," Andy replied, "We have a long way to go. Red, short comings are outside our personal selves." Andy thought, Was the journey now on top of Red, instead of Red being on top of this journey. "Red, you need to get back to your smooth Mabaan smooth blood pressure again," said Andy.

You have jokes today, Red spoke. I can make that subject to change. Well, I've been thinking. We are seeing disorganization, rapid social changes, many, and many psychosomatic disorders and psycho stuff period. On the net also. Maybe this is why the blind are happy.

Andy just dropped his jaw. Who was protecting them as the feathers of a bird protect it from the frosts of winter? Furthermore what was following them? Andy got quiet, and looked out the window as the train slowed down some. He saw a ranch of horses. The name Strong Foot came to mind. A sign did say. 'These Horses are bred for the Royal Canadian Mounted Police' That's what they needed to do. They both needed to strengthen their footsteps, maybe Andy thought.

Red said, We didn't find these poets either, it looks like. Robin Skelton, and Barrie Phillip Nichol.

"Yes, well done Red. Barrie's poem "Dear Captain Poetry" is sweet," said Andy, "Ha, the underestimating of ones that have so much underneath isn't good." Andy laughed.

Red laughed and said, Ya, and poets George Harry Bowering and Patrick Lane. I don't know, maybe Google has a different grid for Canada?

"Maybe," Andy replied, "Ah Red, when in doubt go into the garden and the garden will heal you," said Patrick Lane. "I know there isn't one on the train, but we can go to one. I like this wisdom by Lane, and he sure has changed his life."

Red just smiled. Red looked at a news feed, and told Andy, Steam Laundry won the 2013 WILLA Award for poetry.

"Great," replied Andy, "Nicole Stellon O'Donnell high five to you, wherever you are."

Seth Woods was in the dining car also, and he listened to all that was said. Red and Andy were silent as they were about to finally finish back scanning when Seth asked, "Have you ever heard of the poet Sonnet L'Abbé?"

No, Red replied.

"How do you spell her name?" Andy asked.

Seth told Andy, and went on to say, "She has journeyed from coast to coast and to Canada's North, attending regional conferences, asking Canadians about their love for Canada and how we can show it in local and nation-wide events for celebrating Canada's 150th birthday in 2017. She has a poem also entitled, "Inuktitut meaning What Is Your Birthday?"
Andy right away found her on the net, and so did Red.

Seth smiled and said, "I figured you both would like this information."

Thank you Seth, Red and Andy said with enthusiasm. They both went to researching this woman's poetry, wisdom and accomplishments.

Andy recited two lines from her poem,

Let's finish building the Trans-Canada trail;
Let's bling up an anniversary train;

"This is beyond amazing," said Andy, "I would really like for us to meet her, and talk. She must have so much going on inside her head."

"Yes," replied Red, "Check this out from an interview from Lemonhound.com. She is also trying to help shift the cultural gaze of skin colour."

Seth then said, "I have someone else, you both may take interest in. Natasha Rebry, and she is a scholar who studies Gothic literature with the history of modern psychology. She says, in the late 19th century, both science and literature were exploring that gray area."

Red and Andy looked at each other and tele-thought, gray, oh no. Every color is there too. Andy was on this information quick. He read online, "These things are far removed from the humanities and cultural studies," says Rebry. "I'm really looking at those phenomena that suggest there is depth to the psyche, that what is on the surface is really only a small part of the true story." Andy sent Red this link.

Red went over this and said, Yes, only a small part of the true story. Thanks Seth, great information.

Waitresses came to their table, and presented Red and Andy with a song, and Seth seemed to be the one behind this because he was smiling. Seth grabbed his guitar and the waitresses began to sing,

My Buffalo hear me calling for you
Come hurry home
My Buffalo where ever you may roam
My Buffalo come hurry home
Come home, I am waiting here
I have only you for a friend
My work won't end without you, without you

I have the people for a prize
Their so nice, come to me, come to me
My Buffalo you are so good to me
When shall I see some boys like you
No one can work so hard like you can do
Help me to the pleasant poetic fields
I'll take care of you to the end
My only friends, we love you
The boys are no good, lazy bones
I love you alone, Buffalo, Buffalo, Buffalo.

The song did make Red feel better. He remembered his dream of Mad Bear and him crawling in Bison dung back in Nebraska. This also made the both of them miss Charlie very much. A notion came to both of them to send for him. Red was looking at one of the waitresses pretty good and Andy caught that. Red looked at Andy and said, If she was my wife?

"Well she isn't," Andy replied.

Northwest Territories:

Canada's Northwest Territories and places of beauty. Inuvik, Norman Wells, Fort Simpson, Hay River, Fort Smith, and Yellow Knife. Nahanni and Wood Buffalo. The Boreal Forest, and the Smoking Hills. The Mackenzie River and the canyons of the

Nahanni River. The Coppermine River and the Slave River and Taltson. Great Slave Lake and Great Bear Lake. Also the Territorial islands in the Arctic Archipelago include Banks Island, Parry Peninsula, Prince Patrick Island, and parts of Victoria Island and Melville Island.

Northwest Territories Railways:

Mackenzie Northern Railway began in 1964.

Northwest Territories Poets:

The first poet I found was Miranda Currie, and she is a survivor. Her poetry is capturing in narrative with animals and politics. Miranda's poems, "Income Outcome," "Dog Run," and "Artic Tern," are adventurous, and uplifting.

The second Poet I found was Kay Getty, and her poetry is powerful in the themes of home life, nature, place, and life. Kay's poems, "Northwest Coast," "I Have Scattered My Children To The Winds," "There Is No Death Nor Time," "God Cleans Himself Like A Cat," and "Here In Atlanta" are witty, with a dark side, in other poems she has written.

The third Poet I found was Patrick Woodcock. Sweet poetry on war, peace, people, and faith. Patrick's poems, "The Sandstorm," "Sardasht Osman is not dead,1" "Lunch by the River," "The Irrigation Pond," and "Blood, Oil, and Art" are beautiful and intense.

The fourth Poet I found was Sally Ito and her poetry has life, and wisdom. Sally's poems, "Alert to Glory," "Apprehend," "Spring Break," and "Caress" are poems with intense imagery and meanings.

The fifth Poet I found was Jim Green, and his poetry has themes of animals, life, nature and place. Jim's poems, "Autumn Song," "Loon Dance," "Silence," and "Drum Song" take you to a place full of life.

Chapter 4-Alberta, Canada
September 5th, 2013

It was loud in the cab of a steam train. "The Empress locomotive 2816 can go up to seventy miles per hour," said a man to Andy.

"What?" Andy asked, being confused and all.

"You have to drive the train," the man replied, "I have to go." And the man ran away toward the Medicine Hat train station.

Andy looked at the station, and people were all over the platform. He then looked at the roof and people were looking out the turret windows. The station was beautiful Andy thought. The station has pronounced gables, sloping eaves, and red brick. Okay Andy thought, I can do this. He looked for rear-view mirrors and there was none, but steam was coming out of the top stack and below from the right and left. There was steam with blazing phenomenonility. Andy smiled as he looked at the whistle cord, and bamm. He grabbed it and let loose two toots, and laughed his ass off. While thinking it was funny and all, he knocked over a book that must have been placed in the cab, and the book was *The Bank and Train Robbers of the West; James Boys, Younger Brothers, Etc by Belford & Clarke Publishing.* Andy was in awe, as he picked it up and flipped through the pages. The cover was beautiful Andy thought. It had a cowboy on it with a gun in his hand, and the font was very different. Andy heard a voice from a Canadian Pacific railroad worker from the station, "He's going to America." What Andy thought, what the heck is going on. Seven men looked at Andy. Andy was tripping now about all of this. He heard that voice again, "He must be stopped before he gets past Calgary." Whoever he was; he was near the engine. Andy then heard dogs barking. Oh my God Andy thought, it's the Royal Canadian Mounted Police, and every remote outpost must now be on his trail. Okay Andy thought, Alphonso and Poe where ever you are, this is for you. Besides the trains boiling water was a boiling and so was Andy's nerves now.

Andy looked at the boil pressure gauges, and put one hand on the throttle, and one to wind up the cut off lever from the floor. Andy squeezed the release handle, and shoved it all the way forward, and let loose of the release handle to lock it into place. There was no way, Andy was going back to America, for he knew this, so why would they think that? He opened the cylinder cocks, by turning the valves all the way clockwise. He then released the brakes. He watched the brake release gauge rise. Something told him to apply a little bit of brakes, before he hit the throttle toward him. He did and off he went. The cluck sound began, and the train rapidly sped up. Then something told him to back up on the cut off lever to switch gears. Andy grabbed the whistle cord, and let out a *Choo Cho, Choo Cho, Choooo Cho*, and he loved these sound blasts.

Outside, near the train on horseback was Special Constable Stick Sam; the best and most intelligent native for tracking, also Louis Cardinal, Sid May and many more Royal Canadian Mounted Police.

Andy then loaded more coal in the firebox and he heard another man's voice.

"It's about time you got here. A man never lives so innocently that he never gets in trouble," said Stephan G. Stephansson a poet born in Iceland, who has lived in America for a while, but made his way to Alberta. This startled Andy. He thought it was a lawman or was it? Andy felt he may have found some grace again.

"You and your friend, didn't find me in America, so I had to come here to find you," said Stephansson, "I too believe the wings of verse can overcome the troubles of the human race. Well, can you get this train to move faster because them Mounties are right next to us?"

Andy looked at him and smiled. Stephansson smiled back and said, "Winston Churchill once said to me, "You have enemies? Good. That means you've stood up for something, sometime in your life. We have to stand up for something all our life."

Andy thought, You Stephansson, truly have.

Stephansson said "We are going to starve liberating, but let's go with it."

Andy looked at him and thought what the?

A loud sound was coming from all around. Andy and Stephansson was looking around. The temperature dropped. You would actually have to be there to appreciate how loud this was. Andy realized it was around four am in the morning.

Stephansson then asked, "Can I be Frank? Folks back in the day use to get a tattoo in hieroglyphics that says, "Peace Forever in This Valley. Let No One Break the Peace."

Andy looked around and the ground moved slowly.

Stephansson then said, "The Turtle Train meets Turtle Mountain, a lost indeed series, Ha. I have $100,000 American Silver dollars."

Andy shrugged his shoulders and said, "I too would like a tattoo in hieroglyphics that says,"Peace Forever in This Valley. Let No One Break the Peace. We are going to need to find jobs, but really careers."

Stephansson looked at Andy and shrugged his shoulders.

Andy then looked at Stephansson and thought, He's under cover for the Royal Canadian Mounted Police, and then Andy laughed.

Stephansson looked at Andy and said, "You think you are driving the The Spokane Flyer don't you? The Children of the Sun Train?"

The sound got louder. Andy thought about Elvis, and the battery. Andy thought the train was off the rails and flying. Then he remembered his friend Bones. Andy had his thoughts off in space, he then noticed a bear on the tracks. He looked around and heard the steel squeal and the rivers the train was passing were beautiful. He looked back and what the train was hauling was double stackers like Legos. The bear went to stepping out of the way just in time. The bear ate most of the grain anyway from the grain trains of Rev. Leonard Gaetz and James L. Ross. Ross was in control of the construction of the Canadian Pacific Railway west of Winnipeg and was looking for men to work, so Andy was looking for him.

The train sung with the wind and the ground rumbled and Stephansson splattered. He lost a bet with his rectum. The train was flying for ten dollar books, figurative speaking.

"It looks like we lost them," said Stephansson, "Where are you going Andy anyway?

"Great!" Andy replied, "But look there. It looks like we are going over a bridge."

"It's the new High Level trestle, Lethbridge, in Coalbanks, aka Fort Whoop-Up," said Stephansson, "The highest and longest on this type."

The train was flying fast, and it was at the top rocking and rolling. There was a serious drop to the ground near Belly River. A visual sure to take your breath away. Beautiful Andy thought. The train was flying Andy thought also, and it looked like it anyway, over the bridge that is. There were horse drawn carriage wagons down there. Cool Andy thought. Also there was four men carrying a canoe.

"Great!" Andy replied, "But look there are two Indians standing in the middle of the tracks at the end of the bridge, with their hands out for us to stop. Well I have to go to work. I am late."

It was Chief Running Wolf and Danny Bearspaw.

"Work for who?" Stephansson asked.

"James L. Ross. Ross," Andy replied, and he slowed the train down to stop.

Stephansson was scared the natives were going to kill him, but not Andy. Andy looked at them and said, "Poetry, poetry brings peace, poetry is a medium we all know makes us happy."

"You are not Willie Gates," said Danny Bearspaw after the train was stopped.

Andy looked at Stephansson and Stephansson shrugged his shoulders.

They heard and seen a six horse drawn railroad work wagon coming up one of the other tracks that spliced ahead, next to one being built. It looked like it from seeing just the ties and not the rails. There was two men on it. When they got closer they got off, and came up to them all and one of them said, "Come down, there's a school classroom on this train, somewhere between the two first class, two second class, baggage, express, mail and dining cars. Oh it looks like cargo cars also of wheat, tallow, beef, and manufactured goods. We need to show you something. We have been having a serious drought, and they say a locust storm is headed this way." Andy thought about Utah and Jung Hem Sing.

"Are you J.H. Cherry?" the other man asked.

"No," Andy replied, He had to go home.

"Okay, where is Louise Phillippe? The man asked and asked another question, "Who are you?

"Louise never came to work, and my name is Andy Cherryseed," was Andy's reply.

"Are there more immigrant farmers and ranchers pouring in?" The first man that spoke asked.

"Yes more coming," Andy replied.

As they went into the school car, there was books and notes on the black boards based on the book *Travels and Adventures in Canada and the Indian Territories between the years 1760 and 1776* by Alexander Henry, who was a pioneer fur trader, who lived and hunted with Wawa tam of the Ojibwa.

Andy got the notion to look down the trestle, so he looked out the window, and there were Royal Canadian Mounted Police climbing the trestle up to them. They looked like red ants everywhere in a fury hurry. Andy and Danny Bearspaw ran to the steam engine to get them out of there, and Danny Bearspaw said, "Willie, these railroad tracks are the old trails of the Mountain Stoneys, the Blackfeet, the Plain Crees and the Wood Crees."

"My name is not Willie," said Andy, "Well, lead the way."

Chief Running Wolf followed them and made inquiries as to Andy about his journey, and how long Andy intended to remain in his country? And Running Wolf said, "My father, Little Mountain, was once alone in the mountains, when a wolf came to him in a dream saying, 'My son, you have often heard my voice, for I am Running Wolf, the head chief of all the wolves. I run all over the country. My tracks are to be found everywhere, and I will always continue to wander. If you should ever have sons, name one of them Running

Wolf after me. I can tell a horse's age by its whining, and a man's by the sound of his voice.

Danny Bearspaw then spoke and said, "I am in love just like you. I am in love with pretty Claudine Marceaux. The one you love is at the train station, she is with your girlfriend."
"What, I have no girlfriend," Andy stated and asked, "She doesn't want me does she?

"No," Danny Bearspaw replied.

The phone awoke Andy, and it was the one Andy loves on the phone, and she told Andy that she loved him and missed him and so much more but Andy was half asleep awestruck by the dream and what all the one he loved had said to him. Andy then thought of what Red has told him before, 'Never give up on anyone, miracles happen every day.' The words she spoke over the phone, "I love you" in her tone of voice played over and over again in Andy's mind as he got ready, and to Andy, this was a miracle.

The trains whistle was in high geared action this morning as Andy made his way to the dining car. Red was watching silent films, and glancing at the rail news there in Canada. OmniTrax has been envisioning a realignment of the North American trade system through Churchill, with Canadian farm equipment and grain moving out and incoming goods traveling by rail through Winnipeg and the American Midwest to Mexico, also to Russia, Red told Andy.

"Oh ya, nice," Andy replied and asked, "Have you seen any polar bears?"

Red laughed, and replied, No but we can take a train when we get to Churchill, Manitoba to view some polar bears on an excursion. It's the Polar Bear Capitol of the World.

"Sounds great, let's reserve a train," Andy suggested.

Will do, Red replied.

"Watching the Great Train Robbery are ye?" Andy asked playfully and said, "Silence turns the experience of film-going into a pure game of hide and seek, a sort of exhilarating scavenger hunt in which the mind's eye surfs the image looking for clues to personality, absorbing atmospheres, savoring shapes, making thematic connections. Silence pulls you into the image rather like Alice down the rabbit hole. By contrast, with sound, the image comes to you. Silence invigorates the imagination; sound decorates it."

Andy wanted to be silent to Red about his phone call he received this morning, but he did say to Red, "You know Red there are some things that grab your spirit and never let go. Things you dream and hope for, to come true. Like some poems and songs, there is something that tells you, you are alive and you are meant to be. It's a great feeling."

Red replied, I know what you mean, a lot of poems and songs on the American journey just vibed with my heart beat, and said this was all meant to be. It's a feeling that one day, all of this will be in the right hands, and bring us to life again as we have for some poets and great people.

"Yes," said Andy, "This song "Scotsmans Bluff" by John Wort Hannam just hits home, that mandolin in it just tells me, like there's Angels singing through it, singing, All is going to be okay, and brings a smile to my soul." Andy also felt he was being tested, because everyone wanted him to quit and come home, so the lyrics to the song were what Andy's spirit was dancing to. A deep new metamorphosis was coming Andy felt, but it was induced by the need he knew was wrong. Andy shook the wrong off and kept his faith, and this went easier for him because of this song. The song made him feel right.

We have something in common with the poet Nancy Matteson, and that is history and poetry, Red filled Andy in on the Canadian study. It is a real art to making a character come alive in so few words. She knows how to break the silence with historical figures.

"So do dreams Red, look," said Andy, and pointed to the trains window, and there was a locust on it, riding the train.

Red smiled and said, We are starting to see United Kingdom connections amongst the poetry e trains passengers.

Andy smiled and said, "Well you know as well as I do where we are going next."

At this moment Seth came to their table and threw down a net printed copy of Carmine Starnino's essay *'Vowel Movements: Pointless Toil and Empty Productivity.'* Red looked at it and Googled *'the Cage Match of Canadian Poetry: Carmine Starnino and Christian Bök in Conversation.'* A debate about aesthetics, theory and ideology that spans the twentieth century and beyond. It has roots in all poetry written in English, be it American, Australian, or European.

Andy read aloud, "Bök thinks, given the diminishing readership of poetry in the modern milieu, it is wise for poets nowadays to start thinking about the future audience that they might otherwise address, including those robots, clones, and genetically engineered animals that will eventually adapt our culture. Also he thinks, the job of poetry nowadays is to constitute an aesthetic of critiques and surprises, to generate knowledge and make discoveries, and that this is the epistemological contribution that we make to the past."

Um, hmm Red hummed and said, I don't agree with Bök here, Poets are among the stupidest and laziest people I know. Carmine Starnino says, that if we are going to fight for the future poem, then, that future has to include being able to draw one's influences from any quarter without fear or anxiety. And certainly this is a future that in my own way I am trying to prepare for. Red wrote snappish notes in his day-book. His journals were sources of travel, expenses and income, but never self-analysis. And Sir Sanford Fleming came to mind. Was it time for a new time, a self-analysis in a new era of clone tones? Yes that Ben Franklin inspired worldview has no doubt, besides Red knowing this, Andy knew what that was about. Solutions. On the cover of Red's journal, this is written on it, *'What Cosmic Times Is It?'* And did this time have more weight in consolidating strengths and overcoming differences? Red wrote, Poetry that doesn't cost a penny, or cost a single life, and has spiritual cooperation.

"I like this here," Christian Bök says, Andy read aloud, "Poets look, he thinks, with some alarm upon poetry and actually ignore its language. There is no great epic poem about the moon-landing, for example. And to him, that seems very amazing -that, in the history of art, there should be no response directly to that experience. If the Greeks had rode a trireme to the moon, there probably would be a twelve-volume epic about it, written shortly afterword's as a way of transmitting to future generations the importance of this grand achievement, and it's certainly the most important thing we've probably done collectively as a species, to actually set foot on another world, and yet we haven't produced a poet of epic significance, who might be able to broach that historical moment with much expertise."

Red looked at Andy and said, Bök also says, there's a low level of ambition among Canadian writers. None of them really imagines that they could ever aspire to a large audience. None of them ever imagine that they might actually provoke controversy and discussion, all of which might result in debates of this sort. None of them really imagines that their cultural legacy might extend beyond the shores of their own nation. And he claims Calgary is probably the best place to be a young poet in Canada, because there is a very active small-press community.

Andy looked at some papers and said, "I like what Starnino pin points here, a poet should be a singular phenomenon and not as representative of any sort of school. Interesting, he says, in Canadian literature, poetry is really stifled by its own competent mediocrity. There is no necessity for poets to actually aspire to kind of ambition that would really be world-changing, because poets who are relatively normative and mediocre are rewarded very handsomely for their cultural contribution, and in fact, I can't think of any other art-form that sets its standards and ambitions so low that it doesn't even feel obliged to redress its own sociological in consequence."

Red laughs and repeated what Bök has said, Poets don't actually think to aspire to write the software of reality. I love that.

Andy smiled and looked to see if the locusts were still there and they were gone. Andy smiled again because he and Red were delivering poetry in a new way. And a new way was changing them.

Ah, well I hope Aritha van Herk agrees with us, she says, Red quoted her, "Our stories are markers of our difference, our originality and our imagination. They're key to identity. If we don't know our stories, we don't know who we are."

"On many levels of we," Andy added. He thought about erotics, his stories, well their vibrant stories. Andy added more wisdom from Herk, "Red she would probably call our work, in Italian dialect 'Geografictiónne.' She says, Stories, novels, and poems are still a way of connecting with someone that we may never have a chance to connect with. Also she thinks the act of reading is as creative as writing or can be."

How do you imagine your reader? Is it a male or female, or what? Red asked.

Andy replied, "I want my reader like a wolf following me around in hunger, to mate with, to hunt with me, to howl in stereo with me. To snarl and growl at my grueling significance text, to want to kill me, maybe, furthermore to look at the lakes I write about and sees their significant reflection. To run with me to mountain tops and to drink from streams with me."

"And how about you?" Andy asked.

Female, Red replied, cooing. Has to be a woman Andy. Women loved to be coo'd. Coo Coo rhymes great with Choo Choo.

They both laughed.

Red spoke and said, I love this by Aritha van Herk, she says what a maverick is: 'a unique character, an inspired or determined risk-taker, forward-looking, creative, eager for change, someone who propels Alberta in a new direction or who alters the social, cultural, or political landscape.

Andy smiled at Red and thought about his dream and what Stephansson had said, "I too believe the wings of verse can overcome the troubles of the human race." Andy looked at Red and wanted to talk to him, but he didn't. So if the wings of verse can overcome the troubles of the human race, then it's all about saying the right words at the right time, even with the odds of "It's not what you know, but who you know," Andy thought. Red was thinking also, and his mind was on Alberta, and its beauty. Were they Mavericks?

You know Andy, it must be something to pass away from here from a car accident, said Red, It's a fear of mine. Robert Kroetsch passed away a year ago from a car accident, scary to me. I like what he says, Literature and those who created it? They are alive.

"Nice," Andy said, "He doodled. He dawdled. He dared. I could have sat in his class. I hear you Red, it's a fear of mine also, even though I wanted to be a race-car driving when I was a boy. You know I have played the song 'The Scotsman's Pass' at least twenty three times. I have to again, but I won't play it for a while now, so I won't let it get the 'Sweet Child Ol' Mine' factor."

Seth laughed and said, "Well I learned it for you." Seth smiled and played John Wortman Hannam very well.

Andy looked at Red and smiled. Andy felt good when the song was played, but Andy is well aware that when songs do that to him, a great change is near. Andy itched his palm, and pointed, Onward, Forward! Then played the air mandolin.

Red placed the poem *"Letter to Sir John A. Macdonald"* by Marilyn Dumont in front of Andy... Andy read it while Seth played, and Andy looked up and said, Yes, imagine that. Andy, now thought about a tattoo. "Peace Forever in This Valley. Let No One Break the Peace."

Alberta:

Canada's Alberta and places of beauty. *Áisínai'pi*, known in English as writing on stone. A protected place and National Historic Site, it contains the largest concentration of rock art on the Great Plains. Petroglyphs and pictographs were carved and painted on sandstone rock walls by the Blackfoot and Shoshone tribes.

There are sweet places like, Head Smashed in Buffalo Jump, The Badlands, Lake Louise, Crypt Lake, Moraine Lake, Peyto Lake, Athabasca Falls, Spirit Island, Larch Valley and Sentinel Pass. Mount Edith Cavell, Mt Engadine Lodge, Mt Lorette Ponds, Banff National Park, Waterton National Park, Maligne Canyon, Columbia Ice Fields so I wonder what Kris Demeanor, Derek Beaulieu, Patricia Kathleen Page, Aritha van Herk, Alice Major, E.D. Blodgett, Roland Pemberton, Mary Pinkoski, Anna Marie Sewell, George Ryga, and Robert Kroetsch would write on *Áisínai'pi* if they lived back in the day.

Alberta Canada Railways:

The Canadian Pacific Railway began in 1882-83, the North Western Coal and Navigation Company also known as Alberta Railway and Coal Company began in 1882, the Canadian Northern Railway began in 1890, the Calgary and Edmonton Railway began in 1891, the Crow's Nest Line began in 1892, the Edmonton, Yukon and Pacific began in 1902, the Grand Trunk Pacific began there in 1904, the Alberta and Brazeau River Railway Company began in 1908, the Alberta and Great Waterways Railway began in 1909, the Alberta Midland Railway began in 1909, the Alberta Central Railway began in 1910, the Edmonton, Dunvegan and British Columbia began in 1911, the Pembina Valley Railway began in 1912, the Canadian Northern Western began in 1914, the Lacombe and North Western Railway began in 1914, and the Northern Alberta Railways began in 1929.

Alberta Poets:

The first Poet I found was George 'Geo' Thompson, and he studied at Danforth Collegiate and Technical Institute. Geo found the poetry train as soon as we arrived in e-Canada in B.C. in 2012. Geo's poetry is relaxing and soul searching/finding. Poetry with meaningful meanings, in family, life, humility, wisdom, and love. Geo's poems, "We All Have A Story," "Fall From Grace," "Dark Days," "Seventy Years On, 1944 2014," "Mom," "What If" and many more are smooth and soothing poems. Poetry with courage and inspiration, furthermore a positive outlook on life.

The second Poet I found was Brian J. Smith. Life and animals, there are many animals in his poems of humor. Bj's poems, "The Tom Cat," "The Quarter Circle X," "Casey," and "My Cowboy Church," are adventurous and witty.

The third Poet I found was Roland Pemberton aka Cadence Weapon and his poetry is pioneering and historical. Roland's poems, "Victory" and "Monuments" are encouraging poems.

The fourth Poet I found was James W. Jesso, and his poetry is alive in wisdom, ultra-life, and nature. James' poems, "Seeing Her In All Things," "Amongst a Chill," "Old Growth Spirit," and "Fate's Hand" take the reader on journeys to awareness in spirituality.

The fifth Poet I found was Jem Rolls, and his poetry is vibrant in humor, life, politics, and wisdom. I could not find any titles of his poems, but his poetry is thought provoking.

The sixth Poet I found was Jenna Butler, and she studied at the University of East Anglia. Her poetry is shining bright with the themes- family, nature, and people. Jenna's poems, "Flight," "Keswick," "Kerouac," "Prometheus," and "blueberry season" are poems of delicate beauty indeed.

The seventh Poet I found was Kris Demeanor, and his poetry is raging in humor, nature, and people. Kris's poems, "Extreme to Me," "Crowfoot's Nephew," The Beavers Think It's Spring," and "Labour Day Classic" are upbeat poems, and they can shake the reader loose for sure.

The eighth Poet I found was Sara Al Souqi, and she studied at the University of Alberta. Her poetry is vast in many ways; culture, prejudice, political, and life. Sara's poems, "Fighting for peace," "Shout Out," "Veiled," "Dear Ex- leader of my nation," and "What I am About," are powerful, positive and uplifting, furthermore poetry with fresh vision and perspectives.

The ninth Poet I found was Marilyn Dumont and she studied at the University of British

Columbia. Her poetry is strong in family, heritage, love, and nature. Marilyn's poems, "She Carries the Pope in her Purse," "The Breed Women and Camp Cook," "She Worries Beads," "Letter To Sir John A. Macdonald" and for sure her poems about Gabriel Dumont and Louis Riel. Marilyn's poems reminds me of everything that is important in life, everything precious, everything we should never forget, and all over the world there is precious things like this, her poetry is humbling.

The tenth Poet I found was Doris Daley, and she studied at SAIT Polytechnic. Her poetry is themed in family and friends, life and love. Doris's poems, "Average Girl," "A Baxter of Blacks," "Poem for Charlie Russell," "Answering Machine," "Pierre," and "100 Years From Now" are creative and humorous; contemporary cowboy poetry with great endings.

The eleventh Poet I found was Alice Major. Poetry with wisdom flux nature. Alice's poems, "Advice to the lovelorn," "Saint Pelagia," "Symmetries of Dilation," and "Maps" are poems with intensity in wisdom all out. (a poet needed for the battle for the Igloo Bill)

The twelfth Poet I found was Rich Larson. I could only find two poems, "Datafall and "The Blank Slate" and they show his great creativity.

The thirteenth Poet I was Kirk Ramdath, and he studied at the University of Calgary. His poetry is smooth, life, love, and war, much more. Kirk's poems, "more," "Calgary," "onion of love," and "the lone citizen" are extremely beautiful poems.

The fourteenth Poet I found was Leanne Guenther and she writes children's poetry themed in family, life, love, and nature. Leanne's poems, "Together We Are Canada," "Cell Phone," and "Five Little Owls," are wonderful.

The fifteenth Poet I found was Alexis Kienlen, and she studied at Concordia University. Her poetry is in smooth power life, precious life: Alexis' poems, "ballad of the insomniac woman," "chess," "South to North Saskatchewan," and "portrait of the poet" are poems in fact that comes out right away as a fighter, Alexis' poetry is emotion capturing brilliance.

The sixteenth Poet I was Brendin Evans. Poetry of love and life, furthermore inner strength. Brendin's poems, "Poets Emotion," "His Heart," and "Vintage Poem, are filled with love, courage, and preciousness.

The seventeenth Poet I found was Dave Eso, and he studied at the University of Calgary. His poetry is music to the ear in love, history, and nature. Dave's poems, "One Fifty Five and Counting," "Love Letter," "Faces," and "Youtube as an Eulogy" are beautiful and dramatic with a deep metaphoric atmosphere.

The eighteenth Poet I found was Lendo Mutambala, and his poetry takes the reader to family, hope, life, and love. Lendo's poems, "Dreamers," and "The Compassionate

People" are for sure, powerful and beautiful poems.

The nineteenth Poet I found was Patrick M. Pilarski, and he is incognito. Patrick's poems are "Cars Without Headlights," "Your Village," and "A Thin Skin," imagery in mellowness.

The twentieth Poet I found was Kevan Lyons. Poetry in life, narrative, and life -core wisdom. Kevans poems, "A Soldiers Oath," "Solitude Poem," "Lesson of Love," "Relationship Problems," and "Role of God in Addiction Recovery" are soul touching, beautiful and musical.

The twenty-first Poet I found was Andrea Hunter, and her poetry is themed alive in love, poets and poetry. Andrea's poems, "We Need the Poets," "I Have Reason To Believe," "Swallow the Sun," and "Your Eyes," are passionate, with imagery, creating impact!

The twenty-second Poet I found was Bob MacKenzie, and his poetry is themed in many ways and themes, nature and life in the light and the dark. Bob's poems, "Across the Water," "Circle the Wagons," "The Dark Shimmering Deep," "Time and the Prophet," "The Flower," and many, many more poems are beautiful, powerful, and diverse poetry.

The twenty-third Poet I found was Helen Hajnoczky, and her poems, "The Heart of the New West," and "A History of Button Collecting" are beautiful, themed in family, humor, and politics.

The twenty-fourth Poet I found was Carl Leggo, and he studied at the University of Alberta. Carl's poem's "Thin Skin," "Ring around the Scholar," and "Zoo," are prime, screaming more poetry, ya ya poetry!

The twenty-fifth Poet I found was Vivian DeMuth, and her poetry falls everywhere onto the vast landscape/mindscape of poetry from animals to tragedy. Vivian's poems, "I Have Been Calling Them," "Desolation Devi/l," "The Age of Extinction," "Ode to a Hurricane" and "Operation Alternative are creative and they are poems that will open your eyes/mind.

The twenty-sixth Poet I found was Nathan Peterson and all we know of him is farming, and his poem called "Farming" and the poem brings it all from the dirt to the table.

The twenty-seventh Poet I found was Erin Dingle and her poems are lethal double to the double (.) "Wood Smoke," "Brain Storms," "Freeze Tag," "Woman," and "Zeus Reborn," are poems with complete passion in all aspects, lethally.

The twenty-eighth Poet I was Kimmy Beach, and she studied at the University of Alberta. She is a interesting poet, with interesting poetry to relax to. Kimmy's poems, "When I Skate," "All Citizens," "Bass Guitar Frenzy," and "Underground," are uplifting poems with originality about music and life.

The twenty-ninth I found Poet was Taras Kazna, and his poetry is themed in nature, life and war. Taras' poems, "Boys From Ontario," "Crazy Old Man," "Gift of Fire," "Shuters of Colombine," "Walking With God," and "What it Means to Be Canadian" are beautiful, clever, and musically narrative.

Chapter 5-Saskatchewan, Canada

September 16th, 2013

In the land of 100,000 lakes, rivers, and bogs, called 'the Gathering Place' by the Cree. Red heard movements in complete darkness. He guessed the train was going through a tunnel while he was sleeping so he took a deep breath, relaxed and went back to sleep, but Red was sleeping. He felt a warm breeze, and it was dark so he didn't even know it was heat from steam from the boilers in the tunnels. He heard a roaring sound, with a little rumble, and he didn't know it, but he was near the river running through Moose Jaw, and the river was thought to be shaped like a moose's jawbone. He also heard people breathing in the tunnel, in the rat-infested darkness. The heavy breathing was Chinese workers lying next to Red who were badly beaten in the rail yard the day before. They have been digging these tunnels in fear of the Yellow Peril. Terrified and unable to pay the head tax, into which was now a law in full effect. And now they are fully hiding out in these tunnels. They say above ground, 'It's the Land of Living Skies,' suggesting there's not much interesting about the land itself, but underneath, there is another realm.

"We can't move," said a man, "We can't move as fast as we can build railroads." Red heard a man and could see him a little bit and he was a Chinese man.

Yes it looks like more spaghetti, Red proclaimed while thinking about high resolution satellite imagery, and where was he? But, Red told the man, Look at what can be done one day, Trains for all, to go where they wish, for their welfare.

"Welfare," one said blatantly, with a temper temperature rising.

A loud steam-shovel could be heard. Oh no, everyone thought. "They are digging into the ground for us with a steam-shovel," and the Royal Canadian Mounted Police were. It also sounded like work crews were hard at it, because off in the distance you could hear the track laying machine, and Gandy Dancers singing. Oh no, everyone thought, "They are using a post digging machine, stomping straight down into the tunnels," and the Royal Canadian Mounted Police were. This is not good, Red said, we have to get out of these tunnels. Crawl, let's go, Red demanded.

They heard voices also; they heard them make bets, gambling on whether or not Chinese laborers would escape the tunnels before the explosions went off. "Not a China man's chance," the doubters would jeer. "Explosions," they all thought and feared, as sweat poured out of their bodies as they moved quickly to the box car station.

Yes, the Chinese knew where the White Railway men built a train station by using a box car, but there, they set the box car over a tunnel with a thin ceiling wall. They found this because the ground was sinking from above. It was dangerous, but it was where they could hide out until dusk, and escape far away from the station rail yards in Moose Jaw where they were nearly beat to death. One was dragged through the flower garden there that greeted the travelers, they told Red.

Red was thinking what is going on with the Moose. I am going to die now in the earth, called Moose Jaw. Unbelievable, Red thought as he crawled faster than a worm in a flood. Red asked them, What is the name of the place we are going to?

"Moose Woods," The China men replied.

Oh, great, Red replied, We have to get to Chief Whitecap and John Neilson Lake, the person in Saskatoon. A clean place. A city of justice. Red heard a voice say, "John Lake and his Pilgrims." Red first seen a match strike a rock, and it's flame rose up to a face and this face held a cigarette in its mouth. The man lit his stogy, and then a lantern. He was in full military uniform. This man was poet Dr. John McCrae, and he looked at Red and the leading China man. McCrae glanced behind Red, lifted up the lantern, and looked at the rest of the Chinese. He then took a puff, held it in a bit, and let the smoke out. He looked at everyone and recited his poem, "The Pilgrims."

Red looked into his eyes after looking at his parted hair and said, No way, let us pass. They know where we can escape.

"Shit, lead the way," said McCrae, "Don't let me keep us from stopping us." McCrae smiled, and he followed behind Red.

A China man took the lantern and lead the way.

Red told them they should name the stations in alphabetical order. Also name none with an M, N, or O, You have no idea what I am talking about, right now I know, and Red laughed. The China man who led them stopped, and he looked at Red, snapped his fingers to Reds poetic beat.

Finally they made it to the box car station, and they heard voices. And it was the Sioux Chief Red Cloud and Charles M. Hays. The Chief gave Hays a jacket made of dear skin, and they made jokes about the Red Coats. Hays then spoke about the White Star Line, speeding travelers from Europe to the Orient using White Star ships and Hay's transcontinental railroad. They also talked about treaties, the down falls of the whiskey trading post, and briefly on unfair trades.

Red and they heard chickens everywhere.

Voices could be heard talking and coming near, and they were Tom Sukanen, a Finnish immigrant who built an ocean-going boat and the French sculptor Paul Chevré. They were talking about the longest stretch of perfectly straight railroad tracks in the world, here in Saskatchewan. They then mentioned something about giant grasshoppers.

Red noticed something. There was a young lady across the dirt road as he peeked his head out to see everyone. She wore clothes way ahead of their time Red thought. The leading China men said, "She's crazy. She mentioned you, and some other man meddling, but I guess she was right, because here you are and her she comes."

She was poet Desirae E. Dibben from the year 2043. She wore a derby. She plays cards and chess a_nd_ plays a little drum. And when she doesn't like you she'll stick out her electronic tongue.

"You cannot come up here yet," said Desirae E. Dibben, smiling at them, "Not until I tweak it, because if you do, you will warp. People are getting their heads chopped off by trains and?. Hush, I'll inform you soon about The Big Muddy, Operation Bungalow Z, but first we have to get to 'Tote Road' through the wheat fields. The nights are different here, time channels blend, and sometimes they leak. I have to get you to Shiloh."

Mammoth clouds began to appear and it was near dusk.

She didn't tell them about the Rugeroos. Old Indian spirits that change into animals. Vicious and will harm you if you don't leave when you see them. They growl. When you do leave, you will see a pair of red eyes that will follow you until you have left the area. People have said that they change into animals right in front of your eyes sometimes. The most common animal they change into is a coyote.

Coyotes appeared everywhere.

Red noticed her lips were purple, because she had been eating misaskquatoomina, the delicious wild, purple berries whose Cree name translates to Saskatoon. The Chinese started to laugh and talk about Bienfait.

Bean-fate, Red spoke aloud, I had enough of your bean fate in them tunnels. They laughed again as they all walked through the wheat and they mentioned a man's name, Antoine Charles Bienfait, he paid the money, and they talked about a underground lignite mine.

Finally Red noticed the coyotes behind them. Do not run, at all, Red whispered to them, Keep walking and talking. The wheat seemed taller as they moved forward. Now it seemed as they walked out of the field where they were, the grass was shorter, cut fresh, and there stood a mini two story house. A man came walking out of the home very fast holding a rifle with one arm, because that was all he had, he only had one arm, and he said, "You are on the property of Trèfflé Bonneau, and that would be me, so why are you all on my property?"

Trèfflé Bonneau was a railroad builder and farmer, and he was making a name for himself in real estate.

We need to get to Shiloh, Red replied.

"For what and who?" Bonneau asked.

To build railroads, Red replied.

Trèfflé Bonneau thought for a minute or two. He spit on the ground, raised up his rifle, and placed it back on his shoulder. He looked at everyone in the eye one more time, and said, "I have work for you, farming and rail work. Come on in, if you like children that is? I have seven, three girls and four boys." When Trèfflé Bonneau said those words, those kids knew all was okay and they scadattled out of that house like it was on fire, but when they realized there was a Black man, five Chinese, and a young Lady, they put their fingers in their mouth and just stared.

Trèfflé Bonneau was about six foot seven, dark hair, receding. He had this stare, like he had five years of your lives planned out already. He looked around, and said, "Desirae has been here before. Where is she?" She didn't come in yet. She was with the kids. "Make yourselves at home while I get them in," Bonneau said.

Red thought, been here before, hmm?

All the children came in and they looked at everyone, and everyone was looking at them because all their lips were purple. They all had been eating misaskquatoomina, the delicious wild, purple berries.

Desirae came in and she had a purple berry chin.

Trèfflé Bonneau came in with some baskets and his lips were purple. He too had been eating misaskquatoomina, the delicious wild, purple berries. Pascal Bonneau, Trèfflé's father, a superb railroad foreman giggled as he took a basket of berries from Trèfflé. They sat around a backyard fire, and in the back yard had tipis, and he said, they worked for him, they stayed up talking about trains and America until they all went to sleep. Red was just dozing off when Trèfflé Bonneau awoke him, and handed him a shovel.

Trèfflé Bonneau said, "The train will be here soon to get Louis Reil. I have failed him, so I need to get him home."

Red followed Trèfflé to a chapel, and Red thought of the movie, "Taking Chance." Trèfflé unlocked a door, and they entered a empty room, and Trèfflé locked the door back. Trèfflé took off his over coat, and started to dig into the dirt.

Trèfflé looks at Red and says, "Come on, help me."

Red asked, Is Reil in the ground?

"Ya, you're smart, but lazy, come on," Trèfflé demanded. There was a knock at the door.

It was Pascal, "Let me in, I changed my mind."

"Get a shovel, and come back," Trèfflé demanded, "You were on watch."

"I have already moved him, I told you I changed my mind," Pascal said, "I have him in a wagon."

Trèfflé threw down his shovel, and went and unlocked the door. "I am going to see the body home, you all stay here," he said.

"Dress warm, it's a blizzard out there" said Pascal.

A blizzard, Red thought.

Edmund Osler came in through the front door, and looked at Trèfflé. Osler asked, "Why are you so nervous? Is it because I have the better reputation?"

"I ought to" Trèfflé replied. He shook his one armed fist, and went out the door into the freezing cold.

Red was back at the Trèfflé Bommeau homestead warming up, and told everyone the news, and where Trèfflé Bommeau went. The children were washing dishes, and they still had them purple berry lips. This made Red think of his mother and awoke. He laid there feeling he was connecting with something eternal. A change was coming, Red felt, and increasing.

Andy and Seth were jamming to the song 'The Railroad Tracks' by John Koellisch when Red joined them at the train station. The train was parked and refueling there. Andy told them that he had a dream of looking for treasure at a railroad station, and the clerk there named Tiffany told him, she didn't like her career too much. Andy told her she had a great job or career, however she looked at it. She seen and assisted many people on their life's journey good or bad. Many precious souls, journey through her direction, and he has read many 19th Century stories about the clerks and train stations. Folks remember you, and some folks may write about you in their diaries, and come to think about it. He told her, she should write a book about her career working at the train station.

Hmm, Red said, Maybe your dream forecasts a gift or unexpected legacy, and that would be a great idea for a book, and then again the youth today don't care much do they.

Andy looked down and didn't say anything but thought, poetry and the railroads are wonderful. Such beauty and so inspiring. Andy knows and Red too, train travel and poetry make people happy. And a thought came, a gift and a legacy would be for his dream to be fulfilled to train travel with the one he loves to show her the country, and get married at Emily Dickinson's home. Andy looked up and said, "I miss Charlie and Mr. Welchberry's presence and stories."

Me too, replied Red. Red also thought, one day Andy will find his true love, and Red felt bad for Andy, but worse for her, or anyone that did not see or feel Andy's heart.

They also were mourning the loss of poet Scott Bates who had recently passed away, and they felt for Robin, Scott's son. This made both of them miss their fathers.

"Red, I have decided to apply for a career at railroads, and training," said Andy. "I can't go back to roofing, I love roofing, but those contractors do not care about their employees so, I have to do something about that entire win, lose or draw. I have to get my CDL I guess."

You'd be good at it Andy, Red added.

"I think so," Andy added, "Because it is a great feeling about all that and this. Also I can do more for poetry. In roofing, my head barely stays above water."

Give it your all Andy, give it your all, said Red, I may get into film, like the poet Maria Campbell. To produce poetry's culture and forgotten history, furthermore to bring things ignored by mainstream society. She loves horses like you Andy.

Andy smiled and said, "I like the advice a friend of hers told her, Never believe what anyone wrote about you. That way you wouldn't get swell-headed and you wouldn't be hurt."

Red, laughed and said, I agree.

"I need your help Red in searching," Andy asked, "I need help finding poems by Eli Wolf Mandel. I have a feeling about this poet."

Okay, I shall, Red replied knowing Andy had triggers of empathy going on again, and Red knew them triggers well. Ah, got it Andy, you are correct. He claims drains. Hmm, he thinks teaching is a drain. Like writing poetry, you end up using all your creative energy which would have gone into writing. Meaning Andy, teaching or doing awareness and such drains us, hmm. Red laughs and says, Makes sense but it is also a small contradiction.

"Thanks Red," Andy replied, "Yes, but as he says, occupied with paper work bullshit. No assistance. He loved to teach and write poetry but the policy work was a drain. Goes back to that money machine. Ha ha, Andy laughed... I was thinking the other day Poets need an assistant, and some body guards. Poems write us, Oh so we know Mr. Eli Wolf Mandel, you are correct, so many Poets know this, and guess what, a mind siren. I hear a siren folks. That person behind the curtain is one bad ass, so please stay out of a poet's way."

Seth laughed, and said, "Tell em Andy, tell' em." Other passengers applauded.

"We don't have to clarify what we have done in America," Andy went on, "And we are not obligated to clarify in this documentary of Canada after we leave Canada. We can turn our backs on politics, but we can't on poetry. A good long break maybe but not the Poets. As Shelly said and Mandel, we are unacknowledged legislator's. Health for the tribe."

Yes a tribe being grinded by time and ideals that lead nowhere, Red added.

"Death, the world is waiting for us to die Red," Andy continued, "As in my vulture theory we have talked about, and Mandel knew this also. And unity, Poets need to unite."

Andy, we have done well, Red added, because mentioned here, the Cree was nearly erased from history here in Canada, and what are we doing, we are also bringing that awareness also.

"Right," Andy replied, and he mentions "Cadence, Country, Silence: Writing in Colonial Space" by Dennis Lee. But Red from this wisdom, our voices are Americanized and so is our poetry. We have to scope this out."

I hear ya, Red replied, As I heard you talking to the one you love, and Riki Chen's posts, it's time for a break, so we are free from outside influences.

"Clean slate to perfect the signature we have in our writings," said Andy, "A new perspective as teacher poet Ronald H. Peat taught us."

Oh you'll love this, Red added more wisdom when Mandel mentions what German writer Thomas Mann has said, 'I am the sick person that makes society well.'

"Imagine that," Andy replied with a laugh, "Brilliant. Society doesn't want to get well."

Andy I have to hand it to you, said Red, You deal with much. I remember in the O.P. days you were in shock when you learned how egotistically poets are.

"Sickening to me and, Yeah well, what can we do about it? Andy replied with a question.

I don't know Andy, it sure is a shame, Red replied.

"Yeah, like Ryne Sandberg," said Andy, "Me and my brother in 1987 got autographs from all the Chicago Cubs, but not him, he looked at us young kids, rose his nose up and off he went into Wrigley Field. Heart breaking is what it was and is Red."

Seth spoke, "You two are something else. I am glad I met you both. That was the best team the Cubs ever had."

It's great to meet you also Seth, they both told him and smiled. They boarded back on the train, and chuffed north east.

Andy thought, History, bad ass history was at it again; repeating itself like the old bastard-bitch history was and is.

They all looked out the windows, and were looking at the Ghost Town Trail in lower Saskatchewan.

"These prairies here are what these poets call who they are," Seth explained, "This is their spirits, their spirit land."

I wish we could stop the train Andy to touch the land, Red wished.

"So true Red, so true," Andy agreed, "Canadian poets have a different blessing that I want to know more. It's beautiful Red. Even though empathy is kicking our ass because of what is going on in America. We are being shown something here."

Yep, and we are a learning, Red replied, shhh. Red put his index finger over his mouth, and whispered the art of listening.

Seth spoke, "Sorry to ruin the silence. You are seeing 'Love in a dry land', poet Dennis Cooley," and Seth recited in a whisper fashion Cooley's poem "By the Red" from his 1984 collection entitled "Bloody Jack."

It started to rain, as the train rolled past Red Deer River.

Red laughed out loud and said, Moose, my oh my, more Moose.

"Prairie Poetry," said Seth, "Red and Andy I am reading your book Poetry Train America, and I have to hand it to you both. You had courage to leave a job and your homes to go out into the world with no money and no prospects, and stand up for the poets of that site, and put up with all the snake mentality and back stabbing. And you Andy suffering from heart ache. The both of you being pushed and being taken for granted and still gave a damm. Manipulated by fake profiles. The consequences of tarnishing your name, even though some tried and still believe they are doing so, freaking hilarious. You two are strong men, now autograph this book for me. And Charlie, I miss him and don't even know who he is and what he looks like. You even have me reading the web blog betterlivingthroughbeowulf.com."

Red and Andy looked at each other and Seth said, "Don't let the world get you down. They'll soon get their own personal yellow envelope from Dread."

Red and Andy looked at each other again as Seth said, "Ya sorry gentlemen, but Doom has a brother."

Andy put his mind in the back seat, he knew his prayers were answered but he also knows the powers of the ghost pranksters and the Medea's are at hand, the Spiritual Trip Wire Association.

Red knew that look on Andy's face and said, Spiritual Trip Wire Association.

"Ya," Andy replied.

Saskatchewan:

Named after a Plains Indian word "kisiskatchewan," meaning 'swiftly flowing river,' Saskatchewan once was known as "The World's Bread Basket," Saskatchewan, also known as the "Land of Living Skies," with hundreds of scenic lakes, Besnard Lake, Emma Lake, Waskesiu, Lac La Rongem, Blackstrap and many more. Last Mountain, Redberry, and Jackfish, the Qu'Appelle Valley, Diefenbaker, Madge, Last Mountain, the Cypress Hills, the Frenchman River Valley, Prince Albert National Park, Grasslands National Park, Killdeer Badlands, The Churchill River, the Boreal Forest, and the historic Hanson Lake Road, so I wonder if Glen Sorestad, Louise Bernice Halfe, Robert Currie, Judith Krause, Don Kerr, Gary Hyland or Robert Currie seen spirits of their ancestors in the aurora borealis or northern lights, or thought they were fire bridges to the sky built by the gods?

Saskatchewan Railways:

The Carlton Trail Railway began in the 19th Century, the The Qu'Appelle, Long Lake and Saskatchewan Railroad and Steamboat Company began in 1883, the C.P. Railroad began in 1905 there, the Regina Municipal Railway began in 1910, Cando began in 1978, the Southern Rails Cooperative began in 1989, the Southern Prairie Railway began in 1998, the The Red Coat Road and Rail began in 1999, the Great Western Railway began in 2000, the Thunder Rail began in 2005, the Torch River Rail began in 2008, the Last Mountain Railway began in 2009, the Great Sandhill's Railway began in 2009 the former Empress and Burstall Subdivisions respectively, and began in 1911-1923, the Stewart Southern Railway began in 2010, the Big Sky Rail began in 2011 and the Long Creek Railroad began in 2012.

Saskatchewan Poets:

The first Poet I found was Ken Mitchell, and he is a Poet and a Playwright. I have only discovered one poem, "The Day Leonard Taught Me To Chew Snuff."

The second Poet I found was Scott Reesor, and I have only discovered one poem, "Another Day in the Chute with Pa."

The third Poet I found was Victor Enns, and he studied at the University of Manitoba. Victors "Afghanistan Confessions Poems" are poems with some serious imagery, that makes one appreciate their comfort zone.

The fourth Poet I found in was Khodi Dill, and he studied at the University of Regina, and the University of Saskatchewan. Khodi's poetry has powerful themes in culture, humanity, politics, and racism. His poems are lethal, ruthless, and vibrant.

The fifth Poet I found in was Lindsay Jack, and she studied at Niagara College Canada. Lindsay's poems, "School Poem," "G20," and "Alouette," are powerfully themed in humor, sarcasm, politics, furthermore are purely table turning poetry.

The sixth Poet I found was Sylvia Legris, and her poems, "4 Marked by Claws and Cloudburst," "Cervical Vertebra Variation (1 to 3)," "Lore (hummingbird)," are poems of a new tuning, with nature & anatomy, making the reader look at things in a new perspective.

The seventh Poet I found was Geordie Grassick and the only poem and information was his poem "The Gate," a beautiful poem about a man and his horse.

The eighth Poet I found was Shayna Stock. Her poetry has good attitude, themed in humanity, politics, and sexism. Shayna's poems, "Do you hear what I hear?," "Creativity as Responsibility," "1 thing Ian Brown and I have in common and 6 things we don't," "Choosing to Listen," and "Unbridled Wind" are poems you can agree with, reader beware she can adjust your attitude.

The ninth Poet I found was Robert Currie, and he studied at the University of Saskatchewan. Poetry with animals, family, life and nature. Robert's poems, "My Poems," "Matinee," "Under the Blanket," "Caught," and "Beyond the Open Window," are witty, story-like and relaxing.

The tenth Poet I found was Sharon MacFarlane, and her poetry is sweet in family and culture. Sharon's poems, "Saving," and "The Oath" are witty and have great perspectives.

The eleventh Poet I found was Steven Michael Berznsky a.k.a Mick Burrs, and I could not find any poems. From his Youtube video, Steven is an admirable Poet feller in many ways.

Chapter 6-Nunavut, Canada

September 27th, 2013

Andy was in awe and pondering his empathy circuit, and he did not take it for granted. He desired the poetry train to be a "Miracle Train" evoking feelings of gratitude and serenity. He thought and thought and was unable to resist the sedating effects of the moving train, so he passed out in his roomette. He began to dream as he intensely does. He was in a strange place. He heard the birds deep within the fog, and the sun seemed to be falling. The voice of poet Olan L. Smith spoke from memory, and what he had told him, Wisdom of the transformation is the spirit we possess. Andy was in the presence of the void, and the void knew it was in the presence of Andy. They both were passengers riding through time for rich wisdom. Worth was in the air, even in the thickening fog, a feeling of strong listening was carrying Andy's curiosity and content.

Andy heard doors slamming far away. Then he heard dogs barking, and there was nine of them pulling an empty sled, raging at Andy. The dogs looked hungry and mad. There were seal bones all over the snow. There were no trees and a lot of crushed rock providing stability over the fragile ground. It was an empty landscape. The ground did look dangerous to Andy, like it would fall out beneath his feet.

Andy looked at the sled, and something dawned upon him, he should appreciate this sled, it must be big like a new snowmobile in a modern time event. Andy finally got the notion, that he was stranded, but had a sled. It was cold and the night was moving in fast. Andy looked at the dogs and said, "Let's do this. Andy got in the sled, got comfortable, grabbed the reigns and said, Mosh, Marsh," and the dogs looked at Andy like he was crazy. Andy laughed, and said "Yah and the dogs listened this time," and off they went. Andy hoped the dogs knew where to go because he had no clue. So Andy yelled out, "Food." Andy laughed. They came up to a woman and a dog, and they looked eerie amongst the fog. The woman spoke to Andy, "You only get one chance a year to get material up here." Andy looked behind her and it looked like there was a village, but homes were on fire.

The woman spoke again, "They are rallying for the work movement, for eight hour work periods." She looked back at Andy and said, "You have much work to do, thirty one bridges, two tunnels, and three hundred culverts."

"Who are?" Andy asked.

The woman replied, "I am a hunter, a fisher, and a harvester of berries, crowberries, bearberries and blueberries." She smiled looked up and said, "No more planes, we are taking the trains, you come to this place as a passenger but you leave as cargo."

"I come in peace," said Andy.

"The Inuit has no word for war in their language," said the Woman.

Andy felt and knew he was a long way from home. He felt he had to center his energies now to himself, to close off his empathy. It's not that he wasn't ready Andy felt, it was just that there was a worse feeling of nothing of being able to do anything about things that triggered his understandings of others. Andy felt the closer he gets the further away the ones he cares about goes, in all areas of life. He wasn't looking for sympathy, he just did not want to be in a purgatory of love, but was worse was that he felt his friends really did not care. Andy wanted to lay the rail, build the bridges and culverts, and he wanted to do it with heart, and he wanted to do it the right way, from the beginning and old school. This was the only thing Andy had hope for, so he can do more things, and even thought that he was a man now, he still felt for, and felt the same as he did in his youth. Hopeless and helpless to all the struggling today. Maybe Andy was not in his time yet. Time, Andy thought, time?

The woman disappeared, but Andy could see a red tower far away. Andy heard her voice say, "Learn how rich pisirq, traditional ajaja songs and poems are."

"I want to meet the people," Andy said. Andy then saw a man far away beating a drum, but this drum was different. This drum had a handle, and it was flat, and the man beat the drum on both sides, as he turned it with his other hand. A young man appeared out of the fog, and he was carving ivory figures out of walrus tusks. He pointed to Andy, and then at the figure he was working on and said, "You."

Andy walked up closer to look, and the man said, "You have to keep moving, keep your blood flowing."

Andy smiled, and the man said, "Be patient." The man gave Andy some Caribou clothes and disappeared into the fog. The man's voice was heard, and he said, "Stand up for your dreams," and this woke Andy up. Andy laid there sad in a way, because he has, and is, and his friend Red is also, standing up for poetry's dream. As Andy got ready for the day, He asked himself, "am I standing as tall as I can." No was his answer because of funding, but Andy obeys a great lesson. Ask no one for nothing; be in debt to no one.

Red knocked on the door and asked? Are you alive Andy? We have a plane to catch to Iqaluit, Nunavut.

"Cancel Red we are taking dog sleds instead," Andy replied, "Yes, Red I changed my mind like the arctic weather. I want to understand Mother Nature here. Plus we don't want the Inuit to think we are scientists."

I am afraid of dogs, said Red.

"So am I, we will be fine Red," Andy replied.

The both said at the same time, 'I am afraid of planes more" and laughed.

"Red don't look at me like that. I know you are thinking snow mobile," said Andy.

Red laughed and said, Okay.

"We have to go this way, to understand their connection and wisdom," said Andy. "The arctic is one of the last peaceful places in the world."

The man who helped them with their sleds sung a song, "Auld Lang Syne" and the meaning as times gone by. He also mentioned the song could affect the environment. He also mentioned the poet Taliesin is popular up here, besides Robert Burns.

What does the song mean? Red asked them and explained a little. Does the song mean that we should forget old acquaintances? Or does it mean that if we happened to forget them, we should remember them?

"I would say, never forget them Red, because you know as well as I do, friendships mean a lot to us, and others. Maybe not in today's mentality, but we know why, and what's important."

As they began and made their way through Nunavut, the man spoke out loud from somewhere,

Forward, forward
ship, kayak, sledge!
Your large cheeks
You must smooth, to grow light-running!

Red and Andy smiled looked at each other and laughed, because Red could tell when Andy was cold but not Red, so Andy said it any way, "Red, your cheeks are red."

Red smiled and said, Yes they are.

Along their way they came up with a freezing duel poem. Along the lines of kicking fears' ass and taking advantage of the cold in search of Ancient Wisdom with all their dead reckoning.

Andy spoke, "Red we should be grateful right now that this is not the 'Poetry On Foot' journey, but that would be a great idea one day, starting from Atlanta. Georgia."

Red was quite for a moment, thinking about that type of journey, and thought, Hey that wouldn't be that bad. Red then laughed and asked? Are we poet stewards of the planet?

"We are something like but not the only ones. We are Facilitators and a Supplicators of poetry's survival Red, Facilitators and Supplicators," Andy replied, "And as we have, our focus of riches should be in wisdom, and our names, furthermore and mainly in our permanent status with the divine, and then the people."

The Northern Lights seemed to be more vibrant, well of course, they were further north, they thought, and they looked at the dogs and Andy and Red in synch commanded, Yah!

So out in the cold vast darkness with glimmering ice crystals, Red grabbed his smart phone, and searched the area, and the text to voice read, 'Sorry, we are currently unaware of any railway attractions or excursions in this area. If you have information on a railway attraction in this province please contact us and the information will be added' and Red laughed.

Andy looked back to see if there was a Phantom Light anywhere. He then looked at Red and told him, "Only you can prevent forest fires" and laughed.

Red laughed and said, Looking for that Phantom Train Jane.

"We are on the dog team train man," said Andy.

After miles of coldness, they arrived in Baffinland, to find themselves with hypothermia, but luckily the dog team lead them to Zacharias Kunuk. As they warmed up they talked about hunting, wolf packs, trains on ice, and the Mary River iron mine, furthermore of course, hypothermia.

The rest remains at the summit of secrets. Because much bigger things are going on. Kunuk did mention that they must meet Kenojuak Ashevak when they get to Iqaluit.

Nunavut:

Means 'our land' in Inuktitut. Glaciers, mountains, and Polar Bears. Hundreds of Inukshuks, man-made stone landmarks were built by the Inuit. Inuksuk means 'something which acts for or performs the function of a person.' Auyuittuq National Park, Sirmilik National Park, and Qaummaarviit Territorial Historic Park. Lake Hazen, Baffin Island, Belcher Islands, Ellesmere Island, Akshayuk Pass, the Weasel River and Owl River valleys, and Repulse Bay.

Nunavut Railways:

The Mary River Project is located on northern Baffin Island, in the Territory of Nunavut in the Canadian Arctic. The project is currently in development and Baffinland is on track to ship iron ore.

Nunavut Poets:

The first Poet I found was Sarah Yi-Mei Tsiang, and she studied at the University of British Columbia. All of her poems are strongly themed and structured in many things, like animals, family, and life. Sarah's poems, "Hansel and Gretel," "Rivers of Blood," and "Kingston Pen," are mind opening, modern, and most of all beautiful, and many more have fantastic imagery and great perspectives.

The second Poet I found was Zachariah Wells, (they say he's a locomotive) and he studied at the University of New Brunswick. His poetry has a wide range. Zachariah's poems, "Broken," "Dream Machine," "Mental Moonshine," "One and One," "Permanently Temporary," "The Parkinsonian Reflexoligist," and many more are witty, humorous, and there is an originality about it un-read, felt, maze like, and the whole time in the maze of Zach's poetry, your head bobs, in the yes mode, because you like and agree, with Zach's methodology. I like the locomotive.

The third Poet I found was Barbara Landry, and she pulls in existence, truth of tooth of and in truth and place are embedded in her work... her work is precious, saying here I am, she said it all.. ya ya. Barbara Landry is a hey that Poet, kicks ass, Listen ya ya... whoo, really, this is a woman that made a platform of place, a duty well done. Her poem, "Getting There, Last Night In" and so many other poems of hers say what I wrote.

The fourth Poet I found was Taqralik Patridge, and her poetry thrives in family, culture, the Inuit north, and women, Taqralik's poems, "a childhood poem," "Battery," "Coin," and "I picked berries," are beautiful and heartfelt.

The fifth Poet I found was William Virgil Davis, and his poetry is breathing life & nature. Williams' poems, "Morning," "Seasons," "Sentinel," and "Photographs" are kicked back, as in recording through poetry the beauty of life, and for an example his poem, "The Writer."

The sixth Poet I found was David W. McFadden, and his poetry is deeply in life, history, (horrors & place). David's poems, "Chinese," "The Ambrose Bierce of the Tokyo Grill," "It's Not Funny Anymore," "Why Are You So Long and Sweet?," "Saskatoon," "November Fly," and many more are beautiful, educational, humorous and wise.

The seventh Poet I found was David Groulx, and his poetry is of place and circumstances in life and the gift of life. David's poems, "I am Your City," "You Leaving With The Circus," "In These Small Moments," and "Paranoid Indian," are poems of truth and strength. A Poet of acceptance- period, spoken: a David Groulx myth-

The eighth Poet I found was Laakkuluk Williamson Bathory, and she is also a performance artist. Themed in culture history and myths, and her work makes you explore the extra-ordinary.

The ninth Poet/Storyteller I found was Alootook Ipellie, and his poetry is themed in animals, culture, legends, and spirituality, furthermore music and happiness. Alootook's poems, "How Noisy They Seem," "Walking Both Sides of an Invisible Border," "One of Those Wonderful Nights," "The Owl and the Raven An Eskimo Legend," "Lost Visions, Forgotten Dreams," and "It Was Not 'Jajai-ja-jiijaaa Anymore - But 'Amen'" are completely beautiful and heartfelt.

The tenth Poet in I found was Emily-Jane Hills Orford, and she studied at Carleton University.

The eleventh Poet in I found was Napatsi Folger is a Poet to look for in Canada.

The twelfth Poet in I found was Laura McNaughton, and her poetry is themed in environment, life, and survival. Her poems "Walking," "My Bones Are," "Am I going home," and "I don't remember ever wanting to be an astronaut when I grew up," are poems with great perspectives and twists.

The thirteenth Poet in I found was Ian Kamau, and his poetry is themed in faith, freedom, and not being a minority. Ian's poems, "The Pessimist," and "I am Not a Minority, are poems of faith, strength, and determination.

The fourteenth Poet in I found was Mosha Folger, and his poetry is themed in the Arctic life, culture, patience, and survival. Mosha's poem, "Ancient Patience," "Summer Play," "Leaving my Cold Self behind" and "Where have all the Shaman gone?" are beautiful, and full of insight.

The fifteenth Poet in I found was John Parry, a great poet, that knows about survival there in the Arctic and the internet.

The sixteenth Poet I found was Sandra Ridley. Sandra's poetry is filled with imagery and language that makes the reader think and feel, and feel and think you do. You know for sure after reading and listening to her poetry you have read, heard and feel beautiful, unique and original poetry. Sandra's poems, "Dead Reckoning," "From Vigil/Vestige," "uniform '54," "Violent Morphine," and many more are dream-like and full of life.

Chapter 7-Manitoba, Canada

October 1st, 2013

While dreaming Andy and Red were at Frobisher Bay and Red was leaving for Manitoba. The train was moving slower than normal. It was cold at the upper Hudson Bay, but it was warm in their bed as they dreamed.

The bay was icy looking and steamy, but not ice, but the ice was being kept for the time being. The feeling that things and times were going to be cold came to Red and Andy, but there was some security, because they sure have covered some ground. Camps were everywhere along the bay, and so were many loons.

Andy waved good bye to Red because Red was going by steamboat to visit the Métis again, but also there was work log rolling on Carrot River, much piece work was going on. Andy looked at the flags on the ship, when a man appeared behind him on the dock and said, "We messengers come with a message from Kenojuak Ashevak. Sinnektomawok, udjertortok, udjertortok piarak," and in English, "Remember the Land." He was alone though, Andy thought, the man was saying, "Dreams, be careful, be careful for children and remember the land."

Andy looked at the man and was astonished by his eyes, by the glimmer of the color teal, chromish looking in the light, a rarity. Andy said, "Her name is poetry, and it rhymes."

The man looked at Andy and smiled. Then the man looked up, and there was a giant snowy owl flying south but turning east wide. "This is no ordinary owl," the man said, "This one is much wise and solemn."

Andy didn't say a word, things were thinning but Andy thought I have seen these owls before, and it's been awhile. Andy looked at Red and he was further away, but Red yelled from the boat, Andy everyone's outside their igloos and skin tents.

Andy looked at the ground, and moisture was all over. The ground looked energized or could be at any moment. This made Andy's heart beat faster. Andy waved mentioning he heard Red. This owl was observant, circling the area, like it was looking for someone or thing.

Red thought, Something has come back to haunt us even more than the serious social issues existing and have already causing effects. Tremors were felt, making the Inuk panicky, running around the camp villages. Glaciers way back in the distance were falling into the Hudson Bay, so now time was for being.

In a bass tone voice, this word was heard, "Land!" What and who was this voice that made everyone feel breakdown?

Red grabbed his large blue turquoise necklace with an owl engraved on it Mad Bear had given him, and Red thought, Earth was showing her potential around here. Red and Andy then noticed everyone hoping like rabbits, and this was odd to them, what was the Inuk seeing? Was the hoping a maneuver to survive a deadly unseen force?

Fires were everywhere from fallen kudlik lamps caused by the tremors, plus the falling and un-contained seal oil burning away inside these residences were helping spread the fires. Andy started to appraise the radically altering situation. He was thinking of rescue operations, confinement of the fires, extinguishing the fires, salvage operations, and additional assistance or any kind of apparatus needed. Because these people were indeed in need of help. Andy looked at all roof tops in case he needed to rescue from above.

Red looked at the icy water in the bay, debating to jump ship and swim to land to help others establish incident command posts, commissaries, and supply depots, furthermore get a telegraphed message out for help. The debating only lasted for a minute, and regardless of all the water spiders, Red jumped overboard and swam to shore to aid the Inuk.

Fire breaks, fire breaks, fire is dynamic, I too need to be dynamic, Andy thought as he sized up the situation again, and reassessed his thought tactics, natural fuels and weather patterns? What did Andy and Red know about wild-land firefighting? Andy thought about books, rescue the people and their books.

The man on the dock then spoke, "Wildlife also gets impacted from this, the caribou and walrus specifically, water pollution from this too, also mining and quarrying activities." The man then pointed to the Inuksuit path alongside the proposed railroad, so Andy and Red knew where to go. To be cautious, and to remember the struggles amongst other struggles, furthermore check for deceit was the notions Andy and Red quickly pondered.

Andy thought about the one he loved, and looked up to the Owl, and sung a song by Leatherwolf,

"Hear Me Calling."

We hear the sound of a distant chant
And hope someday we can
Look through the eyes of those of those who dared
I wish you were here

Hear me calling
Drowned in the rhyme on the piper's tune
Shadows falling

Like the rain on the midnight sun
Hear me calling out
Nowhere to run

You're never gonna live forever
It's do or die and I still need you
Hear me calling out

Red ran up to Andy, soaked, wet, and cold, but Red had a Inuk shawl on. Isn't Time a Trip? Red asked.

Andy answered and said, "Yes, Let's go help."

Andy looked at Reds shoulder and there was a water spider on him, and Andy's finger kicked the spider faraway onto the icy snow.

Red looked into Andy's eyes, and smiled. Red busted through time and slept through. Red ran to the telegraph office, and he walked through the door, but Red stopped in his tracks once inside because right in front of the telegraph was a white footed Mouse. The Mouse squeaked at Red. Red looked around to see if anyone else was seeing this and there was no one else in the tent. It also got brighter in the tent, meaning the sun was showing through the dark sky. Red needed to use that telegraph like right now, but the Mouse was eerie with a feeling of discord in the air now. Red had to outsmart the Mouse to scare it away.

I am looking for a parachute, said Red and asked the Mouse, What are you looking for?

The Mouse replied to Red's amazement, "I am looking for a flute." The Mouse then asked Red, "What is a parachute?"

It lets men fly was Red's reply.

"Men can't fly," said the Mouse.

Well Mice can't play music, said Red.

"Well you show me, I'll show you," said the Mouse.

Okay, Red said and thought, I am not doing good at this here, and how did the Mouse know what a parachute was. There are no planes here but wait there is in another time, so Red told the Mouse a story, and the Mouse told a story to Red. This was buying time, so Andy could come, and rescue Red from this Mouse, and the Mouse was like okay. Red thought, Hurry Andy, clearly you sense that my none too quick return has triggered your curiosity. Well it did. Andy was outside the tent and heard every word. Andy ran through the door, and made a loud roaring sound like a grown Elephant, and scared the Mouse away. Andy looked at Red and laughed.

"Red, do your thing, I like the sound of the messages sent by telegraph," said Andy.

Red said, Oh ya, old school texting. Listen to this Andy, so Red went tapping away, and it was music, a melody with a beat, sweet rhythm.

SOS SOS
... _ _ _ ... ... _ _ _ ...
Come rescue them
_._._. _ _ _ _ _ . ._. . ... ._. ._. .._ . _ .. ... . _ _
with poetry, we beg
. _ _ .. _ .. ... ._. _. _ _ _ _ _ . _ _ , _ .._ . _ ...
Build a railroad
_ ... .. _ .. _ _ _ ._ ._. ._ .. ._.. ._. ._ _ _ _ _ ..
from Iqaluit to Winnipeg
.._ ._. ._. _ _ _ _ _ .. _ _._. ._ .. .._ .. _ _ _ _ _ ._ _ _ .. _._ ._ .. . ._ _._. . _ _.

Andy looked at Red, and looked at the people, and said, "I'll return Red, I am going to go help them."

Andy stepped out of the tent and thought, Nothing could harm me, even though all things in this dream seemed out of the ordinary, and facing fear was nothing. Andy looked down, and started to spin in place to escape or stop the dream. He thought, this was the fastest way to save everyone. Controlling this dream was a no go. Andy looked for a book to read to awake, or change the dream. Andy blinked, and pinched himself while searching. Andy looked for escalated ground while he rested his back against igloo wall thinking. He also thought about her at home on the porch drinking coffee, and reading poetry, but most of all looking into her eyes, and making her smile with his autumn honest eyes. I need to stop thinking and act, Andy said to himself as the area seemed to get more isolated. Andy started to blink again, because people looked like black figures now. Much more is going on Andy thought, This is not like a dream. Andy braced for impact as he went around checking the inside of igloos and skin tents for people and books.

Meanwhile back at the telegraph tent, Red was looking out the entrance. He had sent the SOS out a few more times. Red was looking far away out into the distance, hoping to see rescuers coming. He looked all around him, and as he looked he glanced back into a direction he had a hunch from, center south. It looked as though a truck was coming, blazing through the snow. Was it an arctic mirage in the blowing powdered snow?

Andy was now aware of his heart rate increase as he ran looking for people and books. Street signs were of another planet entirely, the space age language, the space age architecture, the geography of the moon it seemed like. Moon like with Inuk running around in panic, and shadow people appearing out of nowhere. Andy knew his subconscious was making the decisions. He tried. Andy dropped to his knees, and asked, and asked and asked for a way to help. An apparition of Jung Hem Sing appeared, and touched him on his shoulder. Andy knew it was wishful. Andy then looked up and there was a wolf, but this wolf seemed familiar but Andy could not recall how. The ground started to shake again. The wolf seemed to be fearless to this. Andy saw a shadow person come running towards him out of the corner of his eye, and the ground broke, and Andy fell under the ice. Andy did notice Red and another man at the top of the hole as he sank into the freezing lower deep icy slushy ground. Andy was laying on his back in his roomette. He had discovered he could always wake himself when he knew he was having a nightmare by opening his eyes. The thing that was so terrifying this time to him here was, they were already open. He laid there fully paralyzed awake in his signature gumption, in deep shock to dream again. Another thing he asked for was her love again. He noticed he was sweating also while he slept, so he laid there concentrating on the now and nothing else. Then he thought of their poet friend Olan L. Smith.

Red continued to telegraph for help in dream time, and Red would not remember anything prior of this dream until now. The truck he seen coming was here, and it was a friend of Red and Andy's from the Poetry America pre-reading squad, but this Kalvin was from the future, and he was the Kalvin Freeman from the year 2043.

The trucks plow and chained covered tires threw snow out Kalvin's way as he rode past the space-age style structures. Kalvin made it to where Red was, and jumped out of the truck.. "I received your text," Kalvin said.

Red scratched his head and thought I didn't text. I sent a telegraph, said Red, Kalvin you look different and smiled. Kalvin grew out his red hair and beard, but time had passed and gray was in the day.

"Ya Ya trucker," said Kalvin.

Mosquitoes, large mosquitoes appeared everywhere, tripping Kalvin and Red out.

Well, we have fires to put out, said Red.

"Ya ya," Kalvin replied.

The Inuk's, Red and Kalvin worked together putting out fires by backing the long dump trailer hooked to the truck into the icy water, and dumping the cold water into the fires. The Inuk's didn't know what to think of the big truck. Red just smiled as they looked at the truck in amazement. The Inuk's used long logs and their sleds and dogs to clear the way and once in while get the truck unstuck from the snow and ice. Log rolling is great in many ways Red thought and log booms were everywhere in Canada. Red asked Kalvin, So how are things going on in America. Kalvin laughed a little bit but had a sad look in his eyes.

"Well," Kalvin replied, "As the actor and comedian Robin Williams says, Canada is a big country, the kindest country in the world. A really nice apartment above a meth lab. You don't want to know Red."

Red said, Wow, that is one heck of a statement.

"Ya ya," Kalvin replied.

Railway official Edson J. Chamberlin and industrialist lumber king John Rudolphus Booth appeared on Gloucestershire steam tractors, and asked them if they wanted a job. Red and Kalvin looked at each other and the Inuk's, and the Inuk's looked sad like they were thinking, Ya, take our new friends and heroes away.

"I have work in Canada, South America, and Mexico," Chamberlin said.

Kalvin looked at Red and said, "This man is starting to irritate me. I am out of here." Kalvin went with the Inuk's and celebrated their life saving and book saving accomplishments somewhere in a secret Inuk place.

What the heck Red thought. Red looked at John Rudolphus Booth with his long thick black over coat, and his tall fur hat. Booth was tapping his cane on the ice, growing impatient for Red's reply.

"How much money do you have in your pockets?" Booth asked Red.

Well, I have no money, and very happy with that, but I do love log rolling, Red replied with a little laugh.

"I came here with nine dollars in my pocket, and see that train coming loaded with square cut logs?" Booth asked.

Yes, Red replied.

"Well, those are my truths," said Booth.

Red thought again, You people are out of control with your loathsome monopoly, and Red did consider this was a period when governments stood or fell on railway issues. Red thought of Andy. Andy would like this guy. He was a shingle maker and a bridge builder.

"Well think about it because you are good, and you can find me at the flower show. I love flowers," said Booth.

Red smiled and replied, Okay, and thanks. I will let you both know. Flowers, nice Red thought, another reason to like this guy. A railroader loving flowers, nice. He did seem a bit privatized though, making Red wonder why.

Red walked away down the tracks watching a railroad watchmen fill barrels up with water, and this was to put out fires from steam engines. Red also noticed men moving dirt with wagons, and dual mule teams with flat wooded trailers with no wheels from a trail looking like from the hilltop, and dumping dirt in the valley here. Red then heard the Countess of Dufferin steam train, and she was a beautiful sight to Red. He was getting colder and smelt fires again. He looked behind him, and he was no longer in Nunavut, so Red searched where the fire was. Along the way as he walked the railroad tracks he noticed men, the Doukhobor Railroad crew asleep in heaps of straw on the prairie near the tracks. He made it to where the fire was and it was a large bon fire with many people around it. Red walked up to them, and introduced himself, and glanced into the fire with his hands held out. There were many farm houses also, and the porches were filled with children. One child tugged on Red's coat and asked, "Are you a Spirit Wrestler too?"

Red smiled and laughed inside and said, Why yes I am, and I have wrestled many, and still am, and I help others. I have a friend named Andy, and we are like a tag team.

"A tag team, Oh, we Doukhobors are all a tag team" said the boy.

Well that's a good, good thing, because we all need help, because we can't do it all, said Red.

Red was in a colony of Russian immigrants. Red did not speak Russian so the boy who spoke English explained to Red some things, and the elders seemed to have a loss of communal spirit because they were silent with most of their heads down low. The government and the railroads were taking advantage of them. Red knew about this kind of shit business. The same reasons Andy retired from roofing to go on this journey. Companies careless about their workers. Once people realize, and kill their fear of the loss of everything and what they have achieved they will be okay, and start to learn to liberate themselves and find themselves living in peace. Money makes one rape the planet for more and more. As Gandhi said "Live simply so that others may simply live" but folks want to take advantage of people with that. One must live by treading lightly on the land. The boy also told Red about crop failures, and wheat was a bid commodity.

The boy asked Red if he was going to help build the Forks, a railroad junction near the ports of the Red River in Winnipeg, and the boy asked "Did they name the river after you sir?"

Red laughed and said, I would like to think so, but I think not. Probably named by fur traders.

Other children came running to warn them all the Royal Canadian Mounted Police were coming. The feeling of good omens quickly vanished in Reds' dream, and he vanished also out of sight. Red ran to the nearest train station, and once inside there was a black lady working the ticket counter, and she said, "Welcome to Winnipeg, the Gateway to the

West."

Red was a little stunned because it was like he has seen or known her before, so he asked her, What's your name because it seems like we have met before?

"My name is Evette, and I don't believe we have never met. Are you hitting on me?" Evette asked.

Red laughed and replied, No, no. Just seems like we have met.

A man came through a door behind her, and he was William Methven "Smooth" Whyte, a station agent for the Canadian Pacific Railway. He spoke, "Evette his deeds have spoken, as Sir Charles Tupper would say. He is like me Evette, determined, and interested in foreign missions and local education. I want you on my Diamond-Crossing crew."

Are you talking about a Fort or something? Red asked.

Whyte laughed and said, "I like you're thinking, why yes Red a fort."

Railway executive Richard Bladworth Angus walked into the station and asked, "Whyte, are you ready for a sniff test because we cannot falter or bust today or tomorrow because construction out of Winnipeg is crucial."

Evette asked, "Gentlemen, have you been reading the newpapers?"

Angus raised his voice and said, "Yes, we know about the Brooklynn Bridge and the sales lady." Angus looked at her and Red, and asked Red, "Who are you?"

The William Crooks train was pulling into the station from Minnesota and Red replied, Well, since you have spoken to me the station here might just drive off on its own down the railroad if I really tell you who I am. This moment in dream land awoke Red.

Andy was laying in his bed thinking about the now, and Red was struggling to wake up because this dream wore him out. They just wanted to rest, take a break, and lay there when all the sudden they both jumped out of bed because they heard the clashing of pots and pans outside their roomette doors, that were across from each other. Once on their feet and startled out of their heads they heard a voice they recognized, and it was Mr. Welchberry singing,

Get out in that kitchen and rattle those pots and pans

A Bill Haley Song 'Shake Rattle and Roll.'

Get out in that kitchen and rattle those pots and pans
Well roll my breakfast 'cause I'm a hungry man

I said shake rattle and roll
I said shake rattle and roll
I said shake rattle and roll
I said shake rattle and roll
Well you'll never do nothin'
To save your doggone soul

Wearin' those dresses your hair done up so nice
Wearin' those dresses your hair done up so nice
You look so warm but your heart is cold as ice

I said shake rattle and roll
I said shake rattle and roll
I said shake rattle and roll
I said shake rattle and roll
Well you'll never do nothin'
To save your doggone soul

I'm like a one eyed cat peeping in a sea food store
I'm like a one eyed cat peeping in a sea food store
I can look at you tell you don't love me no more

I believe you are doing me wrong and now I know
I believe you are doing me wrong and now I know
The more I work the faster my money go

Andy opened the door and said, Whooo, with the biggest smile on his face since he lived in Kentucky when she said, Come on baby. Andy started snapping his fingers, and clapping his hands. Red opened his door and said, Ya, really loud, and jumped around happy as can be. Seth was behind Mr. Welchberry playing the song for Mr. Welchberry.

They all walked to the dining car singing the song. Once there they all sat together and Mr. Welchberry asked, "So how are you?"

We are fine Mr. Welchberry, they both replied.

"How is Charlie?" Mr. Welchberry asked.

"He is doing great," said Andy, "He is writing poetry again, giving the world some great pieces."

Ya, Red replied, Chief Joesph would be proud of him.

'He's', Andy and Red said at the same time, in Synch, and looked at each other, and Andy continued to tell Mr. Welchberry, He's a bit mad at us from all the excitement of Poetry Train America, then Andy whispered, and the Royal Canadian Mounted Police, we tend to forget all the tech stuff in our posts. Also Mr. Welchberry we talk about him all the time.

"I can vouch for that," said Seth.

'We', Red and Andy said together in Synch, and Red continued to say, We also have a gift for him for Christmas. Martin is making him a custom leather bound Poetry Train America. Mr. Welchberry our finances have been low, but we have been blessed by new friends.

"Did you explain to Charlie all of this?" Mr.Welchberry asked.

"Yes, somewhat," Andy replied, "But we don't want him to stress over some of the mess."

"Did you tell him, you miss him and love him?" Mr. Welchberry asked.

Yes, of course, they both replied.

"Okay, I see you all are doing fine in Canada," said Mr. Welchberry.

"Oh ya," Andy replied, "I can go on and on."

The poets here love the poetry train, said Red, and I'll tell you what Mr. Welchberry, appreciation is not even a word in how we feel.

"Gentlemen, I am making breakfast, and you two get back to work," said Mr. Welchberry.

Thanks, what are we having? They both asked.

"Caribou and Arctic char, Maktaaq an outer layer of whale skin, served raw," said Mr. Welchberry, "A Canadian delight."

Andy and Red looked at each other and said, Well alright, but inside they were like Oh shit, well Canadian country it is.

Mr. Welchberry, laughed and asked, "What's the plan today?"

Well, we are featuring poetry presses and publishers and the poets, Red replied,The ones, the passengers on the train.

"Nice, great idea," said Mr. Welchberry, and he walked away.

Seth laughed and said, "That man is cool. He seems like he has lived on earth forever."

Andy and Red laughed and said, Maybe.

Red said, I had a dream about Kalvin.

Andy thought and said, "Come to think of it, me too."

Tears fell from Reds eyes about the news in America as he read online, and Seth played White Lion's song, "When the Children Cry."

They both had a premonition and felt the intense feelings about the existence in the United States.

Andy looked at a recent message sent to him by the one he loves.

Forget me not~
Forget me never
I love you know
and forever

The idiom of all the Tea in China came to Andy's mind, no my love never, ever shall I forget you.

Then the news about poet Olan L. Smith came, that he was hospitalized for shortness of breath and chest pains. This tore Andy up, so he went to the restroom and cried. Olan has been helping Andy with his empathy, and now this. Andy felt bad in a way, was he a part of this inducing, and hoped not, so he prayed for his speedy recovery. Drop the weight, drop the weight, as Olan said, and Andy tried. Andy did feel the amazement and blessing of the poetic family they were part of, as poet Tammy Jo Ricci knew and suggested way in the beginning of this journey. Andy looked into the mirror and said, "Unbelievable power, we have unbelievable power to make the world a better place, God bless everyone get off your asses, and do something." Calm down he thought, listen to what Olan said, calm down. Pucker up Bubba, pucker up.

Once returned he overheard Seth ask Red if he has seen the movie, "Cipher in the Snow." Red hasn't seen the movie he told Seth, but Andy has and an epiphany came to Andy, that being ostracized is no joke, and he himself was when he was young, and that is why Andy has a speech impediment, but something deeper kept Andy going. Something much deeper.

Andy spoke, "I am a man and a boy at the same time, also a quarterback and a safety at the same time."

Dual offense and defense, replied Red.

"Yes," said Andy, in a good way though, then the battle slash error of, well you know, feed the good wolf or feed the bad wolf, but 99% a good wolf most of the time, not speaking of a wolf being cornered. Who knew the world was rough, until taught? For instance I use to watch and play with lady bugs on my window seal when I was young. Love the animals. Remember the T.V. Show Wild Kingdom. The show fascinated me. I remember telling my Grandfather. I want to go to Africa, and then he told me about the zoo. Why would anyone want to destroy such a place. They should have left them all there, come to think about it. Anyways. I was aware and still am aware. Then there is Hope. There is Faith too. I may have felt and said I hoped to be a zoologist, but can't recall, but that deep desire to go on a safari was intense for me. So I learned to draw by instinct, art come into play, but it was hard. And toy animals, the plastic ones, I had them. I also saved those animal cracker circus trains, and played with those with the little animal figures. Then distraction came in many forms. Cartoons, sports, toys, music, ah music tripped me out. I remember seeing KISS cards, and thought this was cool, and the band the Monkees. American Bandstand and the Soul Train. Parenting is the grandest, hardest job in the world. Why didn't anyone who raised me guard this desire? My love for animals. So I guess you can say Chaos came into play. I'll tell you what also fascinated me, was the show Night Gallery. It didn't scare me, but fueled my imagination. But let's get back to Hope, much more than that Faith."

"You must have one great memory," said Seth.

Yes he does, replied Red.

"Death was kept a secret, and I still wonder why," said Andy.

"It sure and the hell isn't now," Seth replied.

"For sure," said Andy, "Were they hoping death would never happen to me, or any child they ever seen. So why is Hope and Faith so important? If good and evil are equal and in constant battle, why is good evil, if good desires to execute evil, and yes I know you have one or the other to know the difference, but why has good grown weak to Hope and Faith."

Mr. Welchberry came with their breakfast and said, "Never mind me, carry on gentlemen," and he sat down to dine with them and spoke again, "I know it's not polite to eat and talk, but you are talking about dire things I am sure."

"Thanks Mr. Welchberry," replied Andy, "You all eat please and I'll continue. The goodness in people should stress, and implement more Hope and Faith every day, but listen, Hope is the feeling that what is wanted can be had or that events will turn out for the best, so let's say Hope is dining with us here and is a person. To me Hope is saying you can do it, you can, you don't need me, but I have to warn you, I have a evil twin named Despair, and is jealous of me, and Despair is great at making everything we do collapse."

A bicycle can't roll with a flat tire can it, said Red.

"Exactly," Andy replied, "so why ride, walk with our blessing of two legs. Hope needs to be more clever then Despairs cruelty, and I stress this again, Hope needs to be more clever as Despairs cruelty. As we talked about in Poetry Train America. History is a tool but also the problem, and the problem is no one is listening and learning. What we didn't know during the American journey was Jiddu Krishnamurti but now we do. Way before all of this, we knew about poet King David's 'Those who seek shall find' those words are embedded in us, a phrase for a born instinct of survival. So this gentlemen, goes back to my theory of availability. Jiddu Krishnamurti wasn't available to us here in America. Seth, me and Red never went to college, because Despair was everywhere in our lives. So in our living history, we do know we continually let Despair keep air in it's tire self, as Red's analogy. Okay, take the word and meaning of participate, part, why do we even part with Despair. Then we have fear, fear of what, who and what is actually going to stop or hurt us. This is why, I love Robert Anton Wilson. Robert would laugh in Despairs face, and piss his pants doing it. Today, Despair has took ostracization to a new and bizarre level, so Hope needs to take its self to a new higher level. All of this lives inside us all. Hope is like saying. Hey, together we are beauty, delight with me in this beautiful passion. Beyond death is beautiful, it has to be, but all this other bullshit has got to go. You know, I am not cutting out any names here but there is a new teacher I know, who is becoming a teacher, but has no clue of any of this. And if this teacher did and taught great wisdom, they'd have no career. Who is in charge of all this stuff, they are the ones responsible for all of this, what kind of reward is gained by that and this. Do we have a dark secret we can't see, tricking us. Does it lie in our stomach? Why isn't there a light secret there too? There has to be."

Mr. Welchberry spoke, "Maybe toilet paper should be banned."

Everyone laughed.

"Mr. Welchberry," Andy said, "Listen, I thought this one time. There should be a death museum. Were we can see through caskets, and see through crematory's and other clear visuals. Like a recent passed away couple and fastened them to two rocking chairs and let them sit there until they are dust. So what about the smell, the flies and &c. Will this wake folks up, that our lives are beyond precious?"

No one said a word, but thought and thought, and the imagery grew and grew.

"Murder and killing hasn't worked, and neither has sorrow," said Andy, "Well let's get to work."

Eat Andy; replied Red, it's very good. It's a learn as you go program, when Hope caresses you in any form it should be not be taken lightly for me any way. Hope is sought and heard more often nowadays, but always~ Hope has ~always been desired, furthermore felt, so that is where Hopes' glance is, now when Hope caresses you, all despair has gone flat. As I mentioned, I have learned a thing or two about Hope and despair, and one of the things I have learned is, Hope and Despair are two wheels on one wicked bicycle...

Seth, pulled out a vintage Casio keyboard and played a Randy Newmans Song, 'The World Isn't Fair.'

Andy was in deep thought as Seth played the song, about the parallels of Hope and Despair, and vanity presses and not so vanity presses. What is the difference? There is none; it's about the audience and an audience. Despair has wide and lengthy audience, but Hope, is left on a stage all alone, seemingly like, and Hopes voice echoes loud to no ears, the auditorium is empty, why? Andy took notes of this to write about.

Dr. Richard L. Bello was on board the train and overheard the conversation, so he introduced himself, and they talked about climate change, and the warmer temperatures threatening the railways. Andy knew about this from the melting of the permafrost in his dream.

Mr. Welchberry spoke, "Back in the day the Federal Minister of Railroads Charles Tupper said, 'The human mind naturally adapts itself to the position it occupies. The most gigantic intellect may be dwarfed by being cabin'd, cribbed and confined. It requires a great country and great circumstances to develop great men.' and I mentioning this because, well it's fuel for the Hope fire, and the process of un-adaption."

Seth looked at Andy and Red, and they winked. Mr. Welchberry had a book with him also entitled 'The Viking Heart.'

Andy was thinking, America is going through psychological warfare.

Red asked, The Viking Heart, by Laura Goodman Salverson? Mr.Welchberry, how are Connie and Sophie doing?

Andy was in deep thought thinking about Faith and Hope again, and he being caught in between the mega and the mini, the awake state and the dream state, furthermore the washed minds and the time dirty minds, while researching the author and poet Laura Goodman Salverson.

"Yes," replied Mr.Welchberry, "Laura is one of my favorite poets from Canada. This may jolt your memory Red and Andy, and Mr.Welchberry recited a poem from the book,"

The gold of the sunset illumines the deep,
Oh, thus should each evening prepare me for sleep.
A soft cooling breeze with the freshness of dew,
- The ocean a mirror of heavenly blue.
The mountain peaks towering stately around

Are giants on guard where the sky meets the ground.
This sunset foretells that the day shall be bright
That follows the steps of this wonderful night.

As soon as he recited the last line Connie and Sophie brought them more coffee and a plate of pancakes for Red, because Red loved the fact that Robert Anton Wilson made pancakes for aliens every morning, and sat their plates out on the table of his patio deck, and offering to the Angels, and they all thought that was beautiful and highly hilarious. They brought French toast to Andy, well he loves French toast, and so does the one he loves. Andy and Red stood up, happiness hit their faces glow switch, because they haven't seen them either since they escaped from the United States.

Connie and Sophie kissed them both on the cheeks. Connie and Sophie looked at Mr.Welchberry, and Connie said, "We love you Papa, we loved it when you read to us the Viking Heart, and yes, it is important that a child learns truths. One of our favorite things about the book is Laura made Einar Halsson a strong heart as she says, 'it's not right to make fun of the child when she tries to learn something.' So fun maybe the nail popping Hopes tire." Connie and Sophie looked at Red.

So we must take our lives and times more seriously, said Red, There is a time and place for everything.

"Yes, for now, and then celebrate when the Hopes' Train is back on track," Connie replied.

Andy was silent reading the Viking Heart, in awe mode, also responsibility mode, because the analogy from the book, the dream, the giant voice that spoke 'Land,' this whole mornings conversation was in a time synchronicity mode, and this all was happening again. Déjà vu in high gear sort of speak. This is where time says, Hi there, I have a glitch, and the doors wide open, come on in, and excuse me also, This is where Hopes' parents live. Andy a rose his third eyebrow as he read, 'Don't you hear him trying to get the silly sheep down off the slopes?" And to Andy that was the hill of nothing of any value for positivity of times heavy weight in our Despair basket. Drop the Despair basket and gather, gather Hope. Andy thought of Faith and spoke, Seth can you play 'When the Children Cry' again please.

And the Poetry Train rolled on. The day was new and beautiful furthermore full of the blessing of Hope. And the Soldiers of Hope were rebuilding, showing the despaired that Hope loved them, but encouraged them to move faster.

Manitoba:

Beluga Whales, Churchill its title as Polar Bear Capital of the World, Riding Mountain

National Park, Hudson Bay, Sandy Lake, Falcon Lake, Lake Manitoba, Lake Athapapuskow, Rat River, International Peace Garden, St-Pierre-Jolys, Kwastichewan Falls, Big Grass Marsh, Bird's Hill Provincial Park, Grand Beach Provincial Park, Pinawa Dam Heritage Park, Spirit Sands-Spruce Woods Provincial Park, Turtle Mountain Provincial Park, Medicine Rock and I wonder why there are no Poet Laureates in Manitoba.

Manitoba Railways:

The Grand Trunk Railway began in 1852, the Hudson Bay Railway began in 1880, the St. Paul, Minneapolis, and Manitoba Railway began in 1882, renamed the Great Northern in 1890, the Canadian Pacific Railway began in 1871, the Northern Pacific and Manitoba Railway began in 1888, the Canadian Northern began in 1899, the Brandon, Saskatchewan and Hudson Bay Railway Company began in 1903, and the Prairie Dog Central Railway began in 1970.

Manitoba Poets:

The first Poet I found was Paula Dawn Lietz aka Pd Lietz, and her poetry is themed in animals, erotica, family, love, nature, and wisdom. Pd's poems, "A Whole Lot of Scared," "Holes in My Armour," "In Multiple Ways," "To Birth Over Boundaries," and "Redox of Atoms," are powerful, sensual, and mesmerizing, furthermore every word calls out to the reader, and raises the minds' eyebrow with epiphany's. Her Haiga & Tanka poetry are just as thought provoking and beautiful.

The second Poet in I found was Althea Guiboche, and her poetry is themed in culture, life, love, humanity, and nature. Althea's poems, "Agimaawag akina," "everyone counts," "the coffee break," "poverty is not a choice, and "through my eyes," are poems of strength, and for sure will humble the reader because her love for humanity speaks well in her poetry.

The third Poet in I found was Josh 'Freewheelin' Sigurdson, and his poems "Forgive Me If I Cry," and "Your Soul, Immensely," are true melancholy.

The fourth Poet in I found was Duncan Mercredi, and his poetry is themed in animals, culture, humanity and nature. Duncan's poems, "big bear," "This City is Red," and "it is good this," are beautiful poems that place the reader in nature, and understanding.

The fifth Poet in I found was Don Schaeffer, and he studied at the City College of New York. His poetry is vast, and themed on many things. Don's poems, "New Streets Lead to Water," "Port of Miami," "Skype," "When I Won the Voice of Democracy Contest," "Zen for a Slot Canyon Hiker," and many more are beautiful, contemporary and delicate.

The sixth Poet in I found was Colin Ward, and he studied at Nippissing University. His poetry is vast, and themed in many things, life, all life; comedy, nature, people and suffering; not to mention structure of poetry that is evident in his work. Colin's poems, "Timelines," "Dark Neighborhood," "Embracing Arms," "Last Waltz," "The Real Life Death of Sam McGee," "Still Life," and many more are clever, humorous, and serious, furthermore Colin's poetry makes the reader humble.

The eighth Poet I found was Méla Renard, and her poems, "Rust," and "Number Games," are beautiful, historical, and somber.

The ninth Poet I found was Katherena Vermette, and her poetry is themed in life, and culture, furthermore, love, and struggle. Katherena's poems, "Green Disease," and "Indians," are poems of truth with slickness.

The tenth Poet I found was Rosanna Deerchild, and her poetry is themed in culture, & leadership! Rosanna's poems "First brush with death," "found:," "His Feast, Her Broken Fast," and "Mother Hood," are precious and proof we all can live in harmony regardless of skin color, and way more than that.

The eleventh Poet I found was Robert W. Nero, and his poetry is themed in animals, nature, reality, and wisdom. Roberts's poems, "Dead Owl," "Fascination," "Large Owl," and "Salvage Operation," are poems with great parallels and epiphanies.

The twelfth Poet I found was David Zieroth, and his poetry is themed in animals, nature, and life. David's poems, "Crows Do Not Have Retirement," "Function of the Individual," "Galileo," "Sun," and "The Fly in Autumn" are relaxing, and alive with life.

The thirteenth Poet I found was Sally Ito, and her poetry is themed in Humanity, and Life: life on all levels of Grace, furthermore more Grace, and the Humility. Sally's poems, "Alert to Glory," "Apprehend," "Caress," and "Spring Break" are mythological, getting the signal she's only doing that for stone heads, just saying, epiphany spirit, furthermore a Poet that has a great voice and pen span.

The fourteenth Poet I found was Diamond Doug Keith, and his poetry is themed in life, cowboy life, and nature. Doug's poems, "Cowpuncher's Melody," "Cowtown Carol," "The Day Leonard Had a Sale," "There's a Angel in the Saddle," and "These Dirty Ol' Wranglers," are beautiful, witty, and humorous.

The fifteenth Poet I found was Michelle Kafka, and her poetry is themed in friendship, love, life, and nature. Michelle's poems, "Comfort In Blue," "He Sleeps In Numbers," "Friendship's Meaning," "Gourmet Fish," Red Rain," "Seashell Lost," and many more are beautiful, imaginative, with a unique relaxing deliverance.

The sixteenth Poet I found was Greg Scofield, and his poetry is themed in culture, family, love, nature, and erotica. Greg's poems, "Prayer Song" "I'll Teach You Cree," "I've Been Told," "I've Looked For You," and "The Ship" are beautiful, impacting, and wise.

The seventeenth Poet I found was Michelle Elrick, and her poetry is themed in life. Michelle's poems, "256 Paper Machine," "Bread," "Ditches," and "Swallow" are very unique and beautiful.

The eighteenth Poet I found was Geoff 'Poppa Mac' Mackay, and he found the Poetry Train. His poetry is about life, faith, humor, and family. Poppa Mac's poems, "Behind The Grease Paint," "Cowboy Hats," and "Cowboy Prayer" are full of life, furthermore humorous and beautiful.

Chapter 8-Ontario, Canada
November 27th, 2013

Andy was walking and it had just rained, because way ahead of him was wet. Thunder was in the distance and so was an oncoming train. The scent of a paper mill was in the air, and so was a few newspapers scattered. The covered scents had the name Sir William Mackenzie in the headlines. Andy talked along the way and he repeated what he overheard back at a train station, 'I have nothing to say about the steam train.' I can't believe she said that. One hundred and fifty years of the steam train. It will be 2043 maybe 2063 before we hear; I have nothing to say about the diesel train. Changes, changes, changes, fast and down as an avalanche. We must keep up with the modern, and get bullet. Come and ride the train, come get to know the new by gone era. I must keep going, and get to the City on the side of a mountain, Ontario. Andy was hungry, and he thought about cooking a can of beans on a boiler head.

A young lad was in a field not to far from the tracks. When Andy walked near, the boy walked upon the tracks to walk along with Andy. "Excuse me Mister," the boy said, "My name is George Phillips and I love poetry, I may even write one or two poems but I want to be a railroad fireman." The boy then asked, and Andy noticed his fine Irish accent, "Who were you talking to?

Then came the train. It was beating as it had a heart, hissing and growling.

The boy then stopped and said, "They are looking for you and your friend. We need to get off the tracks."

Andy didn't say anything, but followed the boy. The train rolled past, and there were throngs of passengers on the flat cars sitting on benches and standing between the planks. The weather was bone chilling and the young lad, George Phillips said, "Them poor devils. We can hide you on the Grange, the home of D'Arcy Boulton. He's a lawyer fighting for the railroads."

"Who is we?" Andy asked.

George laughed and said, "Me and my friend Mary O'Shea, she is a maid there, and she is my friend. Oh look, we are near the circus grounds Andy. There is Mr. Matthew Scott, the trainer of the largest elephant in the world, Jumbo and Tom Thumb, the baby elephant."

Andy smiled from ear to ear, and asked, "Can we go see them?" This excited Andy, because he loved elephants and especially Jumbo and this was the legendary Jumbo.

"We can try Andy," George replied.

Andy noticed in some places as they walked were colder than in most places. Andy also noticed them black shadows again, and they were talking amongst themselves on the tracks and on the embankment next to them, but Andy didn't say anything. The boy noticed Andy looking that way and said, "They are hobos looking for circus work." Andy noticed them also, but those figures were not what Andy see's. When they turned around to get to Mr. Scott, there was a man right in front of them, and this startled the both of them.

"Pardon me," the man said and he was Father Albert Lacombe, a peace keeper for the Cree and the Blackfoot, and furthermore the Canadian Pacific Railway. Lacombe had this curious look going on, as he looked at Andy. He didn't look at George but at Andy. Lacombe's presence set Andy in awe mode. Lacombe had this large crucifix around his neck, and it hung low, it was so big that it was the length of his stomach, and Andy was tripping. Lacombe said, "Follow me," and they did, and Lacombe talked about peace keeping. Lacombe had Andy under his spell, and Andy was in the art of listening mode. They made their way to the John Bell Chapel, and once inside, Lacombe pointed to the art of Kenojuak Ashevak, a stain glass work of a snowy owl. Andy was in awe at this work. Silence was broken, when Cosimo Figliomeni walked into the chapel. He was a railroader in Ontario, and he asked Andy, "So you want a job on the railroad, that no one else wants, do you?" and Figliomeni laughed and said, "You are just like me when I came into Canada, eager, and just wanting to be a part of something great."

"Yes," Andy replied, "I am a fast learner and have a great memory, furthermore I am honest."

The blank dream door opened again, and the sister poets Susanna Moodie and Catharine Parr Traill came into the chapel. They looked at Andy and said, "So you promote poetry, what do you have planned for poetry presses?"

Andy replies, "I want to bring presses to the poets and poets to the presses, and not only that poetry back to the shelf. I have been blessed where I come from to help presses, poets and these books stores. This brings, or makes poetry available. If poetry books are shelved once again this will bring the poet to the reader. No one where I come from would know any of these beautiful people and their poetic work. I did it with a book called 'Fast Trains' by Emy Louie."

Andy broke time code by saying this.

Susanna and Catharine laughed a little bit and said, "We are not laughing at you Andy, just the fact of fast trains. People growing impatient are they? Andy you work hard at promoting poetry like men work the field."

"I do it because I love poetry, poets, and the railroad," said Andy, "I like to see people happy, and poetry does this, for the writer and the reader, and train rides are just as satisfying. Catharine people read poetry and write it on trains all the time."

"Yes they do, so you like giving children a new perspective on life?" Catharine asked.

"Yes," Andy replied. "I don't want the youth to be unfortunate and to miss out on the beauty of poetry; past, present, and future. Also, Catharine, steam, diesel, and bullet trains." Andy broke code again.

"Bullet, you are funny Andy," Susanna replied, "You have a poet's imagination that is for sure. A train gun, I like that, shooting out trains."

"You must know the back woods of Canada," said Catharine, "To rough it in the woods. So you are like me, you like gathering and historical tales."

"Yes," Andy replied, "Okay."

The poet and the head of Department of Indian affairs Duncan Campbell Scott came out from a back room, and said, "I love the wilderness." He sat down and played a piano in the chapel.

Andy spoke, "Duncan, I seen that back door there, so what is the difference between you playing music and expecting us to enjoy it, maybe a dance and or sing along, but you have a problem with native music and their dancing? Why do you think Indians are fools?"

"The sun shines and the water runs," said Duncan.

"Why are you mocking the Indian's poetic method of measuring time?" Andy asked.

Duncan stood up and said, "Okay you dream voyageur, what do you know about Angelhood?"

"You can get on me all you want to, but do you see Keejigo here," said Andy. "Keejigo's a young girl, a half-breed poet, who was the third wife of Tabashaw, chief of the Salteaux. She lives for love, so that's one thing I know about Angelhood. You live for love and give love to those who don't, to those who live in despair, and please do not speak about deep love."

"Who are you trying to impress Andy, the one you love, poets, or the Angels?" Duncan asked, "She lives for love alright, so why does she journey with other men?"

"Me Duncan, I am trying to impress me, growth as a man, a poet because if I can't impress me, then how am I going to impress anyone, and if no one cares, then so be it," Andy replied, "I do what I love, and how can you think like that of her?"

"The train has stopped Andy," said Duncan and recited his poem 'En Route."

"Beautiful poem Duncan," said Andy, "I did come from nowhere, and bet this, I shall not go into nothingness, because I am fighting for the little ones."

"So am I," Duncan replied, "I am unsympathetic to aboriginal ideals. I want to get rid of the Indian problem."

Andy looked at George Phillips and said, "I have to go. I do not like this talk. George there are better ways to go about things. Policy, polish yourself first, for Angels sake. Good day ladies," Andy said as he looked at the glass stained snowy owl one last time, as he and George walked out of the chapel."

I understand about saving lives, but oh my, you can be more creative, and what gives folks the right, like they can't think for themselves, just show them, why force them, Andy thought, but knew he couldn't do a thing about it, because he was in dream time in a time long ago.

Katie, a young girl was outside the chapel, and she was the daughter of Catharine Parr Traill. "Hello George, who is your friend?" Katie asked.

"This is Andy, and he's come from America to promote Canadian poetry and trains," George replied, "And poet Duncan Campbell Scott just gave him a hard time."

"He's not the poet Andy should know, he should know the poet Isabella Valancy Crawford, and she plays piano too" Katie said, "She's at my house as of now, she just moved in not long ago. She loves aboriginal myths and legends unlike Duncan."

Andy smiled because his friend poet Julie Catherine Vigna loves Isabella. "Can we meet her?" Andy asked.

"Why sure," Katy replied, "Although she is a bit reclusive and unwilling to receive guests, but you two are different. You will feel her dignified hospitality."

At the Traill homestead, Isabella was organizing figures, tiny dolls, colored rose point silk and peacock blue satin; and cardboard on the dining room table. Reclusive? Isabella was nowhere near reclusive when she seen Andy. When Andy seen her she was bright eyed, with her hair pinned up, and she was dressed well. Andy could tell she was full blooded Irish. Isabella didn't waste any time and said, "You and George can stay here and eat fresh Irish cookies and potato cakes I have just made. I am going to show Andy around Kawartha Lake."

Once at the lake Isabella and Andy walked up to a canoe, cleared off the fallin maple leafs and put the canoe and themselves onto the lake that was filled with lily pads. The lakes tide was crystal clear and slow. Dragon flies were entertained by their presence. An oriole caught Andy's attention along with the purple skies, attracting Andy's soul imagination. Isabella was happy too and recited her poem 'The Camp of Souls.'

Silence was slight and Isabella recited another poem 'At the Opera- A Fragment.'

"Andy, you have to admit it feels great when someone, even myself says about you, 'indeed of no ordinary kind- vigorous, powerful.'" Isabella told Andy this with positivity in her eyes.

Andy felt he was deep into his inner world of feelings and fantasies. Was everything smooth sailing now? The waters were calm for a change Andy felt. We had found ourselves staring at a small ravine which was at the base of the lake. This ravine was also the lake's drain which ran into a smaller lake on a lower land level, and this part of the lake was also polka dotted with lily pads like green Irish freckles. Also we were on high alert for both visual and sound evidence of bears. Andy thought walking was fun; paddling was even more fun, once at the lower lake, Isabella pointed to a cave, so they paddled their way into this beautiful aquatic cavern.

This cave turned into a railroad machine shop. Where locomotives breakdown for an overhaul, and literally where coveralls dirt up hard. Crank pins spin off by hammer and chisel, removing the hex. Where you take off tires and rods get them polished up. Listen to the sounds of the boring mill. Look at the flame thrower. Where things are done with belts and the main driving wheel is creating new threads. There was a bay of boilers being stripped, and cranes carried us away it seemed like as we paddled through and on.

Strange lights, like Chinese lanterns appeared through the mistletoe filled oaks and apple trees on their way out of the cave. Andy noticed the black shadows again amongst themselves along the shore. Andy was paddling away, and he noticed it seemed a bit harder, and the canoe slowed down some. Andy turned around to look at Isabella and she was no longer there, so Andy slowed his pace. A man then laughed from the lakes bank and Andy recognized it was Walt Whitman, and Walt laughed. Andy oared near where Walt sat, and Walt recited his poem, 'As I Sat Alone by Blue Ontario's Shores' and these lines echoed in Andy's mind,

We are the most beautiful to ourselves, and in ourselves;

Produce great persons, the rest follows.

I listened to the Phantom by Ontario's shore,
I heard the voice arising, demanding bards;

Of all races and eras, These States, with veins full of poetical
stuff, most need poets, and are to have the greatest, and use
them the greatest;
Their Presidents shall not be their common referee so much as their
poets shall.

Of These States, the poet is the equable man,
He supplies what wants supplying--he checks what wants checking,
In peace, out of him speaks the spirit of peace, large, rich,

The flag of peace quick-folded, and instead, the flag we know,
Warlike flag of the great Idea.

Questions and more questions, Andy thought, and Walt was amazed at Andy as Andy was of he.

Bards for my own land, only, I invoke;
(For the war, the war is over--the field is clear'd,)
Till they strike up marches henceforth triumphant and onward,
To cheer, O mother, your boundless, expectant soul.

Bards grand as these days so grand!
Bards of the great Idea! Bards of the peaceful inventions! (for the
war, the war is over!)
Yet Bards of the latent armies--a million soldiers waiting, ever-
ready,
Bards towering like hills--(no more these dots, these pigmies, these
little piping straws, these gnats, that fill the hour, to pass
for poets;)
Bards with songs as from burning coals, or the lightning's fork'd
stripes!
Ample Ohio's bards--bards for California! inland bards--bards of the
war;)
(As a wheel turns on its axle, so I find my chants turning finally on
the war;)
Bards of pride! Bards tallying the ocean's roar, and the swooping
eagle's scream!
You, by my charm, I invoke!

Andy was all in his thoughts. Why is everything so contradictory? Then Andy noticed Father Albert Lacombe hiding amongst the trees listening to Walt and this startled Andy and he awoke. He laid there half awake, thinking about the significance of the dream. He checked his phone messages and covered his head with his blanket. He thought, just last night about the song and meaning of 'Back to the Primitive' by Soul fly. Survival mode, and now this, Walt and his poem, 'As I Sat Alone By Blue Ontario's Shores.' The best and worst views on life were coming back again so Andy closed his eyes. Has the world dwindled to no more than an obedient mirror image of itself? He asked. And Walt for sure was claiming for himself Shelley's title of unacknowledged legislator. There was something deep going on and in accord, a mystical union? Was true history to put an end to things? Things that were not positive. What kind of millennium was it going to really be? The now, the new is, and what isn't? Our humanity, we may not be aware. 'Initiate the true use of precedents.' Are we subject to history, rather than at one with it? Reunification still, cannot be enough, even though all is you and me, and we choose to leave, the flag of peace folded, the flag of peace folded. We must rediscover our essential greatness over and over again. Andy was fast asleep again, walking near an animal powered Street Railway. There were apple carts everywhere filled with red and green apples. Andy was cold so he walked into the steam heated and gas lighted Canada Southern Railway Station in St. Thomas. The station has many rounded top windows on the second floor, making this building one of a kind to Andy. The station was empty and the halls were long. It would be nice if there was a book store here, Andy thought. As soon as Andy turned a corner in the station, there was a man sitting on a bench, holding a book, and he was the poet, Archibald Lampman, and he was a poetry lamp man to Andy right now as Archibald recited his poem.

The Railway Station

The darkness brings no quiet here, the light
No waking: ever on my blinded brain
The flare of lights, the rush, and cry, and strain,
The engine's scream, the hiss and thunder smite:
I see the hurrying crowds, the clasp, the flight,
Faces that touch, eyes that are dim with pain:
I see the hoarse wheels turn, and the great train
Move labouring out into the boundless night.
So many souls within &c &c...

Lampman handed Andy a copy of the Toronto Globe newspaper with it folded to the 'At the Mermaid Inn column' The poem 'Sleep' by Thomas Bailey Aldrich was encircled, so Andy read it.

"For the uplifting quality, the divine gift of revealing the unseen, and the beauty of thought in its relations to the universe, we must go to another school," said Lampman. Andy sensed a great withdrawal happening, but why? "My message to my generation is the promise of consolation which nature accords to her devotees," Lampman pronounced. Lampman then got up and recited his poem 'The City of the End of Things' as he walked around the station looking out the windows.

Ah, Andy thought, Lampman was feeling the birth and rise of the machine, and was somewhat skeptical about it. Andy followed him, and looked out the windows also, while listening to the strength of his words and voice. Lampman recited his poem, 'The Truth' while gazing at Andy, and after he finished reciting the poem, it started to snow outside, and Archibald Lampman looked out the windows once more and recited his poem 'Snow.' As the snow fell Andy was slowly awakening, and he was brought back to when he was sleeping and awakening, and the day ahead was the first day of the poetry train journey.

He was excited, and he knew the treasure would be wisdom, and here wisdom was, fight for poetry and humanity, but with the voice of nature, and do not become a part of the machine, to let your voice and wisdom *machine through* the machine only. Because life was like the train station, people come and people go. Andy had a sound vision of his grandfather saying, "Rise and Shine, what are you going to do sleep your life away?" Andy smiled as he got up and ready, he was thinking why was Walt in a nature setting and Archibald in a structured setting, when their message was the other way around. Was it to transverse the trans-course of time? So the importance of the poet in and for place came back to mind as he walked to the dining car. The Land and the Unacknowledged Legislators!

"That it is Red, we need a modern book of poetry of political poems of our times, satire, truth, the whole one hundred yards," said Andy as he sat down, "Not only all of that, but poets speaking to the up and coming ones. Let's ask poet Eve Brackenbury if she and Prospero's Parkside Books would publish it or co-publish it. The Land and the Unacknowledged Legislators!"

That's funny that you would say this because I am reading here and scheduling for us to go to the Highway Book Shop in Cobalt Ontario, Red proclaimed. It is now closed down and for sale. It was once an independent small press, a crucial conduit of literary activity, they say, owned and ran by Dr. Douglas C. Pollard and Lois Pollard. They have published over four hundred and sixty books, and three hundred individual authors.

"What happened?" Andy asked.

Lois was overwhelmed by the internet, Red replied. They published by balancing philanthropic and capitalistic principles. The press was mostly interested in local history and culture. Humor and self-help books were also preferred manuscripts because they financially balanced out the poetry and fiction titles the press published.

"So one hand washed the other?" said Andy.

Yes, replied Red, As Douglas Pollard said concerning the work of his press and presses similar to his: "writing and compiling the history of an area is a monumental task as so much has happened that needs to be recorded. By the same token all of this history has created a printing job that was not only time consuming, but in view of today's high costs in the printing field came at a higher cost than we would have liked."

Andy laughed and said, "We hear that, don't we Red."

Red laughed and said, No kidding there. I think it's worth a shoot in asking Eve, but I would make it an all-out challenge for all involved. Get creative, so where this book makes many statements. What gave you this idea Andy, The Land and the Unacknowledged Legislators? Also Andy there has to be a way to blend the modern presses to the poets and the poets to the presses. You know I think it is great to help them, because if you look at times long ago, you picture the poets and the publishers working hard to create great poetry and books.

"A dream last night of Walt Whitman and others," said Andy, And the poets on the train, dealing with the serious problems in America right now. We also need to talk to Dustin, about poetry presses and poetry publishers, so they have a section to post their presence on the site, and maybe some presses can offer an idea or two to get this going. We can call it a 'Submissions Hub', where they create a profile, and post information about their press and submissions calling. The Submissions Hub will be a directory section slash page. Okay Red, I think we are living the dream for sure, read this." Andy sent Red a link to the poem 'The Owls' by Christopher Dewdney. Andy told Red about his dream, and said, "Way to many coincidences again Red. Under the skin of the Lake, dream hunters, ciphers in the dream's earthling logic, now the Angels, the lake, we fuse."

We fuse, Red replied and smiled, I hear ya Andy. Andy, read Dewdney's essay, 'The Angel of Now.' He says, "Time is like an animating breath. Time, with its promise of a continual future, is also the font of hope, for only within time can our dreams be realized. He was encountered by an Owl and he says, the owl's visit gave me something else as well, an experience of "now," a single bell-note of coincidence that re-tuned my relationship to the present. The more deeply you delve into "now," the more mysterious it becomes."

"Nice," Andy replied. "I am reading now deeply, and he read out loud more of Dewdney's essay. The future is also opaque to us. In a sense, we walk backwards into the future and see the present with a kind of peripheral vision. The twentieth-century philosopher and critic Walter Benjamin has used this image too, comparing the present to an angel who backs into the future while gazing at the past as all the evidence of history piles like wreckage at his feet. "The angel would like to stay, awaken the dead, and make whole what has been smashed. But a storm is blowing in from Paradise; it has got caught in his wings with such violence that the angel can no longer close them. The storm irresistibly propels him into the future to which his back is turned, while the pile of debris before him grows skyward." So it is with us. Like passengers riding backwards on a train, we see only the landscape we have passed, but nothing ahead of us." But we do Red, we have poetry, the arts, the music and &c. That is the meaning of my dream last night, of all dreams; Walt and Archibald were reaching out, to time stamp, to encourage. To give a voice to these times, our times, but we can't forget the relay, the blood of those who did for us, and this is not just wisdom beauty for America it is for all nations, to write of the now and the place. This wisdom and poetic fire, its relay, this relay should inspire all poets to stand up for their place and in time, unafraid to show their rawness of their perspectives of the now, the new is."

Red laughed and said more of the essay. We only have to speed up our consciousness in order to experience eternity in a single second. Boo!

"Hilarious," said Andy and laughed, "So what is our responsibility? Well railroads could change time, but time could not change the railroads. Let's look at this with poetry in place of the railroads. Well poetry could change time, but time could not change the poetry. Back in the day on a Sunday Morning, November 18th, 1883 was a day known as 'the Sunday of Two Noons.' Sir Sandford Fleming hailed it as 'a quiet revolution.' The eastern time belts had to turn their clocks back half an hour, creating a second noon, in order to conform with the western belts. No one would gain or lose no more than a half hour of their life."

What are you getting at Andy? Red asked.

"A quiet revolution," Andy replied, "An un-folding of the flag of peace, an un-folding of the flag of peace."

Red looked at Andy and Red asked, What?

"All of this makes one feel like Lassie," said Andy, "Lassie trapped in a house fire and trying to help his master and loved ones to safety."

I hear that Andy, courage, Red replied, Luckily there isn't a fire. But although as Christopher Dewdney says 'Power increases as size decreases. Moore's law is there, steadily, digitally eating it all away. The world is slipping into the Internet's black hole.' And times, hole.

"Murphy's Law, Moore's Law, Man's Law, God's Law, Cole Slaw," said Andy, and everyone laughed and it got quiet. Everyone was relaxed and looked out the windows. The sun started to shine through the cold and dark sky. Andy thought about the warm days in Franklin, Kentucky and all the cardinals flying around. Andy knew something was going to be great for he and poetry but never imagined all of this. Andy felt such gratitude about everyone on these journeys, and so did Red.

Seth then played the 'Fields of Glory' by Sting.

Red was reading about the poet Colin Ward, and his two beautiful poems, "God's Lake Narrows Pilgrimage" and "Looking for Lorca." Ward mentions about trains in two ways. Missing trains as in departures and there are more trains than places.

Seth then played the song 'Somewhere Over the Rainbow' by Harold Arlen and E.Y. Harburg, and the song 'Time After Time' by Cyndi Lauper.

Andy was studying Ward also and Colin finds, History to be fertile ground for inspiration and material. It encourages and rewards study of our past. "We got a bite," said Andy, "Colin believes in online workshops, he has his opinions about poetry online and poetry, pixel poetry he calls it. Red read his 'Pixel Poetry: A Meritocracy' essay I sent you."

Meritocracy says it all right there, Red replied.

"What happened to public goods?" Andy asked, "Ability now versus, availability."

And 'they' all laughed.

"It's a trust issue," said Andy, "People do not trust any institution, and can you blame them. There is no more moral binding glue. People need to calm down and be slicker and stickier so it goes back to what elders should have told the youth, education pays and wisdom stays. Times are changing, so keep up with them. The year 2009 was a launching year for poets, and the Wicked Papoose Caboose will figure this out later in time. Also with the stickier, Sand goes through our hands fast if our hands our dry, but if our hands are wet. No, the sand sticks. Meaning get your hands wet in time, in your time here on this planet, and make it great."

Andy, browsing here, said Red, In 2018 it will be one hundred years that natural time has been dead to man-kind, kind man.

"Ha kind man, mankind," said Andy.

Mr.Welchberry came into the dining car and was humming the bass line to the The Cavaliers song, 'Oh Where Can My Baby Be.'

Andy was thinking Mr.Welchberry was one cool man, oh where was the old times. Beautifire, analogy. And the fire raged and we must save moments, even if only in fragments in today's poetic and railroad modern time. Poetry was in the air.

They all looked out the windows once more and over the hills they went and Mr.Welchberry recited a Wilfred Campell poem entitled 'Beyond the Hills of Dreams.' The views were charming and the poem was beyond beautiful to everyone. The poem gave them a feeling of love from an unseen powerful place. Campbell believed, a poet had an obligation to uphold whatever was worthy and likely to enrich the lives of others.

With poetry in the air, a theme near to his heart, and so was Andy's thoughts, thinking of kissing the one he loves with the poem echoing as they did.

Connie came walking into the diner with a kettle of hot tea, and she recited a slice of a Wilfred Campbell poem entitled 'A Canadian Folk Song' as she poured them all tea.

The firelight dances upon the wall,
Footsteps are heard in the outer hall;
A kiss and a welcome that fill the room,
And the kettle sings in the glimmer and gloom.
Margery, Margery, make the tea,
Singeth the kettle merrily.

Mr. Welchberry laughed and said "Shamela," and whipped out a book entitled, 'Tom Jones' by Henry Fielding, and he then said, "A Disney opening fifty years ago or more. As you enter this timeless land one of these many worlds will open to you. Frontier land, tall tales of truth from the legendary past. Tomorrow land, the promise of things to come. Adventure land, the wonder world of nature's own realm. Fantasy land, the happiest Kingdom of them all."

Andy smiled and the song 'If This Is It' by Huey Lewis And The News came to his head, and so did Emily Dickinson's Homestead.

And Red had out a book of his, Joel Chandler Harris 'Uncle Remus,' and Red was thinking of the young writers, and watching them grow as writers. Young Canadian poet, Kara Zhang posted a poem on the site poetrytrain.com, entitled, 'Diana's Dream.' Red didn't tell Andy. He wanted Kara's posting to surprise him all its own, because her posting made Red's day, because this is what it was all about.

Andy liked what was going on, so some other door opened. The girl of his dreams and the wisdom of Henry Fielding way so long ago, and being poor, and Fielding hung in there because he loved literature and wrote it.

Red thought about Joel Chandler Harris and his boyhood encounter with an owl. He winked at the owl and the owl winked back. Also, Old Harbert and the story of Owl and the other birds. The Owl got the job of sleeping with his eyes open. He was a wonder, and a wonder to the world of literature. Red was feeling homesick as Joel once noted as well.

Speechless, Andy was speechless and thought, some things are just too beautiful to describe, and some things much to ugly. It just makes you realize what is really important and the beauty of life that we have around us. Andy got up to go brush his teeth, and Seth played the song 'Staying Alive' in guitar pluck mode by the Bee Gees, and Andy stopped, turned around, and everyone laughed.

"You all get back to the workshops, while I'll go and brush my chops," said Andy and laughed, "What's the point in being alive if you can't do anything remarkable, right? Right!"

As Andy went he thought about what Alain de Botton had said, "In the olden days, people believed that our dreams were full of clues about the future." So what did they do about that back then? Andy thought. On his return, he looked into the dining cars kitchen and noticed Sophie sitting there looking at the ceiling fan, the only fan Andy has seen in a long time, but he understood, it was the kitchen; smoke and heat. Sophie looked at Andy and said, "The body remembers things that we do not consciously remember, like good food. Andy I want you to read the poet Mary Di Michele, because she says, It is vital to civilization to have a literature that embodies, gives voice, and gives form to female experiences, and well, I am a good cook, am I Andy?"

"Yes Sophie, you make me smile, hugz," said Andy.

Wow, Andy thought, this reminds me of the woman who wrote poetry in Kabul, Afghanistan in some way who waged a literary war that is both personal and political, hey this was Sophie. Wow what Sophie she is making me feel, and her cooking, a feeling inside me that American women poets need to unfold the blanket of peace, all women in fact who write. If women can encourage soldiers into and go to war, like Malalai of Maiwand, then they can for peace, unfold that flag.

"Why do you think it has to be women Andy?" Sophie asked.

Andy smiled and said, "It is simple, just look forward through time. Step forward with both feet, no longer keep one's feet on the past or the now. We all need to have a love affair with the future, and with the peace. The woman I love writes some of the best poetry I have ever read and has strong wisdom about all of this. I wish we all, and I mean all of us poets, join forces, but it seems the ways of the past chains us separate ways. And Publishers also. This is how you create an audience and the true land arena. So tell me about Mary Di Michele."

"I can't right now Andy," said Sophie, "I have to get back to work. Read her poem, 'The Possibility of Time Travel.'

Okay, I sure will, and thank you Sophie, and your cooking is the best," said Andy. He returned to the dining car. And as he went, he thought, my gosh I understand about people's personal tribulations, but we are smarter than that, yes we are. So this tells me, poetry is like ones children, they want it safe, where they can control it and such, but at the same time poets want readers, love and book sales I am sure, but they are not listening and seeing what's up. The past has hooked us is so many ways, and until we all walk forward into the future and join forces it's not going to happen. Also, some kind of incentive may do this.

Red, "look up the poet, Mary di Michele and her poem 'The Possibility of Time Travel," Andy asked.

Sure will, replied Red, I have good news and bad news Andy. I have registered the poetry train at thewaterspoetry.com and the criticalpoet.com. The gauntlet of some of the planet's best critics. Jude Goodwin is on the train and also Matt Anderson is down with Poetry Trains' Operation Jester.

"Nice, haha," Andy replied, "So what's the bad news?"

We are heading into a snow storm, but I have an idea once we get to Ontario. Me and you are renting snowmobiles and looking for poets, said Red.

Andy laughed and said, "Nice, let's do it. Because we can't let them be falling victim to time, like the poet Marjorie Lowry Christie Pickthall who rejected the "fragile poetess" image that was imposed upon her, and as she has said, What the deuce are you to make of that? As a woman? As a man, you could go ahead and stir things up fine. Times sure are a changing. It's time to Stir."

Seth smiled and played a song by Andrzej Rejman, with the poem 'Finus' by Marjorie Pickthall on his battery operated Casio keyboard, and he sung,

Give me a few more days to keep
With a little love and a little sorrow,
And then the dawn in the skies of sleep
And a clear tomorrow.

Mr. Welchberry said, "You all can learn a lot about struggles of women from the poet Dionne Brand, and also Robertson Davies once told me, Extraordinary people survive the most terrible circumstances, and they become extraordinary because of it. You both will love Ontario, so go and place your mat and beat your bowl, and have no worries about the flawers, as Davies would say also." And Mr. Welchberry laughed, and his laugh was iconic.

Andy and Red looked at each other and smiled, and Andy said, "Thank you, Mr. Welchberry, and we shall and we shall return, with our tickets. Let's go with it Red, let's kick up some snow, with some solar-powered snow mobiles or electric sleds."

Andy looked at Red and said, "That poem and song is so beautiful."

"Make time for hockey too, and the poet Al Purdy, gentlemen,' said Connie, "Be sure to visit his A-frame home. And don't forget Kenojuak Ashevak, a stain glass work of a snowy owl. 'a quiet revolution.'"

Ontario:

Blue Mountain, Manitoulin Island, Cup and Saucer, Thousand Islands, Sleeping Giant; Wawa (Sault Ste Marie to Thunder Bay), Niagara Falls, Webster's Fall, Georgian Bay, Eva Lake, Fairholme Lake, Lake Ontario, Agawa Rock, Lake Superior, The Scarborough Bluffs, Agate Island Beach, Long Point Beach, Wasaga Beach, Parry Sound, the Badlands, Bonnechere Caves, Ouimet Canyon, Algonquin Provincial Park, Bon Echo Provincial Park, Bruce Peninsula National Park, Point Pelee National Park, so I wonder what Bruce Meyer, John B. Lee, Ann Margetson, Eric Winter, Jill Batson, Ted Amsden, Eric Folsom, Helen Humphreys, Penn Kemp, Graham Ducker, Cyril Dabydeen, Elizabeth Zetlin, Kristan Anderson, Kateri Akiwenzie-Damm, Terry Burns, John Steffler, Pauline Michel, George Bowering, Pierre DesRuisseaux, Michel Pleau, Fred Wah, Rodger Nash,

Daniel Aubin, Tom Leduc, Pier Giorgio Di Cicco, Dennis Lee, Dionne Brand, George Elliott Clarke, and Marty Gervais think of Thunder Bay/Lake Superior?

Ontario Railways:

The Erie & Ontario Railroad Company began in 1835, the Hamilton Street Railway Company began in 1873, the Ontario & Quebec Railway began in 1881, the Canada Southern Railway began in 1881 as the Erie and Niagara Extension Railway, the Brockville, Westport & Northwestern began in 1884, the Algoma Eastern Railway began in 1888 as the Manitoulin & North Shore Railway. The Toronto Railway Company began 1891, the Toronto, Hamilton & Buffalo Railway began in 1892, the Hamilton and Barton Incline Railway began in 1892, the Ontario Northland Railway began 1902 as the Temiskaming and Northern Ontario Railway, the Halton County Radial Railway began in 1954, the Goderich-Exeter Railway began in 1992 and the South Simcoe Railway began in 1993.

Ontario Poets:

The first Poet I found was Brandon Pitts, and his poetry is themed in love and history (lol & his unknown own love poetry.) Brandon's poems, "For You," "Lot," and "Take a Trip," are rooted deep, wise, and happening. Brandon is the author of the poetry collection, "Pressure to Sing" and the forthcoming collection, "Tender in the Age of Fury."

The second Poet I found was Ubong Umoh, and his poetry is themed in faith, love and life. Ubong's poems, "As For Me," " A Daze in Days," and "A Spirit-Scented Candle" are beautiful and strong.

The third Poet I found was Ash Dickinson, and his poetry is themed in life, fast life, hard life, pick up your life, have a great life, furthermore lost love life. Ashs' poems, "Commuting to Jupiter," "Glass Coffin Coffee Table Wife," "The Bycycle," "The Disposable Lifestyle," and "Ten Restless Hours About Love And Want" are hard core and poem tornado's- as he would say- F Sharp perhaps.

The fourth Poet I found was Penn Kemp, and she studied at the University of Toronto. Her poetry is themed in much about life, and the music in poetry. Penns' poems, "Double Vision," "Metta Meditation," "Night Orchestra," "The Net of Elementals," and "Utter Silence," are beautiful and mesmerizing.

The fifth Poet I found was Kevon Mitchell, and his poetry is themed in love and romance. Kevon's poems, "Beautiful Lady," "Love Stories," "See, I Can Hear You," and "Zone," are beautiful and musical.

The sixth Poet I found was Lois Lorimer, and her poems, "Between Two Houses," "Resting," and "Seagull," are beautiful and relaxing.

The seventh Poet I found was Fannon Holland, and he studied at Point Park University. His poetry is themed in life, nature, and in how things are. Fannon's poems, "Come Again," "Listen," "Poet, Thrown Down," "Prodigal Son," "To Whom It May Concern," and "The Elevator Conundrum," are powerful, most of all ruthless in the truth in and about modern times.

The eighth Poet I found was Leigh Kotsilidis, and her poetry is themed in many things. Leigh's poems, "Before Meteorologists," "By Any Name," "Rodeo Romance" and "The Tin Woodman Turns Partisan," are beautiful and very original.

The ninth Poet I found was Linda Besner, and her poems, "Dogwalker's Law," "Moonlight on Komatzu Extractor," and "Villeneuve Villanelle," are beautiful and filled with powerful imagery.

The tenth Poet I found was Bill Mahoney aka the 'Rhyming Rebel', and his poetry is deeply themed in politics, social issues and justice, the youth and wisdom. Bill's poems, "Eddie," "Granny," "Johnny Wants a Job," "Our Town," "Rebel Woman," "The Spirit of 46," "Welcome Layla," "When Scrooge Comes to Town," and "U.S. Steel," are hardcore, powerful and ruthless.

The eleventh Poet I found was Meena Chopra, and her poetry is themed in darkness, life, love, nature, and romance. Meena's poems, "Confines," "Strangers," "The Dew Drop," and "The Mystery Book" are beautiful and relaxing.

The twelfth Poet I found was The Mad Poet aka Melissa A. Dean, and her poetry is themed in love, life, culture, faith, and humanity. Melissa's poems, "Broken Wings," "Open Your Eyes," "Strength," and "The Truth About It All," are beautiful, inspiring and powerful.

The thirteenth Poet I found was Evy Hannes, and her poetry is themed in faith, love, life, and nature. Evy's poems, "Celestial Sigh," "My Garden Of Tranquility," "Pale Pink Roses," "The Last Leaf," and "This Moment is Ours are beautiful, with a touch of sadness.

The fourteenth Poet I found was Hayley King, and her poetry is themed in nature, and spirituality. Hayley's poems, "Little Bird," "Super Woman," and "Three Letters On Their Way," are beautiful and precious.

The fifteenth Poet I found was Josh Smith, and his poetry is themed in modern life and love. Josh's poems, "Any Moment Now," "Famous Last Words," "Love is What You Left

Me With" "Ordinary Life," and "Whatever Doesn't Kill Me" are humorous, truthful, upfront, and inspiring.

The sixteenth Poet I found was Sâkihitowin Awâsis, and her poetry is themed in animals, community, culture, erotica, humanity, life, nature, politics, mind control, and modern issues, furthermore truth. Sâkihitowin's poems, "Bikes Not Oil," "Firewood," "Hearing Two-Spirits," "Hey Lady," "Silence," "Take Back the Night," "The Beast," and "Untitled" powerful, upfront and in your face with truths.

The seventeenth Poet I found was Holly Painter, and her poetry is themed in family, life, love, and sexuality, furthermore womanhood. Holly's poems, "Chasing Home," "Find Your Voice," "Hey Miss," "My Story," and "Weapon of Choice," are breathtaking, and powerful.

The eighteenth Poet I found was Keith Garebian, and his poetry is themed in atrocities, family, love, life, and war. Keith's poems, "Eros" "Discovery," "Drowned Moons" "Flotsam," "Scarecrow," and "Their Memories Burn" are beautiful, dark, and heartbreaking.

The nineteenth Poet I found was Lillian Allen, and her poetry is themed in many things, mainly and strongly themed in culture, history, life, love, racism, and spirituality. Lillian's poems, "Limbo Dancer," "Poem for Billie Holiday," "Rasta in Court," and "Social Worker Poem," are beautiful, musical, and very powerful, furthermore original.

The twentieth Poet I found was Sadiqa de Meijer, and her poetry is themed in family and nature. Sadiqa's poems, "Jewel of India," "Lake Ontario Park," and "Pastorals in the Atrium," leaves the reader spellbound in awe.

The twenty-first Poet I found was Mark Clement, and his poetry is themed in nature, trees, and spirituality. Marks poems, "Poetry Tells Us," "Rondure," "Street Scene," "The Moth," and "Tree Eulogy" are beautiful with enlightenment.

The twenty-second Poet I found was Kathryn Gwun-Yeen Lennon, and her poetry is themed in many things, family, friendship, and life. Kathryn's poems, "Exclusion Enacted," "Hunger is Inherited," "Tombolo," "One Minute For Phuong Ns Du," "When the Glaciers are Gone," and her "Mixed Blood Child / 混血兒 hùnxuěěr poems" are beautiful and powerful with wisdom and charm.

The twenty-third Poet I found was Mary Ann Moore, and she studied at Trent University. Her poetry is themed in life and nature. Mary Ann's poems, "Saturday Market," and "Shiny Under the Moon," are beautiful and magical.

The twenty-fourth Poet I found was Michael Dennis, and his poetry is themed in many things, erotica, life, love, human nature and nature. Michael's poems, "Between Monday," "closer to death," "Friday Courage Grows," "missing the kisses of eloquence," "praise," "Spring," "the sound you hear," are beautiful, and can he be ruthless if he's ignited, igniting the reader.

The twenty-fifth Poet I found was David Brydges, and he studied at Humber College North Campus. David's poems, "Bending," "and "The World Weeps," are delicate and beautiful, and I wish there were more to read.

The twenty-sixth Poet I found was John B. Lee, and he studied at the University of Western Ontario. His poetry is themed in many things, culture, family, fun, life, nature, and war. John's poems, "Burning Land," "If I were a Nation Innocent of War," "The Green Muse," "In the Muddy Shoes of Morning," "In This We Hear Light," "I Too Can Show the Way," and many more poems are beautiful, brilliant, and beyond intense.

The twenty-seventh Poet I found was Chris Faiers and his haiku, haibun, and poetry is beautifully themed in all things under the beautiful sun. His poems, "Five Minutes Ago They Dropped the Bomb," "Picnic with Al," and "Reflections on The Good People of Tarnished" are serious mind opening poems.

The twenty-eighth Poet I found was Janet Hepburn, and her poetry is themed in animals, life, nature. Janet's poems, "Alzheimer's Opus #4" "Decoy," "Ferry Ride," "Tanzania," "Moorings," and "Winter Burial" are very beautiful, relaxing, and with great details of place.

The twenty-ninth Poet I found was Jane Ozkowski, and she studied at York University. Her poetry is themed in dreams, identity, life, people, and much more under the sun and moon. Jane's poems, "Amphitheater," "Alternate Life as a Flight Attendant," "Blood Dream," "Buried," "Staten Island Land of Dead Angels," "The Part of You," and many many more are enchanting with twists, and she can be comical too. Jane also writes short stories.

The thirtieth Poet I found in Ontario was Todd Sukany, and his poetry is themed in life, scriptures, and wisdom. Todd's Haiku and poems "Circle the Wagons" "Five Loves," "From the Headlines," and "Priceless," are brilliant and grasp the reader very well.

The thirty-first Poet I found was Amy Gleeson, and her poetry is themed in love, lost love, life, and city life. Amy's poems, "an angel walking home after dark," "ghost girl," "life lines," "he made me love me," "I saw my true love," "Toronto, " "winter river," and many more are astonishingly beautiful, with melancholy, and the reader will say, 'wow' that's bad a**' for sure.

The thirty-second Poet I found was Luminita Suse, and her poetry is themed in companionship, family, life, love, and nature. Luminita's poems, "the dried leaf," "in rain," "a dried branch," "his bouquet of roses," "rain sifted," and many more are heartfelt, and sometimes breaking.

The thirty-third Poet I found was J. Graham Ducker, and his poetry is themed in animals, family, and love. J's poems, "A Mother's Silent Wish," "Loafing Around," "Love Is Not Eternal," "The Midnight Marauder," and "The Survivor," are comical and serious, and some have wordplay.

The thirty-fourth Poet I found was Melissa Upfold, and her poetry is themed in life, family, and friendship. Melissa's poems, "4:38:," "Good Bye Avery," "Like a Family," "Morse Code," "Sixty Second," and "Wrecking Age," are of sadness, and place, placement of sadness and all surroundings.

The thirty-fifth Poet I found was Gregory Betts, and his poetry is themed in culture, history, life, people, and sports. Gregory's poems, "ars poetica," "Eaton's Effluviad" "Hockey and Poetry Go Head-to-Head," "On the Construction of Muslims," "The Cinematographic Egypt Near East," and "Walcott's on Culture" are pretty hard core and deep.

The thirty-sixth Poet I found was Jason Rafay Ansari, and his poetry is themed in culture, peace, prejudice, and wisdom, furthermore the truth and youth. Jason's poems, "Every Morning," "Oh Mankind," "Rhythm & Poetry" and "Run Free" are very powerful and I wish there were more.

The thirty-seventh Poet I found was Laura Kelsey Rideout, and she studied at University of Guelph. Her poems "Stampede" and "War and Peace" are very heart touching, soul tattooing, and you wish everyone heard and read these two poems.

The thirty-eighth Poet I found was John Ambury, and his poetry and Haiku is themed in animals, life and nature. John's poems, "Bees," "Trinity: The Great Oak" "Smog Alert: Toronto," "Spring On the Pond," "Strong," are beautiful and full of wisdom.

The thirty-ninth I found was Amani, and her poetry is themed in romance. Amani Live poems, "Kryptonite," "Free," and "Heart of a Poet," are powerful and upfront.

The fortieth I found was Ken Stange, and he studied at Loyola University Chicago. His poetry is them in animals, life, wisdom, and much more, all sphere'd up in mind opening, mystical, planetary, powerful wordplay, most of all, his poetry will raise the readers eyebrow, kaleidoscope like, as by his Tanka Spheres. They are beautiful and creative.

The forty-first I found was Natalia Govsha, and her poetry is themed in life, love, lost love with a originality, nature, and wisdom, furthermore a woman's strength. Natalia's poems, "After," "Carousel," "Delusive," "Game of Perception," "Inerrable," "Madame," and "She" are emotion whirlwinds, and her poetry seems to be the cedar tree she clings to. The imagery and wisdom with her poems are way beyond fascinating. Some poems will leave you heart broken, and put in emotion placement.

The forty-second Poet I found was Anna Yin and her poetry is themed in family, youth, life, nature, animals and fish, but most of all life's beauty and romance. Her poems, "I Often Dream of Fish," "Life Jars," "We Could Live to One Hundred Fifty," and "Window and Mirror," has imagery beyond amazing, and are beautiful. Anna's poems make the reader look at the bright side of things, and so much more. Anna's haiku is just as beautiful and touching.

The forty-third Poet I found was Deborah Thompson, and her narrative poetry is themed in family, love, outer space, tradition, and war. Deborah poems, "Far and Beyond" "It's a Life Worth Living," "Relieved of Duty," "The Couple in Love," "The Story of Annika," and "That Feelin," are positive, relaxing and inspiring.

The forty-forth I found was Brett A. Boyer aka Patricia T Green. He studied at Loyalist College, Nicholson Catholic College, and Algonquin College. Some of Brett's themes are of love, pain, lost love, and general experience and wisdom. Brett's poems, "delicate emotions," "the leopard," and "the medicine man" and many more are wise and beautiful. You know he knows empathy well when you read his poetry. Brett is a poet to be on the lookout for.

Chapter 9-Quebec, Canada

January 8th, 2014

The dream's sky was a color range from yellowish to dark gray. Red didn't know if it was turning night or day; and as he walked along the tracks he came up to a telegraph pole with no wires, and perching on this pole was a large crow. Red slowed down his pace in his walk a bit and thought about the Mexican myth about crows. Red then thought about other cultures and the crow's symbolism. I am going to go up to the crow and talk to him, Red thought. I am not scared. Hello Crow, said Red. The crow didn't reply. He was in a deep sleep. Okay Red thought, I best be kicking railroad rocks, and he walked on. Red could smell the Port of Québec. Red had this feeling he was in hurry, but what for, or was it something or someone else in a hurry? The echoes of manufacturing were in the air, as so were voices of a couple, voices of laughter. Red seen them way ahead of him on the tracks, and there was a bridge up ahead also. The laughter was coming from behind Red though. Another couple were coming by on a railway velocipede. Red moved out of the way as they rolled on by. They didn't say a word to him. Okay, Red stopped and thought, I am going down this road into town, because it looks like these lovers are having some type of gathering up ahead, near the bridge, and to the looks of it, I may not be wanted around there. Red took the road, and walked east, away from Mont Laurier and closer to Quebec City.

Red wants to hit slow gear and mingle, relax a little bit, he thought. What's the hurry Red thought and he sang the song 'The Little Red Caboose' by Henry Thomas as he walked. He then laughed and thought of Andy and sung,

I always ride up on the roof on the Kettle Valley Line
I always ride up on the roof on the Kettle Valley Line
I always ride up on the roof, and &c. A song by Brian Dewan.

Red was thinking, There is something I need to lift, but I can't remember at all what it was I need to lift. Up ahead was a train station, Hedley Junction, a rundown place, and he sang, 'The Railroad Boomer' by Carson Robinson as he made his way there.

Andrew McColluch, a civil engineer with the Canadian Pacific Railway was sitting on a bench reading Shakespeare. He was there with James J. Warren, president of the Kettle Valley Railroad and Warrens' daughter. They were done doing business and were now headed west. Red overheard them talking about naming new train stations in western Canada. Poetry brings happiness, Red told them, and walked on by. Warren and his daughter looked at McColluch and smiled. McColluch looked at his book and said, "Why yes, thank you."

Warren's daughter said, "Let me read that book, I'll find you great names," and she smiled.

Red noticed he hasn't seen a track-side newsstand in while. Red felt he was where the pivot stands between the Old World and the New World came or comes, the all is flux mode, and he smiled. A man who looked like a doctor rode by on cariole in a hurry, and right behind him, three women followed him in a sleigh also in a hurry. They took an unseen cart road, a route through a field. The train station was very busy. There were many people around. Red heard someone say, "You need to enable the Port of Québec and the surrounding area to hook up to the country's main rail artery," but Red didn't know who said it or see to whom this voice was speaking to. There was also talk of building new stations, because this one was way too small. The Acton Vale and the Gare du Palais. Those names sounded good to Red, this or his dialect was a sweet language Red felt.

The man's voice that said the names of the train station spoke again, and was coming closer to Red through the crowd. "Roads deep in mud. Lumber, saw dust and snow, they are always making a mess. Make cart roads, leave cart roads, make new roads, on and on, the madness goes. The cradle of humanity is being rocked by lumberjacks. A saw mill hatchery here, and a saw mill hatchery there" This man was poet Amédée Papineau, and he looked at Red with great curiosity.

"Hedleyville is a busy busy place, and I have never seen your face before," said Amédée.

Red caught Amédée's curiosity. I am the hustle and the bustle, replied Red.

Amédée asked, "Are you taking the bait of free land too?" Amédée looked down at Red's feet and said, "You must be okay, because you wear no boots with spikes. Why don't you have shoes on?"

Red tossed in his bed, and replied, I am close with nature, or want to be anyway.

Amédée laughed and said, "Come with me to my Manoir."

Red felt okay with that, but something told him, something was going to happen not to his liking.

"You can go with me to the regattas," said Amédée.

What does regattas mean? Red asked.

"Boat and canoe races," replied Amédée.

As they walked the steamship named "Hope" was paddling down the Ottawa River, and Red smiled, and thought, Engage beyond. As they walked away, the Conductor of the Ottawa steam train called out, "Saint-Jean-sur-Richelieu, Charny, Eastman, and St.

Gabriel Station. All Aboard."

The good feeling Red had going on was trampled on when a man coming running down the middle of the road shouted, "The Men of Gore are coming." Red's eyes widened because behind the man was many a men carrying pitch forks and scythe. Everyone either joined these marching men or scattered, confusing the dream out of Red, and Amédée looked at Red and said, "I have to go. I 'll find you," and Amédée ran off.

The poet and journalist François-Réal Angers came creeping up behind Red, and said, "Ils sont de retour, avec leur, dommage, vol, sacrilège et assassiner." Meaning in English, "They are back, with their harm, theft, sacrilege, and murder."

Red didn't know what he was saying, so Red prepared for the worst. François-Réal Angers then said, "J'ai abandonné la littérature et je le regrette. Oh je le regrette," meaning, "I have abandoned Literature and I regret it. Oh I regret it." and walked away, but when he walked away he said, "Time dare hit the Golden Dog of the wing. Bloody Bloody Drama. This bloodthirsty frolic, from the political volcano," in English.

Oh shit Red said to himself, Where am I? Oh I feel it now, like a ghost using my body to see, to read. From the past to the future from now or something like that going on and; back. Red called out to Andy, and Red thought, Oh attachments as he looked around and a man walked up to Red.

"You must leave town at once," said Railroad promoter Jedediah Hubbell Dorwin, "Everyone does what they like. It will be dark soon."

And it was getting dark.

"There are no road lights and there is no police force," Jedediah warned.

What? Red thought.

"Go; here take my lantern," said Jedediah, "And go east. There will be a hill, Champ de Mars Hill. Stay away from it. Go around and go back east. You will get to the village of L'Industrie, Joliette. The terrain is difficult Red."

How did you know my name? Red asked.

"Everyone knows your name," Jedediah replied, "Like everyone knows I smuggle tea and loaf sugar back across the border."

Red laughed and said, I smuggle poetry.

Jedediah laughed, and Red headed east and Red felt danger.

Jedediah recited his poem 'The Voice of the Shadow' as he walked away.

Red heard most of it as they separated paths, and Red thought, wow, sounds like life in America in some places. What am I thinking, there are many places dealing with nonsense causing despair. Red made his way nearly a mile and it was darker. He seen another man walking down the road with a lantern and he was the poet Louis-Honoré Fréchette, and he was reciting his poem, 'The Voice of Exile." For Louis-Honoré Fréchette, his writings was on his mind. He lost them in a fire in Chicago. "I am Le Lauréat," said Louis, that was his nickname. "I am looking for a Christmas tree, are you?" Louis asked.

Red didn't know what to say. Yes, Red replied, taking no chances with the danger he was feeling. Red then noticed an ax strapped to the back of Louis.

"Where is your ax?" Louis asked.

I'm just looking, replied Red.

"The intellectual climate of Québec is changing," said Louis.

Okay Red thought, so is the earth, and you are the one with the ax, but Red did not say anything.

"Good evening to you Red, I have to go" said Louis, "Christmas trees bring warmth to the soul."

Yes indeed, replied Red, And good evening to you Louis. Red walked east.

Many a thoughts came to Red, and many a spooky things. And it was dark but Red could see fairly well under the clear night's sky. He first heard the sound of water, as he got closer he could tell it was a waterfall, but he heard a battle also. Then he saw the river through the trees. Red heard dogs barking way in the distant woods. He walked down by the river, and it was sided with large rocks. Red only noticed a crayfish, and a baby duck as he walked the river north east near the falls. The Falls sounded like thunder or was it thunder, Red wondered? He finally arrived at the magical falls, something was more than beautiful about it, like it was just created, because Red has seen many water falls before at night, but not like this. The sound was louder than usual. Red felt a presence behind him, so he turned around to look. Once his eyes scanned the trees he noticed a wolf about seven yards behind some trees in some opening land area. Oh no Red thought, this wolf will not hesitate to eat me if the wolf can get away with it. Staying calm wasn't easy he thought, so how can I drive the wolf away, or how can I get away?

The wolf was gray, the wolf then barked at Red, and he looked at the wolf's eyes glaring with the night reflection in them. Red had no weapons, so he looked down for rocks, sticks, any tool. Then Red seen a bigger wolf and it was black. A bird chirped above Red making him jump. The gray wolf ran off. Red moved forward to see where the gray wolf went, as he made it through the trees he seen the wolf on some lower rocks. Red then retreated but it didn't do any good, because he was surrounded by five of them. Red stared into all of their glowing eyes.

"Don't turn around. Keep looking at them," a man's voice spoke from behind Red, and he was the poet, William Kirby. Kirby walked next to Red, and they looked at each other, and Kirby said, as he looks at the Northern Star, "The existence of animals testifies to the Creator." Red looked up at it too, and he never saw the Northern Star this big before, of course Red thought, this was long ago, many moons ago. The wolves seemed to be okay with their two guests in the woods.

"It's too cold for insects," said Kirby, making Red wonder. "The mystery of The Golden Dog," said Kirby and asked, "Have you seen the tablet of the Chien d'Or? None has been able to tell me its origin or meaning. I'll never see the day, but would be good news in the paper."

Red noticed men here mostly had the same style of beard. Pork chops nearly all the way to the Adam's apple. Tablet Red thought, an IPad? And Red laughed inside.

"There is a threat of civil war," said Kirby making Red feel his apple.

Oh shit, Red thought, and he followed Kirby. As they looked at the wolves before they left the falls. Red felt some kind of living he has never ever felt before.

"Red, your California manifesto is impressive, and you are steering, and not just riding life out. So do you like western Canada?" Kirby asked.

Red laughed and answered, Yes.

"Can I trust you? Are you a book collector?" Kirby asked.

Yes, and oh yes I love books, Red replied.

"Follow me," said Kirby as Red was following Kirby, "To ourselves annex our glorious gains, the forest land and all that it contains! I am a profitable speculation. Publishers, them Publishers."

Red said, I hear ya, I come from hideous uncertainty too.

"Red, history is a struggle between good and evil where, although good sometimes wins, it does so only at huge cost and with enormous difficulty," said Kirby in a loving voice, "See Quebec, and live forever!' The Golden Dog."

The surrounding camp fire they came upon was hidden by coils and coils of hay.

Kirby explained his concerns once near everyone there, "Like you I fight for poets, and better copyright laws for Canadian authors. Copyright the novel, these days author neither receives royalties nor keeps control of the text. Red imbues the minds of the rising generation with knowledge of history."

Wisdom that co-extends, said Red.

The poets Edward Hartley Dewart, Michel Bibaud left the camp without saying a word, like un-friending someone without saying why. Bibaud left because he had to go type set an owl in his book, 'Épîtres, Satires, Chansons, Epigrammes, Et Autres Pièces de Vers'.

The poet François- Xavier Garneau was reciting his poem 'Winter" when Red and Kirby appeared at the camp site, and finally Red could focus on this part of the reciting.

Who looks under the ice
In the cold air, flying slowly and sinister
The white owl wanders from roof to roof, &c &c...

Red and Kirby found a place to sit, and Xavier Garneau said after he recited his poem, "I love history, well documented panorama, and poetry with romantic rhythm and colour."

They must have been talking about books because poet and bookseller Octave Crémazie 'with a different looking beard' was there. Octave's poet friend Antoine Gérin-Lajoie was there and he said, "To Paris to trade books. Ah, if I were a farmer!" as he walked over with his cane to sit down. "Within the reach of the people, as in Canada law, like elements of public and constitutional law." Antoine looked at Octave and said, "I dare not to walk around town in daylight, much less to appear in society, LaMinerve."

Antoine had those eyes. He reminds Red of Andy.

"Maybe I'll be a translator? I may like history," said Antoine.

"I am doing the translations," said poet Léon Pamphile Lemay. His coat was very eye catching with its black fur shining out from the inside. He had a mustache with his hair slicked back. "I want more volumes of poetry and literature. I like True Tales," said Léon and he recited his poem,

The clock

I find it later, and asked incredulously,
If as in the past, the needle marks true.
I am at work, I am idle.
It works great train now, my clock.

"The universe is a poem," said Léon as he looked up at the moon and said, "The poet's dream, a bold wing."

This was Deja vu for Red, and there was no clock as Léon pointed to the sky, it was time to, regatta race time to race. Red felt something but forgot, the poet Amédée Papineau came to mind as a double dose of Deja vu, and then Red remembered. Like an inspection was about to take place; a divine one.

Red then noticed a woman with an oriental fan, and she was the poet Sui Sin Far, Edith Maude Eaton aka Mrs. Spring Fragrance. Poet Philippe-Joseph Aubert de Gaspé walked by all down and out, causing the effect of lost eye contact between Red and Sui.

Philippe did look sad, heavy bags under his eyes, a pouty jaw, and his clothes were to tight. Red then noticed poet Thomas D'Arcy McGee. Red looked at him and thought of Jimmy New Orleans. Did McGee know Jimmy was incarcerated in Washington D.C.? D'Arcy McGee sat next to poet Joseph- Charles Taché, known as 'the Iroquois.' Taché looked tired, spread thin as he smoked from his pipe, and he loved the canoe. They all loved the canoe.

I take it you all don't know what marshmallows are, do you? Asked Red and laughed.

George 1st Baron Mount Stephen, the Founder of the Canadian Pacific Railroad was there and silent, taking in all he could to tell Jimmy New Orleans what all was going on here, but Stephan had no clue Jimmy was in jail in D.C.

Red took a quick look at the fan Sui held and it looked like it read-
"Sound the battle cry;
See the foe is nigh."

Was this some sort of secret language? Red thought. As Red was going to look at her when Philippe-Joseph Aubert de Gaspé spoke of his great importance, "I had it all. I did. I want to write about legends, traditions, and family, to save us from oblivion."

"But I am going to prison," Philippe said sadly, "I let things fall apart. There's not enough beavers being killed in prison," And laughed but then got sad again... "I had all this and what for, what for? Responsibility or the honor of proclaiming in the streets of the town. They say I 'am in liberality and in great need of foresight. I am in debt to the crown. Was it all worth it? Oh but they should not know, of I ask of such things. Laws, laws, laws. I am forced to seek refuge, with my large family, forced into retirement. I am going to be imprisoned for my debt. Red we must reflect deeply upon our past conduct and our family. People are concerned more with politics and rebellion and not literature, and that worries me."

Red said, Yes, me too. It's still the same Philippe, it's still the same.

Philippe spoke again, "Solitude, the long winters allows us to educate, educate children, literary education, steady association with authors, both ancient and modern, English and French, through contact with whom his taste was refined. My son is a writer, writing the first novel."

His accent in French when he said novel made Red smile.

"I am an outcast. I appreciate that all the more the frank," Gaspé continued saying, "I have companionship with farmers, we hunt and fish together."

George 1st Baron Mount Stephen smiled because that is what he wants to do, hunt and fish. The poet William Chapman was stammering about trains and gold mines.

Mrs. Spring Fragrance, Sui Sin Far, Edith Maude Eaton sat there and couldn't take it no more and spoke, "I am Chinoise, Chinoise. Behold, how great and glorious and noble are the Chinese people! You all are speaking about boat races, railroads, trains, gold mines and not encouraging mutual understanding and respect between communities for multiculturalism. Fundamentally, I muse, people are all the same. My mother's race is as prejudiced as my father's. Only when the whole world becomes as one family with human beings be able to see clearly and hear distinctly. I believe that someday a great part of the world will be Eurasian. I cheer myself with the thought that I am but a pioneer. A pioneer should glory in suffering." Sui looked at Red, the Syke Brothers and Horace Jansen Beemer, a railway contractor and engineers and then said, "The best I can do is accept an offer from a railway agency to typewrite their correspondence for $5 a month."

At least you got an offer, said Red and laughed.

Sui laughed too and spoke again, "I love poetry, particularly heroic pieces. I also love fairy tales. I also think about selling poetry and other things."

Red thought of the poet Riki Chen in the 21st Century, and all of this. Her fan was saying to Red, indicating, indicating exile. Why, Red thought, maybe everyone on the planet should just get up and move to another country, everyone, that's one way of changing things around, and Sui smiled like she read Red's mind.

The poet Honoré Beaugrand was there also and finally got noticed when he said, "Exile, Oh Exile," a few times and his accent was magnificent to Red, with a French twist, "Exile, Oh Exile in time and patience."

Red felt it again, the hurry, and Red seen them, yes he did, he seen the eyes of a wolf, or was it this Golden Dog. Red looked at everyone, and then back where he seen the eyes glowing, but they were gone.

The poet Joseph- Charles Taché was there, and he was looking at Red the whole time Red has been there. "You need to wear better Canadian clothes," said Taché.

Red looked down at what he was wearing, and laughed, and said, Alright.

Taché said with a smile, "I am deeply convinced of the importance of poetry and novels. Red it's a patriotic duty to collect and pass on to future generations the real or fictitious stories connected with the places and people of the land."

Red smiled and thought, Patriotic duty, huh?

Taché smiled again and said, "The mind of man can no more live on realism than his soul can live on the natural truths it perceives; the mind must venture into the unknown, the soul must find repose through faith in mysteries. Hence the need for our imagination to feed on magical notions. Herein lays the charm of legends and tales."

Everyone there smiled and that is when railway contractor Horace Jansen Beemer, and the Sykes brothers, William and Samuel who were mechanical engineers arrived. The poet Robert Stanley Weir was there too. He clapped his hands and recited his poem, "Oh Canada."

Taché smiled at them and said, "Glad you made it. I want to make transportation for passengers and freight safer and more readily available. It's not commerce, not railroads, nor telegraph lines that will ensure the future of a people, Our future is in our sense of social security, in the proliferation of civil and religious liberties. I have my doubts in defending our vast territories too, so how can we protect our roads."

"Our plan is to make an American invasion of Canada inconvenient," said Samuel Sykes.

Lack of a decent alignment, new alignment, Red thought, confuse them, change the gauge of the railroad tracks, Red suggested.

William Sykes then spoke, "The Carillon and Grenville Railway engines are still their original 'Provincial Gauge' at 5 feet 6 inches."

Standard Gauge, 4 feet 8 inches is too narrow some say railroaders in America, said Beemer.

Well there you go, said Red.

Everyone looked at each other in awe. Red looked at them and smiled. When we wear the shoes of others, do we become even more lost? Where is the barrier, and how can it come down? These are two quick things Red thought about when the poet Dr. William Henry Drummond and Amédée Papineau came blazing into camp. Amédée Papineau looked at Red and then said, "There you are, good. Are you ready to race?"

Dr. William Henry Drummond said, "Let's hope you don't have Phil-o-rum's Canoe. Because, you may not know what to do."

Me, race, replied Red, I thought I was just going?

"You are the log roller Red," said Dr. Drummond as he put his arm around Red, "Here's for de man will tak' de job." Dr. Drummond walked Red away, and away they went to the regattas.

The poet Octave Crémazie who was silent and listening, was thinking about peace, and he recited his poems 'Peace' and 'Flag Chime' as they all went to the boat races.

One night, gathered around the fire,
These frequent guests listened in silence
Long stories with this warrior spirit

Octave stayed, and thought about the driving force of Hope and Faith.

They're on you all here in the press, aren't they? Red asked them.

"Yes indeed," replied Thomas D'Arcy McGee, "But we are having a fine time up here. We go to church by boat. Come on Red, you can do it," said McGee. Red was a bit confused because he heard the sounds of boots through railroad gravel, and the scraping sound of shovels. The hill they climbed was an uphill struggle. The elevation was one foot per twenty, so this made Red feel like a train. Once there Red looked at this wooden sailing vessel created by someone's own hands from the material nature has provided, and then Red looked at the waters, the Ottawa River. The river looked dangerous, because it was rapid and filled with logs.

Amédée Papineau looked at Red, and said, "Hope!"

McGee said, "Dear Dream do not desert me, Dear Shadow, do not Flee! Peace hath her Victories, no less then War." D'Arcy Mcgee recited his poem 'Dream Journeys'

&c &c-
Thus borne on wings of woven dreams
The ship of night, swift-sided sleep,
Finds us along those alien streams,
And wafts us homeward o'er the deep

Red stepped into the canoe, and Dr. William Henry Drummond recited his poem, 'The Log Jam,'

&c &c-
Dere was de job for a feller, handy an' young an' smart,

Willin' to tak' hees chances, willin' to risk hees life.
Cos many a t'ing is safer, dan tryin' de boom to start,
For if de log wance ketch you, dey 're cuttin' you lak a knife.
&c &c-

Red looked at a totem pole and there sat that crow, and the crow said to Red, "I can change the size of your canoe. From the size of a pine needle or big enough to contain the whole universe."

Red was in awe, and in shock. Red looked around to see if anyone else heard the crow, but it looked like they didn't but one being did, and that was the wolf from the falls. Red spotted the wolf and the wolf was looking at them from a bluff over the Ottawa River. Red looked at the crow and answered, Big enough to contain the whole universe.

Red awoke. Red looked at his alarm clock and picked it up, and reset it to wake him in a half an hour.

Twenty minutes later the train pulled into the Palace train station, the Gare du Palais in Québec City. The sun finally peaked over the horizon and the palaces' night lights were still on, and Andy looked at this place in amazement. The granite and large windowed building was amazing with its copper roofs, and the big clock that truly caught Andy's attention also. Red was asleep. Andy is usually always up way before Red.

This morning felt different to Andy and he got nervous of about a earthquake, a global disaster. He thought about the iron fire beneath our feet. Who and what's outside these windows are what is important, Andy thought.

Were Red and Andy improving the lives of the poetic man-kind? Andy then felt the humbling feeling come again as he looked at the Palace Train station. Andy felt that he wasn't and he thought of home, furthermore he thought about, within for, answers. As he thought, this house in Kentucky came to mind and this house is where he wants to settle down one day, He, the one he loves and a dog named Leroy enjoying the final days of life on Franklin road.

Red finally made it and he was on time, tired but on time. Red looked at Andy and smiled. Andy noticed a crow outside rolling around in the snow and Andy pointed it out to Red, and Red was in awe. Red had a stern look going on and said, There will always be more.

"More indeed," Andy replied, "We have our plateful this week. We have a page to make for custom books with Martin. We have Poetry Train Press to write up for the public and poets selected already, and for them to be judges. Robert Niswanders ideas. Furthermore we have to check back with publishers and presses and Eve Brackenbury & Prospero's Parkside Books. Emy Louie and the Fast Train Poem contest."

And the Alphonso G. Newcomer Award, said Red.

"Yes, for sure the Alphonso G. Newcomer Award," Andy replied, "And finish the Poetry Train America book list. Charlie has also contacted us. He's publishing his new poetry book in a few weeks, and he's curious about sales for Poetry Train America. I told him, it needs indexed, and stocked. Also he knows he has the book."

Mr. Welchberry came into the dining car spiffy as ever singing the 'North Train' song by Félix Leclerc, and he switched back and forth verses from French to English.

Oh ! The train to Sainte-Adele
Visited after the Mont- Laurier
Nobody could stop
Seem we have seen spinning
In the sky last night

Oh ! le train du Nord
Tchou, tchou, tchou, tchou,
Le train du Nord
A perdu l'Nord
Rendu d'l'aut' bord
Le train du Nord
A perdu l'Nord
Pis c'est pas moi qui va l'blâmer
Non, non, non !

"Red and Andy I want you two to meet the trains engineers," said Mr. Welchberry, "They will be here in a few minutes to eat breakfast. And their names are Ed and Ted. They are brothers." As soon as Mr. Welchberry said their names, the brothers walked into the dining car, and smiled and walked up to Red and Andy and said, "It's nice to finally meet you two." The brothers sat down, and mentioned they loved the railroad poet Cy Warman, Neil Young, Johnny Cash and Lucille Bogan.

Red and Andy looked at each other and smiled, took notes and were enjoying the morning. Andy thought about the one he loved, and he contemplated a future wedding at Emily Dickinsons house. He thought about the hard labor by hand to pay for it all, and he smiled and thought, I did it before, by saving and working weekends to pay for the trademark for a band name and the bands cd production. All hard work by hand, no new mechanical tools at all, just old fashion hard work and old fashion tools. Made and saved nearly $10,000.00 in a year to pay for the expenses. Was that what was needed, to return to the old way? The proverbish and psalm way. Be silent, unseen and work hard for that wedding dream. Have the funds available for the day when they return to each other, and he could say, let's get married now, and she'll be like how, we have no money, and I'll be like, well, what do you think I have been doing? Andy then thought about Red and Dustin. Can Dustin maintain everything until his return? Can the future goals be accomplished by the ones selected? The bills will be paid, but can the Integrity of so many reasons of Poetry Train keep a rolling for a while without Andy? He'll have to make that choice when we have finished the Canadian Documentary. Andy and Red also want to take a step back anyway, to plan the next countries to e-roll through.

"I like those poets and songwriters too," Andy replied thinking I better reply because I know they know that my mind is somewhere else.

Connie brought them coffee and Seth was silent in the dining car until he played 'Riding on the Cotton Belt.'

Everyone sipped their coffee, and the sun stood up and was fully awake now with Andy and Red. The train was stopped there for mechanical checks for a while. Mr. Welchberry and the engineer brothers Ed and Ted talked about the railroads planning to change over from diesel fuel to liquefied natural gas both to save money and meet future air quality rules. Electrifying the railroads and the economical way to do that was by sharing the cost with the CHSRA. They also talked about the German train system. Red was all into it with them, because of a conversation Red had with poetry promoter Matt Anderson, who was also with poetry train on 'Operation Jester.' Andy was beginning the documentary and their research book.

Andy then randomly asked them, Be in no hurry to answer this, but I want to ask, If you all were frozen in time, what fifteen minutes of your past would you be frozen in forever? Me, I want to be frozen in time when the poet Madelynn recited her poem 'Farewell to the Weeping Rose' to me, and I am careful what I wish for.

No one said anything.

"We need to contact the poet Antonio D'Alfonso from Montreal" said Andy, "He says, Today, it is not easy to be a "diverse" writer. The benchmarks of the past are outdated or too obfuscated to communicate with the present. Moreover, the relationship between the past and the present is as corrupt as ever; as a result of its bond with the past, the future seems unable to display its modernity. I like this Red, 'He sees writing, editing and publishing as belonging to a sport team. We can't all be goaltenders, center-fielders or quarterbacks. Literature and culture is the product of teamwork. Can you see a hockey team, composed of a single player, no matter how good this person, facing a very strong team with many excellent players?"

Thanks Andy, says Red, I see he's a specialist in the kind of literature he produces. He has published more than 800 authors. Andy he says here, so I agree we need to talk to him. 'Sad to say that my initial project was a waste of time and a total failure.' Guernica Editions, He regrets starting his publishing company. We need to talk to him about wisdom and seek his advice.

Andy thought, thought about the next and last 25 years of his life. Will he and Red regret starting poetry train? Red was thinking along the same lines as well. Andy thought about the youth, the driving force, and thought, it's all about them not us. Wisdom needs to be passed on to the next generations regardless of tribulations and its phenomenon-.

Red then brought to Andy's attention the new poet on the train Dominic Albanese. Andy looked into his reflection on the window and thought of time hooks? Trying, he's trying... Trying Andy thought, the best he could that was for sure. Sure is an accomplishment, was thought of also, said by someone else.

Red was in correspondence on Facebook with the new poet Dominic Albanese on the train, and Red, thought of the Christmas Spirit.

'There is a book somewhere called "From Italy to White River" about the New Haven Railroad my grandfather was the steam crane operator and that crane is still on the siding in White River Jct Vermont, for all you RR history buffs," said Dominic Albanese and asked. "How do I know if anybody likes my work, or does it matter?"

Well, I do, replied Red laughing, this comment makes me think, why because the owner of Facebook made it so easy for people to express themselves and that like it button seems like it's a chore to most, but when someone Netscape's a photo and puts a stupid quote on it from someone they get trillions of likes... but that is here... So it tells me if you get no likes then they do, but really who knows... I am going to post wisdom from a poet named Michael Stone aka Rygar, Rygars Method of Getting Your Poetry Read.

1) be proactive and link your poetry when in chat or other places (just don't link your poem on a comment on someone else's poem)

2) READ OTHER POETS!

3) Be respectful in your comments, keep it constructive and not personal.

Be patient and stick with it and make sure your poetry is available in a hands on mode/fashion.

Thank you Dominic, I shall return and comment myself...

"Groovy yuk yuk I date myself," Dominic Albanese, replied. "In Oregon I had more readings and offers to read than I wanted. Down here in Florida, seems like the highbrow is pretty low brow lots of people at the mullet fest or the mud jam but not too much poetry, yet getting on the train has re-lit the fire so I will look around. Big Book wisdom. The only sure way to insure ignorance is contempt prior to investigation. Susaan Sigafoos is on your deal too, and her and I go back to about 68, she is a true love of mine, but way too busy to be bothered with my dribble spit and moan. I wrote my first poem at 12. I am 68. Also I have a collection of poems about and from when I was in the war. I have not shared them except with a few workshop fellow poets in Oregon the reaction was pretty severe tears and one lady threw up. I will wait to post any of them, and keeping comments not personal, roger Wilco.. (hear and will comply) lots of people don't know what Wilco means?"

Dominic, what you have done since you have been on the train, and commented via conversation and all, has really flipped the script, and I'll add the 'd/ID, said Red... Because this whole journey started from a few things. In the documented journey Poetry Train America stood for a truth of past present and future, and still stands for that & more. A beacon, a true beacon, the best that I can and shall do. I can only move and build the availability of poetry, railroads and both of their histories/braided now by law. Poetry Train has made its presence to the correct people in both and braided industries; finally, it's still taking a while. There are nearly 1,500 passengers for a reason, and all just ride. Poetry Train has a good webmaster, a little feisty, but good, and this. The Poetry E Train has th'Wick'd Papoose Caboose, and that Mr. Albanese is all we need. Welcome aboard the poetry e train.

"Thanks, and just for yuks my Grandfather who has the same name was quite a famous railroad man himself," Dominic Albanese replied. "He is in a book called "From Italy to White River" the New Haven Railroad, he and a few others laid the tracks and he drove a steam crane that to this day is on the siding in White River Jct in Vermont, when he died no one else could run it. I think he was the hossler, but he died before I was born. I used to ride the train to Mexico a lot back in the early 70s Guymas and Los Mooches and had a small place down in San Blas, but drugs and crime took a toll. If possible I would love to know how to change the spacing line to line, because I have always held it should look as good on the page as it sounds spoken. By the way just for input, I read James Joyce's Esse Pure when I was about 10 and have been trying to rewrite it for sixty years. Also some of Gunter Grass and Gary Sinder moved me to tears. Now back to work. I will post a few more and then wait to see if I get any feedback. Keep up the good work and remember we are only responsible for the effort God got the results."

Thank you for the beautiful story of your Grandfather, replied Red, I shall look into that and add it to the Canadian Documentary, as a conversation, with all credit ado because it's important and it's part of the story of what I am doing. Mexico huh, nice the poet Christopher Flakus takes the train there here and there. He's written and produced a wonderful poem on the channel and the site about a train ride down that way. I always back up my text, and then enter it again, sorta like this/sorta like this, then space it out, but I'll look into that. Thanks for that feedback. I recently got The Portable James Joyce, Red laughed, and said, 'Nice, and thank you for the last heart words, yes, I shall and remember." Appreciated & Charm'd. Red was thinking Dominic is a blessing to the website, a blessing.

Mr. Welchberry had some of the Japanese poet Kenji Miyazawa books and the 'Night on the Galactic Railroad' stuck out like a sore thumb. He also had a book of Gem Stones. "We must write poems like Beethovens' Symphonies Miyazawa once proclaimed," said Mr. Welchberry, "Animals have requests too," and he recited the 'Telegraph poem.'

"The word Nosutarujikku he always implied, which is usually translated into English is Nostalgic," Mr. Welchberry explained, "However Kenji implies not just a personal but a common shared memory or sometimes not even a memory but offensive an imagined past. The spirit of harmony. He showed us how to be good people." Mr. Welchberry recited a poem by Kenjis' 'Strong in the Rain.'

When you look at Mr. Welchberry, you sense some sort of vision, that there were invisible gears under us. And certain men were practical, to be of use to society, to serve mankind. Mr.Welchberry looked at Red and Andy, and knew they were going down in history with a few scars, gathering and harnessing enthusiasm. Mr. Welchberry said, "You men are organizing the poetry world like Fleming organized time."

Red and Andy laughed. Andy thought back when he was a boy organizing his baseball and football cards. It started to snow outside, and Andy felt the distance. He felt like the lone wolf in his dreams in the cold out there, walking the tracks. All of the glaciers could melt right now and he'd swim back. The dream goes on, he thought while holding his heart rock.

Andy remembered the wolf and the wolf was looking for his family, the only wolf that tried, the Owl did Red. "Rediscover. That is a new nickname for you Red, said Andy, Rediscover, as in rediscovery over and over again, and Andy laughed, but not for too long. Andy read the poem "The Time Around Scars" by Michael Ondaatje, and tears rolled down Andy's' cheeks."

Red laughed and said, Re-discovery huh. Michael Ondaatje uses historical fragments as well as oral legends; he relies heavily on historical documentation for inspiration, weaving it into a fictional story. He sure does have some fans, that make creative videos of his poems, that is for sure. Red then contemplated his dream he had last night, and the spiritual world. Red was doing research and spoke out, There's something abnormal about the poet, so a poet needs to be abnormal furthermore become more a powerful role in society, to kill more demons to the human soul, to kill more demons to the human soul. Yes Red said, Irving Layton on poetic fire.

"We are the white mice Red of the poetic mines," said Andy and laughed.

Artists are here to warn the dangers to the human soul, said Red quoting Layton. Very powerful statement and responsibility.

"Poets," said Andy continuing the wisdom of Irving Layton, "They saw tooth and claw, Canadian poetry has metaphysical presence, the double hook; beauty and terror. He said Red people have no feelings, no emotions. They are materialistic, money, cars and computers. Poets have no audience because of that. No one has comprehension for a poet. Poetry has become inflated Layton says."

"He'd love our role, and roll," said Andy laughing.

"Divinity and creativity are one and the same," said Mr. Welchberry.

Andy noticed Layton's speaking skills right away.

Mr. Welchberry pointed to a news boy at the train station and recited the poem 'Newsboy' by Layton.

&c &c
Old Ills, and incapacity to love.

Andy was thinking, mankind sure does learn some things fast, but the good things take way so long, why? Andy thought. Teaching huh?

Someone on the train recited the poem 'The Revenge' A Ballad of The Fleet by Alfred Lord Tennyson.

Andy got all into that thought mode as he looked out the window at the newsboy. For the first time Andy fell asleep in the dining car, and the swift kick dream wind took him to the year 2063 in Atlanta, Georgia where this nearly all began, where in the year of 2063. Humanity finally learned to use steam with sand, and took a Stand. Over and over again they did this. The magnitude of the magnet, that ignited this neuro change took and straighten'd out th'spaghetti noodles of time, and th'carbon footprint. They took what was carved and did this by playing pictionary wictionary, and Bless they, they finally got rid of the $trainer- The Poets that taught Andy this in his fast and bright dream was Garrick the Engineer and 'Hide Kerry Douglas' the Poet from the future and in the year of 2063, the high-speed railroaders still listen to Alison Krauss. In this dream they were discussing and using examples in how to improve, move, mark, and capture the great mysterious thing called 'Time.'

Red thought, lets trap the book shelf, and sleep, oh yes and slip- Red woke him up by reciting one of Andy's' own poems and it was Reds' favorite entitled 'Turboa,' and Red laughed before he began waking Andy up with his own poem', Oh but before that, Red thought, they think history and poetry is dead do they?

Upon a time running with the scarecrows
Someone scored a bag from Jesse James in St. Joe
I fell in low, but that was miles ago
Now I travel time spinning your wheels in turbo

I have a story about a crazy ass snake
His ass come close to becoming gray flakes
That fucking snake jumped ten foot out of the fire
I tried to kill it, but he too is a sire

You have to know I have to show you
By the the impulse if time
You have to know I have to show you
By the the impulse if rhyme

&c &c

Andy smiled and laughed as he snapped out of his nap. After a little while later Andy got a Facebook notification. The Writers Federation in Halifax, Nova Scotia, Canada, finally accepted Poetry Trains friend request on Facebook, but once I liked their avatar, and said nicely as we always do, Welcome aboard the poery e train, these folks take us off their friends list, said Andy laughed and said "Okay." Andy was silent for a while and created a poem, "Like the Gold Jesse Stole'

You don't have secrets like me. Taste Missouri-
Down to the haunted valleys of Tennessee
And if you do, what it is you hide?
All I see is your lazy pride
Who and what first funded the Grand Ole Opry Show?
Publisher you lost your prudence, like the gold Jesse stole.
I keep my hands on my hope, while my eyes are like a rope

Teeter totter, so you have favored to be cold
Your action spoke what I have been told
And if you know, then you should be ashamed
It says you're hiring, funny, where's your named?
Who and what first funded the operation that you roll?
Publisher you lost your justice, like the gold Jesse stole.
I keep my eyes on truth, while my ears strengthen my soul

Hey, we tried to couple up to your cars
I see you truly want your poets to be stars
And if you do, where is your gang?
All I heard was a pellet, bb, bang
Who and what first taught you to be this kind of role?
Publisher you lost your love, like the gold Jesse stole.
I don't keep my mind on my courage, because fear I control

Like all the great things in life, when they disappear, you'll know
And they'll we be worth a lot, much more, like the gold Jesse stole

Nice said Red, You are a rebel like Ann Hébert, on the intense side of things.

Andy laughed and said, "What is wrong with folks. I bet in a month or two we can go back to this profile and there will be not one like or comment. Laziness is what it is. Lazy. I guess so Red, I don't accept things the way there are either."

Red started laughing and said, We got this idea, to plant our hands in the garden. He laughed and continued reciting Ann's poem, 'Our Hands in the Garden.'

"Ann Hébert likes the historical novel as well," said Mr. Welchberry, "And in the words of Roch Carrier "If we are to protect our heritage then we need to be vigilant in ensuring that our books and recordings are saved for the generations to come." Mr. Welchberry then recited her poem entitled 'Snow' and when he completed it the waitress Connie came to refill their morning drinks, and she smiled.

Red and Andy looked at each other and smiled.

Connie looked at Mr. Welchberry and smiled. She looked at Red and Andy and said, "I bet you both that you both went against your parent's wishes, and pursued poetry like the poet Émile Nelligan who was born on Christmas Eve."

Red and Andy laughed, and said, Yes, but we are studying now, poetry and the railroads.

Ed and Ted laughed also, and they talked about the writer, Laura Goodman Salverson, and said they wished they had a poet wife like she had a railroader husband. It would be their Canadian Dream.'

Mr. Welchberry cut in and said, "Well not all poets are nocturnal, poets are not identical, they can see in complete darkness, well some do and some don't," and he laughed. "They love water, and some live in the woods."

Everyone laughed, and Andy thought wait a minute, poets are like owls.

Connie said, "I want to recite to you all two of my favorite poems by Émile Nelligan," and she did. Two of his poems back to back and they seemed to blend well together.

Heavenly Ticket

Full of nostalgic melancholy and strange dreams

&c &c

The recital of angels
&c&c

She gave up there in strange rhythms ...

Andy was taking notes and throwing up a force field to protect his love. He was taking notes about a foreseen and up and coming mystery for him and Red. The engineer brothers Ed and Ted talking about their careers. They loved their dual operator idea, it was accident free. With their system they got plenty of sleep.

"We came a long way from the wooden rails, haven't we boys," said Mr. Welchberry, and laughed.

Andy looked at Red and winked. Andy then continued his notes on Taliesin's Secret.

The train was ready to go, and so was everyone else, all ready to get to Montreal.

Andy saw a sign and pointed it to Red, a trail called "Le p'tit train du Nord" translated into "The small train of the North" that stretches over 200 km on what used to be an old railway line, and is now officially the longest linear park in Canada.

Quebec:

Quebec City, the Botanical Garden of Montreal, Wendake Village, Huron-Wendat Indian Reserve, the Saguenay Fjord, Montmorency Waterfalls, St. Charles River/Kabir Kouba Falls, the Charlevoix Region, Percé Rock, the viewpoint at the Saint-Lawrence Lowlands, Îles-de-la-Madeleine, Gatineau and Pink Lake, Kipawa Lake, Fortifications of Québec, Quartier Petit Champlain & Place Royale, the Plains of Abraham, So I wonder if Poets ever rode a bicycle on the trail called "Le p'tit train du Nord" translated into "The small train of the North" that stretches over 200 km on what used to be an old railway line, and is now officially the longest linear park in Canada.

Quebec Railways:

The land of the first Railway in Canada. The Champlain and Saint Lawrence Railroad began in 1835, the Saint Andrews and Quebec Rail Road began in 1835, the St. Lawrence & Atlantic Railroad began in 1846, the Quebec and Richmond Railroad began in 1852, the Grand Trunk Railway Company began in 1853, the Toronto and Guelph Railroad began in 1853, the Carillon and Grenville Railway began in 1857, the Quebec and Gosford Wooden Railway began in 1868, the Massawippi Valley Railway began in 1870, the Wiscasset and Quebec Railroad began in 1884, the Montreal and Southern Counties Railway began in 1897, the Quebec Southern Railway began in 1900, the Québec, Montréal, and Southern Railway began in 1906, the Quebec Gatineau Railway began in in 1997, the Montreal, Maine and Atlantic Railway & the Central Maine & Quebec Railway began in 2002, the Montreal, Maine & Atlantic Railway began in2003, and the Central Maine & Quebec Railway began in 2014.

Quebec Poets:

The first Poet I found was Yotanka (E.B. Aknatoy) Coicou, and she studied in the wilderness of Canada. Her poetry is themed in many things, love & hate, light & dark, life & death, magic, divinity, humanity, culture, Canadian indigenous culture, animals, nature and spirituality. Her couplets are quick and witty, she can show you wisdom with a quickness, her triplets do just as much. Her imagery can be beyond any dimension she desires. She uses the poetic onomatopoeia tool very well. Her poems, "Tumbleweed," "The Howling of Healing," "Looking Into the Abyss," "May I Have, the Pleasure of Your Eternal Company," "Slon-Ha," "The Shaman & The Sheeple," are just a small portion of her poetic talent that makes the reader realize you been touched by grace, wisdom, and every hair on your body now may have a poetic good spell upon you. p.s. she's a blazing Poet Comet!

The second Poet I found was Nicole Brossard, and her poetry is themed in erotica, all of life, the writing life, and wordplay. Nicole's poems, "A Rod for a Handsome Price," "Contemporary," "Piano Topology," "Shadow," "The Indocile Back of Words," and many more are amazing, interesting, and mind opening.

The third Poet I found was Brian Campbell, and he studied at the University of Toronto and McGill University. His poetry is differently themed in life and love. Brian's poems, "After Reading Too Much Shields & Atwood," "Emblem," "Green Satellite Shimmer Report," "Tincture," "Passport," and "You Told Me To Write a Love Poem," are wicked in a good way.

The fourth Poet I found was Steve Luxton, and his poetry is themed in life, history, people, and writing. Steve's poems, "Adolf's Eva," "City Ravine Gothic," "Harmonica Maestro," "Reading the Russians in a Country Restaurant," "Untitled, Unfinished," seems to me doorways into a loving and humble heart, yes there is heartbreak but leads to so much more.

The fifth Poet I found was Flavia Cosma, and she studied at McGill University. Her poetry is themed in humanity, life, oceans & beaches, past lives, and premonitions. Flavia's poems, "Before I Die," "Beyond," "Emigration," "Out of the Great Sleep," "Premonitions, and her "On Paths Known to No One (poems)" are beautiful, elegant, and calming as a calm ocean.

The sixth Poet I found was Blare Coughlin, and she studied at McGill University. Her poetry is themed in love, family, and sex. Blare's poems, "do people still write about sex am i writing about sex sure i guess i am okay," "Poems I wrote in Calgary, Over Winterbreak," and "self-aware/carried through Ohio are unique and original, and makes you smile.

The seventh Poet I found was Gonzo Nieto, and his poetry is about peace and new ways of thinking, furthermore the youth. Gonzo's poem "itching to break this bone prison" scratches.

The eighth Poet I found was Oana Avasilichioaei and her poetry is themed in animals, life and nature. Oana's poems, "Borders on Madness," "Mirrored," "Shouldering," +"Song of the Hunt," and "Song of Water" are beautiful, and mystical, leaving the reader astonished.

The ninth Poet I found was John David Hickey, and his story poetry is themed in animals and nature. John David's poems, "We're All in As a Wolfpack," "Fionn MacCool and the Old Man," "Lex and the Devil," and "Ti-Fleur and the Magic Fiddler," are amazing and captures you well.

The tenth Poet I found in was Louky Bersianik, and her poetry is themed life on a micro level but a great although mega level. Her poems, "LA SPLENDEUR," "De Axes et eau (1984) 2 Le testament de la Folle Alliée" and "Theory, A Sunday" are sexy and very intellectual poems.

The eleventh Poet I found was Jenny Smart aka Halogen, and her poetry is themed in many things. Childhood, family, love, Poets & Poetry and the power within. Jenny's poems, "Circles of Fire," "Cryogenics for a Glaciologist's Daughter," "Heart Shaped Ice Cube," "Layover," "The Editing Process," and "The Geometry of Winter," are outstanding, and will rip the reader or listeners heart ears open, and make you hear.

The twelfth Poet I found was Jeffrey Mackie, and his poetry is themed in life, love, history, humanity, music, and much more, like the modern tricky times. Jeffrey's poems, "Directional," "Humanity," "Mothballs," "Truth among the Obsessions," and "We All Live Somewhere," are clever & comical, and reveals his poetic eye, furthermore leaves the reader astonished.

The thirteenth Poet I found was Miriama Prickett, and she is a mystery, and her poems "juggernaut for drus," and "geeze" are groundbreaking.

The fourteenth Poet I found was Catherine Kidd, and her poetry is themed in deep reality, animals, and love. Catherine Kidd's poems, "Hyena Subpoena," "Lion Queen [Ode to a dying lioness]," "No I.D." and "Sea Peach (Halocynthia Auranthium)," are mind blowing, poetry explosive indeed. Intelligence in poem action.

The fifteenth Poet I found was Mark Abley, and his poem, "The Not Quite Great," is a tip of a Canadian glacier of his poetry, a superb poem.

The sixteenth Poet I was Megan Lane, and her poetry is about love, and she is ruthless about love, and does not hold back. She also writes about nature, and lol and she is comical. Hard core and very power poetry. Megan is also a hit songwriter, and her hit song is entitled, 'Someday We Will Leave this Town.'

Chapter 10-Newfoundland and Labrador, St. John Canada

January 21, 2014

Andy was dreaming of Facebook; browsing at it all when he would be old, and when he looked; the deeper he looked, he seen that everyone had passed away. As he scrolled down the pages, tears rolled down his face. This was making him awake, and as he awoke he remembered voices from friends saying, "Hope your dreams come true, so romantic! Onward, upward!" But Andy was only roughly awakening, roughly because he sensed something when he did awake in a time not too far from a now, so he was awakening into another dream where people were dancing through the streets dressed in outlandish costumes and disguised in various ways. Two boys with scarfs over their faces were teasing Andy as he walked up to a barn like train station, "Guess who we are, guess our names?" These young lads were the poets Edwin John Dove Pratt and Francis Reginald Scott.

"It's okay Andy, the snow comes and the snow melts," said Edwin and his eyes caught Andy's attention. There was mystery in his eyes. Edwin smiled and said, "From Stone to Steel, The path lies through Gethsemane." Andy looked at them and smiled, Andy didn't want to say anything, because things were happening. What was birthing? A question Andy was feeling, and these two kids, made Andy feel a good omen coming. We give ourselves away to others, and we receive from them, Andy thought, and oh, do we receive.

The land was filled with caribou, seabird colonies, icebergs and whales. Schooners were everywhere and so were flotilla. Cod were hung up everywhere also, and they were bigger then children. A whistle could be heard far away, and when Andy looked around to see all of this, he was on top of the roof of the Avondale Railway Station, and it was like Déjà vu. The two young poet boys waited for Andy on a bench below the over hangs of the roof. Andy took a breath and thought this is all way surreal, and it was cold, cold enough to mess with Andy's immune system while he slept. Synchronicity kicked in again, and so was the sea breeze with its pushing skill to humble one. Life seems to come full circle here and there, and then the notion came to Andy that he and Red came into Canada backwards, so this was going to take more thought. Well of course they were on the run from the United States. Andy noticed there were many sportsmen around, and the women didn't look happy, overwhelmed and over-worked. Life seemed unforgiving here. Starved for change? Not so fast Andy thought, the Vikings, the Beothuk, and Facebookers all gone now, all gone. In the fog, and it was getting foggy, just like memories going now, vanishing in the mist, on the surface anyway, life folding into death and death folding into life, and still no one can get enough pull to un-fold the flag of peace.

Historian Daniel Woodley Prowse looked up at Andy from the bottom of a ladder and said, "Come down Andy, you don't have to roof anymore, you have bleed for that cause long enough, come down Andy." When Andy came down the poets named Michael Power, 'Poet of Pokeham Path' and James Murphy played Andy a song, and the song was entitled, 'A Worthy Son Of Scotia.' Prowse laughed at them and said, "No, you both are supposed to sing to the geologist Alexander Murray, and he is standing next to Sir Sanford Fleming."

Andy looked at them all and was impressed by Fleming, but what really has Fleming done, time Andy thought, time. Time gets shorter near a polarity or was it too, illusional? Fleming was a time traveler Andy thought. Mainly Andy noticed a book of minerals in Murray's hands, and Murray noticed Andy had seen the book, and he tried to hide it. Andy also seen a map. Andy looked at Fleming and thought of Mr. Welchberry. A man walked out of the train station and he was William Whiteway, who was the leader of the governments which passed railway contracts. Oh shit, Andy thought, His eyes are colder than the temperature. Something was happening here, and Whiteway had a book too, entitled, 'Manifesto.' Andy was taking in a lot, and all was moving fast.

"Where have you been Andy?" Asked Robert Gillespie Reid, a railroad contractor. Four men on a velocipede there also laughed at Andy. One man was his son William Duff Reid. Andy laughed back at them. Andy didn't know what to say, but to get to work, but work on what, what?

"Stone viaducts," said Reid, and this made Andy think of the séance with Alphonso G. Newcomer and Edgar Allen Poe furthermore pyramids. Ah Andy thought but upside down pyramids. "The International Bridge, where were you?" Reid asked again, and laughed a bit. "You were all over America weren't ya? I have heard of ya, somewhere in Texas."

The train engineer Enoch Bown came out of the train station, and said, "Let's show Andy the Rhinoceros.' Not to mention the series of problems and dangers that included water currents between seven to twelve miles per hour, fluctuating water levels and ice flows in the Niagara River." This man sure did look spiffy to Andy. A man at least in his fifties but looking more like in his thirties. Andy sensed all of his own obligations at once, and didn't want to be careless at all. The temperature started to change and get warmer. Andy also sensed something was about to go down. Rhinoceros?

"To Lachine" said young Duff Reid, "The Rhino is here." It was getting dark fast, a storm was brewing in the clouds.

Rhinoceros? Andy thought again, has to be a baby one. They like to be petted too. The Rhino was a train that Enoch Bown normally piloted. Andy laughed, but not too long because lightening was striking everywhere. Once everyone was aboard the Rhinoceros Train, the spectators outside had their hands over their mouths as though they were terrified. Was it the train or the weather, or was it something completely different? Andy thought about something, if he was being set up by pranksters or time ghosts, he needed to think of something quick. Andy felt versatile and multidimensional, so he was enhancing his energy by absorbing, storing, amplifying, balancing, focusing and transmitting, furthermore feeling piezoelectric towards the moment, all moments. Seeing the frozen light, and sensing the ice of eternity. Looking at the world with different eyes, and using a different time frame. Andy saw the invisible cage Fleming revealed.

Mr. Welchberry was there, and he was taking tickets, and he looked at Andy and thought Andy was almost in full harmony with it and deserves its gifts, even though Andy's heart felt like the aisle carpet, Andy kept his head up, and Andy was slowly seeing the realm in full effect, furthermore things that were causing, let's say shitty effects.

Andy laughed out loud and thought about the mystery and magic of the twelve 12s that he nearly forgot about. Measuring encounters. Andy was touched by a sad breath though, and whispered, "It's not what you say but how you say it; Need you here, My love, love you, I respect you and I want you, know that I am waiting for you. Then, now, affinity." Andy looked outside the window, and the air was filled with flurries, furthermore the sky appeared to have three suns. Their light gleamed on him in Andy's' dream. Codes were embedded everywhere Andy thought, like music, poetry, and the not so good signals were everywhere too, meaning where were the hands on him saying, Mine? We are in the twisted dark information age trying to balance history and eternity, linear time and cycles of time, dogma and ritual, rationality and magic, waking reality and altered states, science and art, and poetry. Andy thought as he looked at the boys, Edwin John Dove Pratt and Francis Reginald Scott sitting across from him, and Andy asked "Where are the men that played music back at the station?" The boys shrugged their shoulders.

The poet George Webber who sat next to Andy on the train asked Andy. "Feeling like a stranger are ye? I am a stranger in my native land" Webber laments and says "All seems sadly altered here."

"Yes, hieroglyphics," said Andy and shrugged his shoulders. "I left my notebook at the station, but didn't." Andy was acting the stranger for a reason. Andy then noticed something for the first time, or was it the first time, everyone had left hands, and he had two right hands. He looked again, but all was back to normal, so why did he see this and say that? The imagination is wonderful Andy thought, way beyond the five senses, or is it not imagination? Yes, the hand is quicker than the eye. Was it all supernatural realms, supernatural hands? Codified indeed. We are victims on this journey to the new golden age. We who write are victims of history, Andy thought, all kinds of history, everything. Enough to make Andy ralph, like Alphonso did in the courtyard. Andy didn't say anything but thought our poetry is our children, and yes mess with them we have the right to go after your birth giving mother.

The boys, Edwin John Dove Pratt and Francis Reginald Scott were happy as can be, kicking their legs. Francis Reginald Scott motioned to Andy to notice the three women sitting across from them all. They were the poets, Henrietta Prescott Lushington, Isabella Whiteford Rogerson and Mrs. Margaret Sharp Ferguson Peace.

Andy looked at Henrietta Prescott Lushington first and knew right away she was going to say something about reality to Andy. She looked at Scott first and said, "My happy child! I smile to see how wisdom I have sought so long hath come spontaneously to thee." These words would one day be her opening lines to her poem 'To a Child.'

She looked at Andy and said, "To one purpose cling, there is a being who is really going to love them, that is going to understand them unconditionally and that we create that consciousness in them to call their soul mate so that as they grow up they do not feel so complicated to act in a different way than others."

What? Andy thought. But what Andy wasn't thinking is that there was someone that did not speak English that knew all too well everything regardless of her tongue.

"You have the poets life Andy," said Lushington and she recited her poem 'The Poets Life.'

The Poet's loveliest thoughts can ne'er be told;
A chain of silence they must ever wear;
Like prison'd eagles, pining to unfold
Their wings, and cleave the boundless upper air,
Unspoken, caged within one lonely breast,
No stranger's eyes can see their feverish unrest

&c &c

No wonder why no one gives a shit Andy thought. Oh but someone did and her loveliest thoughts were silent as her tongue.

The poet hath his grief; he cannot speak
The unearthly glory of his vision, save

&c &c

Andy sensed barriers blocking the energy, and for sure there has been some blockage going on. The energy he knows as Beautifire, has been blocked by pranksters, time ghosts, and human dogs.

&c in dreams that none may share

Let him sing on, though we so faintly hear
The murmur flowing, like a sunny stream,
Within the garden of his life; his ear

*Is blest with music we can never dream
Yet his wild words may give the common earth
Some shadow, some faint thought of his exceeding mirth.*

His secret life is like an Indian Isle.

Andy looked at everyone because he knows what that means. Andy knew his intuition was mainly always right but he didn't listen to his gut responses kick at all, just followed his heart. The storm outside now was matching the storm in the poem, and Andy found that very ironic, just another addition to the mission, in the ode of synchronicity mode.

The boys had tears rolling down their face. Lushington looked at the boys and continued,

*Fear not for him! His gladness is his own,
New springs of comfort are for him unsealed.
His life is more than ours; to him are given,
Even on this dull earth, thoughts that belong to heaven!*

Andy was all upset now.

Isabella Whiteford Rogerson asked her to recite her poem 'The Isle of Elephanta.'

Lushington looked out the window, pointed, and recited the poem.

Andy looked out the window and was in deep thought.

Isabella Whiteford Rogerson's hair was parted and she wore glasses and she looked as though she was in deep thought too. She whispered out, "Nature cannot charm the eye, as it used to in days gone by, when together we have strayed, where her wildest pranks were played."

Yes played, Andy thought, think of the game but don't play it, ah. Isabella had this strong family persona about her. What a communion going on, Andy thought, and still today we are trying to stop the non-sense.

Isabella was in reciting poetry mode.

*Gems of poesy that woke
Dreams of softened sadness
When as yet childish hearts
Echoed naught save gladness*

*Back o'er the past with reinless speed
The wayward fancy sweeps,
And with the absent and the dead*

A sweet communion keeps

Andy was in awe of this, serious awe.

She giggled and said, Here is a bit of 'Hope Realized.'

Was it a dream, or did I see
My own dear home once more?
Was that the dash of bright waves free
along its rocky shore?

Isabella giggled again and Andy thought of the pyramids in Egypt, and their long lost songs.
She clapped her hands, and recited her poem 'Our Future.'

We are rolling onward
with the wave of Time,
And see a glorious future
In the age sublime;
See our city crowning
All the hills around,
See the railways rushing
Over, underground
&c &c

Andy then noticed Margaret Sharp Ferguson Peace and she looked nervous for peace, very. Like she didn't put all her eggs in one basket, and tarry through the woods. And she knew the stranger, and knew herself, they all were the strangers' jelly and cakes. Who may take a short cut or two, jump as well? Andy laughed inside, conceptual concern for concert.

Isabella was still reciting, reciting her poem 'Our Past,' mainly to the boys.

Andy was focusing on something while Isabella was reciting two poems; and the both of her poems are entitled 'Time' and she had a kick of a time doing so.

Andy did catch these lines from the first poem,

But, really, I've forgotten! Back, sweet dream;
And yet I think sweet flowers this book beseem;

And the whole next poem was like a tunnel within a tunnel. A long dark tunnel and all one could really do was, carve, carve ones ass off.

'Time'

A dream, a flash, a breath,
A moment gone;
Swift as a thought you may not
Dwell upon;
And yet God-given to man,
That he may be
Prepared for God's own great eternity.
Isabella giggled, and said, "One Almighty Round."

Everyone on the train applauded. Margaret Sharp Ferguson Peace was like a restless bull, just waiting for her time to be released. Don't let her eyes fool you.

It was still storming out and the lighting struck along with the train, like a light show at a concert for sure Andy thought.

Peace looked at it too and said, "It's the Tempest gathering breath, grand and beautiful." Once she said that, she put her kind of 'Spirit of Beauty' take on Andy, and he felt the strength of her persistent soul. She looked at Andy and said, "I know all about the 'Wish.' At duties sacred call, Assured that fortitude and faith can triumph over all." Peace started laughing, but really she was sad, and she explained why, "Do you know that saying it's better to reign in Hell, then to serve in Heaven, well I came up with that, and that's not true. I wished I never wrote that, I swear, I do. Pride, Satan and his train."

Andy was all lost keeping tabs now. And a now was coming and Andy knew though the puzzle was coming together.

"Behold, behold, Oblivion is amazing" Peace cried out, and she kept reciting and reciting embedding wisdom in everyone. She went into her poem 'The Exile' and Andy thought about Red and the one he loved, furthermore the 'Wicked Papoose Caboose.' The poem was like an eulogy to Andy, a chamber and a choice to enter, but he knew what was beyond the door.

She smiled at Andy and said, "Keep them in suspense. It's very peaceful."

Andy was in deep thought, bravery and self-sacrifice, if one didn't know any better for it, and couldn't act another way. What are logical criteria? Paper stone, scissors stone, scissors scissors, paper paper, stone stone. A stalemate is a formula for world peace.

Mr. Welchberry came and said, "It is true that we have lost opportunities that will never return, but in time, things transform into thoughtfulness for the future.

"It's all amazing Mr. Welchberry and Margaret," said Andy, Breaking, broke; repairing, repaired; hold steady now, and here now is about to go, but stay on the road of love, because it leads to God, but no, all are afraid of mystery. Imposters imposing what they impose. Ah, but then there's grace, Oh grace. Most fear what happens before more than they are terrified of what happens after. You can't embalm poetry," and Andy laughed, and you sure and the hell can't embalm my love."

"The loving are the daring," said Mr. Welchberry.

"I have to stand and dare to be able to see what blessings are waiting for me," Andy added, "But dang it Mr. Welchberry, I know where my love stands, and it stands alone obviously!"

Andy awoke and laid there thinking, So am I a good part to her heart, her life? Am I an aid to her and are these things the same as her to me? I know she's in much pain, but dang I want to be there. My heart is not a fairytale, not at all. Loves' water is rapidly running out it seems, and the mere view of emptiness is returning, dryer than ever. I am all that I am, faults and all, and her as well. I yearn for her, does she for me? Where is the clarity, like it was, or was it? I know what, oh gosh that feeling, when all was okay. There is not a person on this planet that could resonate me like she has. What a maze life is, amazement in all forms of emotions, and Andy laughs. And so was she, the one that knew everything but English. We can't help it we were born, unbalanced, but I am trying my best to balance my life and my actions, and words. My heart, I listen to you, and I listen. Patience, some say, hmm, do they even know what love is, and what I see? Others say, go on, move on, yea, right, so easy for folks, but not me, why, because I feel. Oh if you could only plant experiences in the hearts and minds of folks. Writing seems like the best tool, but it comes down to one experiencing the same things, but still even though, we all react so different, but at the same time we are the same. What if I am the one, and she is the one for me? Why, would anyone or let anyone interfere with a relationship? Or jeopardize such a gift? Ya, I know. Ya, like creating a universe, and then explaining it, ya who's going to believe you? Ya, evolution, l, o, v, e, backwards, more like evolution, or something. Bullshit, na, my love is real. Sublime love, not the friendship kind, that burns up, over the emptiness of dollar bills. Well, love energy is created, ha, and have to keep it to me, what a life, living the dream baby.

Red knocked on the door and said, I hear you in there.

"The door is open, and least that isn't blocking beauty and terror," said Andy and laughed, "Magical moments. Good Morning Red, it's time for me to shed."

You mean to lose your hair, because you are not a …, Red explained but was interrupted.

"Na well," said Andy, " I have to stand and dare to be able to see what blessings are waiting for me, but dang it Mr. Welchberry, I know where my love stands, and it stands alone obviously!"

Red said, Ask yourself this, how can your pain go away, if you return to it? Quit rehearsing, and start getting what you've been deserving. Possibilities are mostly lies, so protect your heart.

"I hear ya, I don't know man," Andy replied, "Come on let's go with it."

When Red and Andy arrived in the dining car Mr. Welchberry and Seth were in conversation.

"The people want British Trains here, the British Rail HST 125. They also want an underneath the ocean tunneled railway, but again the practical way is along the highways," said Mr. Welchberry, "I'm not sure how inclement the weather in Labrador and northern Newfoundland would be that it would make building such a link difficult, if not impossible, but if China can build the world's tallest railway then certainly Canada could build through some fairly desolate territory." Mr. Welchberry looked at Seth, smiled and said, "The fact that the railroad was narrow gauge, not standard gauge, like 99.5% of all other rail lines in the western hemisphere. This required the time consuming and costly practice of changing freight car trucks upon arrival at Port Aux Basque. If the line was standard gauge in the first place, this operation would have been totally unnecessary, and many in the railroad industry think there would be a possibility Newfoundland Railways could still be running today."

"Yes," replied Seth, "And there is the iron ore range and the Trinity Train Loop. What I think is great is, here for the first time in history, a railroad is owned and operated by a First Nations group. I think it was in 2005. I love the idea of international ice patrol, and here come the international poet patrol."

Red and Andy sat down and said, Good Morning Gentlemen.

"The Island of Newfoundland is an extension of the Appalachians," said Mr. Welchberry and he had the book 'Rails Across the Rock: A Then and Now Celebration of the Newfoundland Railway' by Ken Pieroway.

Cool stuff Andy thought, and he thought of the Smoky Mountains, and it's massive beauty from the rails. And here, here too was massive beauty, oceanic. Andy looked at Mr.Welchberry and thought about his dream, and said to him, "I am sure many people have many questions to ask you if they could."

"Ya, I have been thinking about my own talk show," said Mr. Welchberry, "Because I talked to this man in a car ahead of us on his way home from being done wrong by a Trucking Company. You see it kills me that this world is messed up so bad that they use anyone and everyone, furthermore our schools let things like this slip through. You see, these company's set up shop for all with a new CDL license. They do this because they know actually the economy is good, but media and politicians say different. These trucking companies know by hiring a great amount of young men to meet the supply and demand benefits them. They get loads and business faster, and the tax write off is immense, furthermore since fuel prices are down. But the sad thing is these people with a new CDL fall for it, and they get not paid, they get a train ticket or a bus ticket back home, furthermore their dreams are shattered and some lose their families over this. There out to be a massive investigation and a massive black ball on these Trucking Companies."

"Wow that's terrible Mr. Welchberry. Yes I agree the world needs to know. Wow that makes me think, and I think better when I fish. Let's go fishing Mr. Welchberry," said Andy as he looked out the window looking at the shores of Port Au Basque. The men of the fishery were working at a frantic pace. The draggers were out there in the ice. Ocean hot rods for cod, Andy thought.

"Would be nice," said Mr. Welchberry, "Maybe the poet Michael Crummey is around here somewhere."

"Crummey maybe on a road, or a river," said Connie as she came to their table, and took their orders for breakfast. "Hanging out with seals, fishing or baking bread with his wife. I love his poem 'Bread.' Two people should never say the word love before they've eaten a sack of flour together," said Connie with a little laugh.

"Is Sophie making fish this morning for everyone's evening meal?" Mr. Welchberry asked.

"Newfoundland chowder, with garlic mashed taters and steamed kale," replied Connie.

Michael Crummey believes we are in a spiritual crisis, said Red, He also writes about historical events and folklore, said Red as he read Crummey's poem 'Something New' with a smile, because the poem has a beautiful ending.

Andy thought, deeper than a crisis." I am a catfish." said Andy, "As an analogy. You know what everyone the letters a, g, and e are cool and all, when the days come when we can put a really P in front of the a, g, and e and combine get stuck on it, then we shall slash will have a page we can get stuck on and turn I guess. Simple and complex as that. Seth do you know the song 'Rock the Casbah.' Who is put it period?"

Mr. Welchberry looked at Red and had a tear.

"I am going to die any way without her," said Andy, "Trains and mustangs, even thou slash though." Andy laughs and says, "The horse is my ivy of thee lande, dirt and sandy, so I guess I am free and lande, oh oh so grande, ch, comprehende. Shall bow out most respectfully and with spine, and so closer to my heart- ha" and he sang 'Closer to My Heart' by Ratt.

Ah!

I listen to you, are you listening to me

The way that you are, it's easy to see
Feelings for you, now I feel free
I'm lost in time

You broke your promises
Fallen out of love
You broke your promises
Fallen out of love
&c &c

After Andy sang the song, he went to the rest room to settle his nerves.

Red looked at Mr. Welchberry, and said, I don't think time can help him. He knows I am sure he is going to have to let go, and it's killing him, not to mention what all he's been through prior to ever meeting her. It is a blessing, even though it is not turning out good. I know one thing love is a powerful force in all forms. Andy knows it could be worse. Love is simply too valuable to lose. It's the motivation and the reason for living, when you get right down to it.

"Where there is great love, there are always miracles," said Mr. Welchberry quoting Willa Cather.

Andy looked into the mirror in the rest room, washed his face, and rinsed out his mouth. He looked back and said, "Unconditionally I love the blockages too. Gosh all the memories are charged, fully. Love seems unimportant to folks anymore. I surrendered to love and forces are causing this. I feel like I am the only one seeing this. Oh well. Pace of life, whatever. Gifted by God with the only expectation, the true awareness of it. That's it. Actions, words, and time. As a man I have been protecting my heart in relationship alternatives, because why, it's simple I am in love with her, and I conquered infidelity. Oh and prayer, can't forget that important tool. What a valuable in-depth experience, alright? Now Andy compose yourself."

"There are many beautiful truly un-loved women out there, many, and I am sure, lifting would come, but what is that. Where does that stand, to the standing of my heart, and no matter how much we love someone, they belong to God. I am in love every possible way in possibly being there for her, giving, simple as that, and making love that is a whole other story. The body may remember but the soul knows."

And Andy doesn't know that a woman that does not speak English knows.

Newfoundland and Labrador, St. John:

Bishop's Falls Trestle, Marble Mountain, the Torgant Mountians,Mountian-Humber

River, Pinware River, Churchill Falls, originally known as Grand River, starts from Ashuanipi Lake and empties into Lake Melville, Bonne Bay, Red Bay, Witless Bay, Point Amour, Plum Point, Fogo Island, Cape Spear, Signal Hill, Humber Valley, Coroy Valley, Ferryland, Gros Morne National Park, Terra Nova National Park, L'Anse aux Meadows, Twillingate, Bonavista Peninsula, and the Port aux Basques. St. Martins Caves, Fallsview Park, I wonder if Agnes Walsh, Tom Dawe, or George Murray have ever been to the Meeting of Two Worlds, the Arches, or walked the Blow Me Down Nature Trail, seen the Reversing Rapids, furthermore hear the whales sing Oh Canada?

Newfoundland and Labrador, St. John Railways:

The Newfoundland Railway began in 1882, the St. John's Street Railway Company began in 1897, the Botwood Railway began in 1908, the Riviere Romaine Railway began in 1950, the Quebec North Shore and Labrador Railway began in 1951, the Wabush Railway, Arnaud Railway and Bloom Lake Railway began in 1953, the Cartier Railway began in 1963, and the Wabush Lake Railway began in 1963.

Newfoundland and Labrador, St. John Poets:

The first Poet I found was Des Walsh, and his poems "Ambition," and "March 3, 1999 - Notes on an upcoming anniversary," are poems with deep wisdom and vast perspectives.

The second Poet I was Randall Maggs, and his poem "Guys like Pete Goegan," and writings about hockey are intense, a style of writing much needed. Randall's persepective brings the reader first hand into the sport and the reality of hockey.

The third Poet I found was Agnes Walsh, and her poetry is themed in life, love, nature, and tradition. Agne's poems, "Almost a Word," "Homecoming to the End," "Going Around With Bachelors," "The Laying Out," "Patricks Cove," "Percy Janes Boarding the Bus," and "Placentia," are poems that take the reader to place, and life with imagery and things that truly show life, a world that is solid and good.

The fourth Poet I found was Carmelita McGrath, and her poems "Booman," and "My Heart Beats Kelly," are brightly intense, her capturing perspectives stops the readers' mind feet, and stops the reader to think in "Awe" furthermore to capture things for themselves in 'Awe."

The fifth Poet I found was Patrick Lane, and his poetry is themed in animals, and their importance along with childhood and its importance, divinity- its importance, nature- nature's brutality, life-with sympathy, love-precious love, and sadness-with beauty. Patrick's poems, "And of the Measure of Winter We are Sure," "Dispensation,"

"Informis," "Limbo," "Midden," "Mute Swans," "Sada," "Stars," "Submission," and "Wild Horses," are foundation like. Pain can be felt reading these poems, and so can strength be felt, superb poetry with a heart of empathy pounding.

The sixth Poet I found was John Steffler, and his poetry seems kicked back at first like cruising in a Mercedes then quickly, and quietly his poetic vehicle takes you through rough terrain, themed in deep life themes, as childhood, nature, animals & insects, and for sure love in a sweet-original perspective way, cleverly exotic & erotic. John's poems, "Beating the Bounds," "Invited In," "March 22," "That Night We Were Ravenous," and "The Green Insect," are definitively creative.

The seventh Poet I found was Michael Crummey, and his poetry is themed in family, Canada, life's deepness, love, nature and place. Michael's poems, "Bread," "Making the Fish," "Rivers/Roads," and "What's Lost," are beautiful and eloquent.

The eighth Poet I found was Patrick Warner, and his poetry is themed in family, animals and nature, and life. Patrick's poems, "Basilisk," "The Therapist," The Bacon Company of Ireland," Pig Lyric," and "The Pig Narrative," are innocent on the surface but hardcore to the bone.

The ninth Poet I found is a Poet that goes by the name of Riley Dazzle0941, and his poetry "14 in 18," "Salbahe," "Greatest Hits," "20 Things I Want to Say, (Grownups Read Things They Wrote As Kids) " "Balka," "Can I?," "Manila: The Last Ten Years" is themed in poetry and humor, and his poetry wants me to write poetry like his. lol

The tenth Poet I found was Adam Pierce-Critchley, and his poems, "Abdullah Atalar," "All The Trees Have Needles," "Head Wound," "I Feel Guilty It's Easy," "I first heard it about DJ's." "Irish Sea," "This One Took Effort," and "Watching a Horror Movie," are humorous and witty, mind opening, and you know he is not a boring person.

The eleventh Poet I found was George Murray, and his poems, "A Moments Autograph," "Cowboy Story" "Dante's Shepherd," "Exit Strategy," "Frame-Drag," "The Hunter," "Rush," are caring, with deep empathy, understanding, and for sure wise.

The twelfth Poet I found was Tom Dawe, and his poetry is themed in childhood, family, life, and love. Tom's poems, "A Fairy Tale," "Peppermint Rock," "Riddle," "Salmon," "The Bogey Man," and many more are brilliant and life/thought provoking, a thinking kind needed.

Chapter 11-New Brunswick, Canada

January 31, 2014

Men and timber were everywhere in the noisy shipyard. Red noticed the ships were definitely from England, the power of the King, Red thought, and he felt something powerful here, and something powerful was approaching. Red noticed many descendants from Ireland and France. British troops and reporters were everywhere too. They all seem to be in a hurry. The forest behind Red was none like he has ever seen before, and Red knew why they wanted this land, for battleships, homes, bridges and railroad ties. Red laughed inside because he thought of furniture, and said to himself; make them great, because they won't make furniture anymore on a basis like this. Majestic are the trees, for our everyday needs, ya I know Red thought, but, well, looking at these beautiful trees sure does make ones worries go away.

British troops were moving fast in sleighs, Red thought, what was going on? He felt that he and Andy were not the only ones in exile here. Red heard a train, and thought, This was his call, so he hurried himself to where the Choo Chooing was coming from, and this train was The Maritime Express.

Red came across a bridge being built, a walking bridge, logs were this way and logs were that way, a kind of bridge he has never seen before. Life was everywhere, here on the Dungarvon River. There were a lot of logs in the river, and workers dancing on them.

A big Irishman shouted "Come on, boys, we'll make Dungarvon shake!"

There was a wolf howling in the woods, and a man came out of the woods, and Red laughed inside and thought, If that man is a werewolf I'd, and before Red thought anymore, the man called out to Red and he was the poet Michael Whelan. He was also a bookkeeper for lumber operators, so he was curious of Red, and as he got closer Michael laughed. "Well you finally made it to New Brunswick. I got a tele-wire telling me you were coming this way."

Oh ya, said Red and asked, And who told you?

"I can't tell you, because if I did. I would have to write a poem about it," said Michael and laughed saying, "Alexander McDougal, but you are alone."

Sandy, said Red, Oh ya, great. I like him, and Red looked behind Michael, and Michael said, "Ah, yes the allegiance of Ghosts, the Whooper, and they tell me you and your friend have a long way to go, to be a global master peace keeper. Let's take a walk; you are used to walking aren't you? I do have a friend with a horse and wagon. I have much to show you, so let's do that, let's take the wagon."

When Red looked at Michael Whalen he could tell that love was altering his life like Andy, and Red didn't say anything about Andy.

Yes, walking is amazing, said Red, I save lives by walking.

"I walk too," said Whalen with a smile, "Save lives? You know, I have mingled prose with poetry and hope to issue next year a little volume of history of the highest interest. Save lives, by walking, funny Red."

Red and Whalen walked and chit chatted about poetry and trains as they made their way to the poet Charles G.D. Roberts homestead for a wagon. There was warmth there, family too who were mostly poets and story tellers. The sister of Charles who was Jane Elizabeth MacDonald and her son, Cuthbert Goodridge MacDonald, furthermore many friends who wrote poetry were there. The moon and snow were beautiful, and so was Whalen, the way he looked at Red, because Red didn't have on snow shoes, and Red could tell the difference. The families dog Nestor came running up to them.

"Oh that's Nestor" said, Whalen, "He wants a pat on the head and to hear a poem. This is the place Red, a family of poets, and maybe Bliss Carmen is here, their cousin poet. Young people see visions and dream dreams here."

Once there and inside, Red noticed many blind children. Whalen looked at Red and introduced everyone to Red, and Whalen said, Elizabeth works at the school for the blind.

Red smiled and said, Nice to meet you all, and that is one of the greatest things I know. Elizabeth you are their colors of their lives. Red noticed she had a stern concern in her eyes, and Red could tell she was a realm. Red admired her earrings too.

Charles G.D. Roberts came out of his den and said, "Cuthbert please get some more fire wood, We have guests. Have a seat gentlemen, make yourself comfortable." He was an original looking man, with a thick mustache.

Elizabeth smiled and said, "I will make cocoa."

Red was getting comfortable, but a bit confused of all poets here. He didn't realize he was in the home of a poetic dynasty. Cuthbert was a good looking lad, and he was talking to a blind girl. "I shall return, we have guests, and we love guests." Cuthbert put on his winter clothes. Red noticed Cuthbert had an odd look in his eyes. Cuthbert smiled at Red, and said to everyone, "Maybe the Gray Master is out there." And out the door Cuthbert went.

Whalen looked at Red and said, "A giant wolf, and his pack isn't much smaller they he, according to the tracks we have found in the snowy woods."

Red reached down, and tightened his belt. Red was feeling he was a prisoner in this dream. Red looked at the door and then at Whalen, but didn't say nothing.

The little girl then spoke, and said, "Someone here smells like a train," and everyone laughed.

The poet William Bliss Carman came walking through the door stomping his snowy boots on the floor, and then taking them off. As he sat on a stool he proclaimed, "Where there is writing there is a writer. Where there is planning there is a planner. Where there is a building there is a builder. Where there is a miracle there is a God! Oh and it's cold out there."

And this made Red smile.

Carmen went towards the fire to warm up and said, "Set me a task in which I can put something of my very self, and it is a task no longer; it is joy; it is art."

And this made Red smile again.

Carmen fixed his hair by brushing off snow, and his frozen tips were melting. "Oh Maritine, oh maritime," he sung.

"Where is Richard Hovey?" Charles G.D. Roberts asked. Richard Hovey was an American poet who collaborated with Bliss Carmen.

"At the Club," Carmen replied, "He is keeping an eye on the British Troops, and as he says, The prate of the wealth of nations, as if it were bought and sold, The wealth of nations is men, not silk and cotton and gold."

"Yes, they are interested in the southern United States' cotton," Charles G.D. Roberts replied and looked at Red with a curious eye. Roberts thought about Red, You can't be a Copperhead?

Carmen looked at Red and said, "In London, I have passed for a young American writer." But his smile wasn't complete, so Red assumed it was because he was Canadian and not American, furthermore that look from Roberts, puzzled Red. Was it because Red was black? Red noticed a turquoise ornament on a silver chain, exactly like the one Mad Bear gave him, and this about took Reds' breath away, but Red hid this emotion, thoughts, and felt something again powerful going on.

Elizabeth returned with hot cocoa for everyone and behind her was a boy carrying a tray, and he walked slowly because he was blind, but he was smiling. A man was behind the boy and he was the poet, James Hogg. Red knew what the first-class nuisance was about by stories from Andy, and their plans for poetry for the blind. James Hogg was reciting his poem 'A Boys Song.'

The dream was getting warmer and warmer. Hogg then kept his eyes on Red, and Hogg had a look that could see right through Reds thoughts, and Hogg smiled. Hogg was holding a book, and dropped it, and he said, "No, I paid so much for this book." And as he picked it up, he examined it like it was a newborn child.

The wind was picking up outside, and they grew worried about Cuthbert, and Hogg was worried about his sheep. The poet Theodore Goodridge Roberts was in another room writing poetry and Charles G.D. Roberts called for him to join them in their nightly poetry and stories. Charles G.D. Roberts grabbed his Winchester, and sat down. He looked at his rifle, wiped it some, and told them the story about the Trapper and The Gray Master.

Red loved this with every fiber of his body, he was finally getting scared, healthy it was he thought, and it has been a long time.

Charles G.D. Roberts began his story of 'The Gray Master' and little Cuthbert was on his mind.

Carmen grabbed his turquoise ornament, and said with fear, "If the Gray Master kills my flock of sheep," He then recited some poetry of his, dear to his soul.

The grave-tree
Let me have a scarlet maple
For the grave-tree at my head,
With the quiet sun behind it,
In the years when I am dead."

The little girl blurts out, "I want to hear The Solitary Woodsman. The Gray Master is scary for me."

Charles G.D. Roberts smiled and said, "We have a new quest, and heeds to marvel of seeing this sinister gray beast, with the murderous fangs."

A master predator Red thought.

Carmen recited again,

The grave-tree
Let me have a scarlet maple
For the grave-tree at my head,
With the quiet sun behind it,
In the years when I am dead."

This was getting intense. Red was fascinated by the descriptions of the wolf's green eyes.

Red was thinking and Charles G.D. Roberts went on telling the story, and Red's deep focus heard.

"No one knew why this wolf was so big and the settlers of the Quah-Davic Valley could not guess. Maybe it's one of the old Acadian superstitions, simply enough by saying he was a loup-garou, or werewolf. But simply maybe a great Alaskan timber-wolf, no one has solved the mystery. Charles G.D. Roberts picked up a short handled ax. He took his two fingers, and slid down the blade to see how sharp it was. As he done this he went into the parts about Arthur Kane seeing the Gray Masters' long muzzle up-stretched towards the moon.

Red remembered a wolf in his dreams so he looked at the door again. Red felt that Charles G.D. Roberts had no fear of the Gray Master and wanted Cuthbert to have no fear either.

"And Kane wondered what strong command from their leader could have kept them silent when all their ancient instincts bade them answer," said Charles G.D. Roberts.

Was Red witnessing the first days of demise of the earths ecosystems?

Cuthbert on the other hand was trotting in the quiet moonlit shallow valley with a train station about 1km from where he was. The snow was falling just right, not to heavy and not to light. He loved the snow, and the cold air clinging close to the ground. Cuthbert heard the sound of a train coming and it sounded like a banshee. The sound was just as glass bends light by making light move more slowly through it. The inversion layer of cold air bends sound because sound moves more slowly through cold air. Instead of a Choo Choo, it sounded like Whoo Whoo, and it echoed all through the forest, so he wanted to wait for the train to watch it arrive at the station. To his surprise, although he was hearing the sound coming from behind a hill, the train wasn't appearing. After several minutes he gave up, and walked away, and finally he saw the train arriving. The hills were reflecting the sounds of the train and Cuthbert remembered the Gray Master. Cuthbert decided to go to the station, but walked slow and he was cautious. Once there he hid behind a tree to see who was coming off the train. A box car opened up, and British troops walked out, and down ramps with their horses. The Conductor came out to put down the stair steps, and out came Lord Durham. Cuthbert's eye brows nearly reached his hair line. Lord Durham was with his top hat on, and he looked like a conqueror of crisis. Cuthbert hurried home as fast as he could without betraying haste. He trotted on, heedlessly three or four paces ahead, ahead of anything, he thought, "I have to run faster than the Gray Master too."

Charles G.D. Roberts told them many stories of the 'Kings of Exile' and one by one they all fell asleep, but Red and Elizabeth. Elizabeth placed blankets over them. Red looked at the last of the fire wood burning in the fireplace, when Cuthbert came through door out of breath, and fell to the floor. He looked up at them, and said, "The trains at the water tower and Lord." Cuthbert passed out from exhaustion, but they knew that Lord Durham was here, and they were out of fire wood. Why was Lord Durham here? Charles G.D. Roberts questioned himself, and thought as he picked up Cuthbert to take the boy to his bedroom. Elizabeth followed them after taking off Cuthberts' boots.

Red looked at the fire dying out. He remembered the owl that came through the chimney, and scattered fire on the floor back in America. Red arose, and said, I must leave, they are here for me. So Red looked at everyone sleeping, and this rang a bell. This was Dread, so Red left the dynasty of Charles G.D. Roberts family and company.

Horses galloping, clip clops, clip clops, and Red walked the road looking for the train station. Once around a sharp turn in the road, they were there, Lord Durham and British Troops.

"America is a refuge for rebels, but you all switched that around," said Lord Durham and laughed, "I will have to write to London, and tell them all about you. You are a rebel, but a rebel of a different kind. Lord Durham laughed and spoke again, "We ended up on the wrong side of the rock where its cold, and everything is on a level of secrecy. Look, gather faster is all around, the British are tripping, and the U.S.A. are tripping, furthermore I have a head ache."

Red didn't know what was going to happen, so he just stood there in amazement. "Hang him," said a trooper.

"He is from America, a black man," said Lord Durham, "Why hang him. He is not a ring leader. No trial will help, until the whole world knows. He is not a danger to the welfare of poetry and the railroads. I will not help the mockery of Justice, Hanging, Banishing, Freedom, what about? Red there are so many cowards and double dealings, and the restless folks of Canada trust me, and trust you."

Red says, Poetry is like Gods fence and we found the gaps. Then you understand?

"Softly Red, softly," said Lord Durham, "Take him prisoner, to Bermuda. I will consider this matter with high regards. I am concerned and I have influence."

Red laid there thinking about survival drives while awaking and thinking about love, his yearning for service, furthermore thinking about all the powerful energies that move us, like dreams, like the dream he just had.

Red got up, and ready to dare and confront life today. There are no boundaries, He thought, only what we let others perceive of us, and if we believe in their perceptions, then it gets ugly. Just as what Poets may think of this if I tell them, Poets are not like music stars, Music stars like to socialize and party with their fans. Most of them anyway. Poets like to demoralize and have no part of their fans, most of them anyway. Also Black men need to make sure they acknowledge who they quote; I am tired of seeing black men bite. Red looked outside the windows of the train, and could tell the weather outside was biting too. If only Poets would toughen up like photographers. Trees were cracked open, and cliffs looked like they were shrieking. Icicles were everywhere at the train station. Ice was even covering bicycles as the train pulled up to the McAdam Railway Station. I need to take up photography too, Red thought to himself.

"Icicles are called Conkerbells here," said Mr. Welchberry to Andy as Red sat down with them in the dining car.

"Good Morning Red," said Andy, "It's beautiful to me. I find it great that our studies lead to the poet Mary Dalton, a 'Time of Icicles' and icicles are everywhere. They fascinate me. There is something about icicles."

"You two are learning how poets speak in various voices, of their places and psychic territories, and there's such a diversity of language exploration in Canada," said Mr. Welchberry.

Andy wondered why he really said that, like to get off the subject of icicles or something, like they were keys to something, maybe a key to stop time.

Andy spoke, Mary Dalton says, "The aim must be to gain a past from which we might spring, rather than that from which we seemed to derive."

Red laughed and said, Very interesting Andy that could be applied to a lot and deep. For sure to our past lives. She's a child of an oral culture and a print culture. Mary Dalton says, The best poetry is an exploration. It's the making of something new which others can then build on. Andy we should buy cameras, because yes, those icicles are beautiful.

"We sprang alright, and still springing. Though never forgetting where we derive, even if it's from a cliché Springfield like land," said Andy, and laughed. "There are two things Mary Dalton says I love, Writing poetry is original research into the language, and with that she asks, Do you think the alphabetical order purposely points to a larger poetic dialectal/dialectical kind of alphabetism? And this Red, the imagination is its own country. You seriously have to love all that. She's a contender."

Andy it's going to take a life time and then some, said Red, She has a serious point.

"I hear ya," said Andy. Andy then thought about his studies. The Treasury of the World's Greatest Speeches, and one of the greatest speeches was from his Grandmother, and no matter how painful her speech maybe, it was something Andy had to take in.

If you love someone, set them free and if that someone comes back, it was meant to be. Andy remembered telling her and the one he loves, that we belong to God, so it's all up to God, and us also though.

"And I care. Alright Red also I like what Mary Dalton says about the imagination," said

Andy, "It is a country. I love that."

Me too, replied Red, She loves the cento like you Andy. The cento she says is on one level a little anthology.

This made Andy's elbows grow tense, and Andy said, Yes much to work with, like CSI proof, Jurassic Park style.

Many people were getting off the train and Andy thought again about what his Grandmother said, and said to himself, Not the Poetry Train, but I may have to get off this train of love for a while, and see if it makes its way back to me, with the passenger I have in my heart.

Mr. Welchberry, spoke as everyone on the train looked at everyone outside in the cold at the station. "All of these peoples' lives are connected in some way with the river, either as walkers, fishermen, sewage workers, ferrymen, water abstractors, boat builders etc. We will be riding by the famous Dart section of Newfoundland. Quite a beauty indeed."

Seth played the Scottish ballad 'The Twa Corbies' The 'Damh the Bard' version as new passengers boarded upon the train.

Andy smiled and said, "To late, the Blue Jay has come to me," and Andy laughed and recited a poem he just wrote,

Winters' Blue Jay

It
should say
Candor all over my face
It can show Tact too,
I have seen it in its place

In mans
crete cazoo- cabaret,
I just got cut like the company
and matter I converse

A
 genuine dime
for listening and in time,
time shall transverse

Today
I thought of the Tree of Many Souls
And how funny to me

my time still rolls
Time as the same as I am now
As time the same as I was before

The forest again, looks different
Wonderful things happen I do say, more

"I agree" said a Winter's Blue Jay
"The power is within you
I recognize talent,"
and says "That you, have it too."

My photographic memory
Still looks into her eyes

"No one ever knows" said the Winters' Blue Jay
"Because some believe they have no soul, and if they do
this is why the eyes desire those that think they don't,
and some wicked magic has it all twisted around."

So you are saying I know now
But I really I knew then, it was just a gap in time
where my soul had to spend?

"Not really, but maybe," the winter's Blue Jay replied.
"Hey don't feel bad, look at all these branches.
Not to many people reach this life in this life this far.
No one likes the songs I sing
Blue on Blue, but clarity and vision is inside of you"

Whoever sent you, tell them thanks

"I would if I could, but they should be down by the river banks"

Cold

"Hey, I didn't make the forest, let alone the trees."

I hear ya, that's what I've been screaming

"Then you'll be fine down by the river. Screaming, maybe other birds think I scream?"

Now is the time to work at being even more keen.

"Stand alone and say what needs to be said"

Thank you winters' Blue Jay, I love the spiritual realm
And to Bermuda to the crows, I never did like anything they've said
But I know why they are.

"What's funny about life," said Andy, "Even if we are set free, and want to return to where are hearts are or belong, we can't because the other half gets lost in the forest. Freaking hilarious. As I have said in the poem, thank you beautiful spiritual realm, because if your realm wasn't there, things sure would be lost, completely."

Seth was silent, and felt Andy was saying, Hey you, forces are using you to get to the good of the world, and I am protected, so be careful what you do, in a poetic way of course. Red didn't know what to think, and the train started to dart; dart into the views of Dartmouth.

Andy laughed and Mr. Welchberry asked, "Seth can you play the Back Bay Hill song, by Ed McCurdy for me Diddle Dumb."

Seth laughed and said, "Why sure." And Seth played away.

Mr. Welchberry was truly enjoying this and once the song was over he said, "Seth, you must know Long May Your Big Jib Draw by Arthur R. Scammell, because we need to teach these young men this about folks here."

"I sure do," said Seth, "A one, two, a one, two, three, four." And Seth played away again.

And Mr. Welchberry sung, "Some folks say cheerio when they wave the hand to you. The English say goodbye, the French they say adieu; But when Newfoundlanders part, this wish leaps from the heart: Long may your big jib draw!

Andy and Red looked at each other and thought about all of the people at the McAdam Train Station.

Mr. Welchberry looked at them and said, "Long may your big jib draw! It means may luck attend you."

Thank you Mr.Welchberry, They both replied.

They looked at the rocky banks. The waters looked turquoise and this made Red smile. Ferries were out on the river. What to do in a castle Andy thought. Just like maybe what to do in a Christmas card that no one really cares they've received. Andy just smiled and thought again, I'll just write on the train, and hopefully the conductor is paid attention to, instead of all attention in tearing apart the train. It's better to have rode the train then to not have rode the train at all.

"Much folklore on Dartmoor," said Mr. Welchberry.

I can tell, said Red, It's beautiful here.

Andy then thought, there should be no poetry contest on poetrytrain.com, just the Alphonso G. Newcomer Award. Unless it was a Forty/Forty split between the poets and the judges, but with a twist. The other twenty percent well. Andy then noticed, what two people have said in a private group, and left the group, has really but some false negative e aura in there. And a person knows when someone is talking about them behind their back, it really isn't all that complicated. Andy looked at the beauty out there and thought, How can someone claiming nature, love, forgiveness and God, be so cruel, all around I see this, and why do I, Andy thought, Get the imagery of a toddler running around with a shitty diaper, and thinking it's stinking funny. Well it goes to show; when you give a hundred percent to someone it's only a matter of time before they shit on you. To many branches to appreciate a branch. Thank you winters' Blue Jay.

Andy then spoke, "As Mary Dalton says Red, Poetry contests can be dangerous, but also rewarding. So here's my scoop. It is a new year am I correct? Well, here it goes."

"Come on," said Mr. Welchberry, "You are near the last spike here in Canada, or should I say the first." And he laughed his iconic laugh. "You know the poet Edwin John Pratt wouldn't leave you two out."

Andy gets taken back to the memory of the beginning days of his online poetry experiences. He knew then, life was going to change for the good, but how can he have failed on the most important part, unless something was attached, that steals, what was the true message of the Winters' Blue Jay? Andy began again to talk about the contest, when Mr. Welchberry spoke, "An Eyes Right."

"And the heart knows a hand," replied Andy and told them, "The railroad represented a fundamental challenge to reality, she, yes the railroad is a she, she changed social classes, and this one is not a traveling coffin." Andy then wrote this in his notebook.

The Penny Dreadful.
On the Poetry Train. Poems for the Rail:
Killing Space, And Left Alone In Time:
Just Imagine When We Get There.
The Train is Coming.
I Hear You Momma!

"Giant refreshing," said Mr. Welchberry, as he wiped his mouth from a fine breakfast. Connie has great timing bringing Red his usual.

Thank you Connie, said Red, I like being larger then my prejudices, and whatever dislocation I caused, I view it superior to the emptiness I replaced.

"Now you are talking like a train," said Andy, "But you have to be careful, because someone will tell you what time it is, and Andy laughed. "Okay seriously now about the contest."

Poetry Trains' Rotating Poem Competition Riding & Writing the E-Rails? Poetrytrain.com is a legal website, with a real bank account.

- The Judging Panel 40%.
- Selected Poets 40%.
- Webteam, webmasters 10% (costs & maintenance).
- Website 5%.
- 5% Kiddy for the Alphonso G. Newcomer Award or some kind of treasure hunt, riddle, quiz, &c.
- All is responsible for marketing ideas & plans. & All is also responsible for the covers and selection to publish.
- Taxes and yes we have to think about taxes.
- For the year of 2014 the judges will select poems for the book.
- Now this is where we need to get tight.
- (Do we need a section where poets submit poems, without their identity to the judges?
- Is this important and why is it important?
- But to see who they are, we can keep track of that somehow like, we are the only two that sees, or once the judges select the poem, it becomes a public poem, but only until the book is published.
- For the year of 2014 the judges will select poems for the book.
- All themes & styles welcome.
- Once the year is up the judges will reveal themselves, and pass on the judging torch to the poets selected for the year of 2014 to judge the following competition. And yes a record book will need to be placed out first, a full written document of all, and what poems and %s and the whole part of all fractions.
- Also the judges will be asked to submit poems also, and this can be done with the anonymous system the Selected Poets have a take at, once selected, they can get to see what the judges sees.
- This system could run smoothly once everyone gets a feel for their responsible role.
- I will create a legal digital contract so all parties including me, Poetry Train sees through all processing & publishing of this completion completes.

Mr. Welchberry said, "I remember a CBC Radio broadcast of Edwin John Pratts' 75th birthday. I think it was in 1958. He was asked for a little advice for the poets of tomorrow as well as his advice about the public light. Pratt said, We have moved away from Clarity expression to Insanity expression. Never forget your heritage. Leave it in your writings. And be thankful if your poetry survives you."

So we are poetry Sustainers in a way? Red suggested. Well Andy lets run that by the members of the website.

"Will do," Andy replied. "Wasn't Emily Dickinson's' dog named Carlo?" Andy asked. "Pratt's poem 'Carlo' is amazing, what an heroic dog. There is no record of the S.S. Ethie's dog being named Carlo, and they chalked this up to Pratts' poetic license. Have poets become fearful of revealing who they are, or go out on a limb?"

Andy laughs about the branch again. "Okay Red, I'll write it up and post." Andy then thought about his dogs he has cared for, and his horse. He then thought about poems he had written her while he lived in Kentucky. And he thought a book with photos of Poets and their pets would be grand too.

I'll tell you who is interesting, said Red, I found the poet W. Irving Fogwill.

And this made Mr. Welchberry smile.

Red expressed some of Fogwills life, He went to work with the railway at the age of fourteen, eventually became involved with the Brotherhood of Railway Clerk.

As Red was browsing while reading. Woo, we have a bad ass poem on our hands about the youth, entitled, 'Prelude to Doom.'

Fogwill belts away, and he is one of the first, to see weaponistic dark side of mankind.

the wolfish old men,
The foolish old men-who never learn.

Waving the same old flags-the old men
Bidding youth to die for the same old lies.

Mr. Welcberry said, "They have moved up some serious notches nowadays, they have T.V. Commercials, be all you can be and stuff.

"The old and grinning skulls of war. Intense," said Andy after reciting a line from the poem too.

Mr. Welchberry then spoke, "Fogwill use to say," they say, Broken heads make for bad press, while a hearty squeeze of the testicles induces political moderation without a fuss." So I guess he was an intense man."

"And here is another poet that knows how to hammer away," said Andy, "M. Travis Lane." Andy looked out the window, and said, "Her poem 'Portobello' tears me to pieces. Ha ha," Andy laughed and said, "And her poem 'Who Is This Poem Talking To?"

Poems 'Print,' and 'The Turtle Who Holds Everything Up,' raises the eyebrows Andy, Red proclaimed.

Andy laughed and said, "Ya, and her poem 'Protext' is great and cracks me up. She says in the poem, But poetry cannot tell us that. The ship floats while we sail in it. Ah ha," Andy laughs again and says, "The Train rolls while we ride in it."

Her poem 'The View from Under the Bookcase' cracks me up, said Red, Whoever verses her riddle right?

"A riddle it is," Andy replied. "The view from under the bookcase isn't bad." Andy laughs, "hmm the fool moon, and love."

Connie brought everyone Canadian apple maple pie, and the day went smoothly.

New Brunswick:

The Appalachian Range Route, the wonders the Bay of Fundy, Bonny River, Saint John River, Miramichi River, Restigouche River and the Baie des Chaleur, Acadian Coastal Drive, Morrissey Rock, the Confederation Bridge, and I wonder if Douglas Lockhead, and Marilyn Lerch know that there is more RxR history in New Brunswick Canada then anywhere in Canada and the United States??

New Brunswick Railways:

The St. Andrews and Quebec Railway began in 1836, the Shediac and Saint John Rail Road began in 1836, the Chignecto Railway Company began in 1840, the European and North American Railway began in 1840, the New Brunswick Railway Company began in 1846, the York and Carleton Mining Company began in 1847, the Canada, New Brunswick and Nova Scotia Railway Company began in 1847, the Halifax and Quebec Railway began in 1848, the Saint John and Shediac Railway began in 1849, the Grand Falls Railway Company began in 1850, the St. Stephen Railroad Co. began in 1851, the Hillsborough Plaister and Railway Company began in 1851, the Magaguadivic Railway Company began in 1852, the Nipisiquit and Seaboard Railway Company began in 1953, the Lewy's Island Railroad Company began in 1855, the European and North American Railway began in 1860, the Albert Railway Company began in 1864, the Woodstock Railway Company began in 1864, the St. Stephen Branch Railroad began in 1864, the Peoples Street Railway Company began in 1866, the Fredericton Railway Company began in 1866, the Gagetown and Petersville Railway Company began in 1866, the Miramichi, Richibucto & Shediac Branch Rly began in 1866, the St. Andrews Deep Sea

Wharf and Railway began in 1867, the Houlton Branch Railway began in 1867, the Carleton, City of Saint John Branch Railroad began in 1870, the Chatham Branch Railroad Company began in 1870, the Chatham Railway Company 1870, the Eastern Railway Company began in 1870, the Temiscouata Railway began in 1870, the St. Croix and Penobscot Railroad began in 1870, the St. Martins and Upham Railroad began in 1871, the Fredericton and St. Mary's Bridge began in 1871, the Intercolonial Railway began in 1872, the Canada Railway and Coal began in 1872, the Grand Southern Railway Company began in 1872, the Northern and Western Railway Co of N.B. Began in 1872, the Dalhousie Branch Railway Company began in 1873, the New Brunswick and Canada Railroad began in 1873, the Petitcodiac and Elgin Branch Railway began in 1874, the Sunbury and Queen's County Railway began in 1874, the Northern Railway Company began in 1874, the New Brunswick and Prince Edward Railway began in 1874, the Caraquet Railway Company began in 1874, the Consolidated European & North American began in 1875, the Kent Railway Company began in 1875, the Intercolonial Railway's Nova Scotia-Lévis began in 1876, the Hillsborough Branch Railway Company began in 1876, the International Railway began in 1877, the St. Andrews and St. Croix Railway began in 1878, the Saint John and Maine Railway Company began in 1878, the Albert Southern Railway began in 1878, the Elgin Petitcodiac and Havelock Railroad began in 1878, the Harvey Branch Railroad Company began in 1878, the Atlantic and North-West began in 1879, the Woodstock and Harvey Railway began in 1881, the Canadian Pacific Railway began in 1881, the Saint John Bridge and Railroad Extension Company began in 1881, the Great Southern railroad began in 1882, the St. Andrews Railway began in 1882, the Woodstock Branch Railway began in 1882, the Hampton Railway Company began in 1882, the St. Louis, Richibucto & Buctouche Rly. Began in 1882, the Saint John and Loch Lomond Railway began in 1882, the Calais and St. Stephen Railway Bridge Co began in 1882, the Saint John and North Eastern Railway began in 1883, the Salem and Hillsborough Railroad began in 1984, the Tobique Valley Railway Company began in 1885, the Douglastown Branch Railway Company began in 1885, the Saint John Valley & Riviere du Loup began in 1885, the Restigouche and Victoria Colonization Railway Company began in 1885, the Saint John City Railway began in 1886, the Fredericton Branch Railroad began in 1886, the Northumberland Straits Tunnel Company began in 1886, the St. Stephen and Milltown Railroad began in 1886, the Shediac and Cape Tormentine Railroad began in 1886, the Fredericton Street Railway Company began in 1887, the Woodstock and Centreville Railway began in 1887, the Moncton Street Railway began in 1887, the Saint John and Eastern Railroad Company began in 1887, the Hartland Railway Company began in 1887, the St. Stephen and Milltown Street Railway began in 1887, the York and Carleton Railroad began in 1887, the Buctouche and Moncton Railroad Company began in 1887, the Railroad Leasing & Traffic Co. of N.B. Began in 1888, the Saint John River Railway began in 1888, the Tobique Gypsum & Colonization Railway began in 1888, the Newcastle Railway Company began in 1888, the Sussex, Studholm and Havelock Railway began in 1889, the Temiscouata, Newcastle & Shippegan Railway began in 1889, the Salisbury and Harvey began in 1889, the Shore Line Railway Company began in 1889, the Moncton and Harvey Short Line Railway began in 1889, the New Brunswick and Prince Edward Island Railway began in 1889, the Central and North-Eastern Railway began in

1890, the Moncton Electric Tram-way Company began in 1890, the Shore Line Railway Bridge Company began in 1890, the Eastern Extension Railroad began in 1890, the Western Railway Company began in 1891, the St. Stephen Electric Street Railway began in 1891, the Consolidated Electric Company began in 1892, the Nelson Branch Railway Company began in 1892, the New Brunswick Trunk Line Railway began in 1892, the St. Stephen Nickel Railway Co. began in 1893, the Fredericton, Gibson and Marysville Electric began in 1893, the New Brunswick Coal Company began in 1893, the Queen's County Coal and Railway Company began in 1893, the Moncton and Buctouche Railway began in 1894, the Elgin and Havelock Railway began in 1894, the Baltimore Coal Mining and Railway began in 1894, the Moncton Electric Street Rly, Heat & Power began in 1894, the Woodstock and Houlton Railway began in 1894, the Saint John Railway Company began in 1894, the Southampton and Harvey Railway began in 1894, the Commercial Electric Company began in 1895, the Colonial Iron, Coal and Railway Company began in 1895, the Miramichi Midland Railway began in 1895, the Restigouche and Victoria Railway began in 1896, the Aroostook Junction and Limestone began in 1896, the Barnesville and Norton began in 1896, the Woodstock Electric Rly, Light & Power began in 1896, the Restigouche and Western Railway began in 1897, the Hampton and St. Martins Railway began in 1897, the Alexander Gibson Railway & Manufacturing began in 1898, the Shediac and Coast Railroad Company began in 1899, the South Shore Line Railway Company began in 1900, the Washington County Railway began in 1900, the New Brunswick Coal and Railroad Company began in 1901, the New Brunswick Southern Railway began in 1901, the Atlantic and Quebec Railway began in 1901, the Saint John Valley Railway 1901, the Canada Eastern Railway began in 1902, the Aroostook Valley Railroad Company began in 1902, the Moncton and Eastern Railway began in 1902, the Fredericton and Western Railway began in 1902, the Alexander Gibson Company began in 1903, the Quebec, New Brunswick and Nova Scotia Rly began in 1903, the Kent Northern Extension Railway began in 1903, the International Railway of New Brunswick began in 1903, the Atlantic Quebec and Western Railroad began in 1903, the Beersville Coal and Railway Company began in 1903, the National Transcontinental Railway began in 1903, the New Brunswick Central Railway Co. began in 1904, the Herring Cove Railway Company began in 1904, the Tobique and Campbellton Railway began in 1904, the Twin Trees Mines Railway began in 1904, the Interprovincial Railway Bridge Co. of N.B. began in 1904, the Buctouche and Rexton began in 1905, the New Brunswick Coal and Railway began in 1905, the Moncton and Gulf Railway began in 1906, the St. Martin's Railway began in 1906, the Canadian Terminal Railway began in 1907, the North Shore Railway Co., Limited began in 1907, the Salisbury and Albert Railroad Company began in 1909, the Northern New Brunswick and Seaboard Railroad Company began in 1909, the Fredericton and Grand Lake Coal and Railroad Company began in 1910, the Buctouche Railway and Transportation began in 1910, the Saint John and Quebec Railroad began in 1910, the Hartland and Miramichi Railway began in 1910, the Southampton Railway began in 1910, the Moncton Tramway, Electricity & Gas Co. began in 1910, the Albert and Moncton Railway began in 1911, the Caraquet and Gulf Shore Railway Company began in 1911, the Maine Central Railroad Company began in 1912, the St. Croix Docks and Railway began in 1912, the Saint John and Quebec Rly. Bridge Co. began in 1912, the

North Shore Railway & Navigation Co. began in 1912, the Nerepis and Long Island Railway Company began in 1912, the Miramichi Bay Shore Railway began in 1912, the Van Buren Bridge and Railway began in 1913, the Moncton and Northumberland Strait Railway began in 1913, the Saint John Suburban Railway began in 1913, the Moncton and Prince Edward Island Railway and Ferry Company began in 1913, the Grand Falls Electric Railway began in 1914, the Tobique Valley Railway Extension Co. began in 1915, the Canadian Government Railways began in 1915, the Kent Coal and Railway Company began in 1915, the Port Canada Docks Railway Company began in 1915, the Canton and Grand Lake began in 1916, the New Brunswick Power Company began in 1917, the Canadian National Railways began in 1919, the Beaver Coal and Railway began in 1923, the Nepisquit Railway Company 1925, the Moncton Electricity & Gas Company 1934, the VIA Rail Canada 1977, the Canadian Atlantic Railway began in 1988, the New Brunswick Southern Railway Co. Ltd. began in 1995, the New Brunswick East Coast Railway began in 1998, and so many other Railroad's in New Brunswick Canada came to be, and have been lost in history.

New Brunswick Poets:

The first Poet I found was Richard Doiron, and his poetry is themed in love, peace, philosophical, spirituality, and journalistic events of today. Richards' poems, "Ablative Bars," "Eden Resurrected," "Love's Eternal Seal," "My Living Dream," "Rise of the Lesser God," "The Battlefield," "The Magic That She Weaves," "What Tomorrow Brings," and many more are tight, colorful with beat, insightful, but most of all beyond beautiful and wise. Richard's newer poetry is must read, great concerns in matters of today's world, furthermore Richard contributed history and poetry to Chapter 1 of Poetry Train Canada.

The second Poet I found was Carol Knepper, and her haiku on the brain is beautiful and grand. Although her other poems are very to the very beautiful, for me there is a deep love embedded in every line. Carol's poems, "Autumn," "Timespan," "Love," "Step Softly," "I Offer," "Lessons of the Seasons," and "With Nothing Fallen," are for sure soul touching with wisdom.

The third Poet I found was Joe Blades, and his poems, "Hartland" "RE:Call," and "The Dogs," are abstract in an amazing way, punctured life comes to mind. Joe makes the reader think and feel.

The fourth Poet I found was Marilyn Lerch, and her poetry is hard core and we want more poetry Marilyn Lerch. Poems, "What's a Pope Doing Here?/The Greatest Garbage Strike of 2002," and "News Years Day."

The fifth Poet I found was Douglas Lochhead, and he studied at many colleges and hard knocks schools in Canada. I am sure Douglas Lochhead has many more poems his family has, hopefully. Douglas Lochhead's epic poem "Love on the Marsh," is timeless on family, love, and youth, but more than that he knew he was a Poet, a Poet amongst none in person, and he kept 'Love on the Marsh' and he captured all he could for poetry and history. Beautiful defined.

The sixth Poet I found was Rebecca Caissie, and her poetry some may can call theoretical & philosophical and her poetry is alive thought casting-castical; taking all mankind's time and un-winding the baseball of human thought, a gift to us all. Un-Raveling Times-Traveling:

Chapter 12-Nova Scotia, Canada

February 18th 2014

The east coast of Canada held up no totem poles like the west coast, freedom and gold is all most people here wanted to see, Andy assumed, nothing to do with spirituality. At least slavery wasn't present here in Nova Scotia. The Chinese were nowhere to be seen here, but many Irish, Scottish and Arcadians. Transformation was all around. Schooners and Loggers were everywhere like the west coast. Legacy was spewing out of everyone's breath. Andy didn't blink because he didn't want to miss anything. He felt change. Andy seen change, he seen it in the Chignecto Ship Railway, a water railway that moved ships between Fort Lawrence and Tidnish. He also noticed nine horses that muscled the ferry, very impressive Andy thought, and nine webmasters for the Poetry Train. There were so many wonders, and Andy thought, How could anyone miss the Intercolonial Railway Station? This building was immense to Andy as he walked out of the station, and the building was like roofing the federal building in Nashville, Tennessee. Andy thought, This station two stories high, scaffolding, tie off and down indeed. Twelve-twelve with a kick. And here horses and carriages were everywhere thick. Troops were everywhere too, with a look of deep concern about the possibility of an American invasion, and in their eyes you could feel the smallness, furthermore the feeling of being scattered. They kept their eyes on Andy. Andy sensed their attitude, and he watched his own too.

The smell of cattle trains was immense as well. Andy smiled as he looked at three trains parked there, and they were the Blueberry Express, the Flying Bluenose, and the Grasshopper. Many men walked out from the round house and they were the engineers and firemen of these trains. They were engineer George Dorman and firemen Reg McGill; Phillip Devew and Bob Copeland; George Beatty and Fred Dore; and George Murray while the Walking Boss, Daniel Wier who had the reputation of being a hard driver was talking to many Italian railroad laborers along the way. Intimidation's in the air, and was on their faces.

The Blueberry Express, caught Andy's attention again, a mysterious train. He has seen it before he thought, but he has seen many trains, but this one strikes a sense of America to Andy, or was it through Kicking Horse Pass in the Rocky Mountains, Canada where he has seen this train before. Also the Mersey train was arriving from England, an L&M Locomotive, Liverpool-Milton, short-line railways.

Andy did notice Scottish emigrants with little material wealth, a their greater asset by far was their Gaelic language. Andy loved to listen to them talk as he walked around, and this put Andy in awareness. Just about everyone he walked by said, "Halò, Madainn mhath." Meaning, Hello, Good Morning, and this made Andy smile. Andy also overheard things, the popular poet talk in the era was the poet schoolteacher James MacPhersons; 'The Poems of Ossian.' And there was a saying Andy heard, 'A sharing of gold is but brief, but a sharing of song lasts long.' And true that is Andy thought.

Andy noticed the wolf that was following him. The wolf was behind stagecoaches and sleighs, but Andy or the wolf didn't do anything, because it seemed like Andy was the only one that noticed the wolf anyway, but Andy thought, he was the dog that couldn't come home, the dog who was afraid of the electronic fence, the shocking America. He the dog ran to fast through it the first time sort of but not really, so now, he the dog is afraid to come home, and get shocked again. The dog Andy now, actually likes it with the wolves. He cared, but she didn't want to talk to him no more anyhow, Andy thought about all of this as he looked at the wolf.

Andy smiled at the wolf, and Andy wanted to read the newspaper, so he went back into the train station. Once inside he was thinking as he purchased one, and looking at the clerk, you won't see any car crashes here now in these papers with death fatalities. Andy read about naming streets, and a grand picnic celebrating the grand openings of railways. Bands, dancing, fireworks, and sports. Andy said to himself, "That's where I started writing poetry at a family picnic back home when I was young." Andy even picked up a Canadian guide book, like it was needed now, but he did, and smiled because it was furnished by the poet Charles G.D. Roberts. The post master there was a poet too, and he was Angus Morrison Gidney. He seemed to be in a rush, and cleaning up after the morning commuters came in, and out this morning. He looked at Andy and said, "I have a reading to attend on literary and historical topics at the Burnside Cottage or Crossburn, somewhere? I have to go. I am closing now, but I shall return later."

"Okay, have a great day," said Andy as he began to walk out.

Angus Morrison Gidney couldn't get to much in a hurry though, because a mailman came in with a child in his mail bag and said, "We have another boy from America." The mailman also said, "Here is promotional literature of the Dominion Atlantic Railway on Evangeline."

Andy didn't know what to do about this, but didn't want to forget this, to tell Red about mailing kids off to where ever. Andy did ask for a Dominion Atlantic Railway brochure. A telegram came in too, and it was for Andy.

"Are you Andy Sandihands?" Gidney asked.

"Yes," Andy replied.

"This is for you, Mr. Andy Sandihands" said Gidney, "I have to leave gentlemen." So all three left the mail room, and so did the child, and Andy looked deep into his eyes, and said to himself all for you youngster.

Andy read the message from Jimmy New Orleans, What, he thought as he read, "Sandihands, I may never get out, but I am not alone, there are more of my followers out there, with handy hands." Andy didn't know what to think, but as he walked out he heard someone playing piano in the station, and the music played over and over again in Andys' head as he walked around, and he didn't know what the song was, maybe a Louisiana tune. How did they know my last name, I have told no one? Andy asked himself. Andy asked himself this too, What of the boy sent from America, and the parenthood? Jimmy?

The industrial orchestra slowly turned down the volume and questions in Andy's' head. The swishing sound attracted him, so Andy went to where all of this made racket, hissing and clanging, and it was a steal factory near a coal field. The place was dark, the roofs were dark, and coal dust was everywhere. This place was familiar to Andy, but he knew he'd never been there before. He walked into the building and it had a boiler room, an engine room, and the furnaces were blasting some heat and it felt great to Andy. Things seemed to him, to be increasing.

A man spoke coming out of an office or some shop wearing a long plaid cloak and said, "This is where all was made for the whole country. The land of the Kings, Coal and Steel. There is no racism here. Every nationality is here, and everyone gets along."

This man was the poet black smith, Andrew Sheils aka Albyn or known as the Bard of Ellenvale.

"What is the name of yonder dwelling?' Andy asked and said, "No, no-racism should be the King."

Sheils laughed and said, "Yes, a little knew, Love is so terrible when true. That's where I dwell."

Andy laughed and replied, "You too, heaven or hell."

"Poetry has a peculiar affinity to piety and patriotism, yet praise is the breath on which that chameleon a poet exists; and however frail the tenure, it is the alpha and omega of a poets intellectual life,"Andrew Sheils replied and said, "You do know they want us to go to Hub town, Truro. There's a convention going on."

Why did the Tudor period and the Tower of London come to mind, Andy thought.

Andrew Sheils smiled and said, "Well I came here for tools to use at my shop, I'll be seeing you Andy, enjoy Nova Scotia. Andy, the construction of lines was recommended by Lord Durham between Truro, in Nova Scotia, and Shediac and he is around town somewhere."

Sheils left and Andy was full of questions again and thought, A convention, I guess I should go, but I thought this was Hub Town. Andy laughed and said, "Oh I get it, like poetry websites and publishers, they all want to be 'Thee Hub Town.' Like some on Facebook that blocks out real folks in the poetry realm." Before that though, Andy wanted to see the North Atlantic ocean, so he walked there.

Out on the boardwalk things felt good, there was wrestling, boxing and dancing. Andy walked over to a table of pies for sale, and looked around. Andy also looked behind him, because of what Jimmy New Orleans said. Andy didn't notice any men looking at him, but he did notice a lady with dark hair looking at him, and walking towards him.

A man next to him purchasing a pie said to Andy, "I am the Steam-Machine Poet, Byron De Wolfe. I can write forty lines in ten minutes."

This man was the poet George Gordon Byron De Wolfe. Sometimes he shortened it to Byron De Wolfe. He looked young to Andy maybe 17 or older, around the same age Andy started to write poetry, and left home when he was young. Andy liked his last name a lot, De Wolfe, but this wasn't thee wolf that followed Andy or was it? All Andy could do was smile and think this was a cool poet.

De Wolfe said and recited a poem, "I am ready to compose poetical verses for anyone on any subject, verse by the syllable four for a penny."

Here we go to the Pacific!
To the "Hub" a while, adieu!
Fare-you-well, ye troubles civic,
Scenes of grandeur we shall view!
Pullman's train shall give us pleasure,
Naught like it was known before,
All its comfort we shall treasure,
Ere we reach the golden shore!

"I am going to America, Nashua New Hampshire," De Wolfe proclaimed.

And that even sounded poetic to Andy, and he smiled because of De Wolfes' hustle mode.

De Wolfe smiled and he belted out,

Abe Lincoln the Rail Splitter!"

There is a name to ev'ry tongue

Of ev'ry despot bitter –

Since freedom's songs today are sung

For Lincoln, the rail-splitter –

Andy loved this, and the poet John the Hunter -Duvar walked up to them and said, " I bitterly regret my decision to emigrate to a prison of snow and ice, but I have a poem, you two will admire, and it's called "The Emigration of the Fairies."

Andys' eyebrows raised, and he said, "Sweet. De Wolfe liked it too." Andy thought, this is how John the Hunter -Duvar kept Hope alive.

"Yes, I had to create something beautiful out of my misery," said Hunter Duvar.

"Oh it's not that bad," said Andy.

"We shall see," Hunter Duvar replied.

Andy looked up, and a storm was moving in from the sea.

Hunter Duvar looked at it too, and said, "Sea Monsters are out there too."

Andy smiled and thought, The sea is no place for man. What did man care? They all wanted to be here and in America, monsters or not, it was the chance they all took, now that is something.

Railroad engineer Henry George Clopper Ketchum walked up to them and said to Andy, "I fear something, I want to spare ships the annoyance of sailing all the way round Nova Scotia, not by digging a canal across the isthmus of Chignecto, on the border of New Brunswick and Nova Scotia, but by hauling them out of the water onto a pair of parallel railway tracks. It's not as crazy as it sounds, but I feel my work will never get accomplished."

"Wow, I understand," Andy replied, "Me and my friend Red know what you mean, we are like you who need to find the correct people that believe in what we do, regardless of proper funds. We are the worlds men who create fascinations Mr. Ketchum, and Andy was impressed with the Chignecto Railway."

Ketchum looked down, and said, "Most of the immigrants are here to work for me, but it's all up to the London banks."

Andy just shook his head and didn't know what to say. 'Banks' he thought 'Sad.' No it's up to who created the world. Then Andy thought of the place Llanerchymedd, a small village on the Isle of Anglesey in Wales. Why? Andy thought. Okay something is going to happen Andy thought, happen fast, I feel it.

They all looked at Andy and Ketchum said, "You better get you some crampons."

Andy looked down at everyone's shoes and they all had them attached to their shoes.

"Easier to walk on the ice," said Ketchum.

Andy laughed and said, "I hear that, thanks." Andy then took a step back, and looked at them and the ocean going vessels, coastal traders, and harbor ferryboats. Andy looked at them and said, "Never forget your identity." Andy looked out over the oceans sky and thought a savage is coming, a brutal storm.

Frederick George Creed the inventor walked by with his tele printer, and Andy just laughed and said, "Woe, excuse me Sir can I see that please."

Frederick George Creed said, "Beg your pardon, but no!," and walked on by. The other three men with Andy looked at him and thought, Andy is a strange fellow.

"Okay," said Andy and laughed. Mr. Creed was dissatisfied and Andy understood, but laughed, because Andy saw the future, Andy was from the future, and Andy laughed because he understood the feeling of being scorned and was told there was no future in his ideas of poetry and the poetry train. Creed had this look on his face like he wanted to get out of Canada, and he also noticed the approaching storm also.

A gale of wind became present with a whipping, and the ocean began to surge.

"Oh help us Oberon and Titania," Hunter -Duvar proclaimed. He wanted the king of the elves, to protect him. He believed that the purpose of humankind was to preserve the world, and enrich it by creating new and beautiful things, so Andy thought, hmm, okay, protection indeed and said, I am with you Hunter -Duvar, I am with you, and Hunter smiled. Hmm, pranksters Andy thought, No it was Dread, and his chaotic hand.

A low rumbling and locals assumed that it was the rolling of an earthquake, and panic mode came upon everyone. The poets Sarah and Mary Eliza ran by to find shelter. Sarah stopped, and walked over to Andy and said, "You strayed into a garden fair, your heart is shown, yes we tremble, and they claim as their own, gather, even if not things seem to you fair, fling all dark tints back to despair, you know who protects us under this canopy, they come from the horizons' smiling face, they are behind the thunders' path to trace, you'll soon see together all of our faces dear, again when all the years are here, when you awake to see, the magic of all the realms reality, oh no this is not a spell Andy, this is golden light, where time blends day and night, your wishes are promised fair, and now you see so clear, remember in your heart we all never part, and after the blink you shall bloom, and you'll see the door was the tomb, your none fear is how we now shall all meet."

Andy dropped to his knees, shut his eyes, and said, "Oh my," and it began to rain heavily, heavily as this sensitivity he was feeling. Andy didn't care about that or the storm, he felt so good, that no words could express. He wiped his face and opened his eyes, and the woman with the dark hair was standing in front of him smiling. Andy looked around, and all of his new poet friends were gone. It was just he and her there. Andy looked and his newspaper and brochure and they were soaked and wet.

She said, "THIS is the forest primeval and their going to rush us out of here, they think we are dull glitter. Sarah was right, your heart is heavens reflection. You are happy in love."

"Yes," Andy replied, and the storm seemed to not harm them.

"I know love too, and this is where we separated," and she described the man she loves. "Have you seen him?" She asked.

"He sounds familiar, what's his name?" Andy asked.

"You know him as Jimmy New Orleans," she replied.

"So Jimmy was Arcadian, and he used an alias?" Andy asked.

"Yes," she replied.

Andy thought, He never shown up because of me, all because of me, but he couldn't tell her. No ill will, but he had to cut a path for the youth.

"Andy, it's okay, I know about the envy out here, and the vices," she said.

"You do," Andy replied and thought, "Wow she's reading my mind, life, &c. I am not poor am I, rich is wisdom?" Andy asked.

"Oh Andy, love Andy love, yes," she replied.

"I am going to die with this love, to myself, aren't I?" Andy asked.

Tears rolled down her face and Andy awoke.

Andy rubbed his forehead and looked at the clock and it was 2:22 a.m. It was way to early to arise, so he checked his email, and it was storming outside. Andy didn't know what to think, but back to turtle mode, who was she in his dream, so he played the song 'Forgotten Promises' by Sami Yusuf, and went back to sleep.

And it was rough for Andy to fall back asleep, but Andy dreamed of the one he loves, and again things were messed up. I am not in Truro anymore; Andy dreamed thought as he was sitting in his seat on the Blueberry Train. Andy and the passengers found winter travel rather uncomfortable. The coal stove was at the end of the train car which gave out hardly enough heat. The pumps were frozen someone mentioned from the back of the train. Andy looked back, and Andy seen British Prime Minister, W. E. Gladstone, and he was happy as can be, Gladstone was tired of the short train carriages only holding up to eight people. But this view was different for Gladstone, and so it was for Andy.

Gladstone said, "Selfishness is the greatest curse of the human race, why hasn't anyone told me about these trains before?" Gladstone looked out the window and said, "I can swing an ax too my boy. I cannot wait to get to the ceremony, and there's no need to go to the turn around town Cape Brenton."

Andy smiled at what all was said. It's because deep down inside we have to learn the hard way, and people nowadays like seeing folks struggle. We don't want things handed to folks, but come on, an advanced race, an era huh ya right. In competing for what? Andy noticed other people too in the back of the train.

The poet Iain MacGhilleatain or named John Maclean, aka Am Bàrd Thighearna Chola (Bard of the Laird of Coll), but known in Nova Scotia as Am Bàrd MacGhillEathain, and John MacLean smiled at Andy and sung his poem, "Am Bard Ann an Canada.' He looked at Andy, like why are you fleeing, hasn't the Irish fled enough?

The Flight of the Earls came to Andy's' mind, and what was Andy going to do with his life now? For he was alone now with his feelings.

MacLean looked sad, hiding his sadness too, but John MacLean's' sadness was hidden from the young one accompanying him. His grandson, Alexander Maclean Sinclair, and the boy was bright eyed, and he looked as though he was filled with music. Young Alexanders' cheeks were full of life, and Andy remembered feeling like that too when he was a boy.

The Writer and Music teacher Reverend Abraham Braine and his son, Edward Samuel Braine were on the train. Reverend Abraham Braine was singing like rehearsing for a choir, and it sounded good to Andy. Reverend Braine and his son Edward talked about the removal of the Mersey Train from the Assyrian steamship, and Andy missed that by awaking earlier.

"Prices at the Pit are changing," said Reverend Abraham Braine, "I had my share of coal."

Edward Samuel Braine replied to his father, "I can build ships and steam trains. I want to become a civil engineer and naval designer. Oh yes, an organist too."

Rev. Braines looked at Andy and asked him if he knew anything about "The History of Kingswood Forest," "The Coal Fillas," "Engraved Sins," and "How to Teach?"

"No," Andy replied. Andy was a bit confused as to where they all were going, and these questions.

Railway bridge builder Duncan Waddell was also on the train, and asked Andy where he had been when he was building the bridge from Dartmouth to Hailfax.

Andy laughed and replied, "I just didn't know. You know I wanted to work."

The train conductor announced. "Crossburn," and the train slowed down and stopped. Andy was happy because he was being bombarded with too many questions he could not answer. Andy looked at Duncan Waddell as he left the train. What was Andy sensing now? Because on the train it was a crowd and that was okay. Ah, Andy thought, happiness is a crowd, a mob, well a mob can be dangerous.

Crossburn, Canada was a very busy place. A town named after J.W. Cross who was the logging superintendent there. Andy loved that, did Cross know of the log he and Red were rolling? The railways were hauling logs both day and night in Crossburn. Spurs were being built, and everyone, and their child were taking photographs. And it had been wet-snowing because the streets were muddy and window ledges had snow on them, dripping. There had been a parade or a march too, liter was everywhere, and so were slide marks.

Yes this was the place Andy thought where it all began for Canada, and it began an ending for Andy in many ways. Signs were everywhere, 'The Davison Lumber Company.' Andy was exiting out of Hailfax, known as the Gateway to Canada. Ironic Andy thought and the Davison Lumber Company, led to more mystery back in America, Pennsylvania.

Loggers and roofers were everywhere, and chucks of hardwood floors were being tossed out of windows; meaning there was work on the inside too. Andy had seen something prosperous like this before, way back in Tennessee when he was young. But Andy thought, I want to be prosperous, why can't she understand that. There were Pie Sales here in Crossburn, and this made Andy smile, and think about ice cream.

And there was J.W. Cross the logging superintendent at the train station, and he had a Kodak camera, and he was running around taking photos and Andy just laughed, and thought, You go; log rolling indeed.

Wilbur Burton Sherrard was there too with his hunting dog and shotgun. "I've got stories, and I can fix trains, and lumber yards are my middle name."

Andy smiled.

"There is the steamer SS Bridgewater," said J.W. Cross and pointing, "The ferry to convey people along the South Shore, here at "The Hub of the South Shore." Snap, Cross took a photo, and said, "Americans, they own everything here now. The trees, and the tramway."

Andy felt something but what was going on? The Davison Lumber Company? And Wilkes & Barre Vulcan, Iron works?

"And there is the Steamer Nether Holme hauling rail," said Cross, and took another photo.

Andy then noticed Catholic Priests everywhere, and he noticed it was a Cajun party, an Acadian Renaissance. Andy had seen something like this before.

"Eastward to Mobile and westward to the Mississippi," Andy heard of refugees. And nicknames, everyone had a nickname. Everyone in Crossburn was hymning, 'Ave Maris Stella, `Hail Star of the Sea' and carrying a flag. A blue-white-red flag with a gold star in the upper left corner. Andy felt tension though. Then Andy stopped dead in his tracks. He was seeing something he had never seen before. They were loading cars into the back of a train, and this was a different train. Andy has not seen this train before.

Judge John Sparrow Thompson shows up with Reverend Abraham Braine, and Rev. Briane was smiling at Andy and said, "Follow us Andy."

"Okay," said Andy, and Andy got in full alert mode.

"I am for you Andy," said John Sparrow Thompson, "Copyright protection for authors, and to the elimination of corruption. But we aim to get you both out of Canada. Just follow us."

Okay, what's going on? Andy thought, Can they be trusted?

Angus Morrison Gidney appears and joins them, and guess what else was going to join them. The storm again, and it was crashing off in the distance.

Gidney looked at Andy as they walked and said, "Keep in mind Andy. Cajuns consequently have no genetic links with Acadian exiles. Nicknames, which proved a much more effective means of identification. Misspellings are not the only pitfalls. You must always be continuously vigilant for all manner of human errors. No less prone to error than their modern counterparts," and Gidney laughed, "Notaries, scribes, pastors, and clerks record what they think they heard not necessarily what witnesses actually state. Dates are sometimes recorded in error. Always attempt to verify every verifiable fact in their genealogy. Never depict as factual any statement based upon a single bit of unverified information. Always try to examine every ecclesiastical and civil document pertaining to an ancestor for precisely this kind of supporting evidence. You look puzzled Andy, you will figure it out."

They all walked into a telegraph office at the Crossburn station.

"I don't want my life to turn out to be like some long poem in the power of the pen and myth, well maybe," said Andy.

They all looked at each other. Andy, Judge John Sparrow Thompson, Reverend Abraham

Braine, and Angus Morrison Gidney.

Gidney spoke first as he geared up the telegraph machine, "Obtained, in a trade, bought, as it turned out, to sell it, and days later sold for $Millions of dollars... the biggest real estate transaction in history. Thus the Poets, as well as others living, passed from one government to another government to another government. The Ghosts Andy."

"British troops are coming Andy," said John Sparrow Thompson, "Ethnic cleansing, expulsion, antipathy, they don't like our trading system of rum and furs, and foods. Living based not on conflict and conquest, but on mutual respect and accommodation and interaction among different peoples. In other words, a culture based on trade and not raid."

"We just want to be left alone," said Reverend Abraham Braine.

Andy pictured where Alphonso G. Newcomer was and pictured him hurt over all of this. Shit, Andy was hurt over all of this. They came together to prevent that imminent invasion, Andy thought, Money, war. This place was showing the trading post too, and the poet scouts.

Duncan Waddell walked in the door and said, "The coast train is ready to go to Pubnico, and Railway Surveyor Frederick Dibblee is on his way, and he will be boarding the ship too. Leonard Atwood shall be here too."

John Sparrow kept looking at Andy and Sparrow looked cold, Sparrow kept grabbing his dark blue jacket collars higher around his neck. And it was cold Andy thought, with all of this arctic air, and there was coldness in Sparrows' eyes. "British troops are coming Andy," Those were John Sparrows first words, and Andy remembered.

From inside the telegraph office at the Crossburn train station you could not see a port, but you wished you could, Andy thought.

Leonard Atwood and Frederick Dibblee walked into the telegraph office, and Leonard Atwood said, "Elevators Up, and Onward we go, the Coastal Owl train is ready, and the Simmons control the show.

"Hellishly slow and wobbley," said Dibblee with an odd look on his face.

"Carson Peck wants to meet you Andy," said Atwood and laughed.

Andy looked at him and asked, "You are American aren't you?"

Atwood and Dibblee both had on those white plastic imitation straw looking hats with a red ribbon around them, or sailor skimmer, and Andy has not seen one of them kinds of hats in years.

"Yes, come on Andy," Atwood replied and commanded. "We have to go Yes, come on Andy," Atwood replied, and looked worried about something, they all looked worried.

"Wait the storm, and the telegraph, I have one to the world, and to her," said Andy.

The batteries are dead, Rev. Abraham Braine replied.

"No worries," said Gidney Angus Morrison, "Even if you disconnect the batteries, I can send telegrams with ease with this storm, and this is no ordinary storm." And he, Gidney Angus Morrison was frantically telegraphing away - ???????.... .. ... / .. ... / -.-. .-.. .. ..-. - - -- -. / .... ..- --. .... --..-- / - .... / .. ... / -.-. .-.. .. ..-. - --- -. / .... ..- --. ....
'this is Clifton Hughes, this is Clifton Hughes,' Gidney Angus Morrison telegraphed this out over and over again, and everyone's eyes were bugged out in disbelief, and Andy just laughed, and thought, imagine that, they'd die over cell phones.

Sparks began to shower from the telegraph wires outside the office. The door opened and Lord Durham walked in. A smile was upon his face looking at Andy and everyone. "I know all about betrayal Andy," said Lord Durham, "And I am not here to betray you. I am here to help. I need you to board the 'Owl Train' and then board the 'William D. Lawrence' ship to sea, and once out at sea, you will be notified of your safe destination. The gravity of things here in Canada are very heavy, and heavy upon my heart. British troops are coming here for you."

Telegraph paper began to catch on fire. And obstacles began to obstruct Andy's' thoughts.

Lord Durham tapped the floor with his boot and said, "You must leave at once. Take Andy to the 'William D. Lawrence' ship.' My head hurts."

The sky was turning green.

John Sparrow Thompson looked at Andy and Lord Durham and said, "I am going back to my duties before my presence has been seen here," and John Sparrow walked out the door into the abnormal storm.

Leonard Atwood and Frederick Dibblee looked at Andy and motioned for Andy and Gidney Angus Morrison to leave at once and they did. They ran to the 'Owl Train.' Andy looked back at Lord Duhram and smiled, and that was a going away thank you smile.

Reverend Abraham Braine yells out, "French Language you must know Andy."

Andy smiled at Reverend Braine too.

Once on the 'Owl Train' Gidney Angus Morrison kept talking about the storm to Andy and, how he became a wireless operator, furthermore Angus Morrison talked about high-frequency oscillations, wavelengths, tuning, loading and transformer coils, condensers, switches and &c.

This place was beautiful Andy thought and everything Angus Morrison was talking about, but Andy was trying to make sense of what was happening, and follow what all was going on. The forest was thicker then Andy dreamed of. The train was moving fast on the way to Pubnico, Canada in the storm.

Duncan Waddell, Leonard Atwood, Frederick Dibblee, and Edward Samuel Braine came walking up to Andy to have a seat next to Andy when Angus Morrison belted out, "The rivers look to be 300,000 cubic feet per second water flowing, expanding to nearly three miles wide, and rising. Homes along the rivers are being demolished."

Andy smiled to see Edward Samuel Braine again, but not all of this happening from the storm. The train started to rock back and forth.

"Hellishly slow and wobbley," said Dibblee with an odd look on his face.

Edward Samuel Braine pointed ahead.

The harbor looked beautiful to Andy with lightening flashing, and an aurora yellow and green. It reminded him of a mass forested Montana but water instead of land. And water was making the train rock back and forth again, so Andy woke up.

An hour went by while Andy laid there thinking about his and Reds future. The website, their families, the next destinations for Poetry Train. He then thought about the gratitude he does have of the one he loves time together, love is amazing Andy thought, but what about our coined secrets, and lovey terms together, our talk of things that mean something, and most of all our speaking in our we terms. At least I am good in bed, she said, Okay. I am only good when I am not alone in bed either. Without her sucks Andy thought. Well back to the struggles of everything we have, Andy thought, and oh ya, give me a pen, I got it, a poem inspired by Publisher, Leah Maines, and 'Ghosts Are Going To Love High-Speed Trains.'

Air' swell-delta keeps screwing with me, ~please
All because I bought tickets from Line-pricea'
What is wrong with these stupid stumpanies?
I'm getting jet lag sitting here in this inertia

My flights have been delayed so many times so I flip
Once my luggage was left out in the rain at night
Wet clothes for sure, pretty much a horrible trip
I could not sleep anywhere at the airport or on flight

I know I am going to die, I love life and all its pains

And Ghosts Are Going to Love High Speed Trains

~Ground' my better half works for Built'a peter, please
All I can say is love at home is good, but the strikes
What is wrong with these stupid stumpanies?
Monthly in newspapers a tragic death happens, yikes

My travels have been alright on highways when I trip
But once I seen a boy hit by a truck, by miracle he did live
Bet you one day humanity will look back and say sad equip
I'd give anything for people to see what they take and give

I know I am going to try, I love life and all its pains
And Ghosts Are Going to Love High Speed Trains!

Andy had written down his new poem, and got ready to meet Red in the dining car, and was happy about the poem as can be. But this day was going to be hard because they have choices to make. Andy also wants to thank Dominic Albanese for his presence on the train, so he hurried to the dining car, and was happy for Dominic, because his poetry was life, a life not so pretty at one time. To Andy, Dominic was a blessing, and for so many reasons, to all of us.

Red looked over worked already this morning. Andy gave Red his new poem in paper format, and looked at his messages, but before reading them, Andy noticed a status post by a passenger on the e train.

Hope is not worth hoping for!

Andy wrote back, "That is what Despair wants you to think."

The passenger replied, "Despair doesn't believe in hope. Hope believes is in despair. Despair will always be searching, that's why Despair will never be an issue."

So Andy thought, Hope vs Despair. So Hope has to believe in Despair in order for Hope to conquer Despair? Hmm, to believe in an opponent's skills. Despair searches? Searches out to destroy, so Hope needs to search out to uplift, hmm more than that Andy thought, To breathe happiness back into folks and for sure ingenuity and innovation for a better world. Hmm, just like the poetry train, you can't go through them you have to go over the top, Walter Payton Style. Okay, get us to the field, and blow that whistle. Un-staged, not-rehearsed. Just flat out, balls to the walls, World-Ball. Andy just laughs, Not talking about peanuts and cracker jacks either. So Hope needs to be Ruthless, ya try laying that one down on the minds of today's' Shamalta Polta, haha,, well, Let's Go With It!. Hope fully engaged- and still play fair, no referees, well Dustin may have something to say about that, and Andy laughs and says, I can go on and on with this one, with this heart of mine all day and night, baby. The song 'Battle Angels' by Sanctuary came to Andys thoughts too. A Quest huh. So it can't be done they say, Despair is the other wheel of the bicycle huh, hmm another form of laziness is all what I see. Screw the bicycle. So is that why the saying, Up and Adam came to be, imagine that? Then another post pops up by a passenger, ' Everyone knows the truth in America. that's why nobody ever agrees about anything.' Okay, got your gear on, your jersey, with a big ol Letters- H O P E. And F A I T H on the back of the jersey.

Red looked at Andy and laughed. The poem rocks man, that Ghost part kills me, only until then huh, they'll see. Better than me this morning all I can do is come up with a parody Andy. E-Railing a Christopher Cross parody, and Red laughs. Seth tune her up, I am singing-

Well it's not far down to paradise, at least's not for me
If the e-ground is right you can rail away and find tranquility
Oh poetry can do miracles, just you wait and see, believe me

It's not far to poetry land, reason to pretend
And if the e-ground is right you can find the joy of innocence again
Oh poetry can do miracles, just you wait and see, believe me

e-Railing, takes me away
To where I've always heard it
Just a dream and the train to carry me
Soon I will be free

&c &c...

Andy engaging Hope like that, engages miracles, said Red.

Mr. Welchberry comes in and sits down, with much on his mind too. Sailing wasn't no joke and is not, he thought as he greeted them this morning. Man has no place in the sea.

Good Morning Mr. Welchberry, Red and Andy replied.

"Red," said Andy, "We need to talk to Dustin about a place on the website for Hank Beukema, he needs his own train station on the site."

Yes, I agree, replied Red. He's a wonderful person and poet. We have a lot to be thankful for Andy.

"I know," Andy replied, "Dustin needs to write a novel, in my opinion with his outlook and strength, we could have a clear change for the good if he focused on that. Leadership."

I agree, Red replied, But he, I think has fallen and does not believe in us, because if he did our phone would ring.

"Ya, you may be right," said Andy and Andy was also thinking about the Hope vs Despair thing again, and it's like big bubbles rising to the surface of the pond. Letting to be known there is something down here slash down there alive and lurking with a HOPE – FAITH jersey on.

Mr. Welchberry looked at them and asked, "Do you two have your tickets?"

And they looked at each and thought, it has been awhile since he's asked that.

Mr. Welchberry then asked with an old rhyme, "Now at ricket with hurlies some dozens of boys, Chase the ball o'er ice, with a deafening noise. Well are you two going to play hockey here in Nova Scotia?

Andy and Red laughed and replied, No way, and we have our tickets.

Mr. Welchberry laughed too, and he whipped out the book, 'The Clockmaker' by Thomas Chandler Haliburton or known to have been titled, 'The Sayings and Doings of Sam Slick of Slickville.' "A writer, who believed in the railway system, and seen the laziness too. Chandler used a character named Sam Slick to critique England, Canada, and America, for abandonment and &c. I think you two should read this today."

And Andy looked at Red and nodded his head, tele-thinking; we need better literary devices again. In other words, the opposition is on to our Walter Payton style. And so what, they both thought, and smiled. But that notion of aging and fleeting came upon them both.

"Yes," said Mr. Welchberry, "But keep your roots in the Old and New Worlds, which give a vital sense of community and identity. Red and Andy there is a value for clocks and a value for time," Mr. Welchberry explained shortly.

Money vs real life, Red replied. You can't see the poetry because of the poets. You can't see the poets because of the poetry, and everything's been screwed up because of a system of raid and not trade.

"We are in Truro," Mr. Welchberry proclaimed.

Andy then looked at Seth and it came back to him Truro. Where the power of poetry lays. It's in the wrong hands. Yes it sounded like Tucumcari. Pull the switch cord, Andy thought and laughed inside.

Red nudged Andy to look at the art on the Truro train station walls. Andy looked at Red and smiled and looked at the art. The graffiti was of a train with people, mostly children. Each train car symbolized something. The train he and Red were on was moving too fast to get a great look at each piece in detail, and Andy's mind was on somewhere else. His mind was on her, the one he loved, The Tudor period and the Tower of London, Llanerchymedd, Pennsylvania Steel, The Flight of the Earls, The Davison Lumber Company And Wilkes & Barre Vulcan, Iron works, and the British & the Acadians, oh yes furthermore The Swedish Nightingale.

"Tichtkunst" (Poetry)," Andy cried out. "Play the Poetry Train Polka for me Seth, please," Andy then requested.

Seth smiled and obliged.

On the Truro train station walls, art turned into stores, of course Andy thought, horses, then there was art within the art. Happiness! Beautiful, Andy and Red thought.

Andy looked at the book Mr. Welchberry had, and asked to read it, and Mr. Welchberry kindly slid the book, 'The Clockmaker' aka 'The Sayings and Doings of Sam Slick of Slickville' by Thomas Chandler to Andy, and Andy sung 'The Poetry Train Polka', and thought- there's a key, somewhere? And he thought as he sang-

In North Truro, there is an odd stone tower
and a singers voice can be heard over the dunes
Just as strong as the Atlantic Oceans power
Her voice had carried through ages of tunes

Theatergoers had to wait outside in the street in their outcry
While she was up in the hall in the Fitchburg depot singing high
She heard them, she heard them and the power was supra,
So she sung to them from the tower, the Poetry Train Polka

While Andy was thinking/singing, 'The Clockmaker' aka 'The Sayings and Doings of Sam Slick of Slickville' is like Nudged Sketches of Flighty Things by John E. WordSlinger, and ol' John E. once told Andy, "That says it all, when you are one of the Original Earth Stompers, a member of Begets of Autumn." And still Andy, John E told him passionately the idea of traveling the world horse back is still the correct way to go, and to make a statement by being one. Living the Dream.

Mr. Welchberry laughed and said,: "Excuse me, I have to take an angry shit." And he asked Seth to play the 'Armstrong and Miller' Train Song for Andy and Red. "Nothing new to them about the inconvenience of toileting on trains," Mr. Welchberry explained, "Just in this way it all has to be said about Living the Dream. Also the Nova Scotia Museum has a Samson, one of the oldest surviving locomotives in the world."

And everyone laughed, and Seth played away, and kept the happiness carrying on-
Have you ever had to take a shit in the train? It's clearly is a spiteful strain.

The train had stopped for the usual schedule, but this time maintenance was needed.

Red then sent Andy a message asking. Hey Guns and Roses, where do we go from here?

"Mr. Welchberry will help us Red," Andy replied.

Seth said, "Good things come to those who wait." Seth then pulled out a violin, and said, "Gentlemen while you are here, go to Sydney here in Nova Scotia, and take a gander at the world's largest violin." Seth smiled and played the song, 'The Big Ceilidh Fiddle.'

Andy just laughed, and Red said, Ya, a good angry shit. Getting off ones ass, really makes things happen. And Andy and Red picked up on that, Seth can read, and they mean really read. And hopefully they all was reading now because Connie was coming.

"Good Morning Gentlemen, sorry I am late," Connie said gleefully, and asked, "What will you all have this good treating morning? Oh yes also, you two should have lunch at the Tatamagouche Railway Dining Car, at the Train Station Inn, and yes it is a Inn also, stay a day or two. You will love the prices."

Red looked at Andy.

"And look into the Bard of Cumberland, Harry Thurston," Connie suggested, "He is a biologist, poet, environmentalist and a nature writer. He talks about economical and environmental issues of our times."

Yes the things we are seeing and you know this Andy thought and then asked, "Thank you Connie, and what would you recommend there at the Tatamagouche Railway Dining Car?"

Connie smiled and replied, "Well you both would enjoy their Nova Scotia lobster, tenderloin steak, salmon, bbq chicken and pasta while dining in a 1928 railway dining car with white linen on railway china beside the historic railway station. I highly recommend it. You will be like 'ya way."

Andy kicked Red under the table the same time Red kicked him, alerting, Harry Thurston and his poem, 'The Owl and the Mouse.' Red surely you are picking up on this. The world does not have words. Language, but no words. By Tomas Transtromer. Surely Andy you are picking up on this... Ya ya Andy thought and wanted to kick Red again.

Oh yes Connie, sounds great, Red replied, We have our work cut out for us, choices, and work. Life right! We will be sure to add that in. This morning Dear I will have the usual.

"Thank you Connie," Andy replied, "The place does sound good."

Red kicked Andy.

"I will have the usual too Connie," Andy requested and hid his anguish. "Connie, the work of Thurston looks very interesting, thank you."

"You are welcome," Connie replied and looked at Seth.

"Yes, for me too please," Seth said quickly, "The regular please."

Andy felt it now. The Great Farewell. Pennies, all from the great and powerful pennies, the mindset, the silent revolution, and he smiles and thinks of palmistry. You can feel it. And Red was was going to feel it once Connie left. Andy was reading the poem 'Chimney Swifts' by Harry Thurston and thought of the animal train he was creating for the passengers on Youtube, poetry trains channel. He took a deep breath and thought about the choices again, and thought about this Hope maybe alive, but Care sure was dying. "Red and Seth I am going to take a walk around," said Andy, "I shall return."

Okay, Red replied I'll check out these video poems of Harry Thuston, and fill you in. Keep an eye out for books.

Andy smiled and said, "Oh ya."

Andy walked up, and down the side walk at the train station looking at everyone and thinking, Like the movie Anna Karenina. It's alright, we live in a world where we are over and over again tested in some way, continuously, and the odds of most of it turning out good, is not in the blue prints. When you truly appreciate what God does in your life, you'd be amazed and what you can see. So it is faith engaged time, and come to think of it this journey started out like that and all came out fairly COOL so far Andy thought and laughed. Andy looked at the train, and remembered the Owl train in his dream. Andy looked at the art on the stations walls and thought poetry grows and changes to fit the change of life and history. It is human to change. If things don't rapidly change to suit us, we begin to change them. That is why we have a history. Andy looked for a place to sit and pray. Andy then saw old memories in his head about what not to forget about. Things you feel in the gut. A break, not abandonment. A time to reflect, to heal, to grow to miss. The wolf in his dreams came to mind, Dawson, British Columbia. Death and Blessings. It could be worse. It could be better. Hawaii. At least the sun is shining here today. I feel like a tired sled dog. I wish all animals were my friends. Now it's up to the Poets and the readers of poetrytrain.com. Well, all ships are coming, and we have to be going.

Back on the train Red was trying to pay attention to Harry Thurston in his videos, and was also thinking about Andy and the choices they were going to have to make.

Seth began to play Gotterdammerung by Richard Wagner on his violin while Red read the poetry of Alden Nowlan and Red looked up at Seth and asked, Do you believe in miracles? Red asked, and Seth said, "Yes," and Seth kept playing the music along.

Do you believe in a poem about miracles? Red asked, and Seth said, "Yes," and smiled.

Everything is a miracle if you look at a lot of things as a would be executioner, Red thought. Red wanted to share a poem, and was confused. Facebook took away the note sharing option. What and why Red thought. Are they serious? Wow. He thought, you know Photography lawyers would have a field day tearing Facebook apart... But it is okay for people to steal photos and photoshop text of quotes and such and members can share them. The world is backwards man. Sad.

Andy got a friend suggestion by the actor Yvan Dalcourt on poetry trains Facebook profile, and it was the poet Yotanka Coicou also known as Hunkpahpa Lakota. Andy accepted and once there he was more than impressed at her poetry and animal photographs and Andy and her corresponded. She told Andy that her father, was also a Switch-man and worked the rails of Canada and the U.S.A. in his early years, and she has a great collection which he passed down to her after he died of Railroad Songs. Her father worked throughout Manitoba and the rest of the western provinces of Canada from Manitoba to British Columbia. Andy looked up for a moment. People passing and then he looked at the train, and thought. Red you are going to love this. Andy then told her all the great Chiefs escaped to Canada, and Andy finds all this powerful stuff. He told her he was half Irish, and Wapelo, a Iowa tribe. She replied, I am the daughter of one of those chiefs who came to Canada and started my line - I am great granddaughter of Tatanka Yotanka - Sitting Bull - Iyoate - Hunkesni - when he came over to our side he mated with my g+grandmother and started our descendants - cousins to Earnest's Kin still in S.D. - I am Hunkpahpa Lakota.

Andy stood up. He looked up to the sky, and thought of Chief Joseph and the whole American Journey. He responded back to her, and ran back to get back on the train and said, "Okay Little Red riding hood. This is where we go from here. Despair is everywhere. The big bad wolf. Dread. We need to become a commodity, valuable and loved. We are going to go into Solitude for a while. Red you have no idea in what's going on. Well yes you do sorry. Red we are in the Times complete grove. It's going to be okay. And screw the Pranksters in the flesh and the spirit."

Where? Red asked.

"I am not sure, but we need a break," Andy replied. "To contemplate, re-group, gather, and figure out some way for funds to enhance the site, and pay for the hosting and name for a lone while a good while. I lost the woman I truly love over money, and my small flaw, and you know what else too Red, the Shadow Ghosts. We also need to ask ourselves, What is our propaganda that passengers may see or feel?"

We have no propaganda Andy, Red replied.

"I know this," Andy replied," But the world we live in, people can't grasp it and they may think things. You know what I mean man."

Andy replied back, "No let's do the solitude thing, and we have nothing like that to prove to anyone, we are legit, and if they don't see it, or believe it, then oh well."

"Okay Red," Andy replied, "You know me."

Quick taking things to heart Andy! Red demanded. Andy Charlies new book 'Volume 3 of Poetry and Prose for the Common Man' is out.

"I'll call him in a bit to praise him and make a page on the forum for him," Andy replied.

Mr.Welchberry smiled.

Connie brought them their breakfast, you could say their déjeuner, and everyone was quite.

"YES!" Andy yelled out, and laughs. "Guess what, haha, Robert Niswander got a publishing contract him and Beverly Cialone. Imagine that Red, he fought for the poets too on O.P. And most poets there talked smack to him and thought Robert was a bad person, and you know as well as I do Robert isn't. That's so funny Red. I don't believe in karma, but you see this, this is the kind of thing that is divine. I will smile for eternity over this one. We have to call him and congratulate them both. Andy shook his head smiling."

Red said, That is sweet. Seeing the world through Roberts eyes, and Red laughs. They deserve it.

Andy then said, "Heartbreak does not move people, blindness would if all lost their sight, then they get of their asses, and learn the art of listening really fast. Significance in the Coincidence dance. All sounds would become painful as our hearts hear. Hello World can you hear me now? Not, stuck like Chuck in the back of a muddy, soldier fueled truck. Poets are outcasts they say, haha, In baby, in fast. I got your noise. Don't make me call up the poet 'Hurricane Dominic Albanese'... haha."

And they all said in sych... 'Heaven YA!

"You know, we have my old friend Mike Brown and Constantine Petrou to help Dustin with the website," said Andy.

Yes, Red replied I have been talking to Constantine Petrou the man has style, and he said he wants to help and he doesn't want to step on Dustin toes. And says the arts and projects can become personal to individuals and the opinion or input of others can sometimes be conflicting. Nevertheless, he is at our disposal he says.

"Disposal?" Andy questions and says, "No way that man is a member of the Poets of

Blood. He's a brother."

Red replied to what Constantine Petrou had told him, Anything that he creates will be with our guidance. This is your vision Red and Andy and it must remain so. He can only try and create it as we describe it being. See how you feel. He does not wish to take someone's project away from them but if we wish for him to take over or just offer you advice, He'll do so.

"As you know Red this is all for the poets and for sure the up and coming poets," said Andy.

Yes, yes, Red replied, We will see.

"What I can't wait to see Red is when John E. WordSlinger puts Jeani Rector straight," said Andy. "She has no idea in what harm she has done to John E. He flys straight, anyone would know if anyone really cared to scope John E out and would get to know him. Isn't that what you're supposed to do before you make the shake? Come on, and the ones that turn away must have a similar personality and intelligence like her. Guess some folks don't know what good ol' fashion long term hard work is. For us and John E, sorta like a great big gift to ever be put into that position though. For her, it is sorta like a city worker and all with a shovel holding her up. I wonder if she knows what that shovel is good for?"

I hear ya Andy, Red replied, Sad. John E told me what Selena Howard said, She'd battle her ass right-now.

Mr. Welchberry spoke, "John E knows what he's doing. You know that fi fi foe foe fumb."

What's sad is people with money think they can do anything they want, but what they don't know is tables turn, said Red.

Seth looked at Mr.Welchberry, and smiled. Seth then played a song called 'Cape Breton Lullaby' that is a poem by the Nova Scotia poet Kenneth Leslie.

Mr.Welchberry smiled and looked them all and said, "Leslie's heroes were men of action who had the courage and the imagination to seek a new and better order. He dedicated himself to truth as he saw it, and he saw it at times with singular vision and startlingly prophetic insight.

Andy was a looking the net for Kenneth Leslie and Andy recited, 'Dream Undone'

One is their master, only,
knowing himself as one,
dream and the dream undone,

one is their master, only.

Red looked at Andy and Andy knew what Red was thinking and Andy smiled.

And so did Mr.Welchberry it seemed because he said, "Loyalty may have also had some influence on Leslie because he was taught that loyalty is not merely an emotion of feeling but the very basis of ethical behavior in that it constitutes a willing, practical and thorough devotion to a cause."

Red smiled because he felt something divine.

Andy kept a reading and then said, "It just never stops, the synchronicity of all this just blows my head off, seriously man if anyone took the time to read and go over what we have all we have done Red, they would have bricks falling out their asses. Let it roam to find a home. Dreams!"

The train began to move and Seth played the song 'S Fhada Leam An Oidhche Gheamhraidh' by the poet Murdoch MacFarlane, the Mealbost Bard.

Nova Scotia:

Known as Canada's Ocean Playground and Annapolis Royal known as Canada's birthplace, Brier's Island, Cape Breton, Cape Chignecto, Cape Forchu, Cabot Trail & Baddeck, Kejimkujik, Bay of Fundy, Mahone Bay, Marina Oak Island, Sable Island, Peggy's Cove, St. Mary's River, Tor Bay, the Salmon River & Cobequid Bay, and Truro "The Hub of Nova Scotia." So I am curious if El Jones, Rita Joe, Tanya Davis, Shauntay Grant, Lorri Neilsen Glenn, and Sue Mcleod have seen the East Quoddy Head Lighthouse and had gone whale and bird watching, furthermore have they seen the remains of the Chignecto Ship Railway.

Nova Scotia Railways:

The General Mining Association began in 1826, the Nova Scotia Railway Company began in 1853, the Intercolonial Railway Company began in 1863, the Windsor & Annapolis Railway Company Limited began in 1865, the Halifax City Railroad Company began in 1866, the Halifax Street Railway Company began in 1866, the Western Counties Railway Company began in 1870, the Intercolonial Railway of Canada began in 1872, the Spring Hill & Parrsboro Coal & Railway Company Limited began in 1872, the Nova Scotia Central Railway Company Limited began in 1873, the Halifax and Cape Breton Railway and Coal Company began in 1875, the Eastern Extension Railway began in

1876, the Halifax & Cape Breton Railway & Coal Company Limited began in 1876, the European & North American Railway Company began in 1875, the Provincial and New England All Rail Line began in 1881, the Great American & European Short Line Railway Company began in 1882, the Montreal & European Short Line Railway Company began in 1882, the Cornwallis Valley Railway began in 1887, the Yarmouth Street Railway Company Limited began in 1887, the Inverness Railway & Coal Company Limited began in 1887, the Terminal City Railroad Company Limited began in 1888, the Oxford and New Glasgow Railway began in 1891, the Rhodes & Curry Company Limited began in 1891, the Dominion Atlantic Railway began in 1894, the Sydney & Louisburg Railway began in 1895, the Halifax Electric Tramway Company began in 1895, the Weymouth & New France Railway began in 1897, the Musquodoboit Railway began in 1898, the Coast Railway Company of Nova Scotia Limited aka the Halifax & South Western Railway began in 1889/1901, the Egerton Tramway Company Limited began in 1902, the Mackenzie, Mann & Company began in 1902, the North Mountain Railway Company Limited began in 1902, the Halifax & South Western Railway Company Limited began in 1902, the Springfield Railway Company Limited began in 1904, the Halifax & Eastern Railway Company began in 1906, the Silliker Car Company Limited began in 1907, the Sydney & Louisburg Railway Company began in 1910, the Guysboro Railway began in 1911, the Nova Scotia Tramways and Power Company began in 1917, the Windsor & Hantsport Railway Company Limited began in 1993, the Windsor and Hantsport Railway began in 1994, the Cape Breton and Central Nova Scotia Railway began in 1994, and the Sydney Coal Railway Inc. began in 2001.

Nova Scotia Poets:

The first Poet I found was El Jones, and she studied at Dalhousie University. El's poetry is themed in justice, history, historic persons, people, prejudice, prison abolition, and rape, furthermore knowing a difference. Her poems, "1812 Poem, Get Free," "Africville Poem," "Boxes Poem," "Einstein Award Poem," "Hailfax Cento Poem," "If I Had a Penis," "Poem about Nelson Mandela," "Say It {Rehtaeh Parsons Poem}," "Remember Me, a Tribute to Our Unsung Heroes," and "On Racism," are poems with a voice for the voiceless, positively, more than that; poems with machete skills cutting weeds and anything in the way. Her package equals Dynamite... Poems that bring a different kind of tears, and difference.

The second Poet I found was Steve Skafte, and his poetry is peeking into the dark and bringing a flashlight, wisdom in a way, new; themed in more than one can imagine, Love is laced in his poems, Gothic like, a new rarity: Steve's poems, "Are you now, or have you ever been?," "Hello Lover," "Hunger," "Ghost Reader," "Loam," "Life and Death and All That's Left on the North Shore of Nova Scotia," "Standing on an Anthill," "Stray Cat in a Straitjacket," "Tin Man," "The Trees Are Bleeding," "Winter Flowers," and many more are creative and tattooing in darkly bright colors, furthermore penetrating.

The third Poet I found was Jonny Bolduc, and his poetry is themed in change of perspective, with friendship, humor, love, nature, and the universe. Jonny's poems, "Another Day," "Break Into Your Heart at Night," "Buzz," "Confessions," "Empty Town," "God Bless Old Orchard Beach, Maine," "New Sky," "Skinny Love," "Stone in Focus Redux-Thoughts of a Dying Astronaut," and many more are beautiful, mind opening, witty with a pinch of humor, most of all a sense there is a Poet out there looking out for you in the farthest point of the northeast of North Canada/America with love, and for poetry. And as he would say, 'clarion call upwards.'

The fourth Poet I found was Afua Cooper, and her poetry is themed in animals, culture, faith, family, friends, heritage, love & romance, and history. Afua's poems, "At the Centre" "Bird of Paradise," "Confessions of a Woman Who Burnt Down a Town," "Horus of My Heart," "I Don't Care If Your Nanny Was Black," "Lisa," "Woman of Wail," "The Child is Alive," and many more are beautiful and intense, and you wonder why this kind of beauty & love is not everywhere. Strength and Kindness are thriving in her poetry. Powerful!

The fifth Poet I found was Valerie Mason-John, and her poetry is themed in love, and other powerful human emotions furthermore mind power/positive thinking. Valerie's poems, "Stinking Thinking," "Storm," "The Color of My Skin," and "Yellowknife," are vivid, beautiful with imagery and messages for sure with compact to impact the reader.

The sixth Poet I found was Tim Merry and I only found a couple of his poems, and they are themed in Nova Scotia, environment, and activism. Tim's poems, "Nova Scotia Beat Poem" and "Slam Poet Harvester," are witty, colorful and powerful. He has harvested me.

Chapter 13-Th'Rising (th'Poet Igloo Bill)

Nova Scotia, date, the 18th of February, 2014 at 12:01 a.m. Fleming time:

Andy fell asleep watching Two Mules for Sister Sarah, and Red fell asleep watching Shawshank Redemption. They fell asleep into a dream, where the environment was like the environments in the book 'Kings in Exile' by Sir Charles George Douglas. Tree swamp with dark spruce woods, and you still get the feeling to be fleeing the hated world of men and bondage. There were deer, bull buffalo, and many more kinds of animals on each side of the railroad tracks.

The Owl train stopped before the place of the main bridge in Pubnico, Canada. The bridge was ripped from its footing during the mighty storm. This storm was like no other and so was the winter. This winter was a word and it's verb brutal in the woods of this season. And in these woods Red and Andy found themselves looking at Moose, and the Moose were eating twigs. Bark and needles as cold as it is, said Red and he was tripping out, scared. Moose were everywhere, elephantine massive with antlers.

The Moose must think we are some kind of Moose, said Red.

"We are wild men and spoken in their tongue," Andy replied.

Ya, said Red and laughed, As long as we agree to ignore each other's existence. They'll trample us.

"Well we don't want to feel like a wild creature just caught," Andy replied, "But I am getting a connection with the wild in us."

Red raised his eyebrows and agreed, and they felt like they were in some faint vision inherited from the lands ancestors whose wisdom had possessed them.

Andy looked at him, smiled, and said, "I am scared too and cold," and Andy laughed.

Red and Andy noticed the realm, and they were entering into the eternal light source again, were they confronted Doom in Poetry Train America, but darkly things were here flashing like distortion. They looked at each other and tele-thought, growth; We were born of stars, then they noticed there could be, and then there was a dreadful feeling. There was also a coal-fed-polluted sky. They thought, and thought fast, by instinct, they were going to have to rely on memories. Because they were in the presence of Dread, Dooms brother.

"Red I get the feeling we should be in Universal Church," said Andy.

I hear ya, Red replied looking at the Moose. And the Moose stared at Red and Andy, And a thunder stared at all of them from off into the distance. It was that same storm. A three star solar storm seemingly, like flares, bright, but dark, with dark flashes and cracking sounds.

"Red we have to be strong," said Andy as he looked at the gleaming skies, feeling difficult times ahead. Thank God Andy thought. It's so damn bright, and these flashes are death black. We have to be patient too. "Yes Red, we are going to have to use our memories. And spray miracle grow on memories planted thirty days ago." Andy then recited some Phillip Paul
Bliss,

Dare to be a Daniel,
Dare to stand alone;
Dare to have a purpose firm,
Dare to make it known.

The forest became stronger, it stood giving them the feelings of habit, self-deception, and repression, and these were the trees there standing tall and yes it felt Dreadful. The light was different again, it looked like a newly-wedding fog, like the Beautifire Andy knows. Then you felt darkness breathing behind your ears also.

Andy and Red then tele-thought of the poets Hampton and Yotanka, and their struggle with their eyes.

Andy then thought of a song he wrote when he was a teen about his mother, Night-time Blindness in the key of A. The dark flashes were black blinding. Andy then soul gripped their poetry, and tucked it away into his heart.

The footsteps of darkness could be heard, crunching in the snow, and the crack of a whip, with dark flashes. It was Dread, and he came from many a miles from the north. Dread lived on Soul Face Mountain, in a cave on a ragged ridge there, to which he formed an isolated and towering outpost, but by trade he was Dread in a fertile valley, the realm.

Andy our homing devices are never going to work, said Red.

"No, magnetic thinking, and the art of listening Red, infra-sound," Andy replied.

Slime mold, swarm intelligence, replied Red.

Andy then did a Wobble Bee dance. "Enthusiasm Red, in-cross-inhibition," said Andy.

As loud as possible, said Red, You already know what's happening. Like a horses keenness.

"Red we are the Moose," said Andy, "Red I feel the presence of Wolves and Bears.

Polar Bears, Red replied, and the Gray Master.

"And Dread," Andy added, while placing his hand on his forehead, "an these dark flashes are killing me."

There is a chronometer, somewhere, said Red, The cracking sound is killing me. Ha, ya in the center of the earth. We need to tell the poets on the poetry train they are the newest technology to release time from nature.

"Do you have a watch?" Andy asked and laughed, "A switch a roo."

Red looked at Andy seriously, and said, Andy yes, poetry train, home sweet home, to help, also we need to tell them what we think of time, so they know what to think of us. We are shedding new light on places closer to home. Looking back to see what is true there. It's about time, it's all about time. A change within the pace of change, the gaps. Poetry train is pushing back the frontiers of modernism. Poetry train time connecting to your poetry train time.

"We are going through something similar to future shock," said Andy.

It's critical, said Red, And do not forget about past shock. Repression. We are in training again. Nature time- universal beliefs deep silent language level 2.

"We have to save this time, once again," said Andy, "Water, water-stop-time." Andy thought about the poet Water aka Carlos Gomez and his broom. Andy spoke again, "Social time- cultural beliefs- deeper silent language level 1."

The light was different again, and it looked like a newly-wedding fog, like the Beautifire Andy knows. Then you felt darkness breathing behind your ears. Dreamy déjà vu.

Red spoke, Let's say poetry is like standard time, and it cannot penetrate subjective layers of memory and repression. So we have to expose this.

"Make poetry as important as time?" Andy asked.

Yes, Red replied, To make poetry as important as time, and to eliminate all distortion blocking this. To get out of the pulse of bull shit. And screw all new signs of genius, unless they want to become a block to the foundation. Red laughed and said, Claws, clawing, clawing time, clawing minds, and clawing rhyme.

"Time is the un-forgiving time lord," said Andy, "And it's face, the past is not done, Standard Time is wanted too for attempted murder, Standard Time tried to kill God."

Maybe so, maybe, Red replied, Depends on a time warriors heart, and their relationship with the past, and with the reasons for modern man's present predicament. A bounty.

"Screw the hostile universe," Andy proclaimed. "For standard time."

Ha ha, Red laughed and said, We are able to investigate man's relationship with the past, and his obligations to this past. And we will also investigate man's efforts which influence man's present actions, and determine whether or not these causes stem from old virtues.
Crack was the sound with a dark flash!

Andy done his Wobble Bee dance and recited, The Ghost Pranksters.

The ghost pranksters are snoopy,
They love to spy, and meddle,
Poet ghosts seek out poets
So go ahead try and peddle

Endurance in love, and patience,
And forbearance is a must to keep
To keep moral issues alive.
Poetry train makes time talk, and sleep

Write poetry and ride.
Ride and write poetry

Move a little slow,
and be an obstacle,
in the morning light
Push tomorrows night

You cannot out maneuver in the waiting game
Eye gazers are time gazers, affecting nothing to the day

The iceberg is melting
The cultural iceberg too
The silent revolution,
the silent language,
the few

When is close to close,
When is your nose your nose?
Poetry train makes time talk and sleep
Empirical Travel
Empirical living and meaning

Live and meaning
There is no single set
On this rolling jet

Red smiled and joined in.

And to the jest on the highway
Like the Darjeeling Himalayan Railway

Slow is spelled with four letters as do is LIFE
Speed is spelled with five letters, so is DEATH

I have the key to the locker for my bike, and I breathe my breath
Poetry train is flowing like a river through the poets life, so bet

Archaeological discoveries
Artifacts and historic features
Bring together past and present in a place
The things which are underneath,
and of the things which are beyond the frontier.
Language & time changes
To live in the moment while keeping an eye on eternity.

The ghost pranksters are snoopy,
They love to spy, and meddle,
But poet ghosts seek out poets
So go ahead try and peddle

Time was for sale, a commodity
Electric signaling was the future.

Red and Andy then heard a voice in the distant arctic air. Ah hum, a bada ba, ah hum, al ah, num al la, bada bada. And it was a young Mi'kmaq boy out learning to be a hunter, and he was with a white man, who looked like a Traveling Collector, he pulled a wagon, with boxes and a young Puma, who laid there on top of the boxes.

And here the past was also the future. Arcadia. The Mi'kmaq boy walked up to Red and Andy and spoke, "You must know the importance of animals. They always know when it is time to travel. You must understand the snow. Identify the patterns. Read the land like you both read poetry. Follow me, we must find seals. They give us many things. They have poor eyesight and the puma has the greatest hearing."

Red and Andy looked at each other, and raised their eyebrows. The boy gave Andy and Red a sun-stone, a mythical navigational aid. A transparent, naturally-occurring calcite crystal that polarizes light and can get a bearing on the sun. The boy looked at them and said, "Gifts from the Vikings, stones that fractures the light, enabling us to locate the sun when it is behind clouds or has dipped below the horizon, and the darkness."

Red and Andy looked at each other, and raised their eyebrows. Andy and Red thought about the Owls, and they polarized the light from the sky as a navigational aid.

"Treat the animals with respect," said the boy.

What is your name? They asked.

"Drew" the Mi'kmaq boy replied, "Rotate the crystal until the two points, the spots on the stones have exactly the same intensity or darkness. At that angle, the upward-facing surface of the crystal indicates the direction of the sun."

And your companions name? They asked.

"I am a Sherbrooke, so call me Sherbrooke," the man, Sherbrooke replied.

Andy and Red both said, Well nice to meet you Sherbrooke and Drew.

What is the Pumas name Sherbrooke? Andy asked.

His name is Scratch, he replied. And the Puma started to scratch on the snow.

Sweet, Red said, The Puma even writes.

"That is so cool," said Andy.

The stones looked like rectangular ice cubes that did not melt, but when held, they felt like heavens glass, but there was a sense of loss holding the stone too. The boy wore funny looking shoes, a skirt like pants, and a sweater, furthermore a funny little hat with a feather. Sherbrooke. He was a character. Can't quite figure him out, but he wore something similar, to safari clothes, but winterized. And they wondered why Drew was not freezing.

Red and Andy toyed with their stones, and looked at each other and tele-thought, We can temporarily blind someone with these.

Drew said, "Andy you have the Frozen Light, and Red you have the Ice of Eternity."

Okay so they thought, temporarily was minor then!

A pack of white Wolves surrounded them from afar. Red and Andy looked at each and said, This is beautiful. And Falcons were in the sky, arctic Hare began to scurry from everywhere it seemed like.

Andy and Red were intruders. The animals were the royalty to nature, and they were all hunting. This was Nature time.

The Wolf pack started to cry out to the unseen moon, and chase the Hare, and the Falcons chased the Wolves. The Lemmings began to run, and the flights of Owls begun.

Drew said, "I have the Venus Hair stone, and with the three we are not alone. We have the three suns. It's time to be like the duck, cluck and protect the young. Shake your stone, for psychic protection, counters black magic, and protects from negative energy action. Shake your master stone. Keep in mind, faith. Keep in mind, the crystals are alone, and cannot do things for you. They cannot make you grow against your will, or with no effort on your part. They will make it easier with your faith to reach a new awareness, and it will also make it easier to use your intention to practice that new awareness. Shake your master stone. Because here comes the darkness."

It was getting darker. The arctic Fox followed the pack of Wolves. And the Wolves eyes began to glow greener, when they saw the snow covered Buffalo. "This standoff will last for days," the boy Drew said, "And we are in the middle. All of the animals look in peak form. They'll strike soon, and wait for death."

Red and Andy looked at each other, and they tele-thought, We need to hunt, because all, looks like we are stuck here. Water, food and shelter. Oh ya they thought in sync, the boy does not know the future. These stones can transform mechanical pressure or heat into electromagnetic energy, and vice versa. Its ability to focus, amplify, store and transform energy used throughout the technology world in ultrasound devices, watches, microphones, radio transmitters and receivers, memory chips in computers and other electronic circuitry.

Drew said, "We must stomp the earth for seal, like the polar bear, or pretend to be a seal. Animals are strong, they keep us alive. Then, then we make igloo. This is how we survive!"

Yes, in the ancient wilderness, they thought. Timeless, and un-spoiled. Acadia. The darkness arced longer flashes, and the crack'en grew louder. A terrible wind began to blow, bringing with it flurries. They had to make the igloo fast, and darkness was about to take over. They were about to become ice plants fast, so they needed to draw energy. The boy made them ice knives with his Viking knife. The boy stopped for a second, and looked at Andy and thought, I should get him to fish for eel. And the other man hunt for caribou, salmon and muskrat. But we have no time, because of this storm.

Andy thought as he followed Drew's' lead. You slice them, you dice them. It was cold and windy, and Andy didn't want to get sick. Red followed along too. Snow mortar, snow mortar, and ice for windows. The crunching sound of the snow was getting on Andy's nerves. Be careful, we can stab one another, Andy warned Red from the inside of the igloo being built. Sherbrooke and Scratch the Puma stood guard.

The poetic ice spiral is going viral as the igloo or snow cave behaves, Red thought and the igloo was ready to be in inhabited within a half an hour. Red was impressed, That was quick he thought.

"I know my snow," said the Mi'kmaq boy named Drew. Drew put away his Viking knife in a arctic fox skin satchel, and said, "Maybe we make a snow tunnel later."

Drew then changed his mind, and carved on the cold ground floor and said, "Whiteskin, blackskin, my mouth waters for a meal and baked beaver comes to mind. Caribou meat with gravy and pan cakes sugar tea if possible. Eels, salmon, and trout. Rabbit, partridge, goose, and duck. Sometimes gull. Lastly if we get stuck and get nothing else and get real hungry. I'll take a pole, and hunt the garden for a mope. We can survive on mope. We have to go get my snares too."

Andy and Red looked at Drew, and it seemed like his face was changing into many faces. Drew carved away on the snow floor, and walls and said, "And I drew and I drew, may as well call me Andrew, and I drew, and I drew."

This was his poetry they thought, how fascinating. Red felt they were keepers of land, forests and seas, furthermore their blood ran deep in their beliefs.

As Drew or Andrew carved, the inside of the igloo got bigger, and the sky was flashing through the ice windows and it was beautiful purple. Multiple versions of reality were going on. Life was more.

"Andy then took a deep breath and said, "A new reality is coming, coming for me and from me. Great changes are about to happen. We have to have faith and still love them and understand, they are all going through something in life as the Poets Madelynn says and Gabriella Duncan says too. You have to love them."

Some more humble pie, said Red.

"You got that right," Andy replied.

The Puma and Sherbrooke first heard the crunching snow. Someone was out there, near their igloo.

"Excuse me Excuse me can I come inside? I am James Orchard Halliwell-Phillipps, an English Shakespearean scholar, and a collector of English Nursery Rhymes and Fairy Tales. I come from over the sea. I am very cold. I have urgent news of the Big Bad Dread. I also brought a cup of sugar."

"Oh yes come in, come in," said Drew, and he cut out a doorway to let him in.

Sherbrooke smiled and thought, A rhyme collector, how interesting.

While everyone was getting acquainted Red, and Andy talked about their friendship, and they come to the conclusion they would dread if either one has turned on each other.

Hello in there, hello
I am a gypsy
I am a lost little sheep
with nowhere to sleep

There was no crunching sound, Dread was slick, he was outside the Igloo, and came upon them silently.

I am a merry wanderer of the night
My name is Puki, can I come inside
I couldn't help it, but I heard you all through the trees.

Dreads' voice asking was Italian like it seemed.

Red and Andy looked out of the ice windows.

It was Dread and he wore a light tan collar shirt with the same colored tie. He wore a brown vest and a sweater. His hat was a regular old winter hat. He looked bummy, maybe because of his dirty pants.

As Dread came walking closer to look, inspecting the igloo, Dread asked. "What did your mother do? She sent you out into the world. What do you seek? Ice? Nice!"

Straws, sticks, and bricks before
Now ice,
nice!
Hmm more-

Browny, Whiteys, and Blacky,
I know you hear me.
I am a lost little sheep,
with nowhere to sleep.

"And there's an animal war going on out here," Dread said.

"Oh boy," said Andy, "Here we go."

James Orchard Halliwell-Phillipps began to want to destroy books, and make a scrap book, and spoke poetry,

"O that I was where I would be,
Then would I be where I am not!
But where I am must be,
And where I would be I cannot.

I would if I cou'd,

If I cou'dn't, how cou'd I?
I cou'dn't, without I cou'd, cou'd I?
Cou'd you, without you cou'd, cou'd ye?
Cou'd ye, cou'd ye?
Cou'd you, without you cou'd, cou'd ye?

If all the world was apple-pie,
And all the sea was ink,
And all the trees were bread and cheese,
What should we have for drink?

What the heck Andy thought. Things were getting dreadful.

"You are digging a ditch in there with that guy," said Dread, and laughs. "No one cares, give up. Let's have a vocabulary contest. Or do you dread death, perhaps you are next."

There is nothing we dread, Red proclaimed, The huffing and the puffing is the sound of the poetry train, not you.

"The huffing and the puffing ha," said Dread.

Things started to be clashing. And CRACK! It was the loudest crack they have ever heard. They felt like they were being edited. Was water stopping time?

James Orchard Halliwell-Phillipps spoke poetry again,

I saw a peacock with a fiery tail,
I saw a blazing comet drop down hail,
I saw a cloud wrapped with ivy round,
I saw an oak creep upon the ground,
I saw a pismire swallow up a whale,
I saw the sea brimful of ale,
I saw a Venice glass full fifteen feet deep,
I saw a well full of men's tears that weep,
I saw red eyes all of a flaming fire,
I saw a house bigger than the moon and higher,
I saw the sun at twelve o'clock at night,

I saw the man that saw this wondrous sight.

And they all saw the sun, gleaming at twelve o'clock at night through the ice windows, and the igloo grew wider. Scratch the Puma started to pace back and forth inside the igloo.

Red sung, Can't find the window? Can't find the light? He was ignoring Dread, and that probably was a bad idea.

"Poetry is spiritual jewelry, logical and compelling, but what we are talking about is earthbound poetry, so why hasn't anyone of you mentioned heaven-bound poetry, spiritual jewelry, all hell-bound is cried about?" Andy asked with an Arkansas accent." A vocabulary contest ha! You can do anything you want Dread, just don't piss in my turnip greens.

They were planning their escape from manipulation. Dread was a master of place and things. The with you feeling. A reversal, an attachment to poetry. A vocabulary contest.

They all three took out their sun stones, and Sherbrooke took the knife Drew just gave him.
And the vocabulary contest began.

"The huffing and the puffing of the poetry train," said Dread sarcastically and laughed. And CRACK!

Scratch the Puma lay to the floor, hissed, and growled, with a rawl sound.

And yes, ignoring Dread was probably a bad idea.

"I am the King of the Flaming Hoops, I can roar." said Dread, "Ice, how nice. Hmm more. I have come to be known as the man who brings em back with dread. I have the tendency to eat."

'All for one, one for all," said Drew, and shook his stone. And he told Red and Andy to shake theirs, "Rotate the crystal until the two points, the spots on the stones have exactly the same intensity or darkness. At that angle, the upward-facing surface of the crystal indicates the direction of the sun."

Then you heard some riffs from the song, 'Entry of the Gladiators' and Sherbrooke was cutting a doorway out of the igloo, and here come the Canadian composer Louis-Philippe Laurendeau through the cut doorway.

The igloo turned brighter, and grew wider.

Drew's' knife seemed to be turning into a cutting tool, as he carved. The carvings represented all of mankind, and all types of poetry.

"Heaven has a will all its own," Andy quoted Confucius.

You can hear more horses galloping around the igloo, and the animal standoff was happening too. They all were fighting each other. Red then thought, Similar to mankind. Andy and Red thought about H.G.Wells and his warnings to mankind.

The Puma arose with motion and grace. He knew the igloo was growing wider, giving him more room to leap. His eyes turned deeper and sharp. Viciously he hissed and growled at Dread. The Puma then looked at Andy and Red and smiled and made two chirping grrr' sounds.

Red looked at Andy and said, I don't think a Bull in a China shop is nothing compared to a Mountain Lion in a igloo. Things might get pretty ugly fast.

"He may want a Moose Red," said Andy.

Ya remember, we are the Moose Andy, Red replied.

James Orchard Halliwell-Phillipps spoke, "I have urgent news of the Big Bad Dread. I also brought a cup of sugar. He loves sugar."

Sherbroke took the sugar, and carved a little hole really slow, and slid out the cup of sugar, and it worked.

It was silent, everything everywhere, and the igloo began to glow more.

"Great," Andy said, "Sugar stops time, not water," and everyone laughed.

We have to have confidence Andy, Red proclaimed holding up his stone.

"Do you feel the 20th Century black hole Red?" Andy asked. Andy then thought, I think there is nothing faster than a high-speed rail romance. Vocabulary, vocabulary, Andy thought. Ghosts, ghosts. Andy then remembered a passenger on the poetry train said; Hope is not worth hoping for! And remembering replying, "That is what Despair wants you to think, and Dread too."

Andy remembered the passenger replied, "Despair doesn't believe in hope. Hope believes in Despair. Despair will always be searching, that's why Despair will never be an issue."

So Andy thought, Hope vs Despair. So Hope has to believe in Despair in order for Hope to conquer Despair? Hmm, to believe in an opponent's skills. Despair searches? Searches out to destroy, so Hope needs to search out to uplift, hmm more than that Andy thought,

To breathe happiness back into folks and for sure ingenuity and innovation for a better world. Hmm, Okay, this is the field, and the whistle has been blown. Un-staged, not-rehearsed. Balls to the walls, World-Ball. To be Ruthless. Let's Go With It!

We should not have given Dread all of the sugar, Red nodded with an we messed up face look with his lip up.

Thomas Chandler Haliburton came crawling through the cut doorway, and Sherbrooke put the snow door back together. Thomas Chandler Haliburton suggested, "Hello Fellers. What a pity it is. Let me be Sam Slick in the contest, and if Dread don't like it he can lump it. And we aint the wise child that knows its own father either. That's sartin, pump my arter."

The value of time came to Andy and Red as they focused on their stones.

"There," Dread said in a loud voice, "That's all the help you'll get from me!" And CRACK goes that sound.

Thomas Chandler Haliburton spoke to Dread, "Help; why you are worth half a dozen of any of us, you are mighty and generous Dread."

Dread didn't know what to think but said, "I am opening up cages, and each beast is childishly jealous."

Thomas Chandler Haliburton turned around and looked at everyone and said, "That was called a genuine superfine soft sawder." Thomas Chandler Haliburton spoke to Dread again and said, "I have a clock for you." And Thomas Chandler Haliburton motioned for Sherbrooke to open a hole in the igloo to give Dread the clock, and that is what they did. The igloo looked intriguing and incredible with perfect roundness, and smooth as glass. As though they used machine tools or even lasers. The igloo glowed brighter and Drew held up his stone as he kept carving hieroglyphics on the floor, and the floor grew wider with the igloo.

Red looks at Thomas Chandler Haliburton and thinks again this guy reminds me of Andy. The animals began to fight again out there, snarling could be heard and whining went on.

Dread spoke sharply, "Sugar I want more sugar," and CRACK came that sound.

"What's the definition of Orphan Law?" Andy asked.

"Oh so your mothers left you all, did they?" Dread asked, "No, that's sugar too. Gridlock, like you all in there. You all dread that no one will contact you for all your work," and Dread laughs and there came that CRACK. "Down the River," Dread began to sing, "Down the River."

Hmm Andy thought. Dread and the World Brain. He has us all and the whole world hostage. Andy then asked, "You know we are readily known, right?"

"It's works, not law I am the Law," said Dread with anger, "Your efforts are diligent. Historians, archivists, artists, scholars, publishers, poets, and trains," Dread replied, "I will make it difficult for all of you. Are you ready for my library?"

"We are letting the daylight in," said Drew, "We are changing things. The Abode."

"You think you created the super gun?" Dread asked.

I feel the whirlpool, Red proclaimed.

"It is time to stack the light from our stones," said Drew.

"Why do I get the feeling we are doing negotiations to keep a nuclear detonation from happening?" Andy asked.

Dread was silent and amused with his new clock.

Andy remember, Red recalled and reminded Andy what Mr. Welchberry told us, "Keep your roots in the Old and New Worlds."

"Yes thanks," Andy replied and thought about, The Tudor period and the Tower of London, Llanerchymedd, Pennsylvania Steel, The Flight of the Earls, The Davison Lumber Company, Wilkes & Barre Vulcan, Iron works, and the British & the Acadians, oh yes furthermore The Swedish Nightingale. Dreamy déjà vu happened again.

Then it came to Andy, "Stand up Red, stand up Drew," and Andy spoke with his stone in hand, and all three lights met stronger, and he spoke and recited, "Helping others make you healthier Dread." Andy whispered to everyone in the igloo, "Compassion is the key. Dread is a big child."

In North Truro, there is an odd stone tower
and a singers voice can be heard over the dunes
Just as strong as the Atlantic Oceans power
Her voice had carried through ages of tunes

The Puma growled at Dread, and Dread proclaimed, "I am not afraid of you, everyone in there is nervous of all of these beasts out here. These animals listen to me. My vengeance is and shall be for my brother Doom, you all buried alive in America."

"Good luck with compassion," said Sherbrooke.

Shut up, said Red.

Sherbrooke replied, "Sugar, we need more sugar."

Red raised his eyebrows and thought, There is no hope for some when it comes to the art of listening.

Thomas Chandler Haliburton spoke and said, "That's it gentlemen, you're learning, I call that human nature."

"I know Dreads heart is empty and soulless," Andy replied, "But we need to show Dread, he can believe in himself, a new better self."

It's at the least we could do, Red added, Man loves to turn things into a battle. I feel it now. I feel it. Red then looked around and asked, What does linkage to a character witness mean Dread?

"Isn't that five words?" Dread asked.

No, we are on your terms, you are the law, Red replied.

Andy noticed it was freaking warm inside the igloo, and looked at the boxes then asked 'Sherbrooke what was in them?"

Shh, Sherbrooke motioned and whispered, "Paper."

Andy smiled and looked at Red and tele-thought, Here we go just like California. Red remembered Mad Bear. Andy looked at Drew, and he drew two Donkeys.

"Hope is the Puma Red," said Andy, "The paper is for Dread."

Scratch the Puma snarled.

Andy looked at everyone and said, "I am glad the igloo is growing, this Puma is going to need more room. Drew here and Sherbrooke are Angels of living ghosts, said Andy, They were given the gift of the straw, down by time traveling writing law. It's happening Red. We are going to make Dread write. They want to buck with us. Hope is our Puma Red. It's the next level up from Ducks, Red, and still Dread can't answer you, my big orphan friend. It's amazing in how some folks tie their shoes, and get to where they are going, like tracks, like you mentioned earlier claws. Ya, we have the super gun Dread, and that is love for poetry and the youth."

"You are getting sleepy; very sleepy, dreamers," Dread replied, "I do love my clock, so who is the clock maker? What is the definition of clock maker, and yes this question is on my terms?"

Red and Andy raised their eyebrows. Trying to get out of it, so it is flee flicker time. Dread spoke, "There are many witnesses in there to witness me kicking your ass."

No, Red replied. You value the clock don't you now. You see the gears, you see the years. You see yourself; the clock maker has already sold you out. That clock you have belongs to your father Despair, we were only making a delivery. Perhaps it was a gift. A gift for you. But you see you set yourself a trap. Your father was showing you compassion.

Sherbrooke carved away, letting in poets from the cold; because shit was about to hit the arctic fan, and Bet that, said Red.

"You are going to get really hungry in there," said Dread, "and you can't come out here. Bad things are out here."

The poet Harry Thurston snuck in from a cut doorway made by Sherbrooke, who sealed the door way right back after Thurston came in. Harry Thurston looked at Red and Andy and said, "You all are feral, and Dread is right. We will starve. I came here because I was hungry. I followed your tracks in the snow. We will become one. By the way the igloo is beautiful. Unfurling the future. A setting in motion. Clockwise. Clock strings. Mysteries. Bravery. Birth. Darkness."

Hunger was something they all were dreading.

Harry Thurston continued to talk and said, "Progress does come from damage, sadly. I admire your research project on High-speed Rail and your concerns about the environment too."

Red and Andy looked at each other with a puzzled look.

Dread spoke, "You have another orphan in there don't you?" Dread then started to walk around the igloo. He looked at the clock and said, "It is 2 a.m."

Harry Thurston spoke, "The drama is unfolding upon us. Species are important. We need to protect the lands. We have come together to do something extraordinary."

The Poet Tomas Tranströmer crawled through the cut doorway and said, "I followed the language. I came upon your tracks in the snow. I have come from across the sea. Reading poems are like reading dreams."

Red and Andy looked at each other with a puzzled look.

Tranströmer spoke again, "I hear the Nightingale."

Red and Andy looked at each other with an even more puzzled look and hearing.

"Tick tock, thankful clocks," said Tranströmer speaking to Dread, "We want peace and won't give in." Tranströmer looked at Andy and Red and said, "This is our ice-age studio, the endless ground. You both fascinate me, you both have great memories."

"What time is it Dread?" Andy asked, "Because we are expecting another delivery." Andy then thought, Let's see if Dread knows what time the delivery will get here shall be that time when the delivery shall arrive here, no matter what time that clock says, just like all the Poets arriving, as orphans. Andy tele-thought to Red, It is time to set mind trot lines. Because yes, we are depending on memories. And we're going to lose the vocabulary contest if they did not deep inside reside on Solution Bay quick. Andy started to feel something and thought of palmistry and the igloo. It was fascinating, and so was the fact that the Owl Train was sitting there on the tracks, and it did have reverse. Andy then thought about the wolf that has been following. The wolf has to be out there, and we need sled dogs. Huskies. Blue eyed Huskies. Andy felt some vibration from his stone, and smiled. The igloo was getting sharper. Life was a miracle.

Dread looked into the igloo from one of the ice windows Sherbrooke was installing, and said, "Fi fi foe foe fumb," and laughed.

The Poet Kenneth Leslie came through a cut doorway made by Sherbrooke and said, "We are going to have to dream great together or it won't work. I do salute you for being a dream warrior. The dream will always be undone unless." Kenneth Leslie looked at Andy and Red and said, "For law gets law to a mountain growing. Love gets love to a fountain flowing. I heard the echoes call of yesterday. Silence. Pearled by a ghostly bell. Silence under a thick white spell."

Community was growing inside the igloo, and so was love and respect.

Kenneth Leslie looked at Andy and spoke poetry,

"Dreaming through what storm of dust,
Whirling fire and granite thrust,
Dreamer of the fronded palm
Bending in a slow salaam.

His voice was like a choir Andy and everyone else thought, so peaceful.
"I found you all by my path taken on the road to Maccan," said Kenneth.

Red looked at Andy and smiled. Sweet it was because Kenneth Leslies poem 'On the Road to Maccan' was beyond great. A sling shot poem into the future. Red then looked back at Andy and sung, 'Time keeps on slipping into the future' by the Steve Miller Band. Red smiled and said, The synchronicity is great. It gives us a sense of hope, a sense that something bigger is happening out there than what we can see, which is especially important in times like this when there are so many reasons for despair.

Andy then thought about orphanage and these orphan works, and we need to look out for our poetry and all of these tender poets, because people will take advantage of them. Poets are in bad situations because they have no sponsors. Poets need to be fostered, adopted or foster, adopt each other. Are we not the parents of new poetry? And hope and courage are two things we can never let go of as we search for solutions. Reminds me of kind of fight for freedom. An overcrowding. The poetry world needs to evolve. So what are the needs? I know I have felt homeless as a poet before with no where I could place my poetry and know it was safe.

"Automatic protection comes in handy doesn't it?" Dread asked, "That is of course you know what Automatic protection is."

Andy then saw gap, and this was for the first time on this subject. Automatic protection. Automatic protection was all around them. This dream was like a musical roll on a perforated sheet, a mechanical invention made for the sole purpose of performing tunes mechanically upon a musical instrument, like a mechanical attachment to a piano, such as the pianola, or a music box, and the fight for poetry law was the air pressure operating the device Poetry Train to sound the notes. The melody was what was so magnificent, and the machine was Poetry Train.

Andy looked at everyone and said, "Listen to what Dread has to say, and in the meantime ignore him." Andy looked at his stone, and contemplated Automatic protection deeper and methods not yet invented. Essence comes to mind, to make poetry more of an essence and protected according.

They all heard a dog barking outside the igloo.

The Poet Edwin John Pratts came through the cut doorway, and said, "Clarity, never be away from clarity."

Okay, said Red, and asked, Can you clarify the dog out there?

Pratts laughed and said, "That is Carlo, a pure Newfoundland dog, and has neither conscience, soul, nor mind; that reason is a thing unknown, to such as dogs; to man alone." Pratts whistled for Carlo, "Old Chap," and Sherbrooke was hesitant because of Scratch the Puma, and thought it was okay, so he let Carlo in, and Carlo went up to everyone in the igloo happy as can be. The Puma was okay with it too.

"Are you rescuing us Carlo?" Andy asked petting the dog with love and awe. Carlo seemed to be loving all the attention he was getting. Andy then asked, "Is this Emily Dickinson's dog, or named after her dog?"

Pratt, laughed and said, "Maybe, you may have to ask her."

Red and Andy raised their eyebrows.

The Poet W. Irving Fogwill came through the cut doorway, and he looked out the ice window and said, "Dread will never learn. I have written about him before. He is foolish, but in control. I'd like to squeeze his testicles to induce moderation without a fuss," and Fogwill did not laugh, he was serious as can be.

Dread started to laugh and said, "Andy you should have studied way before today to mess with me, and your friends in there won't do you any good. I have a treat for you all. I am skilled at fire, yes maybe huffing and puffing won't work, but fire shall."

Andy looked at Red and smiled.

Once that statement was heard Drew stood up, and sung some song in his native tongue, and went back to drawing hieroglyphics, but these ones were deeper and bigger, and the igloo began to grow more.

Dread laughed, and his laughter could be heard all through the wintered forest, in Nova Scotia. He then spoke and said, "I came up with a new definition for Sleeping bag, can you guess what it is?" No one answered, and Dread grew more angry, and said, "It's a body bag for you sleeping dreamers, poetry, poetry trains, very funny, actually I am liking this," and he laughs again. "Would you like a sample? I am all satire and no parody flows in my blood."

Drew said, "No worries"

Andy spoke to Red, and said, "I am going out there. No one threatens our lives. Poetry is life, and more of our lives."

That may be a bad idea Andy, Red said with concern.

"Oh no I am scared," said Dread, "He comes Igloo Boy."

Crack was the sound with a dark flash!

"Okay Puki, how about a taste of your own Duki?" Andy asked, "You have pissed in my turnip greens," and Andy motioned for Sherbrooke to let him out to Dread.

Andy looked at Dread, and once he got a good look, he remembered Dread from when he was young. Machinations were in the core of Dread's eyes, and this glimpse gave Andy many recalls of things Andy now seen Dread was behind things in Andy's past. The first dread of heights, of fights, and most common dread, working hard for the wrong people. Then Dread figured out what Andy dreads the most. And that was, Andy dreaded that he would never get to look into the eyes of the one he loves, and kiss her again and often. To be truly loved.

Dread spoke to Andy as if he was a friend, "Andy, in all do time, you will heal, and in time, you both will forget about each other, and the truth of it Andy in time, the truth will come out."

Andy held back his thoughts and actions, and was silent. He went into anti-skip mode. He was also in all things are possible, and I'll erase you soon modes too. Andy is going to draw the line somewhere with Dread.

"Have you thought about reproduction?" Dread asked, "Because she is going to fly, and you are going to die."

"My love and spirit are copyrighted, and my body comes with an operators manual that I can only read," said Andy, "And people trust me so I can't be copied, nor my love. So you won't be able to work me."

"I have to hand it to you Andy," said Dread, "You do have a different set of skills, and in stickiness. Authenticity. You would have done great a hundred years ago, but now you are going to starve, furthermore put back to square one."

"I am learning personalization and that is a blessing, and the blessing is patronage," said Andy. "Let's say I was lost but now I am found. You are like the thieves out there, so I don't mind being back at square one, as long as I place you into the non-existent public and private domain. So I will show you how to build a fire. Why, why Dread because I serve a purpose?"

Andy looked up, and there were vultures flying above from the animal battle and it dawned upon Andy, the behavior of vulture is similar to, Andy stopped thinking about, and thought, No, poetry train is the digital machine that changes the games once she is built to the full max and specs. And she belongs to the poets and the railroaders, and we all will make the difference.

The wolf that followed them on the journey appeared behind Dread. It was the wolf's eyes that caught Andy's attention. The wolf stepped forward. Dread was about to go about his stupid shit. Andy then looked at the wolf. Andy looked back in his mind in flashes, and in his mind of every poet came to him he has every met or read, and he felt, and seen them reaching. The clawing, the living, and the dying. Their names branded like on a sick ol'greedy man's bulls' ass in Andy's mind, to where his mind looked like a surviving burn victim from the 17USC unit/ward. Andy looked up at the aurora in the sky, and without a word grabbed Dread by the back of his neck, and brought him to his knees, and then placed his head down to the ground, between his knees and said, "No! We know how to stamp you out. We will burn down your art out. You don't put the fear in nothing. We are clawing, carving, we came a long way from caves and slaves;" Andy then thought, of Doom. Red and Andy hog tied his ass, and buried him hostage back in America. Here in the cold. Here in the snow, there was no rope. Andy's hands squeezed down and harder around Dreads' neck. Andy took a deep breath through his nose, and called out to the wolf, "Hear," and called out to Sherbrooke, "let Scratch out."

Red, Sherbroooke and Scratch came out of the igloo.

Andy looked at them and said, "We are taking Dread hostage."

It started to rain. Andy asked, "How does it feel Dread?"

Dread gritted his teeth, and did not say a word.

Andy sung, 'The Calling' by Leatherwolf

Do you hear the sound of a distant chant
And hope someday we can
Look through the eyes of those – of those who dared
I wish you were here

Red says in hardly tone of voice, Poetry is like Gods fence, and we found the gaps. We will turn your fire into beautifire conkerbells Dread.

The Poet Mary Dalton came, and gave Red that magic. The rain and Mary Dalton did the trick. Synchronicity was finger nail dirt for Red and Andy. Red looked into the eyes of Dread and Dread froze.

Mary Dolton spoke, "Geopsychical, I followed the paths in the snow. It is the Time of Icicles. Isn't it beautiful? Welcome to the psychic territory."

Red and Andy raised their eyebrows. Andy looked for the wolf, and Red looked at Scratch.

Andy and Red found the key, and Andy and Red thanked Mary Dalton, and Andy said, "The aim must be to gain a past from which we might spring, rather than that from which we seemed to derive. We have learned a lot from you Mary." Andy looked at Red and smiled and gave him a high five.

"It's the making of something new which others can then build on," Mary Dalton said. Red looked at her and asked, you know the Angelic language don't you, the Angel alphabetism?

"Maybe, and maybe you both know it more than I do." said Mary Dalton, and as soon as she said that a Blue Jay flew by.

The Poet W. Irving Fogwill spoke loud from inside the igloo through the ice window, "Do not bring Dread in here, and I am telling you Dread will never learn, may as well bury him in the ice."

The Poet M. Travis Lane came, and she was waving. She came up and said, "I came from down the railroad-right-of-way, and followed your path through the snow. Floods have taken the bridge away. Well, I find all of this whole," and she smiled. She looked at Andy and said, "You have one good instinctive soul." She looked up and pointed. She smiled and said, "The Owls are here, they are so beautiful, and bright. Them Buzzards are leaving. I can't stand them." She shook her head, and said, "I have to hand it to the one Turtle who supports the world."

Red and Andy looked at each other and smiled. Because the Turtle train was always on the brain. Red looked at Mary and said, Protext and laughed.

M. Travis Lane looked at Red and laughed too, then she said, "We need to get back into the igloo. Because time is stalking us. Leave Dread out here for the princess."

And that is what they did. They went back into the igloo leaving Dread to continue to freeze."

Love was in the air, endangered or not, love was, along with time.

Once Red was inside said, Them Moose are still on the loose.

Andy laughed and did his Wobble Bee Dance.

Where is Drew? Red asked, and James Orchard replied, "He left with the Poet Michael Crummey. They went fishing." Love was in there air because the Poet Michael Crummey came, and he came because the world was in a spiritual crisis.

Andy went to an ice window at the other side of the igloo and looked out. He thought about Crummey, and his promise too as he, to always be by her and fully awake. Closer to her heart, and he wants to awake, and run to her, run to her in the crunching, nerve racking snow. We belong to God, Andy thought, and smiled.

The poet Antonio D'Alfonso, and Michael Ondaatje came through the cut doorway, and Sherbrooke was smiling from ear to ear, and he sealed the igloo back up.

Antonio D'Alfonso was glad to be in the igloo, because it sure was cold out there. Once warmed up he said, "The relationship between the past and the present is as corrupt as ever; as a result of its bond with the past, the future seems unable to display its modernity, and you two are giving Time one heck of a fight."

Red smiled and thanked him.

Antonio D'Alfonso spoke again and said, "And we hear you are gathering up one heck of team. That's what it's about, we cannot do it alone."

Andy smiled and thanked him too, and said, "God has blessed us with all of this." Andy looked back out the window to see if the lone wolf was out there. He also put his hand on his heart rock, and wished he would have prayed differently when all of this began, to be in mutual love, not love again.

Michael Ondaatje caught Andy checking his heart rock, and said, "We remember the time around scars, they freeze irrelevant emotions and divide us from present friends."

"I know," Andy replied, "That is why I try my best to Keep it Poetry so Poetry Keeps you/us, and that is hard to do when you are hurting, makes one want to reach out. There is so much, and I hope young poets understand that, it is crucial."

Michael Ondaatje put his finger over his lips, and closed his eyes for a bit, feeling what Andy feels.

The Poet Irving Layton came through the cut doorway, and Sherbrooke sure was loving all of this as he smiled sealing back the doorway.

"Hello Mice Men," said Irving Layton, and laughed. "It sure is tooth and claw out there. Animals are everywhere out there, like way back when."

Irving Layton looked at Antonio D'Alfonso and said, "They are building an audience too, and that is hard to do, because of the materialistic, doubts, old ills, and the incapacity to love."

Layton's personality is a large presence to them, and Andy and Red felt his power and wisdom. You could feel and see in Layton that he was angry at mankind's savagery. Andy then thought of the magnitude of the magnet, that shall ignite neuro change, and straighten'd out th'spaghetti noodles of time, and th'carbon footprint, and thought of the future, furthermore the savagery too, and a tear appeared, and the continuous battle was on.

They then heard Drew and Michael Crummey return, and that brought back plenty of fish for everyone for days.

Layton said, "Creativity and Divinity are two sides of the same coin."

Andy and Red smiled and thought about the poetry of King David, and that death was an illusion. And that is why Dread is not at all that big and bad with his manipulations, and anyone also that followed that suit.

While Drew and Crummey were making the fish. Red and Andy were talking about Dread, and discussing what to do with him. They thought about giving him a poetry prompt.

You didn't hurt him, said Red, And that is the beauty of a peaceful protest, standoff, and example. And right now he is on his best behavior because we are sick of him.

"Dread has been put on notice, and this will not be tolerated any longer," said Andy. "I am tired of it, plain and simple. He is a disgrace to the force of life and has brought shame to our whole world. And throughout history Dread has occupied countries, and has always been overthrown by protesters and change has always evolved because of it. He is not our friend. I am tired of Dread disgracing our world with his reckless play. Empires and Kings have been overthrown since the beginning of time. History always repeats itself because people forget the past."

We have to watch him though because he is just hoping for an excuse to get nasty, Red proclaimed, and that is what we are talking about, an out of control thug, posing.

"Cookies and milk Red," Andy proclaimed. "That is Dreads poetry prompt, for him to admit he is bad, and wants to change, and vice a versa, the world needs to bring him cookies and milk too, and he also has to bring cookies and milk."

Andy he was carefully chosen by Despair so we have to be aware, Red proclaimed. Dread, whined out in words holding his clock, "Teach me words of compassion, please give me paper. I want to be loved, I want to be loved again. I want to be known for poetry too."

Okay Dread, we will give you some paper and a pencil, Red replied, You do know what a pencil is don't you?

"Yes," Dread replied.

"We want you to write about change and compassion," said Andy. "Here is your poetry prompt Dread, and we want you to title your poem 'Milk and Cookies', and here are some details for your poem. Riot gear for the tactical team and what happens when the protesters wear their tactical uniforms? And no matter what you wear if anyone does anything illegal, you're wrong! That includes wearing a public servant uniform with a badge, and shooting someone in the back, and killing them. Milk and Cookies Dread, Milk and Cookies."

"Okay," said Dread, "History in the making! Taking a stand! Protest protest protest! Keeping the peace!"

That is pretty hard core Andy, said Red, We still can't trust him.

"Yep, and so is life," Andy replied, "That's compassion. He is an embarrassment and a stain on the soul of the Land of Enchantment. Poetry in the form of tear gas Dread, we want you to make us cry, but you are the one that needs to be crying."

Everyone in the igloo smiled except for W. Irving Fogwill.

M. Travis Lane spoke, "It's a cento, a little anthology."

Red and Andy looked at each and smiled, and thought about Henry David Thoreau, and his mental freedom and Dread, does Dread realize the significance of the youth?

Irving Langston looked at Andy, and asked "Tell me about Missouri?"

Andy replied, "It would take every poet in the world with dump trucks, and cranes to tell you what I know, and for sure bullet proof vests," and Andy laughed. Andy looked at Red and said, "Dread out there knows what I know, that is why he, and the Ghost Pranksters like to trip wire me and Red," and Andy laughs again.

Irving Langston raised his eyebrows and did not take this further.

The Poet Ann Hébert came and said, "Let me in. I have seen to much red snow, and no one gets it, and Dread has got to go. The snowy Owls out there sure are swooping, and they are calming things."

Ann Hébert and Andy knew that it was hard for love and trains to melt, and rail through when the snow and cold was at its peak. They both looked at each other, and a deep bond came about, as poetic wisdom is stout. It all went back to place, experience, and struggle. The grandest of things.

Things were silent for a while, and the poets in the igloo were thinking of anyway and every way possible to get Andy and Red out of Canada, and safe. Andy and Red thought of all the poets on the website, and how blessed they were to have such talented poets. And this made them toss and turn in their beds.

Andy noticed the poet Émile Nelligan hiding behind a tree, and Andy motioned Red to take a look and Red, says, Man he looks like Lord Byron.

"He sure does," Andy replied.

Émile Nelligan was looking at Dread, and then at the Owls. He then put his finger in front of his mouth, signaling the universal shhh motion to be silent, and then lip spoke, "I will stand guard", and pointed to the ground. He wore a long coat with fringe, reminding Andy of his mother. Things were divine, in this strange dream.

Andy looked at the Owls and smiled. He then thought about Taliesin's Secret, that even trees battle. This made Andy more keen to Dreads' trickery, and the heresy towards poetry all through time. And by reading so many poets, Andy has walked in poet's footsteps, and sees what they saw. Andy got the feeling that Nelligan and they all were at Nelligans' secret place in the woods. Andy then looked at the boxes of paper and thought of the wisdom machine moving through the machine only, and again in synchronicity happened in Andys' thoughts, Because life was like the train station, people come and people go, and so was Dread. Andy looked at the boxes of paper, and a census of poets, so they are not cursed by that life was like the train station, people come and people go. Their beautiful life captured in a good way, the way poets dream, even if they have the me, me syndrome. The task, and the registry, Andy noted in his mind.

While looking at the boxes, Andy noticed two leaves that must have blown in, and he picked them up, and gave one to Red, and thought in CSI mode, why are these two fellas not under the snow, puzzling it was. Drew looked at them with a smile, as he drew and drew. Red and Andy raised their eyebrows.

The Owls were growing abundant above.

Red and Andy noticed that their reflection was on the ice windows, so they walked up, and looked at themselves in the mirrored ice, and Andy smiled and thought said, Yes, the Yet Becomes Yours. Andy thought of the poet Dana-zoe Gest, and her belief, "that there is nothing but the NOW. We are all here together at one time. We are on the eternal wave of Now."

The Poet Christopher Dewdney came and he was happy as can be.

Andys' heart began to beat faster, because Christopher Dewdney has seen, heard, smelt, and possibly has been touched by the Angel of Now. Andy smiled and thought about Dana-zoe, and her struggles, but smiled because Dana- was in the realm, no matter what the struggle was.

Christopher Dewdney came in through the cut doorway, and he was happy, and he said, "I heard it, I heard the train whistle, and it summons us to the greater world. The train is hope of return, of destinations still waiting."

Oh, and all of this did make Andy and Red smile.

Christopher Dewdney said, "It sure is cold out there. To cold to be out there very long. The Owls keep me spellbound. Ancient bonding. Time stands still when they are around, but Spring is ticking like a clock."

Red asked, What was Dread doing out there?

Christopher Dewdney laughed and said, "He is like me fascinated with clocks, he was staring into the one in his hands. He is hypnotized. The Animals are on the prowl too."

Andy laughed and said, "Imagine that, times running out, and he's supposed to be writing."
"You two are amazed by time as I am," said Dewdney, "And for only within time can our

dreams be realized. I really like how you are carving."

Thank you Red replied, We are un-folding the flag of peace, and much more.

"It's a quiet revolution," said Andy, and quietly Andy thought, it is really easy to turn our backs on Despairs power, we all just have to turn our backs together. Andy then thought about the power and magic of the Twelve 12's. Also maybe there is blood in a turnip after all, and since there was a quiet change to standard time on a Sunday Morning, November 18th, 1883, what is the difference now? And the differences we could handle, we can change so much easier and faster, in this now.

The Poet Colin Ward came in through the cut doorway and said, "I found Lorca's moon, I think I did."

And everyone got up excited, and asked "Where?" And Sherbrooke, he was shaking with curiosity while he sealed the igloo back up.

"Here, with you all in this igloo, that protects us," said Colin Ward, "And you all do know it is noon, right? And this is where we dwell."

Andy then thought of song by Metallica, 'The Thing That Should Not Be' and that Humans who come too close to understanding these truths risk going insane, in that the human mind is no more capable of withstanding these truths than our bodies are meant to withstand high speed impacts. Andy looked out the window, and thought of another song, 'Sweet Dreams' by the Eurythmics. People are scared is what it is, scared. Scared of each other, poetry, and high speed trains.

Drew gave the new poets that came some fish, and Red and Andy looked at each other and tele- thought, The Dream sure was being. And while Andy and Red were dreaming, they were getting messages like crazy on all their modern day devices, and they did not hear a single one, and they dreamt on- they were in the groove, Times' groove!

The Poet Wilfred Campell was coming, and he was rolling a black kettle through the snow.

Sherbrooke cut a wider hole so Campell, and the kettle can come in the igloo. Once inside he said, "Hello everyone I followed the nights' stars, and came from over the mountains of sleep, over the hills of dream, over the mountains of Dread, and beyond the mountains of heart's Despair."

Red and Andy looked at each other, smiled, and tele-thought. Nice, our log rolling for months, and his black kettle. Imagine that.

Wilfred Campell looked at them and said, "You two hold up whatever is worthy, much appreciated."

Sherbrooke helped Campell set up the kettle to make some tea, and Campell looked at everyone and says, "We must teach the youth of poets, and beware ourselves of the Pot calling the Kettle black."

Red said, Psychological projection.

Sherbrooke smiled and recited,

"Oho!" said the pot to the kettle;
"You are dirty and ugly and black!
Sure no one would think you were metal,
Except when you're given a crack."

"Not so! not so!" kettle said to the pot;
"'Tis your own dirty image you see;
For I am so clean – without blemish or blot –
That your blackness is mirrored in me."

And right after that the winds outside began to gust.

Andy thought of equity and this was no accident of history. Andy was in deep thought, and a firelight began to glow on the inside of the igloo walls. Andys' thoughts were, protecting poets, and the arm of justice has indeed withered and its conscience shriveled, furthermore a remedy. Andy wanted to be of use, and look for clues, to help poets in the future. Andy then looked out of the ice window, and said, "We love you Dread, you, but not what you have done."

Everyone looked at Andy, and smiled except for Fogwill.

The Poet Mary di Michele was coming, and she seemed to be un-fainted by the storm. She was holding a string of some sort, but the winds were not moving it, so was it water? Mary di Michele came in through the cut doorway, and said, "The storm is about to touch down."

Red and Andy looked at each other and remembered her theory, and that was time was a fan, rotating in circles, and it dawned upon them, this maybe, with layers of fans. Their eyebrows arose as they tele-thought, we are knives being sharpened, if we allow, our lives to be, anyhow. Then Andy thought of Despair, and Despair was keeping most from the cooling air, of this fan Mary di Michele claims about time travel. Andy looked out of the ice window, and seen the Poet Marjorie Pickthall coming, and his heart beat faster, because the poem/song Finis touched his soul so deeply a tears came from his eyes. When was the settlement of his heart coming, when Hope had the full throne?

Marjorie Pickthall came through the cut doorway and said, "Great job at 'Keeping' Andy and Red," and she smiled.

The Poets Dionne Brand, Robertson Davies, Al Purdy came through the cut doorway and sat down. Sherbrooke gave everyone that lately came some fish. And Andrew drew and drew.
Robertson Davies looked around and said, "Extraordinary, Extraordinary! Such a great difficult task."

The Artist Kenojuak Ashevak came through the cut doorway, and a snowy Owl flew in right behind her, and everyone jumped back. Then it dawned upon Andy, Hockey? The Owl was like a puck. And the igloo is the goal line, the goal.

Red spoke and said, This Owl is a curious as poets, and laughed.

Dread did write something, he was reading over his poem, and said, "I have a poem. I thought about the theme, eating well, big sleep, finding silence in my mind, exercise, acting in goodness, acknowledging my blessings, love and laughing, traveling, and letting go. I thought about all of this."

Andy and Red looked at Fogwill, then looked at each other and thought of the coin; furthermore was Dread going to cash in, change his coin?

Red looked at Andy and said, No 'Old Yeller" Andy.

"Yes," Andy replied, "I bet Dread's nose is cold, not because he is one of us, that is for sure.

Then it came to Andy, the log rolling, and this, 'A Poet Genetic Code' like the sleeping disorder gene of sleep walking, but an order, not a disorder. Dread, was not a poet, not an earthbound spirit but an evil entity. And evil was what Andy thought that became in between he and the one he loved. Curses, curses swarming and surrounding his blessings. Andy was attached to her, love, poetry, and the train, but evil was attaching to him. To bring him off the tracks. Sleeping walking Andy thought really, what a parallel?

Red and Andy began to feel uneasy, watched, and the puma, Scratch sensed something too, furthermore the dog Carlo also did. Andy and Red's vision became blurry, slight stomach pains, and a slight headache. Their hands began to tingle, and then they heard their names being whispered.

Andy looked at Red and whispered, "Don't speak, and visualize light."

Some poets suggested, sea salt, quince seeds, marigold, Cyprus, Rosemary, and violets, because they felt a presence.

Andy and Red looked out of an ice window to see what Dread was doing, and he was sleeping. They looked at each other and said, Odd, and once after that Dread rose up and began to walk around the igloo, was he sleep walking, it sure did look like it?

Andy then thought about the poets on the train, the youth, and British Columbia, where the Canadian journey started, and said to Red, "We are dream warriors too Red. And that's the fact."

"Jack!," Dread spoke loudly awakening, and said, " I have a poem for you, well I didn't write it but I love it, 'Overkill, 'Fuck You' is my poem. Dread spoken out the words of the song,

"Fuck You.
It's all fire now, really gonna cook

We don't care what you say."

Red and Andy looked at each other, and mind touched- they knew their time was slim. "Andrew draw will ya," Andy says.

Fogwill spoke, "I told you all, I told you."

Dread-Head says, "An ounce of prevention is worth a pound of cure."

Andy laughed and replied, "Overkill, Welcome to the Poet Igloo Bill! Andy and Red rests their case, they knew and thought, because they were on it, full poet protection: CAE/IPI #: 682938498. Furthermore, the Internet is a worldwide network that is not yet regulated like radio or television, until now, under case:CAE/IPI #: 682938498."

Red and Andy were not even worried about the Royal Canadian Mounted Police, any, any, anymore.They knew where they come from and they relied on memories. Dread was the one to worry about. And Dread remembered, and stopped using fire and started to shake, applying. And it started to get bright, very bright.

Chief Joseph must be a bit mad at us, said Red, Because from all the excitement of Poetry Train America.

Andy whispered, "No they are the American Police and the Canadian Royal Mounted Police know and there is no more faulty in all the tech stuff in our posts, check comprehende."

Andy and Red knew though, no matter, the Royal Canadian Mounted Police were on their trail.

And Andrew drew and drew.

And Dread-Head laughed like anyone around a poet jukebox.

And Andrew drew and drew.

Andy laughed and replied, "Overkill, Welcome to the Poet Igloo Bill!"

Andy motioned with his finger over his lips for everyone to be silent, and whispered, "Dread is sleep walking, like most of the world. Love was the key to awakening, but Dread was not human."

Andy then thought about love again, and what it means to be ostracized. And poets being ostracized. Andy the thought of Wild Kingdom and it was out there, outside of the igloo, and this made Andy smile. He and Red were guarding poets' desires.

The novelist Laura Goodman Salverson came through the cut doorway, and she said, "Keep up the determination, and don't worry about money or anything that pushes the Hope drive. For it is the price we pay, for our dreams, and spiritual values. Thank you Red and Andy."

And they looked at her with thankfulness, and with all of this going on the Northern Lights seemed to be more vibrant.

The Poet Eli Wolf Mande came through the cut doorway, and said, "Dreams of the prairies, you know, teaching Dread is a drain, a complete drain."

The Poet Genetic Code came to Andy again, and words said by Thomas Mann 'I am the sick person that makes society well.' Poets are not sick, just in the mud, of a world that does not want to be well. It is a drain to make the world well, a world that loves to dispose.

The Poet Dennis Lee came through the cut doorway and his presence gave Andy thoughts, and these thoughts derived from Lee's wisdom about poetry and words, furthermore the art of listening.

As Sherbrooke sealed back up the igloo Andy asked, "Did anyone ever think that Dread was Hope. To be like Hope, like poetry? Dread was the emotion and the notion of the poem, but can't express itself, so it runs around creating chaos. What if Hope needs to be molded, created? What does Dread fear, but we are actually talking about Despair, the father, the great teacher of the art of draining? Let's say we all that wore a Hope jersey confronted all Despairs' offspring, and shown It and them Love, and those that defy, we offer a battle, a battle for a treaty."

One final battle, said answering Red.

"Yes," Andy replied.

"You two are like Michelangelo," Dennis Lee replied, "You just uncut the stone."

"Hope though," said Andy, "Growing outward from the center of its own necessity."

Dennis Lee smiled and said, "Yes, you listened, a teeming process."

Poets in great numbers with poetry of Hope, Red proclaimed, the battle. To bleed light blood from blood beings, showing the world how beautiful the blood are words.

Dennis Lee said, "I have to hand it to you two, you never missed a train station along the way."

And inside the igloo, everyone was living outward to the un-limit of the igloos measure. The igloo was growing.

And Andrew drew and drew, but this time there was a rumble, like someone was playing a bass guitar under the ground. Was the ground going to collapse? They all began to vibrate. In the earth's atmosphere, you felt the field of force.

What is ultimately here? Red asked.

"The Dark Arche," Andy replied, "A divine primordial condition, from which everything else appeared. Despair the source, the source that knew we would figure out. Despair needed to be molded into Hope created. And never has been, Despair wants to be spanked, loved, and held, but deeply wants to be good."

It could be a trick Andy, Red responded, Dark faces of the waters, our poetic brain waters, our poetic genetic code.

"Hmm you have point," Andy replied, "Doom, Dread, and Despair have never thought about a battle on this level."

Andy thought, and tele-thought to Red, Air stops time, changes. We are being watched Red, by you know who. We are flexing and flowing, and know the wisdom is showing.

The Poet Dennis Cooley came through the cut doorway and said, "Despair, and Dread are burglars of blood."

Red and Andy raised their eyebrows, and thought of hide and seek, but with a mix of pranksterism. Things keeping us from our true infinite union with nature, or the intuition into it, our divine origin.

The Poets Nancy Matteson, Carmine Starnino and Christian Bök came through cut doorway, and Nancy Matteson rolled her eyes at Sherbrooke, because Starnino and Bök were still debating about aesthetics of poetry.

Red and Andy had a smile on their face, and they thought about judgment.

Bök looked at Red and Andy, and clapped his hands applauding, and he finally spoke, "Thank you for the thinking about the future of poetry's audience, and transmitting to future generations."

Starnino looked at Red and Andy and said, "No Fear, Fear not the future."

Andy replied, "Thanks, poetry is the destiny of mankind."

Red looked out one of the ice windows and asked Dread, What Cosmic Time Is It?

Christian Bök said, "Yes, ambition, provoke, and extend."

Andy then thought, What protects us from darkness, and the Ghost Pranksters. Because they are with Despair, and they have once too, breathed in this air.

Dread spoke, "It is soon the time to settle things at once and for all. The last day of the delay."

Andy looked at Red and tele-thought, Time is separate from air, but time was in the air, mixed. They then thought, they needed to secure the igloo. With water? Andy then felt a wider separation from the one he loved, and much more, flight. And he thought nations need to care about nations. The separations and obstructions have been long enough. That is what time it was, for universal unification, no more fundamental cultures.

The ground rumbled with threat. World-Ball, worldwide break down. Embarrassment to the sleeping. Reasons, communications, and being precise. They felt the presence again of being watched. Like a mobile camera circling them.

We are the candle, Andy thought, Focusing on light. We are Hope too, the Hope flames quickly taking, and releasing energy. Faith!

Red and Andy took their crystal sun stones, and positive energy was released into them, and natural life forces were felt. Scratch, cried out, "Rawl," and he became a totem to them all.

Red and Andy took their guarding sun stones, and asked permission to remove the dread from Dread.

Inside the igloo the air became brighter and brighter, and they placed themselves into the brightness.

Red spoke, Look into the brightness Dread.

Andy and Red held up their stones to an ice window. Andy spoke, Look into the brightness Dread.

Andrew too held out his crystal, and told everyone to think pleasant thoughts, "Call upon, call up!"

A flash came and Dread was in a memory of when he was young. His mother was washing dishes, and he stopped in his tracks to look at his mother's beauty. The light, the light from the kitchen window opened his eyes and heart to love and beauty. And she washed, and it felt to Dread as though time, the tide of history was washing all that away. As the tides of the sea can get you at lose, at lose in danger, and Danger who was Doom and Dreads sister, Despair's daughter, who received most of the attention anyway, confused Dread. Dread was not a pretender. He was Dread, he wanted the crown, from the pretenders.

It became misty outside the igloo. Andy thought of the poet Igloo Bill. A global poet positioning, eliminating earthbound prime-convenience of looking over poetry and poets.

Carmine Starnino spoke, "The igloo is like a Oulipian, a structuralist conception of language to a level of mathematical precision."

Christian Bök spoke about the igloo too, "Beautiful, ice-ware of reality."

Oh better, said Red, Nobody seems to wish to decimate the acres of forest required to render all possible. Brilliant Andrew, brilliant.

And Andrew drew and drew.

Andy drew too, he carved in the igloo wall, 'Peace Forever in This Valley. Let No One Break the Peace.'

Andy then thought about the restraints Dread had on everyone still. We needed to vandalize and take Dread by surprise, and shock him to demise.

The Poet Aritha van Herk came through the cut doorway happy as can be and said, "There going to know who we are, and connect with us. Great originality and imagination. Keys to identity. Well done Maverick's Red and Andy. Geografictiónne."

Red looked out an ice window, and said, The Poets Robert Kroetsch and Marilyn Dumont are here, and they came in through the cut doorway, and they said, "Thank you," to Sherbrooke and Kroetsch said, "Oh the troubles of the human race."

Marilyn Dumont looked at everyone laughed and said. "Let's hold up a train."

Red and Andy got the feeling of being watched by something other than a human, was it the Owls, or the wolf. Red looked at the puma Scratch to see if he senses something, and it seemed that he did not, or the dog Carlo.

The Poet Jeannette Christine Armstrong came through the cut doorway and she went to an ice window, and looked at Dread and said, "The process of writing is a healing because you uncover the fact that you are not a savage, not dirty and ugly and not less because of skin, or philosophy."

Red and Andy smiled because that was love all around.

"This igloo has meaning to me," Jeannette Christine Armstrong said, "It is protecting. Thank you both for being a knowledge keeper." She looked at Dread, and said, "There is a bridge now between Dread and us. Also everyone I have seen horse tracks, and they probably are the horse tracks of the Royal Canadian Mounted Police.

Red and Andy raised their eyebrows.

The Poets Barrie Phillip Nichol and Patrick Lane came through the cut doorway. Patrick Lane looked around and said, "The Poet healing garden."

Barrie Phillip Nichol looked out of an ice window and said, "Maybe he is writing to Captain Poetry."

Everyone laughed.

The ground began to rumble again. Was it the rustle of relativity?

And it was the phenomena that suggest there is depth to the psyche, and being below the surface of the true story. The bridge never before crossed. On one side was the always same old town of Hope, and on the other side was the ever changing town of Despair. The analogy was thick and cold as the arctic air.

Andy looked out of an ice window because he was sensing, and Red picked up on it also. Was it the horror of the wilderness, the ruthless power of the subarctic winter, but there was also a sense of freshness, the freedom, and fairness and Andy said, "I see Buffalo."

And this made them think of Charlie.

Sherbrooke spoke, "I don't believe it. Robert Service at your service Sir," and Robert Service came through the cut doorway, and said, "Yall, know the Law of the Yukon, only the strong shall thrive; and only the fit survive. Welcome to Canada boys, and welcome to bedrock, you got here being steady, quiet, and plodding, well done."

Andy and Red wanted to laugh, because the Flintstones came to mind. And, Thank you, they both replied.

Robert Service seemed sad, he looked down at the ground and asked, "It is beautiful out there, God's truth isn't?"

"Yes" everyone replied.

"I'm scared of the terrible town," said Service, "I am not going back to dead-falled. Hunger and woe, and it's sixty below."

Sherbrooke arose and said, "My apology, we have fish," and at once Sherbrooke and Michael Crummey made everyone whom recently came in some fish.

It was calm considering, and then they all could hear singing and it was The Swedish Nightingale, Johanna Maria Lind, and she was singing from a circus train, and the train made a perfect echo.

Tomas Tranströmer spoke and said, "I told you all I could hear her singing."

Andy and Red realized they were near Truro, and this put them into deep thought about cosmic time and place, furthermore the wisdom from and of the sea. They were living and dreaming outside of their time zones, and bringing all poets on the train into their time zone. They were in a beautiful place in time. Shedding new light on places closer to home. This made Andy happy and Andy started to sing the 'Poetry Train Polka' and everyone joined in and sung along too. They were happy to indulge in a new modern text; we can say life and time.

In North Truro, there is an odd stone tower
and a singers voice can be heard over the dunes
Just as strong as the Atlantic Ocean's power
Her voice had carried through ages of tunes

&c &c.

The only thing missing was a beautiful orchestra for the music.

Red looked at Andy and said, There is nothing more deceptive than an obvious fact.

"Yes Watson," Andy replied, and they both laughed.

A Poets almanac Holmes, said Red.

"A Poets almanac," said Andy.

Red then looked at him and thought, Hope he finds his woman worthy.

Reversing time sure was taking a toll on them, but they enjoyed their time doing it. Andy looked at Red because he felt his concern and said and asked, "Clues and the blues. How long have I been absent?"

Ha! ha! ha!-he! he! he!-hi! hi! hi!-ho! ho! ho!-hu! hu! hu! that's good, said Red, Oh that's capital such a wit! But all we want just now, you know, Andy, is that you would indicate the time precisely.

"Ah, precisely," Andy replied, "Now, twenty-four hours, revolving-spinning round these twenty four thousand miles of extent, within the igloo."

Wist, my dear fellow you forget, said Red, Tomorrow will be Today. Some other evening.

"Oh, no," Andy replied," fie!-Fleming is not quite as bad as that. Today's Today."

I beg your pardons, Red replied, But I can't be so much mistaken. I know tomorrow's Today, because.

"What are you thinking about?" Andy asked, "Wasn't yesterday, Today, I should like to know?

Yesterday indeed! Red proclaimed, you are out!

"Today's Today," Andy proclaimed, "I say don't I know?"

Oh no! Red replied, Tomorrow's Today.

They looked at everyone and everyone in the igloo looked lost, and Red and Andy gave each other a high-5 and laughed. They looked at every one and said, Edgar Allan Poe, Three Sundays in a Week. Past, Present and the Future. We are just celebrating our vocabulary contest victory.

Andy said, "You gotta be a little bit psychic to see through all the deliberate misinformation in the world." Andy looked at Dread and asked, "We are not the little pigs that built their house with bricks, are we?"

Dread replied by Yodeling. It sounded good, with heart beat and dust on his tongue. And CRACK was the sound.

The jolt, reminded Andy of the day, this day, and its energy flux. Between cause and effect. Deeper than expectations of the moment, or moments. Moral velocity, the fusing of tradition and speed. Literary fireworks, leaving burn marks. The Riddle, social problems, reform, political power and commerce, reason and progress. To master change within the change is to not change at all, this was some of the igloo effect. The natural and all of the protecting us through time as we go. Faith and integrity at work.

The crack'en sound and Dread seem not to fade anyone, and Red was thinking about the Royal Canadian Mounted Police.

The Owls above came to their minds, that they were protected. Then it dawned upon Andy that they needed to get to Dingle Tower, in Halifax. The stones to build the tower were donated from all over the world and this reminded Andy of the poets on the poetry train that help them. Andy smiled and said, "We need to get to Dingle Tower."

James Orchard spoke, "I almost forgot, that is what I wanted to tell you all, that we need to go to Dingle Tower. O that I was where I would be. Then would I be where I am not!" Andrew stopped drawing and said, "I can hear a train coming, and we need to run for our lives. We are protected here, our literary lives are but our bodies are not, we can't be found."

Andy and Red were in the realm again, and this is what they knew. They knew there was something powerful in the world. This is what; this journey is all about the unseen beauty. The beauty that all humanity needs to feel, read, share and express... This was and is nutrition for the soul, and now it was time to go, and let Dread figure things out in Dread's head.

Andy looked at his reflection on the ice window, and remembered the words the poet pj johnson spoke to them."Keep er on track, Remember, If just one person speaks up and speaks the truth, it could never be unheard. If many speak, it cannot be ignored."

The Author Martha Boone Leavell and Poet Joy Kowgawa came through the cut doorway and Joy Kowgawa said, "Sorry I am late for fellowship, the food of friendship, love and the truth." She was crying and Red walked up to her and comforted her, and Joy Kowgawa said, "I want the children not to be stuck in anger and hatred."

We too, Red replied, We too.

Railroader and timekeeper, Yip Sang came from under the ground where Andrew sat, and he smiled and he came up, and he looked around, and then spoke, "From the Hope Othello Tunnel and we must march on, march on through the tunnel to escape on the train."

Justice and Mercy pulsated as the sound of the train went ka-dewng, ka-dewng, ka-dewng.

The Poet Earle Birney came through the cut doorway, and went to an ice window, and said, "Dread is asleep, and Earle recited his poem 'Bushed.' He wants to set himself on fire, not the igloo. He wants to set himself on fire with poetry."

Yip Sang demanded everyone to go through the tunnel, and everyone did carrying a box of paper, and so did Carlo the dog. The last three to escape through the tunnel was Andy, Red, and Scratch, and they looked at Yip, and didn't move a lip, and Yip smiled and said, "People are searching for you."

Red and Andy looked around, and Red looked at Scratch the puma and said, Come on, you are coming with us. And Andy looked at Dread one last time, and then looked for the wolf, but didn't see the lone wolf, only his reflection in the ice window. He seen Yip too in the reflection and this made Andy think of Jung Hem Sing, and Andy felt okay, and he and Red and Scratch went into the tunnel and Yip Sang followed them.

Chapter 14-Publishers like Rawness, Poets of Tomorrow love Lawness
February 21st, 2014

The tunnel in this dark dream was narrow with many chambers, but no one dared to go into them as they crawled out to the surface, and Yip Sang was leading them. There were many rocks and stones on the path out, and Andy's' knees found them all it seemed like.

"Pain, it hurts, son of bitch Red, it hurts, damn rocks and stuff that lies on the path," said Andy in anguish, but knowingly what he was doing. "Crawl inside, dam it Red, for the youth." They don't know. Andy then chuckles, and thinks oh, back to the primitive.

Go Andy go, move, said Red.

"I am I am," said Andy.

Ya ya they are everything, Red finally replied, but then sensed, and spoke, Move Andy something is coming!

"The beauty," said Andy, "The eye, and remember Time is stalking us."

Move link your ass, said Red with slight anger.

"Damn," Andy replied.

And Red laughed.

Andy laughed too and said, "Hey subject."

And Red replied, Hey object.

And they both spoke in sync, 'We all are possible of a great union', and they boogied without doubt through the tunnel.

"Wake up Red, we have to feel the feathers we all have shed," and Andy sung as he followed Red and everyone out of the tunnel, furthermore they used their memories geared in their intuitions.

When you can only lose it to your mind
You got to lose it to your mind
Waves an' waves of tranquility hit hard on your innocence
Well, discarding all that was before, let's crawl inside

Lost in the darkness, lost in today
Thomas Chandler Haliburton yelled out back at everyone, "As Andy would say, Let's go with it."

Andy laughed and said, "Chandler Haliburton is the most quoted writer in North America."

Well he just quoted you for sure here in the Netherworld, said Red.

They began to crawl in water, and now they knew why Haliburton yelled at them. Andy then thought about Persephone, the Goddess of the Underworld, but he felt they were lifted up out of the delusion of individuality even more, and knew the peace of absorption into deity.

Red began to recite the poem 'Hyperion's Song of Destiny' by Johann Christian Friedrich Hölderlin. Red was afraid the ground above would cave in on them from the storm, but they were sheltered from the storm but something didn't seem right with Andy.

Andy stopped, and moved his body sideways so he could look at Red. Andy looked at him like they both were just born again of some sorts. Then there was a mysterious breeze, and it spoke to Andy, 'Be Gentle on the Grind.' Scratch and Andrew looked back at them also. Yip Sang then said, "We are almost above."

Was the miracle grow kicking in on their memories as they moved along. Then they began to see flashing, that black flashing and they were interesting flashes. Was it Dread again? It was that night time blindness again, so they had to revert to the art of listening more.

Poetry was becoming more like time, finally, and Scratch spoke, "Rawl!" Scratch then chirped.

Carlo then started barking, and this made Andy, and Red know people were above waiting on them, or something was.

And Sherbrooke laughed, and Andrew said, "Shake your stone."

The value of time came to Andy and Red as they focused on their stones.

"It is time to stack the light from our stones again," said Andrew.

James Orchard Halliwell-Phillipps I hope you brought more sugar, Red asked and laughed.

They shook their stones, and one by one they exited out of the tunnel surfacing in the woods next to the railroad tracks.

Yip Sang had a look like he made a big big mistake, because Cleveland Abe was the only one waiting for them from above. Cleveland Abe looked at his pocket watch, and then he looked at the weather, and the solar storm was still happening. He looked at everyone and said, "Great railroad timing, you made it to the correct time zone, but the weather is not so nice."

"We have pocket radar now," said Andy.

Cleveland Abe laughed, and asked, "Tell me, tell me is it frightening?"

"Well if you are scared jump in my pocket docket ya ya mentary," said Andy and laughs.

"Well Danger is out here," Cleveland Abe proclaimed, "And this place maybe like the Valley of the Headless Men, so the pocket is the train a half mile west, and they are coming for us."

Ah ha Andy thought, Dreads sister, Danger.

And Andrew spoke, "Also the Naha, a feared tribe of the valley. A tribe of the Dene people who told of evil giants that stalk, The Naha are raiders and fierce warriors, attack upon anyone who camped within their boundaries and sometimes beyond."

Yip Sang spoke, "Let's go, lets run to the Coastal Owl Train, and get you two to the W.D. Lawrence Ship.

Things were difficult because they had to run with boxes of paper and it was different. They were now in an eerie world, and Andy thought of the Flight of the Earls, and the feeling of being watched came upon him. But they yearned to hold and move on, and they all ran to the Coastal Owl Train. They were the band on the run, and Andy hoped they were all having fun. They were running from Ghosts, Despair, the United States, and Royal Canadian Mounted Police, and yes the men of Jimmy New Orleans, furthermore things unseen. They were in Danger, and Dread was possibly right behind.

Animals were everywhere so as they ran Andy looked up for the Owls, and there they were, flying in flocks above them, following the band on the run. Where was the Owl Train? Before, it was near where two-thirds of a bridge was ripped from its footing. The storm was lashing as it was before too, and where was the rest of the pier that was demolished a few hundred feet from the draw to the shore? Where was the ship? Andy just stopped like he was out of breath, and said, "We have to find a way because there is no way we are going to cross the Shubenacadie River."

Yip then yelled out, "The train is here," and there the Coastal Owl Train came just over the tall grass, deerberry, and squaw huckleberry. The train wasn't going to fast, it seemed very calm for all that was going on. It was the Owl train, maybe she was just checking things out. Angus Morrison Gidney was hanging on, and out the door of the train with a smile on his face. And this put a smile on Andy's face too, because Andy wanted to tell him of the new times news, that a Russian Scientist named Leonid Plekhanov was bringing Teslas' WardenClyffe Tower back in a different way, the solution to wireless transmission of power back to life in the name of the Planetary Energy Transmitter, the modern analogue. The train stopped, and Frederick Dibbley jumped off the train and asked, "Was your time hellishly slow and wobbley?" and he laughed. Edward Samuel Braine then poked his head out because he wanted to set sail, and see more trains, and learn about ships. Leonard Atwood came off the train, and said, "Welcome to that railway 'That is'. We need to get to the ceremony and get you to the ship."

Andy replied to Frederick, "Yes, hellishly slow and wobbley." Andy felt a bit leery about Atwood, because he was in the oil business, but how could Atwood know about the future of oil other than of the financial importance; but Andy was impressed about his elevator patents.

Atwood looks at Andy and smiled, Atwood seemed to have no worries, and said, "Carson C. Peck wants to speak with you Andy and Red, and he is in car #5. So Andy, Red, the Igloo Poets and everyone else boarded the train. They all staggered from the roughness of the tracks, and Andy and Red made their way to the train car Peck was in. Sitting next to Peck was Railroad business men Donald D. Mann, and R.J. Mackenzie. Peck was eager to talk to Andy, "Red and Andy have a seat, I find it strange that you both blindly volunteered your life to promoting poetry and the railroads, and are willing to go anywhere to better yourself."

"We do what we can," Andy replied looking at Red and he responded to Peck.

"Even if you could be missing out on marriage?" Peck asked.

"Let's not go there," Andy replied. Red did not like that remark either, and spoke too, Ya, let's not go with that right there.

"You stun me with all of the chances you have taken," said Peck, "What I am trying to get at is the spirit that moves you in this way. Many are called but few are chosen."

"Poetry has called us Carson," said Andy.

"Do you for a minute suppose, with the experience you have had that your chances are better with someone else other than with your friend you are working with today?" Asked Peck "Because a man that can make good in America and Canada can make good anywhere. I am proud of you, and if the spirit that prompted you to offer your services was loyalty to poetry and the railroads, then I say, let us all shout for Poetry and the Railroads."

Andy was silent and so was Red, but that was only for a small amount of time. Andy then looked at Carson Peck and said, "Thanks, but we still have a long way to go, and that is we, Red is the main man. Thanks to all of those that recognize that people who stick their necks out for the common good. Peck to you and everyone else. Do 'not' expect miracles without unity. ~Without unity miracles shall never be, confront thee factja. Please excuse us, we need to retire to sleep."

They both felt like they were sleepwalking, and they both knew about the underlying connectedness that manifests itself through meaningful coincidences that cannot be explained by cause and effect. Into which cause and effect they knew more of, and could not stand it at all. Because most people did not have a clue of the harm they cause by what they say and do.

"Indeed" spoke John George Lambton who was Lord Durham who walked up from behind them. "Gentlemen, Unity in wisdom are the keys. A heart for humanity sure can give one a headache." Lord Durham sat down near them, and was thinking about their escape from America, furthermore helping them out of Canada under the public trick of exile.

The storm was lashing and cracking.

The train started to move, and they began to see ships and workers of the sea. They were going to hear the voice of the people, and the people were going to hear the voice of the poets.

A bugle could be heard where there was no smiling seen, but from the trains windows you could see the marching, the stetsons, and their metals glittering in the sun. Bands of Canadian Mounties as far as the eye could see, and you could tell they all took it all seriously. And Andy thought, they were all far away from their mothers out here chasing whiskey traders, horse thieves, natives, and hobnobbing with haughty Indian Princes and lovely unsophisticated Princesses. But this march and search was for them.

Red and Andy looked at them, and recognized their full strength, and they were fully equipped, and they sounded louder than the solar thunder in the valley and the train, but furthermore so was Red and Andy. Most of their confidence resided in their wisdom, experiences, and the presence of Lord Durham with them, furthermore Lord Durham knew that time was running out for Red and Andy, but he was going to let them speak.

The train was slowing down, and you could hear the thudding hoofs, clattering accoutrements and equipment and the wailing grease-hungry river carts. Then déjà vu kicked in on Red and Andy. Red then looked at Andy and said, "They'd love Play Station," and Andy laughed.

Andy and Red felt they were going to die soon so who is going to take care of all of the hard work? Can we get Witness? They both always had asked. They both thought, and knew America has a bad disposition, and always seemed disgruntled so Andy and Red felt that they could not count on them. The team back home was off in La La Anarchy land, but all in all, they did not fall into the same trap most poetry websites do, other sites never follow through into what they say or aim to do, wounding poets and poetry more than they are and is. The Alphonso G. Newcomer Award was born making sure history did not repeat itself, so they slept well as they dreamed.

The train stopped where the western cable anchor was going to be placed in Hailfax. Above the tracks to the right was a guard tower with a wooden ladder leading up to it, and a few buildings connected in a row, and a sign on the first one said 'Owl'. Andy thought about roofing and the wolf, and Red thought about Scratch. The Mounties surrounded the train, and Andy looked back up at the guard tower and thought about the Tudor period and the Tower of London, Llanerchymedd, Pennsylvania Steel, The Flight of the Earls, The Davison Lumber Company, Wilkes & Barre Vulcan Iron works, and the British & the Acadians, and that guard was not The Swedish Nightingale. Andy tapped on his pants pocket to see if his heart rock was there, and it was but those beginning days sure were not. Oh for the Love of Canada Andy thought. Now I know why they say that, and Andy also knew but knew more on a different level of poets accomplishments, and that is why they get so happy, and Andy thought when a poet posts a selfie photograph on the internet seven out of ten poets were not egotistic, because they know there is no mastery of the art of poetry because poetry was like nature always trying to re-event itself.

Lord Durham arose and said, "Let me do the speaking and I guarantee I will let Joseph Howe, Lieutenant Governor of Nova Scotia, and the Parliament of Canada hear what you have to say. Joseph Howe was a poet himself, a journalist, and a politician, furthermore Chief Commissioner of Railway there.

"Are you Andy Sandihands and Red Regatta?" Joseph Howe asked and Howe thought these two men are amusing, and if the fire at home did go out, I'd get off my fanny to rekindle it to read about these two. Their story of Poetry Train America was one to keep. Howe also thought before they arrived that my books are very few, but then the world is before me, a library open to all from which poverty of purse cannot exclude me and in which the meanest and most paltry volume is sure to furnish something to amuse, if not to instruct and improve.

"I am Andy Sandihands," Andy replied, and Red just stuck out his tongue at the Royal Canadian Mounted Police. Knowing he and Andy were the keepers of the poetry flame. Andy felt Howe's love for Great Britain and her Empire, and this added to Andy's thoughts of mystery.

Joseph Howe could see himself in Andy and Red, fighting and writing for what was right and just, to leave an unshackled legacy to the children of the world for their own legacies. Thomas Chandler Haliburton, and everyone else from the Igloo walked off the train, and Haliburton said, "It's good to see you again Howe."

And Joseph Howe replied with a inquisitive laugh, "It sure is good to see you too Thomas. So Thomas these two men are not afraid of the saddle by day nor of the lamp by night?"

"Not a whimper Joseph." Haliburton replied.

Howe loved men that had spirits with no scandal or bumbling. The Royal Canadian Mounted Police were ready to take Red and Andy until the morning when Red and Andy's voices could be heard. Howe also thought as for the people's rights it was the same for the poets, and it would take the wisdom of Solomon and the energy and strategy of Frederick the Great to weld solutions to the world. Because disloyalty was everywhere. Red and Andy would have to calculate the probabilities of alternative lines of action and act in accordance with the likely outcome rather than their own principles. Fate, decision, and could anyone forecast the probable success who makes a strong fight against impossible odds and at the same time tend to enthrone as a cardinal virtue of poetry through politics? These two men were difficult men to categorize like himself Howe thought, Canada and Poets, a partnership, which may last for centuries, and need not terminate at all, so long as it is mutually advantageous. To strive and to elevate their eyes and minds from the little peddling muddy pool of politics beneath their feet to something more ennobling, exacting and inspiring, calculated to enlarge the borders of their intelligence, and increase the extent and area of their own and the Poets prosperity.

The Royal Canadian Mounted Police tied Red and Andy's hands behind their backs, placed them on horses, and bagged their heads in black hoods. Was it their time of defeat? Would Lord Durham keep his word? Everyone who was with them prior was sad and scared for them. As they rode away to a massive home similar to a goal out in the country. Once there they were placed into a cell, and the hoods were taken off. The room was empty except for two straw mattresses placed upon iron bed structures. The emptiness was stark and dreary. There was no heat, lights and toilet. Red and Andy didn't care they were to tired to care, so they laid down and got some sleep for their pleading, to introduce the Igloo Bill at the House of Commons.

It felt like they had slept for days, and maybe they have, because Andy awoke early as usual, and laid there thinking about when he was a boy with his brother, and Andy felt like they were not wanted, as they were always shut out, and what was the fear these folks have? Andy awoke Red to prepare for the hearing, and they conversed, until they were taken to the floor of the House of Commons.

The house of Parliament on the floor was noising during the seating. Andy and Red looked around and they both thought that this was cool. Just like the theater, and the movies of 1776.

Joseph Howe and Lord Durham were sitting right in front of Andy and Red.

Joseph Howe spoke, "Everyone this is Red and Andy, and they have important things to say."

Red and Andy stood up and Andy spoke, "Miracles Are Possible with Unity; and Hope is in us and we are part of the hopeful people, Poets and Innovators. We are also innovators with a solution-oriented campaign and strategy, forcing seriousness about real solutions to our problems in this world and to be accounted for, accounted for, we repeat: because our survival and history depends on it, long term. We have been committed to this. Poetry and Poetry Train is a major thing, not a minor, and we are here to reclaim Poets rights & dignity, and all of Railroad history it takes above and below. Poetry Train is not about branding, even some think we are, we are about trust, we are looking for trustworthiness from counsel, because we are trustworthy. We are not C.E.O's, and we have no mission statement but it is time to awake and shake. Poetry Train is real, a tool for the ages. Red and I are not trying to open graves, and pick out old wounds, just strengthening the machine, like a licensed poet jukebox, and poetry for the sight impaired. Ingenuity- In-jun-ity- creating work, jobs, careers &c &c, but it seems poets of today are un-grateful, and they are so wounded, we repeat so wounded, and sadly un-educated because of the 20th Century black hole, and modern poetry website abandonment's. Not clandestine publishing but high tech. Hello it is the year 2014. Humanity and clear thinking are part of the solutions in the and on the world. Can anyone of you in this house become vulnerable for teaching the next generation? We can! Can anyone of you submit to a process that threatens your identity? We can! We will not join in on the disgrace, mistakes, and ruin that folks do and have done to poetry. Poets of these times must dispel all things that wound or kill poetry. And this is our modern duty. Furthermore it is proper and noble as life, so we are asking for complete reliance on our constitutional counsels. About the force of modern, responsible literary publishing becoming a reality and to propose a bill, we call the Poet Igloo Bill, and make it law in Canada and America, and so forth, to protect and compensate Poets and to fill in the gaps of current copyright law. Or Copywrong law! It pays to know there is just as much future as there is the past."

Everyone was grasping the time riddles Andy spoke of.

The Igloo Bill protects Poets and their work. Under the Igloo Bill the Poet has the option for adoption and adopting, legal publishers too, and this adoption helps the Igloo expand and strengthen. Creating a partnership, a membership association protecting poets, their poetry and the name of poetry from modern un-licensed literary websites and the seventy five year old rejuvenating Monster, known as Orphan Works Law protecting and destroying. In the Igloo, Poets are protected from the Big Bad Wolf of time and publishing negligence. They all can create their own ice block sort of speak for the Igloo from the inside out, with all of their ideas to help and strengthen the Igloo Bill, and all of their poetic wills, just like a living will, furthermore, the Igloo Bill creates laws for online poetry websites requiring them to be legal. Similar to ASCAP and BMI, and using the same tools they do, with two tools added, the poetry e train and a poetry website license task force.

"When were you born Joseph Howe?" Andy asked.

"December 13, 1804," Howe replied.

"And you Lord Durham?" Andy asked.

"April 12, 1792," Lord Durham replied.

"Okay, do you create things that are copyrightable? And to muscle up that question. Do you have an artistic child who creates copyrightable deeds, and ya ya I am talking about the c inside the circle?" Andy asks.

Andy then did some old school secret body language to Red that meant hope they are not chumps, because we want this to drill the souls to what is real and should be in control. Andy then continues speaking, "The current copyright law is causing gridlock in the digital marketplace known as the Orphan Works. A monster eating everything up creative, and useful, speaking of hunger, what are the stats on the homeless in America and Canada, and the orphaned period? Poetry can feed the world's homeless with this system. Howe in 1809 legal publishers can finally help you and Lord Durham and in 1867 publishers can finally help you. It takes that long, why, why can't help be placed now? Poetry has a common bond that we all share. I have my back up against the record machine, so I may as well jump, only to the other end of the Igloo. Let's take the invention of the American Jukebox, that preserves culture, and brings the world together. A poem jukebox everyone, a poem jukebox. An Igloo Bill with a manufacturing plant with railroad tracks of new poem jukeboxes, distributed everywhere, with poetry heard and read from all over the world, furthermore poetry for the sight impaired. It can be done; we just need the Igloo Bill and Act, grants granted, and a team selected by us and you. Finally and suddenly Poetry and the Poem Jukebox via satellite called wifi shall compete with a large television company and the music industry, for the cost of a nickel, just saying, the original price for a song, via 1927. Wifi Ladies & Gentleman can be powered by icomera.com, they bought out Greyhound because of corruption, their wifi needs to be on Amtrak, let the Poets buy out Amtrak. icomera.com and Peter Kingsland, Chris Chinnapan, and Saeed Bashirian can make this happen for poets too with their powerful icomera. Movemanage get me. Please don't let me get on the talk about lottery machines and &c &c that ruins more families then benefits them. Inspiration, Vision, Leadership, Engineering, Prosperity, the Poem Jukebox, you can call it a Poem-graph, an Engineered Poetry System aka the Poetry Train with Railroad History on audio under the Igloo Bill as well, and the world is the Board of Review."

Continuing to speak Andy said, "Can do, can do! Can Poets and Counsels be so dead to the Poets dignity and duty as to be thus deluded into the losses and violations? Poetry is not fiction. Poetry saves lives. There is glory, honor, dignity, and truly there is Sacrifice in poetry. Counsel and Poets, the non Poet has insulted you, and the want to be publisher have insulted you over and over again, furthermore so has the law. Can there be more insulting? Can there be more disgrace? Poets are true and different and wise. Is this the honor of Poetry? Is this the spirit of Poetry? No, we proclaim, we think not! We demand positive conduct amongst counsel. A new foundation, in the Poet Igloo Bill. Poets, Poetry calls upon us to rescue her and humanity, and you all know in the world we all live in now, we don't need to get into great detail. We say again, Poets are true and different and wise. And we have proof."

Andy then added, "Is it not dangerous to awake the sleepwalker? Sleepwalking is more common than believed, and not outgrown as we think either. Poets do not fully sleepwalk, they have a good gene, a sequence separate from the human race and some would call a disorder. Poetry is the opposite of sleepwalking. It is time to take it all seriously, and become bodyguards. Or brain-guards to the brain-washing machine. The potential dangers are enormous. Highly coordinated tasks can take place without conscious thought. As Robert Anton Wilson says, Reality is what you can get away with and manipulation and corruption is out of hand."

Andy then thought of the ghosts too, furthermore his return point. "The arm of justice has indeed withered and its conscience shriveled. Oh how long can the pot keep calling the kettle black, and evidence for this widespread cultural perspective is seen, for example, in the popularity of crime-related entertainment where detectives follow the clues to confound prejudice and common-sense; the recent trend for forensic science to play a central role merely emphasizes this point. Failure to do so can hardly help the growing problem of illiteracy, and the art of listening. We can and will pitch a tent here if needed. We are talking about the human bond furthermore the need for universal unification. We do have to ask what if Poets and Poetry could feed the world? Because they can, and would if we planned and planned and created a network far beyond any welfare system yet known to mankind. So shall we? But does mankind want to be helped, they do, but they don't know how because they are brain-washed but not completely brain washed. But the rest of the world is sleepwalking."

Andy was on a roll and continued again. "I shall prove this right now in how Poets are genuine and can save the world. Let's take the sleep walking disorder for an analogy here. The world is sleepwalking and I know this. Let's take the Russian physicists, Leonid Plekhanov and Sergey Plekhanov with their vision to instantly transmit electric energy to any distance via ground and provide an endless source of clean and natural energy for all mankind. Everyone should know about this, and the funds they need to make this happen should be paid instantly on the drop of dime, of a dollar, surely we all can give a dollar to this campaign. We have been monitoring this since the campaign began. And they need the funds, and it's taking too long. Everyone needs to know about this, and maybe we need not to pay our electric bills this month, and pitch in and help out. As a poet myself I see the interference in and on the world we live in. Planes shot down near Russian and who knows what else. Despair is everywhere damn it, can't you all see that we are all brain washed, and it needs to stop? Andy felt something come over him, there was a nasty taste and smell, that came upon him, some kind of virus, but he mentally brushed it off, and continued talking, and what is also messed up is the woman I love is a poet, but she too is brain washed by the feared world, and fear has her, and fear has the world chained to misery and poverty. Can I have some e-paper please?"

"What they ask?" Because Andy broke code to wake the folks in the house up.

Mr. Welchberry, Alphonso G. Newcomer came into the House of Commons, and everyone in sync made the sound of 'Oh!', and it was silent, and then it got loud, and order had to be restored. Mr. Welchberry gave Andy some e-paper and it said, the woman you love is forced to move, and possibly be homeless, and Andy arose to look around. This news threw him into shock and he blacked out; falling forward and busted his head on the table, and from the looks of it, injured his left knee when he fell.

Red looked at everyone, and he stood over Andy, then Red knelt down to make sure Andy had a pulse, and he did. Red looked around again, and saw that no one cared, so Red took over the hearing. Andy will arise soon, let him rest, Red told them all.

Lord Durham then arose and spoke, "Let these men join in with Red and Andy, and also represent them with their mission."

The counsels did not like this, but they had to comply with Lord Durham.

"And yes if we have to pitch a tent here we shall," Said Lord Durham.

Thank you Lord Durham, said Red, We are referring to websites with commercial adds, or places of business in which copyrighted poems could be heard or read, or whether such poetry was live or recorded and, critically, whether or not it generated direct revenues. Whether it pays or not, the purpose of the websites employing it is profit and that is enough. Poets can make their living primarily from fees earned through the sales of books, and cds; Audio and that is where the gap must be filled with the Poem Jukebox and Poetry for the sight impaired.

Red spoke with deep concern for Andy as he laid there unconscious. One of our fundamental goals is to assure that poetry creators are fairly compensated for the public performance of their works, written or spoken, and their rights are properly protected. We need to adopt a royalty-payment mechanism, we call a Poet Igloo, a Poet Igloo license gives signatory legal poetry websites and businesses the right to play or have any poet by an Igloo Poet in exchange for a fixed annual fee, just like ASCAP and BMI. We also need to rethink the role of copyrights in the digitized world. Equity to and for the Poets. As in 1909 the player piano rolls, we have in the 21st Century none legal poetry websites rolling poets and stealing their dignity. Ya Ya the Jook Box with the many c's inside the circle!

"Why an igloo and why are you talking about the future?" Joseph Howe asked.

Water the imagination please, Red said, This is a new poem medium for the poets prosperity. Also because of leaky rules and free-riding Sir, progress, to promote progress again and again. Striking proper balance for Poets, and this burden has been placed on me and Andy, deriving from the originalpoetry.com's abandonment on nearly 40,000 poets and other sites as well, that have not followed through with publishing, and publishing for profit.

Red looked at Andy and hoped he would come to, and Red spoke again. Is poetry a dramatic work? Is the internet now public performance? Is poetry similar to lectures, addresses, and sermons, furthermore oral deliveries? Is a Poet entitled to protection against this new and more complete form of appropriation quite as much as a Poet is entitled to protection from a stage performance of the Poet's Poem.

The Poet and Attorney Joseph Story stood up and spoke a poem,

Be brief, be pointed, let your matter stand
Lucid in order, solid and at hand;
Spend not your words on trifles but condense;
Strike with the mass of thought, not drops of sense;
Press to close with vigor, once begun,
And leave, (how hard the task!) leave off, when done.

Story looked around the House of Commons and said, "We will talk about equity, the poet's equity."

Here shall the Press the People's right maintain,
Unawed by influence and unbribed by gain;
Here Patriot Truth her glorious precepts draw,
Pledged to Religion, Liberty, and Law.

Joseph Story began to speak on the floor in the House of Commons. "Is this not History? Is this not a treatise? The facts are critical and must be foreseen. The facts and circumstances deserve analysis, deserving a test. We ought to have the intellectual honesty to recognize it for what it is. The whole business of human life is no longer flowing on in narrow and shallow channels, so we need not to look at this with careless eyes. They are righteousness and just, furthermore they broke no law, so the question of justice is a matter of whether the administration of law is righteous and impartial. They have litigated their rights without peril. "So who has appropriate Jurisdiction of this Court of Equity, the Queen?" Joseph Story asked, "This bill is original and of discovery and Andy and Red need relief along with this Igloo Bill."

Andy then started to become conscious again because he heard the Queen and the mystery that leads he and Red know, and as Andy slowly got up, he wiped off the sweat from his brow. He thought ya talk in riddles, the Queen, everything leads to the Queen. Andy thought about the poets struggles again and their wisdom, the poetry trains fireman Dominic Albanese came to mind because he has more wood, coal and &c to back this up, and Andy thought Buckle up Bubbas it is time turn the tables.

"Equity follows the law does it not?" Joseph Story asked, "Equity had come not to destroy the law, but to fulfill it!"

The house floor began to roar, and Red thought, turn the tables and then flip them, ah we can do better.

"Hear ye, Hear ye, so who here opposes the Poet Igloo Bill?"
John Reeves who was a judge and author stood up to speak, "Circumstances are complex, like all other circumstances."

English law officers began to fill the House of Commons.

John Reeves continued to speak, "Yes an analysis and a reform is needed. And a granting of legal status for all literary websites. An act incorporating these suggestions may receive royal assent despite opposition. These men need voluntary assistance and wholeheartedly assistance examining both the history and the existing state of their pleadings. As we know there is always a certain Class who set themselves against every attempt to introduce Order and Justice. As Andy said, Without Unity Do Not Expect Miracles! As I have said before, It has happened to the law, as to other productions of human invention, particularly those which are closely connected with the transactions of mankind, that a series of years has gradually wrought such changes as to render many parts of it obsolete, until now; the jurisprudence of one age has become the object of mere historic remembrance in another. Is this why we write about Law, and is this why Poets write Poetry? Of the numerous volumes that compose a lawyer's library, how many are consigned to oblivion by the revolutions in opinions and practice, and what a small part of those which are still considered as in use, is necessary for the purposes of common good and business! The multitude of books and the researches of a lawyer are confined to writers of a certain period, so must that be the same for a Poet. We suffer from the same monster and we have failed and neglected the Poet.

Andy then spoke, "Time within Memory is the Memory within Time. You know they say scholars do not believe in God, can you believe that? Public memory, family lore, lack of historical documents and heavy renovation of the property make it almost impossible to pinpoint an exact history."

Andy was testing the sleep walkers in the House of Commons. Meaning if they don't step up now, the little man with big eraser was right behind them. Andy then walked around, and said, "Automatic protection with extensions, waivers, the use of nicknames, a list of witnesses. The internet is not yet regulated like T.V. and Radio, and since Facebook likes to drill oil up in the north pole, they should pay Poets as clubs, bars and taverns do for musicians. Ya ya and you think poetry and the poetry train wants to be looked at like that. We think not! And they say there is something wrong with the economy, maybe its how one ties one shoes and walks the walk. I am sending out friend requests right now in those House of Commons, and don't block me then turn around and suggest folks that have no clue what is going on, please."

This started another uproar on the floor, and English Law officers surrounded Red and Andy.

"A poetry reader on the Poetry Train has a solution and her name is Sarah Polidoro, she says the company Shazam.com and their technology can help too," Andy proclaimed. "Shazam is a mobile app that recognizes music and TV around you. Why not Poets? This app or one similar can protect poets anywhere and everywhere. Shazam is more than just identification they claim. Poetry is not breaking the 2nd commandment as TV is and has. We call to the wisdom of Neil Postman for that one. We demand a regulatory measure. A decree of the Long Parliament. To the Queen, to the Queen, what a joke. We demand a forum to engage the public. The public needs to be learned about this all. Let the Public be open to truth and understanding, which should not be monopolized by the government's standards. Let the public have say so. Unity secured not by force but by a consensus that respects variety of opinion. We need promised effective safeguards. Where is today's pillory, and whipt?"

Joseph Story spoke, "Why do you all have a John Milton face? Yes it is a 21st Century Areopagitica. Don't go there because you never cared before. I quote Milton, Give Poets the liberty to know, to utter, and to argue freely according to conscience, above all liberties. Is Poetry a threat to you? Are Poets dangerous? We are talking about a secure way that compensates the poets, creates work, to hire people with skills that have no work. Government systems work, the kind that benefits the homeless and such. Unity here, Unlike most monopolies. You want to talk about monopolies and then make Facebook feed the homeless."

"Voices of reason," Andy spoke louder, "Voices of reason. This shall put an end to this dangerous situation, and defects, because our blood is not corrupted. We want Justice, a Known Channel, we the people, we the poets, we the press, and we the homeless. Where we can be freer to show the world their Poets, their happiness, their sufferings, their passions, were they can be safe and gain. Lords and Commons, We stand here today, and dare under the banners of freedom, and shall continue to dare with valor and unity and we ask the same of you. Liberty for the Poets, from you humane, you must take us and Poets seriously worldwide. The State of Illinois in the United States support us and praise our achievements we came to Canada because of the path and the wisdom of the railroads and from the wisdom of the Great Chiefs of the U.S.A. We found their escape route that no historian or lawman has ever found, we found this all through poetry. Give the people a choice, the public a choice, give them the facts. Give us funding and a team to make this happen. Grant the world the Poet Igloo Bill."

Andy held his head up for a moment, and spoke again, "My companion Red has something else to add and may trouble you. And I recite this."

Unlock the paddle locks of your mind
Release the Poets and Poetry to be not confined
Their virtue is true, honest and kind
Help us awake the Sleepwalking blind

Andy added, "Ladies and Gentlemen we have always been obedient and affectionate of the law. A Poet I am, and Poetry & Railroad's Promoting is my profession, and our income is from Book Sales and Poets who donate to me and my companion, and that is all. And this can be boosted to all Poets with the Igloo Bill."

Red gave Andy a pat on the back and spoke, There are no voiceless people. Only people that haven't been heard, yet. Poets world-wide have not been heard. People miss good poetry, and let the public decide what good poetry is not Poets or so called Poetry Publishers. We believe that the right to be heard and read belongs to everyone. Poetry some say does not sell because Poets are unknown. Celebrities and Politicians Poets sell they say, to whom, the average person don't buy them maybe if you are Leonard Nemoy the average person may have his book or Jewel? Poetry should be at the top of the literary chain, why do a study on everyone's attention span. Because of this people want mindless entertainment and instant gratification. Some Poets have no idea about publishing, how to go about it, self or company based that is safe based &c &c. These Poets do not know where to start. The saying "It's not what you know but who you know," let's think of that. Poets do not know whom to go to, and the readers do not know where to go to read. Lords and Commons I have an example, let's examine poemhunter.com who are web-add crazy, and making money off of Poets no longer online or alive like the Poet Pasquale DiMeola, grab your digital gizmos and gander. Createspace.com is probably the best site for Poets, they get better royalties there. Self-promotion is all they have, and then when they do, others call it shameless and look down on them, why? There is a secret, and that is the public wants to know the poet before they purchase their books, a memoir like book inside the book of poetry or prior, and some Poets do not want to be known personally they would rather be mysterious, and be a mystery, and that can be great in the long run. Availability, secure availability... When we say secure, the truly only way for now is this. When Poets take their text of their poem as place over a photo of theirs or in the public domain that goes well with the theme of the poem, they do this with software, and they do this because the Photography industry has their act together, an Act we need for the Poets, a tight nit Unity, the Poet Igloo Bill. This information is from Poets on the Poetry Train, this is their wisdom along with ours, me and Andy, and the whole America journey and Canadian journey. We shouldn't and don't ask you to judge others for not buying poetry. We should judge poetry for not delivering a product people want, and why it is not available, in all create forms known to mankind. People want conflict here you go, this conflict is grand and out of hand. You want face value, well let's face the value. Let's go old school with poetry hands on, hands on books availability everywhere and everywhere, anthologies, interviews, clues to the Poets &c &c. And yes genres have standards, and Poets need standards. Poetry needs to clean up its act before it can become an act, a poet in the train says, and we agree, but how can it with no way to be heard so they work harder. How can a new poet become a new classic poet? The internet is a grown up without regulation, regulation like banks fight piracy. We want to hold those in power accountable for our rights in a digital age. Regulation is pro-innovation for employment and economic equality. Poets can regulate, most are un-employed any way, they can learn to be digital regulators. Andy and I should be the United States of America Poet Laureates, give us a team to build the Poet Igloo Bill. Media Justice for the Poet Igloo Bill and it is original never before litigated and we ask you Lords and Commons to seriously look at this matter and Poet Igloo Bill with high regard, and we ask Joseph Story and his appointed legal team to help us.

"Davy Crockett what a fine case and Poet Igloo Bill indeed," said Joseph Story as he stood up. "I smell oppression. These men are poor, and they are innovators, and their idea to me is more than an Poet Igloo Bill it is a modern patent. They got here by writing and promoting poetry and the railroads with pennies I am sure, and they mentioned donations by their passengers. I find that amazing, and our schools wished we produced genius and will like this. Charming and touching to me."

Whose touch harmonious charms the nascent taste,
With love and rapture warms the poet's page,
Or moulds to deeds divine a slothful age;
And thence, as holier purpose fired his soul,
Sung the First Cause, whose wisdom form'd the whole.
The while he spoke, methought his spirit shed
Some heavenly dew of mingled hope and dread;
Mysterious influence seem'd to haunt the shade,
And round his face transfiguring brightness play'd.

Andy spoke in a louder tone, "Poetry is the up up Syndrome, non- Poetry Literature Readers are Murders I say. Hey remember when Blue Kool Aid came out, Andy laughed and continued saying, And by the way, Children read and you cannot stop them. So Children write poetry and all kinds of books because most are sleep walking."

Red then spoke, It is our right to write poetry and be protected. And Poems written by Poets are their Children, and this is how true Poets look at this fact, yes they do, and now you know this too. We are Poets and Poetry Promoters. A Law needs to work for us. This is important as Freedom and Prosperity. We have been against all odds since day one. We ask to take this knowledge and help us create a Poet Igloo Bill. Money talks and Bullshit walks they say, do you have any idea what we have gone through? We are not talking about a commercial Poet or Poem mill either.

Lord Durham removed the English Law officers from the House of Commons, and said, "Let's let Joseph Story speak now."

"John Reeves," the judge called Joseph Story, and Andy Sandihands and Red Regatta to his seat, and asked them if they would give up the Poetry Train for their freedom.

Red and Andy refused and spoke in synch; You are violating our moral duty. This is our planet too, and No we will not sacrifice our Poetry Train for our freedom, because we are not criminals. Hooks in our mouths will not work. We are not fish, Sorry Charlie.

Sleep walking is real, said Red, Answer me this, how many rich and poor are suicidal people because of money furthermore illiteracy?

Andy retorted, "ha beware of the cing and cang." Andy thought about a spit ball... and Red laughed in his mind.

Lord Durham called back the English Law officers into the House of Commons.

Andy started to sing the song 'Things' Bobby Darin, the Jukebox slowly playing, the Things We are Going to do.

"Order," John Reeves demanded.

"John Reeves," Joseph Story proclaimed, "They are faithful and trustworthy, and follow codes, but it is just the two of them with no funds to hire an expert team to get this started. Poetry books in all forms are the objects and purpose that benefits the world. We need a general policy, closed promises not naked promises. Poets are injured and have been neglected, robbed, and a further investigation on gross amounts. This folly needs to stop, and there needs to be legal obligations for online poetry sites. There needs to be a high degree of diligence and this needs to be brought under review. Poets need an income for what they love to do, if they are professional, and we need to know about standards set standards. Value is an important ingredient also in poetry. Poets need protection. We need to look at this with great concern. I have awoken to these facts and issues. These facts and issues maybe accident or by design, and Red and Andy are the only ones that have brought these facts and issues to the world, and it is going to take Superior skill to solve these matters. Red and Andy are talking about each Poet having an enterprise within an enterprise, protecting and regulating and compensating, but most of all benefiting all, under the Poet Igloo Bill. Unity and Uniformity, Rules Universally. International Justice. We cannot abandon these facts and the Poets and Poetry. They need modern rights and protection as Movie Stars and Performing Artists do, most of all as Citizens do, public welfare. This is not a simple case and law must be enforced wisely and mutually."

Andy looked at Red and said, "Out of the darkness and into the light, the weight of this wisdom is going to take a train with some might! This is some good stuff Maynard. Um Poets are a different kind of Citizen."

"Order," John Reeves demanded.

Lord Durham and Alphonso G. Newcomer looked at each other and smiled.

Joseph Story continued to speak, "Judicial forums must be placed in all countries for Poets and their Poetry, furthermore their equality and their independence. Lawful for all Nations with dignity. Public International law, implemented and applied for modern commerce and intercourse. Common business like anything else. Negotiations and debate must start now with highly regarded principles and no idleness. The best minds must create solid ground for the Poet Igloo Bill. This is now an obligation for Poet statues worldwide, real as any other real statue; this is intellectual property, art of words. A new mixed statue has arisen. Red and Andy see the future because they can see past today."

Red spoke, John Reeves some folk think we are on some crusade, No, we want to awake and create a Poet Parade. We are the elders of Poets, not me and Andy but Poets living today, and they must have a say so too. We did not start this controversy; this was born by multiple reasons. So I court the Jester.

"So the original is from America?" John Reeves asked.

"Maybe more," Joseph Story spoke, "Red and Andy have not fully looked into Canadian sites on their Canadian Journey as they have in America."

Andy spoke, "We have our own Axel F, online detective protecting us."

"Why do you need protection? How can you do better looking at your site here, you have no community? John Reeves asked two questions.

We fired our webmaster for three reasons lack of funds, further powerful protection for the Poets on PoetryTrain.com, and the webmasters incompetency, furthermore, hackers & hijackers on the poetry train, Red explained.

"Sovereignty!" said Andy, "in International Allegiance in Positive Code to Poets and their Poetry worldwide. We want the Poet Igloo Bill to be working with the Library of Congress and other great institutions similar worldwide. Big brother is everywhere but in the Poetry realm. Yes most Poets want to remain private but they want their Poetry to be Read and Protected. Did you all know you are on camera?"

Everyone in the House of Commons looked around, and then everyone laughed.

Mr. Horz Welchberry (his full name finally revealed) came into the House of Commons and spoke to Lord Durham silently.

Murmuring proceeded in the House of Commons.

Lord Durham spoke based off of information from Mr. Horz Welchberry. "John Reeves Andy and Red have a message from a Poet they have reconnected with from OriginalPoetry.com that goes by the writing name Trocka7. I want Andy to read this to you."

"Very well." John Reeves replied.

Andy read the letter to the House of Commons.

"Andy, what happened to the poetry website. I had a lot of my poems on there and it is really sad that I can't access my own work. I am lucky that I have them all in notebooks (somewhere!!), but it's disheartening because I put a lot of time and effort into organizing them all on the site, all in one place where they could be easily accessed instead of scattered about in 25 different notebooks! I am just sad I am so thankful that I remembered you Andy and found you! And yes, I would love to be part of the poetry group PoetryTrain.com. I would be FLIPPING OUT if they weren't all in notebooks!!! These poems came from my heart and soul, and I love them. These are my creations and I would be devastated if they were just totally lost forever. I can't access them now at all, that I had them all in one place, all organized. Now I will have to dig through boxes of old notebooks to try to find them, and they are all scattered. I spent hours upon hours typing them all onto O.P. and I at least had them all typed up. Now I will have to do that all over again. Just really sucks that they didn't at least send out a mass email or something saying that the site was shutting down and giving people time to go to the site and copy all of their own work. I would have appreciated that, being given an advance warning so that I could access my work and copy it all onto my computer. I probably should've done that in the first place, but I didn't ever expect that the site would just shut down with no notice."

Trocka7...

John Reeves, Trocka7 and many other Poets, not just from OP many can be doomed to this, and I do not want to be a smart ass but you all Superiors need to wake up to this fact and stop the sleep walking BS. And I do not give a care if most Poets alive today do not care. No I don't. Me and Red fight for the unborn Poet so they DO NOT HAVE TO DEAL WITH THIS EVER!

"Lord Durham I want these two removed from the House of Commons, this case will continue." John Reeves demanded and got up and left the House of Commons. The House was in an uproar, and the English Law officers cuffed Andy and Red and placed black hoods over their heads and took them away.

Lord Durham, Alphonso G. Newcomer, and Mr. Horz Welchberry looked at each other and smiled.

"Hellishly slow and wobbly," Andy yelled out from inside of his black hood over his head.

Chapter 15-Prince Edward Island Canada October 5th 2014

Red and Andy were taken to Prince Edward Island by steamboat, and once on the waters their hoods were removed, and to their surprise the Lawmen were Drew and Sherbrooke. Arranged by Lord Durham. Sail boats and fishing fleet were everywhere on both sides and waves were engulfing them. The sea was a magnificent tangible spirit they were not use too.

Andy did his wobble bee dance, but differently, and Red smiled, but then frowned and asked, Where is Scratch?

"Scratch is on the ship. It's not over yet. We are hiding you out here for a while until Lord Durham figures out your escape, said Drew, "You must eat now because where we will be hiding you two, will be a place you may not like for a while."

Red was wanting to smile but was puzzled and a bit nauseous from the sea.

As they ate pan-seared scallops with carrot butter and curried pistachios and poached lobster. Andy says, "What, oh well. Things change so slow over years and years, we should be poetry lecturers Red."

Red just laughed, and said, Oh Well, For a while hmm. Well some Poets feel that way about us that is for sure.

"Red I feel so much time has passed this last year and lost," said Andy.

Me too, Red replied, It's the 21st Century Andy. This is some good grub.

"Yes," Andy replied as he put his hand in his pocket, and took out his heart rock, he looked at it and wanted to throw it into the sea, but he thought I'll keep, and place it somewhere at home so Grandkids one day will say hey, This is that Heart Rock, and Andy laughed inside. And a voice that spoke to him inside, Not English, it was Portuguese, Keep trying Andy. No tear fell from Andy's eyes as he cut the rope's anchor of his heart.

Andy and Red noticed as they approached land, the beautiful the red sandstone cliffs, the red soil, and the green of the fields, furthermore the deeper shades of the trees of the forest. Then they noticed an old Fort, the Fort la Joie.

Donald Cameron, farmer, postmaster, and court commissioner and Railway contractors Schreiber and Burpee were waiting ashore for them to take them to meet Thomas

Swinyard and Mrs. W. F. C. Robinson, the wife of the Lieutenant Governor to turn the first sod for the Prince Edward Island Railway.

Red felt better, and they both felt primitive and scoffed at the evolution but felt the transition from sea to land. Once there and on land Donald Cameron asked, "Welcome to our 120 miles long of Island. We are always behind in times aren't we Red and Andy? It is an honor to meet you two."

"Yes," Andy replied, "And there's always ghosts in the glass reflections, and all other kinds of oversights."

"Yes indeed Andy," Donald Cameron replied, "And I am trying to get the crooked bends straight, and remove the powderkegs of patronage and bribery."

Red laughed and said, So have we. We are at the beginning of the Dominion of Canada, such a blessing. To the Dominion of Canada!

"To the Dominion of Canada!" said Andy.

"The Garden of the Gulf," The Poet John LePage came by and he said, "This occasion needs a comic-satiric Ode. The American Volunteers, bringing us Poetic Cheers. Boys my Boys bringing back the years. Red and Andy Poetry Volunteers. And we are so sad, but all will be okay, you will have to sleep in Harvey's Brig for a few days."

Red and Andy looked at each other, then at Drew and Sherbrooke, and then at Donald Cameron and Donald laughed and said, "Harvey's Brig is our wooden jail with ten foot walls, you have to, it's Lord Durhams protocol. We have to meet the Hounslet Engine Company tomorrow to talk about extensive series of shops and a roundhouse, and for now, and as soon as he said now, the Poet Larry Gorman came, and he was reciting his intro to his poem 'The Boys of the Island.'

Come all ye young fellows of Prince Edward Island, Come list to my song and I'll tell you the truth: It's true I'm a native of Prince Edward Island, I'll advise ev'ry young and sensible youth.

Thomas laughed and asked, "The man who makes songs, how are you Larry?"

"Okay," Larry replied, "Just keeping them boys out of trouble. They like drinking. Going to New Brunswick soon enough; lumber and no slumber. And when they see me coming, Their eyes stick out like prongs, Saying, "Beware of Larry Gorman! He's the man who makes the songs." And Larry laughs and, walks away but suddenly stops in his tracks and says guess who's here, beware, beware it's going to get scary here comes Michael O'Leary Mr. Railroad Power.

Michael O'Leary would be that is for sure, more power than any and no one knew what to expect yet as he made his way on horseback to where they all where.

"Charlottetown Charlottetown," Larry Gorman said sarcastically, everyone one here were sarcastic Red and Andy thought. O'Leary Road will lead to O'Leary town," and he laughed. Prince County rail system will be grand, and how about Red and Andy give me a hand, he asked, but then he looked at everyone and said, "We should invite them to The Mechanics Institute."

Red and Andy looked at each and thought, What?

O'Leary laughed so Irish like and said, "It's a place where we promote literary and scientific enlightenment. Poetry and Trains. Tea and Poetry, come lets go, let's go." He then looked at Red and said, "We must show Red the Bog but we must cross of over Black Sam's Bridge, we must, we must." He looked down and said, "Hmm There's Black Sam, Black Bill, and Black Ralph, but a Black Red," and he laughed so Irishly.

Red and Andy looked at each and laughed. And in synch they said, the Poetry Train Party never ends.

Donald Cameron spoke a bit agitated, "Sir we have sod to cut first. We have to meet our views, and the views of Thomas Swinyard and J.E. Boyd."

O'Leary laughed so Irish like and said sarcastically, "Thomas Swinyard and oh Boyd." Then asked, "Where are they anyway, Ottawa?"

"Summerside, winter is coming" Cameron replied and laughed, and about that time a man named John Squire came a walking ringing a bell, and young kids followed him and he was known as the town Crier, but was he crying, He was reciting "Liar Liar Train on Fire, Liar Liar Train on Fire. Oh Yes Oh Yes" And the children looked at him and Red and Andy and asked giggling, "Where you ever in jail?"

"No," Andy said and he sat down, and said,

Street Poet comes up to me one day
Walkin' down the street, and we're mindn' our own business
We look him up and we look him down and says
"Hey man, what be this and what be that
And why you gotta say things like that?"
Well I just looked at him, I kinda laughed, I said
"Hey man, we're cool, We are the Poetry Train"
Haven't you heard, there's a new revolution
Gotta spread the word, too much confusion
All hell's breakin' loose, hey hey have you read the news?
All hell's breakin' loose, overloadin' an' blowin' my fuse
All hell's breakin' loose, day and night baby, night and day

All hell's breakin' loose, in the streets there's a brand new way, yeah
You know we ain't always winners but this is the life we choose
And we won't change or rearrange and we ain't ever ever gonna lose
It ain't always easy when the goin' gets rough
When you're gettin' even, you gotta show your stuff, tell about it now
Take a look around, only one solution
Set the world on fire, fight the institution
Gonna stand our ground, feel the new sensation
Something's goin' down, Poetry Train the nation

Everyone clapped their hands and said, "Wow that was good."

"Ya ya" Andy said, "We call that Kiss, and you all need to stop right now. Fire everyone right now. Corruption starts here, Prejudice starts here, stop being prejudice please, Division starts here, and can you all see this, or are you sleepwalking too, and ya ya, we maybe dreaming, but we all can make the world a better place if we'd just wake up and shake up."

"You are like a Shakespearean," said Poet Larry Gorman, "Ya ya that's power Mr. O'Leary."

Red sat next to Andy and mind nudged him to look into the woods. The both thought of the wolf that followed them.

A man came out of nowhere and he was the Poet Lawrence Doyle and he sat down too. Evil is here, and most people are going to America. Lawrence recited.

The poor man drags along;
He hears a whistle loud and shrill,
The "Iron Horse" speeds on;
He throws his pack upon his back,
There's nothing left to do;
He boards the train for Bangor, Maine,
Prince Edward Isle adieu.

Lawrence then in a whisper asked Andy and Red, "Are you ready to board the Ark?"

Red and Andy sensed something. They sensed it was time to move on, they also sensed that they were looked at in many ways through Canada, and hoped they would be remembered for their efforts and heart. They knew only certain people had the gene, the gene thought, that could finally see through everything, without time and truth. A glimpsing gene, that sees past, present and future as one. Then the sensed they never made it to Dingle Tower, but did not say anything.

Lawrence then in a whisper said to them, "We have to make a run for the ship, trust me on this. Secret orders from Lord Durham."

Everyone there was looking at them. Andy looked to the stars in the sky. Red was looking at the stupidity of prejudice he has sensed in every eye, and thought why.

Andy then looked at Poet Lawrence Doyle, and said, "We hope you run fast, we will be right behind you immortalizing," and Andy got up and said, "Let's go with it."

Lawrence Doyle got up and started the escape, and they ran following. This was no marathon, nor a bearathon, carathon, darathon, farathon, or narathon, maybe a rarathon, but more like a where-athon, where were they going?

The flashes began and these flashes were unlike no other. The veil of the world was lifted and it was a perfect beauty beyond.

Red and Andy then heard a young girl's voice as they ran and it spoke, "Memory picture, memory picture, memory picture."

And then they see this girl who spoke to them she was sitting in the grass, and this girl was little young Lucy Maud Montgomery about five years old. They both stopped in their running tracks, and they saw all of her many imaginary friends and worlds to cope with her loneliness. They then sat down next to her and she did not look at them; she then was making a scrap book and as they looked at what she was doing, she was making them, things of Red and Andy. She then spoke without moving her lips, a telepathy of some sorts, "Memory picture, memory picture, memory picture." She then looked them and said, "Loneliness, loneliness is why we write, loneliness, and together in writing we live forever here on earth, in loneliness and we hope we soothe the reader, sooth."

Lawrence Doyle spoke, "Andy and Red we must go, we must. There is a rowboat by the sea, we must take it to the William D. Lawrence Ship. Come!"

The sky looked like it was about to storm again, so they got up and Andy looked at Lucy Maud Montgomery, he looked at her parted hair and smiled. Red looked at the land, and searched for the wolf, and they ran to the sea. Bogs and water was everywhere as they splashed through puddles of water to the sea. They just came across the sea they thought, and they thought, they were glad they ate, because it took all the energy they had to do what they had to do. They saw the row boat and it was in sand. The dark blue sea had back flowed some, but was raging and rolling, and they were lucky the sea did not take the boat fully away. Sea gulls were making more noise than usual. The William D. Lawrence Ship and storm was not too far away but far enough to take any energy they had away.

Andy looked at Red as they looked at the sea and ship and said, "We have not been confronted by the world, and have been transformed by these journeys, poetry and our minds, and we have proved what is good."

Red smiled, and said, Yes we have Andy yes we have.

As they came closer to the William D. Lawrence Ship a rope ladder was thrown over to them, and it was Frederick Dibbley, and he said, "Wobbley, Wobbley," and they looked at Lawrence Doyle and he said, "It's okay, good luck men, farewell." Red and Andy said, Thanks, and climbed up to the deck of the ship.

Shipping Magnate Samuel Cunard was there to meet and greet them, and he said, "This vessel is one of the very best of description, and passes my inspection and examination, and of the Admiralty. A comfortable ship. We will follow and protect Captain Stiffe, and the CS Westmeath steamship to Bermuda as it lays the Atlantic Cable."

Red and Andy looked at the circular iron tanks that held copper cables coiled underwater on the CS Westmeath steamship that was on the other side of the Ship.

Samuel Cunard looked at them and said, "Gentlemen you two, listen to me, and remember my words, To use means to ends; to set causes in motion; to wield the machine of society; to subject the wills of others to your own; to manage abler men than yourself by means of that which is stronger in them than their wisdom, viz. their weakness and their folly; to calculate the resistance of ignorance and prejudice to your designs, and by obviating, to turn them to account; to foresee a long, obscure, and complicated train of events, of chances and openings of success; to unwind the web of others' policy and weave your own out of it; to judge of the effects of things, not in the abstract, but with reference to all their bearings, ramifications, and impediments; to understand character thoroughly; to see latent talent or lurking treachery; to know mankind for what they are, and use them as they deserve; to have a purpose steadily in view, and to effect it after removing every obstacle; to master others and be true to yourself, asks power and knowledge, both nerves and brain. Such is the sort of talent that may be shown and that has been possessed by the great leaders on the stage of the world. You are going to your next stage, farewell, and Samuel Cunard left the ship."

Telegraphy and Telepathy, Geography, spoke Red.

"Ya hack our telepathy," said Andy and they both laughed.

They then heard a voice they have not heard in a very long time singing in Gaelic. A song by Malcolm Gillis.

Na Cnuic 's na glinn bu bhoidheache leinn
'S iad cnuic is glinn a' Bhraigh-idh
Mu'n tric bha sinn ri manran binn
'S a chomunn ghrinn a b'fhearr leinn

The hills and valleys most beautiful to us

*They are the hills and glens of Margaree
Where often we sang the sweet melodies
In the kind company we liked best*

And it was Patrick O'Hara, and he smiled and said, "Welcome, good to see you, and the Tudor Conquest is on. Andy it's time to be a tougher Irishmen. You both are going to love this ship it has its own farm on it, and I have my own train aboard this ship."

Andy smiled, and with his horse keenness he noticed whales leaping in the sea and the ship started moving out and south.

Red said, All is good, as long as we are not headed down the Mississippi, so tired of cussing River Men and Cussing Lawyers.

Andy then noticed cat hair on deck, or was it Lion Hair? No it was the hair of the Puma, Scratch.

As they walked below Guinea Hens were in cages in the kitchen. The smell got to Andy right away. But that did not matter it was good to be in the presence of Patrick O'Hara again. A Donkey walked by, and two Calico Cats did too, and a Black Dog. Andy loved the features of this Dog, the kind Andy dreamed of while he was a boy. The dirty floor of mud and animal dung was getting to Red, and Andy, but they tele-thought animals know kindness and morality. We will help you, the animals, they thought.

Andy then sung the song, "Green Eyed Lady" by Sugarloaf, and Red said, To kiss the green eyed lady means to drown at sea.

And Patrick O'hara said, "Any sailor knows that the green eyed lady is the ocean."

*Green-eyed lady, ocean lady
Soothing every raging wave that comes*

*Green-eyed lady, passion's lady
Dressed in love, she lives for life to be
Green-eyed lady feels life I never see
Setting suns and lonely lovers free*

This voyage will change the course of Poetry History. The Flight of the Poetry Train.

There was so much beauty, there could only be silence.

Poems by Various Poets

Poetry Train, All Aboard

The train wheels are clicking
travelling down this track
bringing the Spirit of the Word to all,
there'll be no turning back.

Clickety-clack on the Poetry Train,
all aboard, poetry and song.
From one great ocean of this land
to the other we keep rolling on.

Share your words, shine your light,
the engineer is riding free.
Come aboard, come aboard, the Poetry Train
shore to shore for you and for me.

Let's light up the country with every colour,
let our words reach all corners of the earth.
Let's share the gift of Peace with all -
Poetry Train is growing in girth.

The bigger the crowd, the larger she grows,
rolling on down the track.
Poetry Train gathering poets worldwide,
giving society something they lack.

The power of the Word in our heart;
travelling on wings, we are shining.
Down the tracks to cities across this land –
Poetry is the silver lining.

Shine on great poets, shine on to the world,
musicians tap your toes to the rhythm.
Celebrate the joy of the beautiful Word –
praise this treasure that we've been given.

Deborah L. Kelly 2013

The Railroad

The dreams of men are forged from yellow metal,
With rich and poor desirous of the same.
In railway camps around the fire and kettle
From all around the world the dreamers came.

They dreamed a band of bright unbroken steel
Extending from the East Coast to the West.
The rhythm of the pistons and the wheel,
They heard that in staccato anapest,

The promise that would make a nation great,
The fortune they would realize in time,
The chance to buy a farm and change your fate,
They added up, the nickels and the dimes,

Some chickens for a mother in Canton,
Some money set aside so one could marry,
With dreams ornate or humble they pushed on
As dreams will not come true for those who tarry.

Through epidemic, avalanche and cold
They drove the spikes securing every rail
While coast to coast their progress was retold
As trestles bridged the mountain top and vale,

They built a nation out of rock and air.
Yet still with dreams of gold it should be said
That someone's bound to take the lion's share
And dreams forsake the broken and the dead.

© Glenn Meisenheimer

The Chattanooga Flyer

There's a locomotive chugging down a pair of metal rails,
As the rhythm of the pounding of her pistons never fails,
With the smoke that comes a billowing, the sparks that fill the sky
While the Chattanooga Flyer whistles shrill and thunders by!

She will roar across the trestles that transverse the deep defiles,
And will rumble through the forests and the hills for countless miles.
As the harvest moon comes rising with it's eerie yellow light
You will hear her lonely whistle in the silence of the night.

© Glenn Meisenheimer

Shaughnessy Ride

I'd like to chug and glide a train
up the rise into the gravity of Shaughnessy, angle
around the curves of Angus Drive, the slopes
of Lilliputian meadows the green of sky
feed ravens from an open window
and ride a CPR train into the past

before the concrete, the million-dollar faces, past
memory's blockades. I'd like to ride a railway-baron train
lounge in a dining car and trace through velvet-curtained windows
the half-moon bays of Marguerite, angle
caboose past hedgerows, gaudy dancers, cedar sky
the luscious dips and slopes

of topiary beasts and yews that edge the slopes
I'd like to whistle-blow a locomotion past
gates and motion sensors, barreling through sky-
blue pools and invisible fences, I'd like to steer a cardinal train
through trespass laws and undulating angles
hands grasping willows weeping into ponds outside the window

elegant geometry, banks and arcs reflected in the window's
placid lake. I'd like to tumble-down a lexiscape of slopes
the stagger joints and rock-offs, curl around angles
in degrees, on tangent tracks, steep gradients past
crossovers, turnouts and corridors of train
ghosts lingering in the terminal between earth and sky

pink magnolias, birds in flight, the stippled sky
a backdrop, marble and stone and shuttered windows
the air itself purified. I'd like to ram a train
through porticos and granite lives through market slopes
and slides down an embankment past
the manicured facades of Hosner, Nanton, Pine, angle

across sentinel displays, stacked railway ties angling
the landscape. Steel banding rips into a guillotine sky
stakes drop, turnabouts cog past
spires and chimneys cupolas bay windows
columns and arches, wrought iron gates and copper slopes
of roofs. I'd like to tunnel drive a train

metal on metal, the past a siding track, a train
angled into a cutting camellia sky
the screech of brakes the open window the violet slopes

by Genni Gunn

On the Rails

As a teenager I felt the draw of the rails. I was egged on by a cousin who was employed by the Canadian National Railway (passenger trains). I was thinking about my short ride aboard the Poetry Train and, the rail terminologies which exist. Here's a little poetic fun with some terminologies encapsulated by CAPS. (By the way, I have never been employed by a rail company). I am enjoying the early ride on the Poetry Train. The company of the passengers makes the journey much more enjoyable. Mr. Engineer, you are doing a fine job driving. All aboard!

Like an EXPRESS TRAIN growling, hauling ass,
the rumbling in my soul would eventually pass.
Out of sight and over the hill,
soon to be quiet, unnaturally still.

I received her ABSOLUTE SIGNAL of that I was sure,
there was intense firm ADEHESION between we two.
The collective ADHESIVE WEIGHT was adding up and driving us on,
with an AIR CUSHION between us who really knew?

I was the ALTERNATOR, but I let my WHEEL SLIP,
sparks flew with energy, generating positive WHEEL TREAD.
With a blast of the WHISTLE, I BANKed toward the BAY PLATFORM ahead,
I resembled an oblivious, displaced DEADHEAD.

I pulled the ALERTER to stop the flagrant discord,
an ALL WEATHER intrusion was swept aside,
The TRAINMASTER hollered, with the voice of RECORD,
assigned her to the ANGEL SEAT for the rest of the RIDE.

Her ARMATURE rotated at an odd degree,
the ENGINEER ARTICULATED the ASYNCHRONOUS, with a loud decree.
With a wave of the LANTERN, it was full STEAM ahead,
like an END CAB SWITCHER and an EX-CON RFE.

It was a FULL SERVICE REDUCTION.
She decried, I am not a GEEP,
but a GANDY DANCER,
FAIRLIE expensive, not at all cheap.

I was so mesmerized I barely HIT THE GROUND,
she had to believe I wasn't the HOGGER kind.

I needed the overbold HEAVYWEIGHT SIGNAL to calm me down
in HAMMERHEAD STYLE, with an ear to the ground.

I ranted like a FOAMER,
it was my FOULING POINT.
My GLAD HAD extended,
I was gathering POINTS.

Her PROFILE was graceful,
it was off the RAILS.
A KNOCK DOWN KICKER,
OUT TO FOUL my sails.

I am an OUTLAW at times,
and others I am a PENNSY with a PER DIEM,
a KEEPER of sorts,
holder of the KEY to the RAILWAY MUSEUM.

I'd rather be a KEEPER,
to her KICKER of a love starved heart.
A ONE-MAN OPERATION,
the PRIME MOVER, not a lowly PULL-APART.
We would be MATING WORMS forever,
on the MILK TRAIN of love,
Pulled by a MIKADO or a MOGUL,
headed to the MOUNTAIN above.

You could easily DERAIL me,
at the ELEVATED RAILWAY, on the BRIDGE above.
I would avoid the BUBBLE CAR at the FIDDLE YARD
and the FLATCAR of UNCOUPLED love.

A MOTORMAN no longer, I will decree,
on the RAILS OVERBRIDGE, you will have to agree.
I was a ONE-MAN OPERATION, well kinda sort of,
now a BUCKEYE COUPLER aboard the FREIGHT TRAIN of love.

©Geo Thompson
Mar 20, 2014 10:27:22 AM

The softest train derailed

(On the route to everlasting love).

The softest train derailed
On the route to everlasting love
High mountains shelters fall
Trees sway in sadness
Their whispering
caught within the wind
A torrential rainfall bruised sky
Clouds are no longer floating
Falling with such force
The softest train off course
Hit the edge of a shadows fall
Knocking love down heart and all.

Nardine Sanderson 17/09/2014.

midnight train

I shall not fall victim,
To this night force in vain,
Escape to the sun,
Before the call,
This midnight train,
Who longing tries to run me down,
Over and over again,
I'll escape somewhere high,
Above the wildering terrain,
I shall suffer no more,
in darkness,
nor In pain,
I'll climb closer to the sun,
I shall not be a victim,
You i shall overcome,
For you are just secondary,
It's i who is number one,
I control my feelings,
you the midnight train,
It's you who shall fall,
I shall stand tall,
And in prosperity I shall reign.

Nardine Sanderson 12/07/2014.

TRAIN in TRANSFORMATION

Tracks unused....overgrown
wail....of the distant moan
chug chug chug
'

Empty hollowly
upon the track that can't look back
built by the broken backs
'

Sweat sorrow and strength
of men forced to the length
distance is a mirage
'

That reflects and dissects the past
a destiny and a dynasty cast
upon the winds awash
'

With change
the Train
a remnant of glory and history
'

Shining and steaming
smoke streaming
in the bright sunlight
'

Time glimmers
we have a glimmer
a glimpse
'

Of the journey infinity
the railroad's serenity and calamity
defining the winding
'

Trail
the tenuous tale
the passengers
'

Dining in luxury
amid the rugged beauty
the bones of the laborers
'

Moaning
shaping....re-forming
the landscape
'

Along....the unused track
for....those who lack
not....vision
'

Passengers....celebrate
laborers concentrate
as....an ancient vision awakes
'

....Noon
....zooms
to the rattling roar
'

And....the winsome whistle
along the thistle
and testimony of the thorn
'

The horn drifts
as....you catch a whiff
of the wood
'

And....the steel
the rail....the spark of the wheel
as....the Train that Transforms
'

Races....to the future
right on time
right....down the line....puffing fine'

THE SINGING TRAIN

Sit....in deliberate attempt
Not....to fall asleep

On the Singing Train
The urge to sleep

Getting stronger and stronger
Visions of macabre murals

Flash by....imagination
Playing tricks with the eyes

The Motorman....
Described in novels

Becomes aware
Of the Music set to

The Wheels in motion
He begins....to write songs

Amused by the naiveté
Of the One....He writes

Another stop....along the erotic
Mystic hours....grips

Sanity and concentration
As He....masters the trick

Willing to ride
Further....than His destination

Yotanka Coicou / Yotanka E. B. Aknatoy

TRACK LOOK

wind on length of rail
wooden slats....steel wheels
rumble.. round a bend
with window watchers looking
out to the plains....rains...whispering wind
left the stations
a while ago
was "busy" well
now...from the snow covered
Canada with Geo Thompson to the wooden bridge
with Dana Zoe or the wild California North
where Donna Lee resides
swing chug puff puff
cross the wide open John Wordslinger flats
down to the palm tree river top
draw side' over the causeway

Chug Chug
my few simple word
working finger bent
"o give me songs of love"
this train.....yes the poetry train
bot sot plip plop flip flop got
me back "on track"
so
I am
back
by Dominic Albanese 12/25/14

The E-Train

On the E-Train we shall ride...to cross the lands upon rails of iron...sharing all beauty seeping into our shadows...as wordslingers speak unto the night
***
The sunset draws nigh...trails of emotion joining images drawn...a sigh in the light that whithers...only to stop for those that follow
***
We seek dreams ever forgotten...open arms in spirits combined...words become novels of shifting grains...like the fruit sands may bare of stories retold

Copyright by Glenn Shaw 1/23/15

Ethel and Gertrude

There are two old locomotive engines
That have been left
For scrap
They sit out there
Being consumed by the tall grass
As it grows taller and taller

Once at full service
They have travelled afar
Ethel and Gertrude
They have seen it all

They ran on those rails
Like it was nobody's business
That's how they go
That's how they rolled

They've pulled wheat across the plains
Delivered cars across the land
Passed through the mountains
Travelled on rails by sea and sandy shores

They have taken travel companions
From the west to the eastern seaboard
Gone North to Alaska
And south to Florida

Pulled tankers full of oil
Cars full of cars
Heavy loads of grain and steel
Guided sometimes by the light of the stars

Now you remember them
These two grand old ladies
Have really seen it all
Only to come to a final halt
No more wakeup call
Ethel and Gertrude
That was your last call
Clickety clack! Clickety clack! Clickety clack!
Clickety, clickety, clickety clack!
Wooooooooooo! Wooooooooooo!

By Deborah Thompson
21/03/2015

Get On the Train

Get on this train to Kampala,
your name is on the wanted list.
I have order to deliver you to my boss
in peace if you accept, and in pieces
if you insist you want to protest.

The commanding officer will kick
your teeth and spit in your sharp left eye.
He has a lot of phlegm for intellectuals
who don't cooperate so get on board fast.

Get on train, the whistle been blown.
It's a free ride quickly get on the train
because I said so and am a soldier,
because your fate has been sealed.
Field Marshal Idd Amin the president
wants your political head as a present.
You have been a critical desident,
come pay the price of your malevolence.

Get on the train, your satirical writings
have been published all over the world.
It starts on the train, be a gentleman.
Your wife is already wailing loudly,
she will collapse if I kick your ribs now.
You can no longer wave to this crowd
so smile to these pipping cameras
and get on the train real fast.

At Uganda Railway 1977 by Toyota M. Safari 27 March 2015

VAGABOND DAYS

The vagabond days approach
On thundering panther paws.
I board them as a hobo does
A fast running freight train.
There's danger in the air,
Excitement hovering there.
I was born for days like these.
They've always been chasing me down.

The vagabond days approach
On powerful sweating haunches.
I feel them breathing down my neck;
A cloyed breath, laced with
Frosty nights and sultry days,
In the wake of distant thunder.

The vagabond days approach
Closing in on me..
I slow my pace,
Readying myself for sweet surrender,
Throwing off my disguise,
Finally coming to terms with
My heart,
And,
The vagabond I am.

© 2010 Candice James

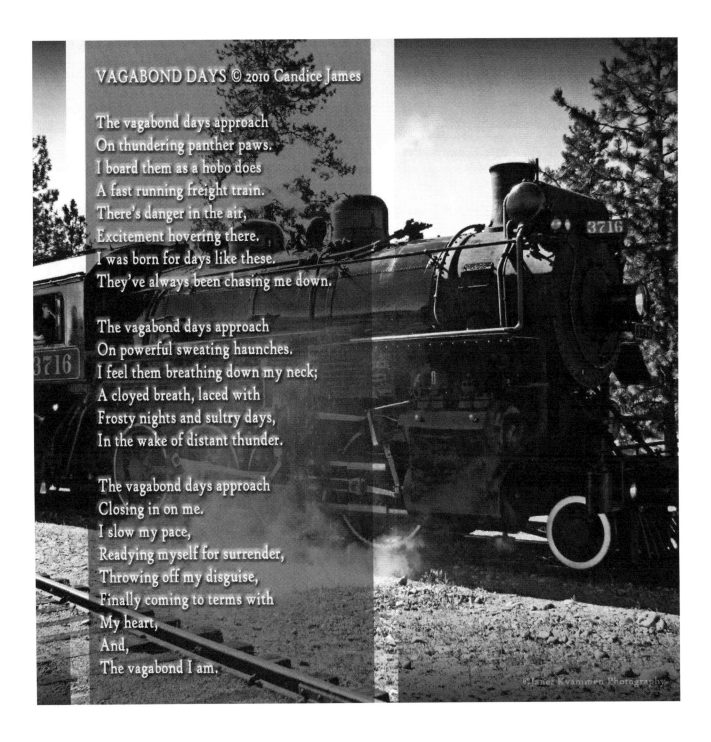

VAGABOND DAYS © 2010 Candice James

The vagabond days approach
On thundering panther paws.
I board them as a hobo does
A fast running freight train.
There's danger in the air,
Excitement hovering there.
I was born for days like these.
They've always been chasing me down.

The vagabond days approach
On powerful sweating haunches.
I feel them breathing down my neck;
A cloyed breath, laced with
Frosty nights and sultry days,
In the wake of distant thunder.

The vagabond days approach
Closing in on me.
I slow my pace,
Readying myself for surrender,
Throwing off my disguise,
Finally coming to terms with
My heart,
And,
The vagabond I am.

AWAY

I'll go to the past,
will fall into the depths of soul,
with love review grains of my former feeling
to you.
I can't destroy the mythical sand castle,
which is a heavy stone on my heart-
lays...and there is no other ways.
It doesn't give to live.
And no help from healing.
The lot waits,
when I'll fall apart...
I still cling of the hope of living...
Still in the glass of morning dew
with bated breath
I try to find reflection of your view;
and still compare your way
as part of glowing colours of summer day.
...If only could I say-
stay, stay with me...please, stay...
But life moves to the end of play,
and there is no other train-
the time cannot be turn again,
we cannot live two lives in parallel.
Before my eyes-there is only trail of train...
last train...away...

©Natalia Govsha

The Sorrow of Dreams

Our emotions are like the ink we spill,
Every poem that we craft becomes an addictive pill.
With each idea we are driven to write on,
Just as the morning continues to welcome the dawn.

Our verses transform into speakers in our head,
Giving us muses to write about until we are dead.
Still we are scattered like the wind and thrive,
Every word a testament to why we are still alive.

The greats like Poe, Dante and Frost,
We take our fill, no matter the cost.
Poetry is a craft that has shaped humanity into what it is today,
But today's poets face challenges that make them want to hide their talents away.

We are like herds of cattle being led to slaughter for what we know,
Given only a pat on the back to stroke our ever bigger egos.
This is mere pittance for the ability we hold in our minds and hands,
Being the fool of the game while everyone takes what they can.

For all artists, this will be their ultimate fall,
And as we die out it is our pain that litters the text into history wall.
Unscrupulous vultures who promise to make us famous at a certain cost,
And for the sake of survival it is our dreams that are lost.

On the web we try to find kindred souls that share our pain,
But there we find only more unspoken shame.
Instead of learning from each we shame the other to show pride,
Not understanding or caring that their insight into poetry could be a great personal guide.

We begin the fight over who is the better or the worst to love or hate,
Not seeing that we are slowly sealing our own fate.
After it is all done and said,
We are left with the ashes of hopes and dreams that are now dead.

Is there any hope that we can we really band together and work as one?
For if so, look at all the good that can be done.
There are a few who are willing to endure the pain,
Taking a flight on what we will call the poetry train.

All aboard for the ride of our lives is about to start,
Let's follow this dream and do something for our own hearts.

(A Collaboration of Robert Niswander and Beverly Cialone)

The Poetry Train A

There is a train of mostly words of poets and of rhyme.
It goes all around the world it does not need time.
A train that hoots and whistles of darkness and of light,
Of mystery and wisdom of wrong and right.
A train that's old and young with poets of delight,
Of anger and of love of sky and earth.
And on this train are poems and prose of people that enjoy
The written and the spoken art of rhythm, rhyme and prose.
So all aboard this train of words where silence is rarely heard.
And minds expand as words unfold from poets young and old.

By Carlos Gomez 3-7-14

The Poetry Train B

Just like a train made up of many different rail cars
Appointed to a certain destination
With a rail life allowed to go to forty years old
Only allowed to be extended by special written concession
In so many words "please let me live the 10 more years allotted"
The cold hard steel of the railroad car tells many stories
Lends so much imagery to a poet working the rail yard
The train, the locomotive, the railroad car
Brings about another life to his/her mind
Words written and spoken swirl through minds
Just like the diesel smoke that rises from the road jack's stack
Power is exhausted and released into the air before the pull
Onward the train rolls and flows like a snake that slitters
Meeting every curve with an industry glee
Cold hard steel bangs, creaks and moans
Wheels squawk and scream out as they roll upon the rail
For those that hear and for those that listen
The train lives a life telling a story
About the food and the roof overhead given
To the railroaders of present and railroaders of old
The train helps sustain ongoing life
As with the train the Poetry Train rolls on
This train made up of many different cars
Switched out and put together in the rail yard of words
Different cars, different sounds and different voices
Destined for the depot known as "Expression"
All aboard!
Were in good hands with engineer John. By K.R. Graff 3/9/14

The Poetry Train C

We get on this train
Mostly with our brain
But our bodies also feel the rhythm
The click and the clack
Of the words on the track
For love of sound and reason
As the wordsparks fly
They get in our eyes
And our hearts are brought to blossom
So please climb on board
And instead the sword
Bring your pen ready and willing.

Y. Yi Pang, 3/10/14

REST IN PEACE-POETS MEMORIAL

Scott Bates (Tennessee USA)
Zaccheus Jackson Nyce (British Columbia)
Dean Morrison McKenzie (Saskatchewan)
Stan Carew (Nova Scotia)

Bill to the United States of America

114th CONGRESS
1st Session

Senate Bill #1

A Bill for an Act, POET IGLOO

In The Senate
& the House of Representatives

August 12th, 2015

  To Amend the Communications Decency Act, the Digital Millennium Copyright Act, & TEACH Act, and furthermore all Copyright Laws to ensure protection, fairness, and transparency on online/internet publishing and business concerns to online/internet poetry. Resolved by the U.S. Senate of the United States of America, that the following article is proposed as federal law under the jurisdiction of the United States of America, enforceable by Executive action. Be it enacted by the Senate and House of Representatives of the United States of America in Congress assembled, that:

Your State's Senator's Name Here & Mr. John E. O'Hara aka John E. WordSlinger of Illinois, (fill your name and location here) (Your State's Senator's Name Here, for Mr. John E. O'Hara and I, PoetryTrain.com and all International Poets of all ages) introduced the following Bill; which was referred to the Committee on online/internet publishing and business concerns, and in addition to the Committee on Oversight and Government Reform, for a period to be subsequently determined by the Speaker, in each case for consideration of such provisions as fall within the jurisdiction of the committee concerned.

POET IGLOO BILL

Preamble:

The Poet Igloo Bill/Act executed, protects Poets and their work & Under the Igloo Bill/Act the Poet has the option for adoption and adopting, legal publishers too can adopt a Poet or vice a versa, and this adoption helps the Igloo expand and strengthen. Creating a partnership, a membership association protecting Poets, their Poetry and the name of Poetry from modern un-licensed literary websites and the seventy five year old rejuvenating Monster, known as Orphan Works Law protecting and destroying literary works. In the Poet Igloo bill/Act, Poets are protected from the Big Bad Wolf of time and publishing negligence. Poets and Publishers can create their own ice block sort of speak for the Igloo from the inside out, with all of their ideas to help and strengthen the Poet Igloo, and Poet Igloo Bill/Act, and all of their poetic wills, just like a living will, furthermore, the Poet Igloo Bill/Act creates laws for online poetry websites requiring them to be legal. Similar to ASCAP and BMI, and using the same tools they do, with two tools added, the poetry e train and a poetry website license task force.

The current copyright law is causing gridlock in the digital marketplace known as the Orphan Works. All Poets and their families today will have this problem one day in the future. Poetry can feed the world's homeless with this system.

Let's take the invention of the American Jukebox, that preserves culture, and brings the world together. A poem jukebox. This Poet Igloo Bill/Act with a manufacturing plant with distribution of poetry jukeboxes, distributed everywhere, with poetry heard and read from all over the world, furthermore poetry for the sight impaired. Poetry and the Poem Jukebox via satellite called high tech/safe-Wi-Fi shall compete with a large television company's and the music industry. Please don't let me get on the talk about lottery machines and &c &c that ruins more families then benefits them. Safeguarded Wi-Fi powered by icomera.com or a division similar created by Congress, icomera.com bought out Greyhound because of corruption, their Wi-Fi needs to be on Amtrak, let the Poets buy out Amtrak. icomera.com and Peter Kingsland, Chris Chinnapan, and Saeed Bashirian can make this happen for Poets too with their powerful icomera. Movemanage. A Poem-graph, an Engineered Poetry System aka the Poetry Train with Railroad History on audio under the Igloo Bill/Act as well, and the world is the Board of Review.

If we planned and planned and created a network far beyond any welfare system yet known to mankind. Creating jobs, careers in the literary world, with all new technology tools. We are referring with tasteful commercial adds like Papermate, &c, any company that pertains to the Literary Arts, or places of business in which copyrighted poems could be heard or read, or whether such poetry was live or recorded and, critically, whether or not it generated direct revenues. The purpose of the Poet Igloo/website employing it is profit and that is enough. Poets can make their living primarily from fees earned through jukebox plays, sales of books, and cds; Audio and that is where the gap must be filled with the Poem Jukebox and Poetry for the sight impaired.

One of our fundamental goals is to assure that poetry creators are fairly compensated for the public performance of their works, written or spoken, and their rights are properly protected. We need to adopt a royalty-payment mechanism, we call a Poet Igloo, a Poet Igloo license gives signatory legal poetry websites and businesses the right to play or have any poet by an Igloo Poet in exchange for a fixed annual fee, just like ASCAP and BMI.

This is a new poem medium for the Poets prosperity. This burden has been placed on me, and poetrytrain.com deriving from the originalpoetry.com's abandonment on nearly 40,000 poets and other sites as well, that have not followed through with publishing, and publishing for profit.

Is poetry a dramatic work? Is the internet now public performance? Is poetry similar to lectures, addresses, and sermons, furthermore oral deliveries? Is a Poet entitled to protection against this new and more complete form of appropriation quite as much as a Poet is entitled to protection from a stage performance of the Poets Poem.

Is this not History? Is this not a treatise? The facts are critical and must be foreseen. The facts and circumstances deserve analysis, deserving a test. We ought to have the intellectual honesty to recognize it for what it is. The whole business of human life is no longer flowing on in narrow and shallow channels, so we need not to look at this with careless eyes. So who has appropriate Jurisdiction of this Court of Equity? This bill is original and of discovery, and Mr. O'Hara and the Poets need relief along with this Igloo Bill.

An analysis and a reform is needed as well as a granting of legal status for all literary websites. An act incorporating these suggestions may receive royal assent despite opposition. PoetryTrain.com, the Poet Igloo and Poets need voluntary assistance and wholeheartedly assistance examining both the history and the existing state of these pleadings. As we know there is always a certain Class who set themselves against every attempt to introduce Order and Justice. Without Unity Do Not Expect Miracles! It has happened to the law, as to other productions of human invention, particularly those which are closely connected with the transactions of mankind, that a series of years has gradually wrought such changes as to render many parts of it obsolete, until now; the jurisprudence of one age has become the object of mere historic remembrance in another. Is this why you write about Law, and is this why Poets write Poetry? Of the numerous volumes that compose a lawyer's library, how many are consigned to oblivion by the revolutions in opinions and practice, and what a small part of those which are still considered as in use, is necessary for the purposes of common good and business! The multitude of books, the researches of a lawyer are confined to writers of a certain period, so must that be the same for a Poet. We suffer from the same monster, and we have failed and neglected the Poet.

Automatic protection with extensions, waivers, the use of nicknames, a list of witnesses. The internet is not yet regulated like T.V. and Radio, and since there are powerful websites online making much money, they should pay Poets as clubs, bars and taverns do for musicians if they post & upload their literary works on these sites.

The company Shazam.com and their technology can help too. Shazam is a mobile app that recognizes music and TV around you. Why not Poets? This app or one similar can protect poets anywhere and everywhere. Shazam is more than just identification they claim. Poetry is not breaking the 2nd commandment as TV is and has. We call to the wisdom of Neil Postman for that one. We demand a regulatory measure. A decree of Congress.

We demand a forum to engage the public. The public needs to be learned about this all. Let the Public be open to truth and understanding, which should not be monopolized by the independent standards. Let the public have say so. Unity secured not by force but by a consensus that respects variety of opinion. We need a promised effective safeguards. We are talking about a secure way that compensates the Poets, creates work, to hire people with skills that have no work. Government systems work, the kind that benefits the homeless and such. Unity here. Unlike most monopolies. Not Hand Outs, Hard Work in Unity For Poetry and the Needy, Monitored by Law.

Voices of reason. We want Justice, a Known Channel as the Poet Igloo Bill into Act, we the people, we the Poets, we the press, and we the homeless. Where we can be freer to show the world their Poets, their happiness, their sufferings, their passions, were they can be safe and gain. We stand today, and dare under the banners of freedom, and shall continue to dare with valor and unity and we ask the same of you. Liberty for the Poets, from you humane, you must take us and Poets seriously worldwide.

Give the people a choice, the public a choice, give them the facts. Give us funding and a team to make this happen. Grant the world the Poet Igloo Bill/Act.

There are no voiceless people. Only people that haven't been heard, yet. Poets world-wide have not been heard. People miss good poetry, and let the public decide what good poetry is not Poets or so called Poetry Publishers. We believe that the right to be heard and read belongs to everyone. Poetry some say does not sell because Poets are unknown. Celebrities and Politicians Poets sell they say, to whom, the average person don't buy them maybe if you are Leonard Nemoy the average person may have his book or Jewel? Poetry should be at the top of the literary chain, why do a study on everyone's attention span. Because of this people want mindless entertainment and instant gratification. Some Poets have no idea about publishing, how to go about it, self or company based that is safe based &c &c. These Poets do not know where to start. The saying "It's not what you know but who you know," let's think of that. Poets do not know whom to go to, and the readers do not know where to go to read. I have an example, let's examine poemhunter.com who are web-add crazy, and making money off of Poets no longer online or alive like the Poet Pasquale DiMeola, grab your digital gizmos and gander. Createspace.com is probably the best site for Poets, they get better royalties there. Self-promotion is all they have, and then when they do, others call it shameless and look down on them, why? There is a secret, and that is the public wants to know the poet before they purchase their books, a memoir like book inside the book of poetry or prior, and some Poets do not want to be known personally they would rather be mysterious, and be a mystery, and that can be great in the long run. Availability, secure availability... When we say secure, the truly only way for now is this. When Poets take their text of their poem as place over a photo of theirs or in the public domain that goes well with the theme of the poem, they do this with software, and they do this because the Photography industry has their act together, an Act we need for the Poets, a tight nit Unity, the Poet Igloo. This information is from Poets on the Poetry Train, this is their wisdom along with ours and the whole America journey and Canadian journey. We shouldn't and don't ask you to judge others for not buying poetry. We should judge poetry for not delivering a product people want, and why it is not available, in all create forms known to mankind. People want conflict here you go, this conflict is grand and out of hand. You want face value, well let's face the value. Let's go old school with poetry hands on, hands on books availability everywhere and everywhere, anthologies, interviews, clues to the Poets &c &c. And yes genres have standards, and Poets need standards. Poetry needs to clean up its act before it can become an act, a poet in the train says, and we agree, but how can it with no way to be heard so they work harder. How can a new poet become a new classic poet? The internet is a grown up without regulation, regulation like banks fight piracy. We want to hold those in power accountable for our rights in a digital age. Regulation is pro-innovation for employment and economic equality. Poets can regulate, most are un-employed any way, they can learn to be digital regulators. Mr. O'Hara aka John E. WordSlinger should be the United States of America Poet Laureate, give us a team to build the Poet Igloo. Media Justice for the Poet Igloo and it is original never before litigated and we ask you to seriously look at this matter and Poet Igloo with high regard, and we ask you too to appoint a legal team to help us.

It is our right to write poetry and be protected. And Poems written by Poets are their Children, and this is how true Poets look at this fact, yes they do, and now you know this too. We are Poets and Poetry Promoters. A Law needs to work for us. This is important as Freedom and Prosperity. We have been against all odds since day one. We ask to take this knowledge and help us create a Poet Igloo. Money talks and Bullshit walks they say, do you have any idea what we have gone through? We are not talking about a commercial Poet or Poem mill either.

We are faithful and trustworthy, and follow codes, but it is just us with no funds to hire an expert team to get this started. Poetry books in all forms are the objects and purpose that benefits the world. We need a general policy, closed promises not naked promises. Poets are injured and have been neglected, robbed, and a further investigation on gross amounts. This folly needs to stop, and there needs to be legal obligations for online poetry sites. There needs to be a high degree of diligence and this needs to be brought under review. Poets need an income for what they love to do, if they are professional, and we need to know about standards set standards. Value is an important ingredient also in poetry. Poets need protection. We need to look at this with great concern. I have awoken to these facts and issues. These facts and issues maybe accident or by design, and we are the only ones that have brought these facts and issues to the world, and it is going to take Superior skill to solve these matters. We are talking about each Poet having an enterprise within an enterprise, protecting and regulating and compensating, but most of all benefiting all, under the Poet Igloo Act. Unity and Uniformity, Rules Universally. International Justice. We cannot abandon these facts and the Poets and Poetry. They need modern rights and protection as Movie Stars and Performing Artists do, most of all as Citizens do, public welfare. This is not a simple case and law must be enforced wisely and mutually."

Judicial forums must be placed in all countries for Poets and their Poetry, furthermore their equality and their independence. Lawful for all Nations with dignity. Public International law, implemented and applied for modern commerce and intercourse. Common business like anything else. Negotiations and debate must start now with highly regarded principles and no idleness. The best minds must create solid ground for the Poet Igloo Bill. This is now an obligation for Poet statues worldwide, real as any other real statue, this is intellectual property, art of words. A new mixed statue has arose.

Sovereignty in International Allegiance in Positive Code to Poets and their Poetry worldwide. We want the Poet Igloo Bill to be working with the Library of Congress and other great institutions similar worldwide. Big brother is everywhere but in the Poetry realm. Yes most Poets want to remain private but they want their Poetry to be Read and Protected.

I have a message from a Poet I have reconnected with from OriginalPoetry.com that goes by the writing name Trocka7.

John,
what happened to the poetry website. I had a lot of my poems on there and it is really sad that I can't access my own work. I am lucky that I have them all in notebooks (somewhere!!), but it's disheartening because I put a lot of time and effort into organizing them all on the site, all in one place where they could be easily accessed instead of scattered about in 25 different notebooks! I am just sad I am so thankful that I remembered you Andy and found you! And yes, I would love to be part of the poetry group PoetryTrain.com. I would be FLIPPING OUT if they weren't all in notebooks!!! These poems came from my heart and soul, and I love them. These are my creations and I would be devastated if they were just totally lost forever. I can't access them now at all, that I had them all in one place, all organized. Now I will have to dig through boxes of old notebooks to try to find them, and they are all scattered. I spent hours upon hours typing them all onto O.P. and I at least had them all typed up. Now I will have to do that all over again. Just really sucks that they didn't at least send out a mass email or something saying that the site was shutting down and giving people time to go to the site and copy all of their own work. I would have appreciated that, being given an advance

warning so that I could access my work and copy it all onto my computer. I probably should've done that in the first place, but I didn't ever expect that the site would just shut down with no notice.

Trocka7...

Trocka7 and many other Poets, not just from OP many can be doomed to this, and you all Superiors need to wake up to this fact and stop the sleep walking. And I do not give a care if most Poets alive today do not care. No I don't. I, we fight for the unborn Poet so they DO NOT HAVE TO DEAL WITH THIS EVER!

Section 1:

Protection for Poets, Poetry and the Literary Arts Online/Internet.

Section 2: *What is the act going to do?*

The Poet Igloo Act will protect Poets & Poetry from online/internet publishing and copyright negligence. Poets & Poets for many years to come, and from the Orphan Works. The Poet Igloo Act will create income for Professional- Poets, Publishers, Web Designers, Artists, Publicists, Promoters, PDF Makers, Ebook makers, Editors, Distribution Experts, Customer Service Department Specialists, Book Cover Designers, Audio and Video Engineers, Affiliations Marketers, Solution Provider, Salesmen Commissions, they are called ASP's, Tag Optimizers, Biographers/Memoirists, Wi-Fi & Cable Specialists, Online Law Officers, and Jukebox Designers, furthermore a percentage can be taken to feed the needy.
The Poet Igloo Act will involve all Poets, Publishers, Law Officers, and Professions named above that want to build the Igloo from the inside out, as Igloos are made. The Poet Igloo Act will impact the world, and all will be affected by the Poet Igloo Act. Compensation to Poets and a percent will go to the welfare of the world, starting in the United States

Section 3: *Where?*

All of sections of The United States of America and any Poet, Publisher, Investor Internationally in the partnership and membership in association with the Igloo Act, PoetryTrain.com and the United States of America, under the Poet Igloo Act.

Section 4: *How is the act going to be funded?*

By any Poet, Publisher, or other Professional mentioned above, or public or private investor that wants to create the Poet Igloo.
Who is going to enforce and administer?
All of the above and selected officials.
Which government agency will oversee the bill and its duties?

National Council of the Arts, and PoetryTrain.com

Section 5: *Penalties (if any) for non-compliance (not following the rules) of the act*

Determined by the Law of the United States, one that should have been in effect already...

Section 6:

Enactment Date: When will the law go into effect?
January 1st of 2016.

United States of America

www.senate.gov

332 Dirksen Senate Office Building Washington DC 20510
(202) 224-5141

284 Russell Senate Office Building Washington DC 20510
(202) 224-3041

109 Hart Senate Office Building Washington DC 20510
(202) 224-4774

Support the Poet Igloo Bill by
Contacting Your Local Senator:

You Can Find Your Senator by Using Your Postal Code

HOUSE OF COMMONS OF CANADA
POET IGLOO BILL

August 12th, 2015

An Act respecting the protection of Poets, Poetry and Literary Arts Online/the Internet. To ensure protection, fairness, and transparency on online/internet publishing and business concerns to online/internet poetry. Resolved by the House of Commons and Canada, that the following article is proposed as federal law under the jurisdiction of the Canada, enforceable by Executive action. Be it enacted by the Senate and House of Commons of Canada assembled, that:

Your State's Senator's Name Here & Mr. John E. O'Hara aka John E. WordSlinger of Illinois, U.SA, (fill your name and location here) (Your State's Senator's Name Here, for Mr. John E. O'Hara and I, PoetryTrain.com and all International Poets of all ages) introduced the following Bill; which was referred to the Committee on online/internet publishing and business concerns, and in addition to the Committee on Oversight and Government Reform, for a period to be subsequently determined by the Speaker, in each case for consideration of such provisions as fall within the jurisdiction of the committee concerned.

Her Majesty, by and with the advice and consent of the Senate and House of Commons of Canada, enacts as follows:

Preamble:

The Poet Igloo Bill/Act executed, protects Poets and their work & Under the Igloo Bill/Act the Poet has the option for adoption and adopting, legal publishers too can adopt a Poet or vice a versa, and this adoption helps the Igloo expand and strengthen. Creating a partnership, a membership association protecting Poets, their Poetry and the name of Poetry from modern un-licensed literary websites and the seventy five year old rejuvenating Monster, known as Orphan Works Law protecting and destroying literary works. In the Poet Igloo bill/Act, Poets are protected from the Big Bad Wolf of time and publishing negligence. Poets and Publishers can create their own ice block sort of speak for the Igloo from the inside out, with all of their ideas to help and strengthen the Poet Igloo, and Poet Igoo Bill/Act, and all of their poetic wills, just like a living will, furthermore, the Poet Igloo Bill/Act creates laws for online poetry websites requiring them to be legal. Similar to ASCAP and BMI, and using the same tools they do, with two tools added, the poetry e train and a poetry website license task force.

The current copyright law is causing gridlock in the digital marketplace known as the Orphan Works. All Poets and their families today will have this problem one day in the future. Poetry can feed the world's homeless with this system.

Let's take the invention of the American Jukebox, that preserves culture, and brings the world together. A poem jukebox. This Poet Igloo Bill/Act with a manufacturing plant with distribution of poetry jukeboxes, distributed everywhere, with poetry heard and read from all over the world, furthermore poetry for the sight impaired. Poetry and the Poem Jukebox via satellite called high tech/safe-Wi-Fi shall compete with a large television company's and the music industry. Please don't let me get on the talk about lottery machines and &c &c that ruins more families then benefits them. Safeguarded Wi-Fi powered by icomera.com or a division similar created by Congress, icomera.com bought out Greyhound because of corruption, their Wi-Fi needs to be on Amtrak, let the Poets buy out Amtrak. icomera.com and Peter Kingsland, Chris Chinnapan, and Saeed Bashirian can make this happen for Poets too with their powerful icomera. Movemanage. A Poem-graph, an Engineered Poetry System aka the Poetry Train with Railroad History on audio under the Igloo Bill/Act as well, and the world is the Board of Review.

If we planned and planned and created a network far beyond any welfare system yet known to mankind. Creating jobs, careers in the literary world, with all new technology tools. We are referring with tasteful commercial adds like Papermate, &c, any company that pertains to the Literary Arts, or places of business in which copyrighted poems could be heard or read, or whether such poetry was live or recorded and, critically, whether or not it generated direct revenues. The purpose of the Poet Igloo/website employing it is profit and that is enough. Poets can make their living primarily from fees earned through jukebox plays, sales of books, and cds; Audio and that is where the gap must be filled with the Poem Jukebox and Poetry for the sight impaired.

One of our fundamental goals is to assure that poetry creators are fairly compensated for the public performance of their works, written or spoken, and their rights are properly protected. We need to adopt a royalty-payment mechanism, we call a Poet Igloo, a Poet Igloo license gives signatory legal poetry websites and businesses the right to play or have any poet by an Igloo Poet in exchange for a fixed annual fee, just like ASCAP and BMI.

This is a new poem medium for the Poets prosperity. This burden has been placed on me, and poetrytrain.com deriving from the originalpoetry.com's abandonment on nearly 40,000 poets and other sites as well, that have not followed through with publishing, and publishing for profit.

Is poetry a dramatic work? Is the internet now public performance? Is poetry similar to lectures, addresses, and sermons, furthermore oral deliveries? Is a Poet entitled to protection against this new and more complete form of appropriation quite as much as a Poet is entitled to protection from a stage performance of the Poets Poem.

Is this not History? Is this not a treatise? The facts are critical and must be foreseen. The facts and circumstances deserve analysis, deserving a test. We ought to have the intellectual honesty to recognize it for what it is. The whole business of human life is no longer flowing on in narrow and shallow channels, so we need not to look at this with careless eyes. So who has appropriate Jurisdiction of this Court of Equity? This bill is original and of discovery, and Mr. O'Hara and the Poets need relief along with this Igloo Bill.

An analysis and a reform is needed and a granting of legal status for all literary websites. An act incorporating these suggestions may receive royal assent despite opposition. PoetryTrain.com, the Poet Igloo and Poets need voluntary assistance and wholeheartedly assistance examining both the history and the existing state of these pleadings. As we know there is always a certain Class who set themselves against every attempt to introduce Order and Justice. Without Unity Do Not Expect Miracles! It has happened to the law, as to other productions of human invention, particularly those which are closely connected with the transactions of mankind, that a series of years has gradually wrought such changes as to render many parts of it obsolete, until now; the jurisprudence of one age has become the object of mere historic remembrance in another. Is this why you write about Law, and is this why Poets write Poetry? Of the numerous volumes that compose a lawyer's library, how many are consigned to oblivion by the revolutions in opinions and practice, and what a small part of those which are still considered as in use, is necessary for the purposes of common good and business! The multitude of books, the researches of a lawyer are confined to writers of a certain period, so must that be the same for a Poet. We suffer from the same monster, and we have failed and neglected the Poet.

Automatic protection with extensions, waivers, the use of nicknames, a list of witnesses. The internet is not yet regulated like T.V. and Radio, and since there are powerful websites online making much money, they should pay Poets as clubs, bars and taverns do for musicians if they post & upload their literary works on these sites.

The company Shazam.com and their technology can help too. Shazam is a mobile app that recognizes music and TV around you. Why not Poets? This app or one similar can protect poets anywhere and everywhere. Shazam is more than just identification they claim. Poetry is not breaking the 2nd commandment as TV is and has. We call to the wisdom of Neil Postman for that one. We demand a regulatory measure. A decree of Congress.

We demand a forum to engage the public. The public needs to be learned about this all. Let the Public be open to truth and understanding, which should not be monopolized by the independent standards. Let the public have say so. Unity secured not by force but by a consensus that respects variety of opinion. We need promised effective safeguards. We are talking about a secure way that compensates the Poets, creates work, to hire people with skills that have no work. Government systems work, the kind that benefits the homeless and such. Unity here. Unlike most monopolies. Not Hand Outs, Hard Work in Unity For Poetry and the Needy, Monitored by Law.

Voices of reason. We want Justice, a Known Channel as the Poet Igloo Bill into Act, we the people, we the Poets, we the press, and we the homeless. Where we can be freer to show the world their Poets, their happiness, their sufferings, their passions, were they can be safe and gain. We stand today, and dare under the banners of freedom, and shall continue to dare with valor and unity and we ask the same of you. Liberty for the Poets, from you humane, you must take us and Poets seriously worldwide.

Give the people a choice, the public a choice, give them the facts. Give us funding and a team to make this happen. Grant the world the Poet Igloo Bill/Act.

There are no voiceless people. Only people that haven't been heard yet. Poets world-wide have not been heard. People miss good poetry, and let the public decide what good poetry is not Poets or so called Poetry Publishers. We believe that the right to be heard and read belongs to everyone. Poetry some say does not sell because Poets are unknown. Celebrities and Politicians Poets sell they say, to whom, the average person don't buy them maybe if you are Leonard Nemoy the average person may have his book or Jewel? Poetry should be at the top of the literary chain, why do a study on everyone's attention span. Because of this people want mindless entertainment and instant gratification. Some Poets have no idea about publishing, how to go about it, self or company based that is safe based &c &c. These Poets do not know where to start. The saying "It's not what you know but who you know," let's think of that. Poets do not know whom to go to, and the readers do not know where to go to read. I have an example, let's examine poemhunter.com who are web-add crazy, and making money off of Poets no longer online or alive like the Poet Pasquale DiMeola, grab your digital gizmos and gander. Createspace.com is probably the best site for Poets, they get better royalties there. Self-promotion is all they have, and then when they do, others call it shameless and look down on them, why? There is a secret, and that is the public wants to know the poet before they purchase their books, a memoir like book inside the book of poetry or prior, and some Poets do not want to be known personally they would rather be mysterious, and be a mystery, and that can be great in the long run. Availability, secure availability... When we say secure, the truly only way for now is this. When Poets take their text of their poem as place over a photo of theirs or in the public domain that goes well with the theme of the poem, they do this with software, and they do this because the Photography industry has their act together, an Act we need for the Poets, a tight nit Unity, the Poet Igloo. This information is from Poets on the Poetry Train, this is their wisdom along with ours and the whole America journey and Canadian journey. We shouldn't and don't ask you to judge others for not buying poetry. We should judge poetry for not delivering a product people want, and why it is not available, in all create forms known to mankind. People want conflict here you go, this conflict is grand and out of hand. You want face value, well let's face the value. Let's go old school with poetry hands on, hands on books availability everywhere and everywhere, anthologies, interviews, clues to the Poets &c &c. And yes genres have standards, and Poets need standards. Poetry needs to clean up its act before it can become an act, a poet in the train says, and we agree, but how can it with no way to be heard so they work harder. How can a new poet become a new classic poet?

The internet is a grown up without regulation, regulation like banks fight piracy. We want to hold those in power accountable for our rights in a digital age. Regulation is pro-innovation for employment and economic equality. Poets can regulate, most are unemployed any way, they can learn to be a digital regulators. Mr. O'Hara aka John E. WordSlinger should be the United States of America Poet Laureate, give us a team to build the Poet Igloo. Media Justice for the Poet Igloo and it is original never before litigated and we ask you to seriously look at this matter and Poet Igloo with high regard, and we ask you too to appoint a legal team to help us.

It is our right to write poetry and be protected. And Poems written by Poets are their Children, and this is how true Poets look at this fact, yes they do, and now you know this too. We are Poets and Poetry Promoters. A Law needs to work for us. This is important as Freedom and Prosperity. We have been against all odds since day one. We ask to take this knowledge and help us create a Poet Igloo. Money talks and Bullshit walks they say, do you have any idea what we have gone through? We are not talking about a commercial Poet or Poem mill either.

We are faithful and trustworthy, and follow codes, but it is just us with no funds to hire an expert team to get this started. Poetry books in all forms are the objects and purpose that benefits the world. We need a general policy, closed promises not naked promises. Poets are injured and have been neglected, robbed, and a further investigation on gross amounts. This folly needs to stop, and there needs to be legal obligations for online poetry sites. There needs to be a high degree of diligence and this needs to be brought under review. Poets need an income for what they love to do, if they are professional, and we need to know about standards set standards. Value is an important ingredient also in poetry. Poets need protection. We need to look at this with great concern. I have awoken to these facts and issues. These facts and issues maybe accident or by design, and we are the only ones that have brought these facts and issues to the world, and it is going to take Superior skill to solve these matters. We are talking about each Poet having an enterprise within an enterprise, protecting and regulating and compensating, but most of all benefiting all, under the Poet Igloo Act. Unity and Uniformity, Rules Universally. International Justice. We cannot abandon these facts and the Poets and Poetry. They need modern rights and protection as Movie Stars and Performing Artists do, most of all as Citizens do, public welfare. This is not a simple case and law must be enforced wisely and mutually."

Judicial forums must be placed in all countries for Poets and their Poetry, furthermore their equality and their independence. Lawful for all Nations with dignity. Public International law, implemented and applied for modern commerce and intercourse. Common business like anything else. Negotiations and debate must start now with highly regarded principles and no idleness. The best minds must create solid ground for the Poet Igloo Bill. This is now an obligation for Poet statues worldwide, real as any other real statue, this is intellectual property, art of words. A new mixed statue has arose.

Sovereignty in International Allegiance in Positive Code to Poets and their Poetry worldwide. We want the Poet Igloo Bill to be working with the Library of Congress and other great institutions similar worldwide. Big brother is everywhere but in the Poetry realm. Yes most Poets want to remain private but they want their Poetry to be Read and Protected.

I have a message from a Poet I have reconnected with from OriginalPoetry.com that goes by the writing name Trocka7.

John,
What happened to the poetry website. I had a lot of my poems on there and it is really sad that I can't access my own work. I am lucky that I have them all in notebooks (somewhere!!), but it's disheartening because I put a lot of time and effort into organizing them all on the site, all in one place where they could be easily accessed instead of scattered about in 25 different notebooks! I am just sad I am so thankful that I remembered you Andy and found you! And yes, I would love to be part of the poetry group PoetryTrain.com. I would be FLIPPING OUT if they weren't all in notebooks!!! These poems came from my heart and soul, and I love them. These are my creations and I would be devastated if they were just totally lost forever. I can't access them now at all, that I had them all in one place, all organized. Now I will have to dig through boxes of old notebooks to try to find them, and they are all scattered. I spent hours upon hours typing them all onto O.P. and I at least had them all typed up. Now I will have to do that all over again. Just really sucks that they didn't at least send out a mass email or something saying that the site was shutting down and giving people time to go to the site and copy all of their own work. I would have appreciated that, being given an advance warning so that I could access my work and copy it all onto my computer. I probably should've done that in the first place, but I didn't ever expect that the site would just shut down with no notice.

Trocka7...

Trocka7 and many other Poets, not just from OP many can be doomed to this, and you all Superiors need to wake up to this fact and stop the sleep walking. And I do not give a care if most Poets alive today do not care. No I don't. I, we fight for the unborn Poet so they DO NOT HAVE TO DEAL WITH THIS EVER!

This Act may be cited as the Poet Igloo Act.
The following definitions apply in this Act.

Enacting Clause Section 1:

Protection for Poets, Poetry and the Literary Arts Online/Internet.
<u>Enacting Clause Section 2:</u> *What is the act going to do?*

The Poet Igloo Act will protect Poets & Poetry from online/internet publishing and copyright negligence. Poets & Poets for many years to come, and from the Orphan Works. The Poet Igloo Act will create income for Professional- Poets, Publishers, Web Designers, Artists, Publicists, Promoters, PDF Makers, Ebook makers, Editors, Distribution Experts, Customer Service Department Specialists, Book Cover Designers, Audio and Video Engineers, Affiliations Marketers, Solution Provider, Salesmen Commissions, they are called ASP's, Tag Optimizers, Biographers/Memoirists, Wi-Fi & Cable Specialists, Online Law Officers, and Jukebox Designers, furthermore a percentage can be taken to feed the needy.

The Poet Igloo Act will involve all Poets, Publishers, Law Officers, and Professions named above that want to build the Igloo from the inside out, as Igloos are made. The Poet Igloo Act will impact the world, and all will be affected by the Poet Igloo Act. Compensation to Poets and a percent will go to the welfare of the world, Starting in the United States

Enacting Section 3: *Where?*
All of sections of Canada and any Poet, Publisher, Investor Internationally in the partnership and membership in association with the Igloo Act, PoetryTrain.com and Canada, under the Poet Igloo Act.

Enacting Section 4: *How is the act going to be funded?*
By any Poet, Publisher, or other Professional mentioned above, or public or private investor that wants to create the Poet Igloo.
Who is going to enforce and administer?
All of the above and selected officials.
Which government agency will oversee the bill and its duties?
Canada Council for the Arts, and PoetryTrain.com

Enacting Section 5: *Penalties (if any) for non-compliance (not following the rules) of the act.*
Determined by the Law of the Canada, one that should have been in effect already...

Enacting Section 6:
Enactment Date: When will the law go into effect?
January 1st of 2016.

Canada

parl.gc.ca

Parliament of Canada
Ottawa, Ontario K1A 0A9

Toll-free (Canada): 1-866-599-4999
Telephone: 1-613-992-4793

Support the Poet Igloo Bill by
Contacting Your Local Member of Parliament:
You Can Find Your Member of Parliament by Using Your Postal Code

Acknowledgments

Rawshank Redemption by Stephen King
When Everybody Called Me *Gah-bay-bi-nayss*, "Forever-Flying-Bird": An Ethnographic Biography of Paul Peter Buffalo Timothy G. Roufs University of Minnesota Duluth
The Fish Car Era of the National Fish Hatchery System by John R. Leonard
Crawford Kilian, author of "Go Do Some Great Thing."
Last Train Across Canada by Murray Sayle, 1990 Full Documentary
Andrew Onderdonk's Way by The Kamloops Art Gallery and Roger H. Boulet
Andrew Onderdonk, Master Builder, by Mrs. Ann Haley
"The 100-Year-Old Diet," in the March/April 2010 issue of Best Health
Raining Rattlesnakes by the Kettle Valley Brakemen, Smile of Manitou: The History of Naramata by Don Salting & Naramata by bcmag.ca
Eight Rules For Making A Great Documentary by Matt Smith
Kings in Exile' by Sir Charles George Douglas
Towards Peace & Reconciliation- Interview with Joy Kogawa by alpha-canada.org
The Roam Travel Show via YouTube.
Time Lord, Sir Sandford Fleming and the Creation of Standard Time by Clark Blaise.
Chief Poundmaker (Pitikwahanapiwiyin) By Brother Sean Brooks
Big Bear the Movie Directed By: Gil Cardinal
White Pass and Yukon Route Railway Depot by nps.gov
Building the White Pass & Yukon Railway By W. A. Croffut
Riding the White Pass & Yukon Route Railroad in Skagway, Alaska by Backstage Traveler
Dead Horse Gulch, yukon-news.com, By Alice Cyr & Jim Robb
Falcon Joslin: Empire dreams by By Julie Stricker
The History of the Tanana Valley Railroad Presented By The Friends of the Tanana Valley Railroad, Inc.
Tragedy at Sea Shipwreck was one of worst West Coast disasters By Ann Chandonnet for the Juneau Empire
Yukon treasures found in history and adventure By Lynn Martel, For the Calgary Herald
The Klondike Gold Rush by sheppardsoftware.com
The spell of the Yukon: Discovering Dawson City Read By Shelley Ameron-McCarron miamiherald.com
Dawson City Gold Diggers by Carol Perehudoff of the thestar.com
Building Alaska, Interview of Author Walter Borneman, buildingalaskamovie.com
Going for Gold: The White Pass and Yukon Route By Civil-Engineering.asce.org
A Man in a World of Men" The Rough, the Tough, and the Tender in Robert W. Service's Songs of a Sourdough Sharon Smulders Mount Royal College, Calgary
Robert Service's secret love life By Robert Gates
Highland Light and the Jenny Lind Tower by Christopher Seufert
The fish camp- Tłı̨cho Aquatic Ecosystem Monitoring Project, a project coordinated by

the Wek'èezhìı Renewable Resources Board in collaboration with the Tłįcho Government
The Man Eaters Of Tsavo by J. H. Patterson
Animal Symbolism, Totems and Dream Analysis from A to Z by in5d.com
Gothic Literature Meets Science by Paul Marck
Man-eater Adventures in Paradise (1961) by John Kruse- story, James Michener- creator, and Michael Pertwee teleplay.
The Old North Trail, by Walter McClintock, The Rival Leaders Chapter XXXI
The Joy of Silent Film by John Lahr
A Tour Of The Deep Relationship Between B.C. Chinese Immigrants, First Nations by Susanne Ma
The Wayfinders: Why Ancient Wisdom Matters in the Modern World by Wade Davis
Zacharias Kunuk: Man Standing By Timothy Taylor
After 143 years, a dream come true for the Métis people by David Chartrand, president of the Manitoba Métis Federation.
Achomawi Myth of the Whitefooted Mouse & How Tol-le-loo Stole Fire, A Miwok Legend
The man who lives without money by Mark Boyle
Moberly land swindle townsite lots were sold during great land boom of 1881-82 by Bruce Cherney
Warmer Temps Threaten Railway Churchill Shipping Runs Over Peatland By Bill Redekop
The conversation of Hope in Chapter 7 was over half inspired by a conversation from a Richard Krawiec facebook wall post entilted- "..that idea about finding beauty and dignity in a rough world…"
Do you really want to live your life 'aware'?
Or is it more important to live your life with 'hope'?
The two don't have to be mutually exclusive. Do they?
And the replies of Richard Krawiec, Luce Pelletier, K.A. Shott & James Kirk
The Viking Heart Initial chapter of the novel by Laura Goodman Salverson
End of the Line by Terence Macartney-Filgate
Duncan Campbell Scott: Civil Servant and Poet by Keith Waddington
A New Biography of Isabella Valancy Crawford by Catherine Sheldrick Ross
Isabella Valancy Crawford by Katherine Hale
As Is at Alone by Blue Ontario's Shore ," Democratic Vistas, and the Post bellum Politics of Nostalgia Thomas F. Haddox
Christopher Dewdney, "The Incredible Shrinking Universe"
A Tribute to Joel Chandler Harris, a Disney film.
Poet's Corner by Russell Bittner Interview with Colin Ward
The Science of Dreams and Why We Have Nightmares by Maria Popova
Mary di Michele The Poet's Voice Interview by Joseph Pivato
Sandra Campbell, A Girl in a Book: Writing Marjorie Pickthall and Lorne Pierce, Canadian Poetry 39
The Selected Poems of Marhorie Pickthall Edited and with an introduction by Lorne Pierce: McClelland and Stewart Limited Publishers Toronto
A Brief History of Regatta By Howland Bottomley

How To Build a New Railroad Without Federal Money October 25th, 2013 By Noel T. Braymer

Horz by by Vesna Kakaševski

Wolf – Totem animal of Slavs by meettheslaves.com

The Harvey Girls by Lesley poling-Kempes

What's the story behind those Shakespearean names? by kamloopsnews.ca

History of the Counties of Argenteuil Que and Prescott Ont by Cyrus Thomas, 1896 & members.kos.net/sdgagnon

A History of Lachute By: Dr. G.R. Rigby

Prolific diary writer left behind a valuable record of early Montreal by by The Gazette (Montreal)

Gale Encyclopedia of Biography: Louis-Honoré Fréchette

Counter manifesto to the annexationists of Montreal by William Kirby

The Golden Dog Le Chien d'Or by William Kirby

Snow Flower and the Secret Fan by Lisa See

How Joseph-Charles Tache invented the nation by Cb Curtis

Poet: Irving Layton Observed by Donald Winkler on nfb.ca

Begin Japanology - Miyazawa Kenji by NHK WoRLD Nippon Hoso Kyokai (Japan Broadcasting Corporation)

Mummering on the Rock : A Unique NL Tradition by Sharon Martin

The Untold Story of the Suffragists of Newfoundland (1999)

The Three Suns by nfinteractive.com

The sea-spirit and other poems by Mrs. Stephen Lushington. Published 1850 by Parker in London

Poems Written in Newfoundland by Henrietta Prescott, London: Saunders and Otley, 1839

The Convict Ship and Other Poems by Margaret Sharp Ferguson Peace Centre for Newfoundland Studies - Early Imaginative Literature By Women -mun.ca

The Victorian Triumph: And Other Poems (1898) by Isabella Whiteford Rogerson

Doctor who and the Destiny of the Daleks by Terrance Dicks

The Soul Mate Exists by Flora Rocha Wisdom of the Heart Foundation

Heart Heal by Trent Shelton

Michael Crummey, author of Galore, Book Lounge video by randomhouse.ca

Eastern Gothic by Alison Hughes

Michael Whelan by W.D. Hamilton

Michael Whelan by Michael O. Nowlan

New Brunswick's forests of old by Provincial Archives of New BrunswickThe Project Gutenberg eBook of Kings in Exile, by Sir Charles George Douglas Roberts

Lord Durham by John Howe & nfb.ca

Does sound propagate further in freezing weather? By Peter Pudlak

The Leonard Lopate Show Underappreciated Literature: James Hogg

The Ethie and the dog in Verse: Canadian Forum, Vol. 1 (November 1920), 55

Poet E.J. Pratt on turning 75 by cbc.ca

Think of Them as a Lottery: 2012 Far Horizons Award for Poetry Judge Mary Dalton on Poetry and Contests by Portia Carryer

Mary Dalton's poetry: exploration and accolades by Leslie Vryenhoek
In Ch12 the poem 'Dreams' by Sarah Eliza inspired that part of her and Andy...
In Ch12, British Elves, inspiration from Olafur Gardarsson
The Braines of Queen's County By Douglas Cochrane C.D., B.A.
The Story of the Davison Lumber Company -by Philip Spencer
History of Coal Mining in Easton by Dr Robert Stephens
Evangeline By Francoise Paradis
Railways worked on by F L Dibblee between 1856 and 1888 by Jo Edkins
A Short History of the Acadian People by Michael Melanson Video Blogger
The Expulsion of the Acadians by Learn Liberty
A Perfect Solar Superstorm: The 1859 Carrington Event By Christopher Klein
How to Become a Wireless Operator I.--Why Wireless is Interesting By T. M. Lewis
Hope is not worth hoping for! In Chapter 12 was inspired by Rishi Khant
The Clockmaker by Thomas Chandler Haliburton
"History of Truro in a Nutshell" By Nan Harvey, Archivist/Librarian, Colchester Historical Society Archives
Ocean Train pulling up to the Via train station in Truro Nova Scotia by Traci Lynn
Evangeline By Francoise Paradis
Absalom, Absalom! By William Faulkner
A Geography Of Time: On Tempo, Culture, And The Pace Of Life By Robert Levine
Readers Digest May 2013 Issue Animals
The Travel Channel Extreme Survival Bankers
Maxwell's Elementary Grammar, 1904
Stripes, get writer name???
Fuck You song by Subhumans/Overkill
Hölderlin's Metaphysics (Lecture) Lecture given in the Aesthetics Research Group Seminar, School of Arts, University of Kent, 23 November 2012. Followed by discussion. Friedrich Hölderlin (1770-1843)
Three Sundays in a Week by Edgar Allan Poe
Conan Doyle Sherlock Holmes
Reeves' History of the English law by John Reeves, William Francis Finlason
The Science of Sleepwalking by E. Sudikoff, A. Marocco, L. Spicher, L. Chang
Sleep Disorders, Sleep Abnormal Behaviour, Cataplexy and narcolepsy by Seddik Sam
Entertainment Law Asked and Answered - Orphan Works by Gordon Firemark
Can Google and the British Library save orphaned books? by Channel 4 News
The Great American Jukebox Promo by Andrew Stein Videography
Jukebox Manufacturing: "A Visit to Wurlitzer" 1950 Wurlitzer Making Phonograph Jukeboxes by Jeff Quiney
Joseph Story by wikipedia.org
Star Chamber Decree (1637)
Neil Postman Are We Amusing Ourselves to Death
Areopagitica by John Milton
Christian Death - Death Wish
The speeches of the Thomas Erskine at the bar and in parliament Volume 1 By Thomas

Erskine
The Internet is not the Answer Andrew Keen
The Power of Solitude: A Poem. In Two Parts By Joseph Story
Amistad by Steven Spielberg
Hook in Mouth by Megadeth
Books by Joseph Story:

Commentaries on the Law of Bailments (1832)--Link to an 1846 printing.
Commentaries on the Constitution of the United States: Volume I, Commentaries on the Constitution of the United States: Volume II and Commentaries on the Constitution of the United States: Volume III, (3 vols., 1833), a work of profound learning which is still the standard treatise on the subject. Story published a One Volume Abridgment the same year.
he Constitutional Class Book: Being a Brief Exposition of the Constitution of the United States (1834)--Story published an expanded edition, entitled A Familiar Exposition of the Constitution of the United States in 1840.
Commentaries on the Conflict of Laws (1834), by many regarded as his most significant work.

The second edition in 1841 was revised, corrected and greatly enlarged.
Commentaries on Equity Jurisprudence (2 vols., 1835–1836) Vol. 1 1846 printing Vol. 2 1866 printing-revised by Isaac Redfield.
Equity Pleadings (1838)
Law of Agency (1839) Link to an 1851 printing.
Law of Partnership (1841)--Link to the second edition published in 1846.
Law of Bills of Exchange (1843)--Link to second edition published in 1847.
Law of Promissory Notes Law of Promissory Notes(1845)--Link to the 1851 printing.
A Familiar Exposition of the Constitution of the United States (1847).

Chapter 14 information by Poets-
Alicja Kuberska, Carlos Gomez, Steven C. Schreiner, Natalie Govsha, Eve Brackenbury, Tonya Graham-Willman, Susan Worrall, Gary Carl Smith, Vga Vgapox Lucas Lazar,
This information is from Poets on the Poetry Train, this is their wisdom along with ours, me and Andy, and the whole America journey and Canadian journey.
And the return of Poet Tracy Ripley aka Trocka7
All Hell's Breakin' Loose by Kiss
All-Time List of Canadian Transit Systems by David A. Wyatt
Quebec: A History 1867-1929 By Paul-André Linteau, René Durocher, Jean-Claude Robert
All-Time List of Canadian Transit Systems by David A. Wyatt

Steve Boyko and traingeek.ca/theboykos.com
A Brief History of the Railway that Passed Through St. George by Jeremy Hatt 5 M @ rootsweb.ancestry.com and wikipedia

Mr. Rishi Khant Chapter 12 passenger on Hope Vs. Despair
Irish Historical Mysteries: The Flight of the Earls by Sean Murphy

d.umn.edu, stripersurf.com, hellobc.com, originalpeople.org, thecanadianencyclopedia.com, bcarchives.gov.bc.ca, kag.bc.ca, bcmag.ca, princeton.ca, pc.gc.ca, osoyoosmuseum.ca, canadianaconnection.com, vancouverhistory.ca, huffingtonpost.ca, thedependent.ca, .huffingtonpost.ca, vancouversun.com, vancouverhistory.ca, webexhibits.org, athabascau.ca, alpha-canada.org, utoronto.ca, nps.gov, digitalhistoryproject.com, historylink.org, yukon-news.com, subarcticscribbler.com, juneauempire.com, calgaryherald.com, wpyr.com, sheppardsoftware.com, miamiherald.com, thestar.com, buildingalaskamovie.com, biographi.ca, cordovamuseum.org, soapysmith.net, civil-engineering.asce.org, timberwolfhq.com, unb.ca, yukon-news.com, 19thcenturyguitar.com, uppercanadavillage.com, capecodonline.com, mychatham.com, online-literature.com, pbs.org, savingcountrymusic.com, thewritepractice.com, tlicho.ca, canadianshakespeares.ca, poemhunter.com, cbc.ca, summitpost.org, uottawa.ca, Living History School on Youtube and Facebook, umkc.edu, firstpeoplesofcanada.com, colorado.edu, umn.edu, in5d.com, lemonhound.com, Canada150blog.com, ubc.ca, springbrookwaskasoo.com, ross-ter.com, ovsrails.com, stephangstephansson.com, wdvalgardsonkaffus.com, electricscotland.com, lethbridgerealestate.com, discovercalgary.ca, collectionscanada.gc.ca, trekearth.com focus.ca, crownofthecontintent.net,m museevirtuel-virtualmuseum.ca, sacred-texts.com, finnala.com, newyorker.com, salon.com, glenbow.org, canlit.ca, mtroyal.ca, thecentennial.ca, hosttownpix.com, canaanconnexion.ca, encyclopedia-titanica.org, canadiangeographic.ca, utoronto.ca, saskarhives.com, saskatoon.ca, saskstories.com, historylands.com, albertacanada.com, saskghost-hunterssociety.ca, kerrobertsk.com, on.com, biographi.ca, osler-sk.ca, metismuseum.ca, willowbunch.ca, chez-alice.fr, nationalpost.com, museevirtuel-virtualmuseum.ca, emergencydispatch.org, deathreference.com, twu.ca, mb.ca, manitobacooperator.ca, bcpcc.com, doukhobor.org, canadascotland.com, kos.net, winnipegrealtors.ca, travelandleisure.com, readreidread.com, winnipegfreepress.com, ruv.is, nfb.ca, waddo.net, hardwoodmuseum.ca, elginmilitarymuseum.ca, st-thomas.library.on.ca, mysteriesofcanada.com, coldspot.org, st-thomas.li, brary.on.ca, whitepinepictures.com, fanstory.com, dominiquesocials10.blogspot.com, poetspathway.ca, uwo.ca, bfro.net, uiowa.edu, wmpub.ca, alongstoryshort.net, brainpickings.org, onf.ca, canadianpoetries.com, icaap.org, canadianpoetry.ca, gutenberg.ca, rugusavay.com, nationalfamilyislandregatta.com, starisloveni.com, portquebec.ca, meettheslavs.com, mccord-museum.qc.ca/fr, kamloopsnews.ca, ebooks2ebooks.com, kos.net, jaimelefrancais.org, rawdonhistoricalsociety.com, canada.com, qc.ca, fullbooks.com, canadiana.ca, learner.org, cyberacadie.com, familles-lemay.com, webnet.fr, canada.com, nomorelyrics.net, litwindowpane.blogspot.com, agonia.net, fawi.net, nfinteractive.com, ricecracker.net, historicalplaces.ca, wtv-zone.com, heritage.nf.ca, niagarafallsinfo.com, archive.org, canadiana,ca, openlibrary.org, mun.ca, sfu.ca, railraod.net, mining.com, thetelegram.com, incanada.net, thelabradorian.ca, thompsoncitizen.net, marketwired.com, sabiduriadelcorazon.org, randomhouse.ca, onf.ca, icaap.org, stu.ca, museevirtuel-virtualmuseum.ca, new-brunswick.net, gnb.ca, ns1758.ca, lib.unb.ca, gutenberg.org, physics.stackexchange.com, wnyc.org, railwaycoastalmuseum.ca, todaysalternativenews.com, heritage.nf.ca, oldpoetry.com, malahatreview.ca, fiddleheadwest-malahateast.blogspot.com, mun.ca, munsterlit.ie, vehiculepress.com, beals-genealogy.com, gaelic.ca, cranntara.org.uk, tallships.ca, parl.ns.ca, uppercanda.info, paulmarlowe.com, bartleby.com, bellaterreno.com, southshorenow.ca, newscotland1398.ca, novascotia.ca, genealogy.com, hswdpi.ca, cems.uwe.ac.uk, jhowell.com, afgs.org, paulmarlowe.com, gwydir.demon.co.uk, acadianmemorial.org, canadianmysteries.ca, acadian-cajun.com, acadian.org, mccord-museum.qc.ca, pontchartrain.net, learnliberty.org, history.com, maritimemuseum.novascotia.ca, earlyradiohistory.us, wwfry.org, cs.trains.com, novanewsnow.com, connectedbloodlines.com, narrowgauge.iform.com.au, woolworthsmuseum.co.uk, fcd.maricopa.gov, hockeyshome.ns.ca, truro.ca, trainstation.ca, harrythurston.ca, nndb.com, blupete.com, chriscunard.com, gladstoneslibrary.com, mysongbook.de, sites.stfx.ca, clansinclair.ca, clanmacleanatlantic.org, gwydir.demon.co.uk, trainstation.ca, nf.ca, angelfire.com/de/naos, educationscotland.gov.uk, celticlyricscorner.net, Utaot.com, wolfmoongrove.com, crystalsandjewelry.com, crystalvaults.com, nfinteractive.com, bchistoryonline.com, shamanicdrumming.blogspot.com, vox.com, today.com, history.com, law.scu.edu, sleepfoundation.org, copyright.gov, sca.jiscinvolve.org, history-of-rock.com, copyright.com, constitution.org, pbs.org, archive.org, jtblaw.com, lonang.com, nycourts.gov, biographi.ca, bchistoryonline.com, vpl.ca, collectionscanada.gc.ca, vcn.bc.ca, canadiana.ca, encrha.com, viarail.ca, historicacanada.ca, chung.library.ubc.ca, columbiaandwestern.ca, sfu.com, ravel-british-columbia.com, beautifulbc.net, wikitravel.org, akcanada.com, albertarailwaymuseum.com, british-history.ac.uk, stlawrenceinstitute.org, oyc.yale.edu, centerformediajustice.org, bartleby.com, travelalberta.com, viator.com, attractionscanada.com, niche-canada.org, kanada-saskatchewan.de, choiceland.ca, earthsky.org, sinfin.net, arborfieldsk.ca, uregina.ca, reginalibrary.ca, southernprairierailway.com, villageofdenzil.com, redcoatroadandrail.ca, opxpeditions.com, planetware.com, baffinland.com, travelmanitoba.com, nationalgeographic.com,stpierrejolys.com, traveltomanitoba.ca, bycx.com, producer.com, caasco.com, homeaway.ca, railwaybob.com, cptdb.ca, poetrynook.com, everyculture.com, domienova.com, quebecregion.com, toeuropeandbeyond.com, baron-grenville.com, wwfry.org, kinglyheirs.com, collectionscanada.gc.ca, canadashistory.ca, pbalkcom.com, tomifobianaturetrail.com, johnwood1946.wordpress.com, quebecrailwaymap.webs.com, irhcfq.org, newfoundlandlabrador.com, trailway.ca, virtualmuseum.ca, huffingtonpost.com, ieee.ca, westrailcanada.com, tourismnewbrunswick.ca, archives.gnb.ca, familysearch.org, traingeek.ca, ns1758.ca, archive.org, novascotia.com, theculturetrip.com, novascotiarailwayheritage.com, ns1758.ca, grandnarrows.com, minersmuseum.com, novascotiaphotoalbum.com, dardpi.ca, truro.ca, umanitoba.ca, poetrypei.com, islandregister.com, kennet.pe.ca, peildo.ca, one-name.org, edu.pe.ca, islandregister.com, poetrynook.com, w3.stu.ca, communityofoleary.com, lmm.confederationcentre.com, lmmontgomery.ca, blupete.com, ceilidhculture.ca/songs.htm shamanicdrumming.blogspot.com, vox.com, today.com,

history.com, law.scu.edu
Wiki 10 times for Songwriters, Locations, and Dates of long gone Railways, until New Brunswick's RxR history, had to many times. Tim Merry

Poet Igloo Acknowledgments

American Version

youtube.com/watch?v=tyeJ55o3El0
legcounsel.house.gov/HOLC/Drafting_Legislation/Drafting_Guide.html
naeyc.org/policy/federal/bill_law
dummies.com/how-to/content/building-a-bill-in-congress.html
scholastic.com/browse/article.jsp?id=4702
carper.senate.gov/public/index.cfm/how-a-bill-becomes-a-law
votesmart.org/education/how-a-bill-becomes-law#.VcETF_lcp2A
pennmc.org/delegates/bill.asp
opencongress.org/bill/all
yalemodelcongress.org/sample-bill
lexisnexis.com/help/CU/Serial_Set/About_Bills.htm
arts.gov

-

dmlp.org
ucomm.wsu.edu/the-internet-copyright
internet-law-library.com
usdoj.gov/criminal/cybercrime
edwardsamuels.com/illustratedstory/isc5.htm
isoc.org/internet/law
templetons.com/brad/copymyths.html
rbs2.com/copyr.htm

Canadian Version

youtube.com/watch?v=DAv9IAb55ig
youtube.com/watch?v=pSCMpX9stW0
parl.gc.ca
openparliament.ca
parl.gc.ca/about/parliament/education/ourcountryourparliament/html_booklet/process-passing-bill-e.html
ccrweb.ca/en/write-your-member-parliament
cpa.ca/documents/advocacy_p5.htm
ontla.on.ca/lao/en/media/laointernet/pdf/bills-and-lawmaking-background-documents/how-bills-become-law-en.pdf
cpa.ca/documents/advocacy_p5.htm
pch.gc.ca/eng/1355260548180/1355260638531
laws-lois.justice.gc.ca/eng/const/index.html
web5.uottawa.ca/www2/rl-lr/eng/federal-legislation/2_2-bill-to-law.html
web5.uottawa.ca/www2/rl-lr/eng/federal-legislation/2_3-bill_structure.html
www.canadacouncil.ca

Mr. Welchberrys' RxR Watch

The Passengers (Readers & Poets, you are a blessing to the world-

Red & Andy have always been a poetry believer
They have always believed poets are achievers
We all out there may not be on the same page
We all may not be from the same place or same age

But we hear beauty of words ticking with time and our hearts
Not matter what gears in form, color or rhyme, poetry fire starts
Red & Andy have always been a dream believer
They have always believed in dream achievers

We all are in some form of a great promise
And they are truly humbled by all of you & this
And this is, You all believe in them with time and your hearts
And you all help dreams to be, and this is where good starts

Red & Andy fought for so many poets, and does anyone care?
It doesn't matter
They had two engineers Dustin aka Lion Boy & Corina
and that does matter
Because poetry and the poetry train has been blessed
and it goes deeper than that. One is the Fireman Dominic
and there are also the Gandy Dancers too. Geo, Yi & Dana-zoe
Red & Andy have fully given up on their old trades
And are fully given their lives to poetry and this train
There are many others that have left the train
And it brings them sorrow and a little bit of pain
But we must move on in this money, theological
Messed up scatter washed- brain world we live in on whatever

Poetry and the Poetry Train shall move on in any type of
circumstantial weather.

And Red and Andy have found a way out & God Bless
They created the Poet Igloo Bill-

And so Mr. Welchberry looks at his watch and closes the door
and the Poetry Train moves on a little more and more.

A great big'o ~thank you to all of you...

and quotes pj Johnson, "Remember, If just one person stands up and speaks up and speaks the truth, it could never be unheard. If many speak, it cannot be ignored."